Which London School? and the South-East

1997–98

Eighth Edition

Editor: Derek Bingham

 John Catt Educational Ltd

Published 1997
by John Catt Educational Ltd, Great Glemham,
Saxmundham, Suffolk IP17 2DH.
Tel: 01728 663666 Fax: 01728 663415.

The Sex Discrimination Act 1975.
The publishers have taken all reasonable steps to avoid a
contravention of section 38 of the Sex Discrimination Act 1975.
However, it should be noted that (save where there is an express
provision to the contrary) where words have been used which denote
the masculine gender only, they shall, pursuant and subject to the
said Act, for the purpose of this publication, be deemed to include
the feminine gender and vice versa.

ISBN: 1 869863 99 2
ISSN: 0959 - 7271

Designed and typeset by John Catt Educational Limited,
Great Glemham, Saxmundham, Suffolk IP17 2DH.

Printed and bound in Great Britain
by Bell & Bain Ltd, Glasgow, Scotland.

Contents

Introduction

When age teaches us a thing or two about survival

During 1997 nine independent schools will celebrate centenaries. In addition Radley College in Oxfordshire and Taunton School in Somerset will celebrate 150 years, Churchers College in Hampshire 275, Aldenham 400, Harrow 425, Norwich School 450 and The Prebendal School 500. Eight others will have anniversaries of more than 500 years. Two York schools, The Minster and St Peters, will achieve 1370 years of age and The King's School, Canterbury, can trace its origins to 30 years before theirs. It will be 1400 years old.

So what, you ask. There are many old institutions in our country, possibly too many, and on first appearance there is nothing very remarkable about a few old schools. But the 262 independent schools which celebrate a major anniversary in 1997 (and there will be another 200 in 1998, including St Albans School which will be 1050 years old) represent more than 50,000 years of accumulated wisdom in teaching. This must count for something. Arguably the old independent schools made this country what it was, and the fact that her influence affected so much of the world for so long must have been due in no small way to the learning process.

With the coming of state education the influence of the independents should have at least waned, or even ceased to exist altogether. But that has not been the case. Cynics may argue that the reason a strong independent sector not only continues but thrives says more about standards in state schools than anything else. There is some truth in this, in that independents consistently score better in exam league tables.

But the independents would not have survived if only that was the case. In fact they owe their survival entirely to their own strengths and merits, despite discouragement in some degree or other from successive governments.

First among the reasons for survival is that very venerability: age teaches a thing or two about survival. Over the years schools have learned how to benefit from good times and how to weather the bad. They have long discovered that one of the pillars on which survival depends is sound management. Most have also discovered that survival depends on not having an ethos bogged down by baggage from the past: an ability to anticipate, cope with modern demands, retain only those traditions worth keeping and jettison the rest. They have learned to adapt and, as the pace of change in life quickens, they have also been able to adapt correspondingly faster.

They have successfully appealed to successive generations by offering genuine parental choice - single sex education or coeducation, boarding or day or convenience boarding - in a way

1

which no state school can, however much the government crows about it. Parents can find a school that really suits their child.

Most important, across the board they have consistently produced the academic results. Parents who send their children, regardless of their academic prowess, to an independent school expect optimum results to be achieved. In return for passing over considerable sums of money they demand good teaching facilities, small class sizes and highly qualified teachers who both know their subjects and can motivate their pupils to learn. Independent schools do not (yet) have to stick to the National Curriculum. Most regard it as no more than a starting point and in most cases the scope of the curriculum offered is both wider and more intense.

Other strengths are those of pastoral care and extra-curricular activities, ranging across a broad spectrum from the arts to sports. The reason that such emphasis is still placed on them is because they encourage aspects such as self-dependence, leadership, of learning to have to live with other people and of making long-lasting friendships, of helping others, of understanding that at times you must depend on others in the same way they will want to depend on you.

It also involves the matter of self-confidence, which is so important; a boy or girl who is only average in the classroom can often find another field in which to excel. There may also be pointers for directions to take in later life, a factor not lost on parents because if there is one thing which worries them more than anything else, and which encourages them to look at private education, it is the job situation. Although, arguably, it should not be part of their role, independent schools now place far more emphasis than they used to on preparing pupils for the next stages. The approach takes two forms.

One is that of actually identifying what the next stage should be and taking the necessary steps to achieve it. There may be the practical aspects of lectures, work experience, job application and interview techniques, creating CVs, of communication and appearance. The second is less easy to identify but goes to the heart of proper education. It is simply that of maximising the potential of each boy or girl, of emphasising strengths and identifying and eliminating weaknesses, of generating awareness, of encouraging the qualities of loyalty, integrity, teamwork, versatility, flexibility and hard work which employers look for.

It is also a matter of turning out potentially decent citizens, of producing good eggs even at a time when bad eggs seem to get a disproportionate share of the limelight. But then the old school is used to doing that; it has done it for generations. In it abides part of the soul of the nation.

How to use the Guide

However long you have lived in London, the prospect of finding the right independent school is full of difficulties. After all, it is only when you begin your research that you can appreciate how great the choice is - and the chance of making the wrong one. And what do you do if the school you have selected is full up with a long waiting list?

In this eighth edition of **Which London School?** we do two things. One is to provide as much useful advice as possible for parents. The second is to provide as much information as possible about the schools themselves.

Articles

If you turn to the contents you will find a list of articles. Do read them. The information they contain may save you a great deal of time. There are also lists of schools offering Reserved Entrance Awards and Assisted Places as well as schools offering entry at 16+ for both A levels and vocational courses, and schools providing Learning Support, to help you.

Schools

Schools are divided into four sections. The first covers schools in London and is divided into two parts. One covers those schools in the Central postal areas. Schools are sub-divided into the eight main points of the compass, then into postal areas and then into alphabetical order. They range from nursery and pre-preparatory up to sixth form day and boarding schools, boys', girls', and co-educational. The second part of the first section gives details of schools in the outer London area up to the M25 motorway. We also include, for the first time, a Directory of Nursery Schools in Central London.

Section two covers day, weekly and full boarding schools in the remainder of the South East - Berkshire, Buckinghamshire, Essex, Hampshire, Hertfordshire, Kent, Surrey and Sussex. They are listed by county and alphabetical order. Again they include boys', girls' and co-educational establishments, up to sixth form.

The third section provides details of independent schools and colleges of further education, listed in alphabetical order.

Each section is divided into two parts. The Listings provide schools with the opportunity to add a great deal more information about themselves than the limited space of the Directory allows. If you study them you will discover much more fully what each school has to offer. The Directory contains basic information about every independent school which might come within a parent's field of choice.

If an entry in the Directory is accompanied by a ★ it means that the particular school or college also appears in the Listings.

Educational Associations

At the back of the book you will find the names and addresses of the various educational associations which can offer specialist advice. There are also maps of London and surrounds.

Index

At the back is an index of all the schools which appear in the publication. The first figure indicates where it can be found in the Listings section. The letter D preceding each page number indicates where a school appears in the Directory.

There are many ways to use this book to best advantage. If you seek schools in a certain area of London or in the Home Counties, look first at the appropriate Directory. It will give you the basic information about every independent school in the area.

After you have selected schools which may be suitable, look and see if they have taken a Listing. This will provide you with much more information about them before you make a direct approach. If you know of a school, but are not sure where it is located, turn to the index. From it you will find the information you need. If you want more information about schools, there is a free Reader Enquiry card at the back of the book.

Hopefully, when you have used this book you will have found a selection of suitable schools - and even options you had not been previously aware of.

The real value of Value Added

While schools which head the exam league tables attract the plaudits, real merit may be found in those further down the order, says Paddy Heazell, a former Head

'Value Added' is an expression that seems rather suddenly to have entered the vocabulary of educationalists and politicians who bandy it about with all the glib assurance of those who imagine that everyone understands what they are talking about. It has emerged largely as a product of the now well-entrenched league table culture. Unfortunately, the maintained and independent sectors have a far from identical understanding of what Value Added means. Unless this can be clarified, perplexed parents are going to be misled and the perfectly laudable ideas involved will become discredited and devalued.

In fact there are two aspects of education to which Added Value can apply, the academic and the extra-curricular, but it is the former with which we are mainly concerned. In the academic sense, claims for the Value Added factor in maintained schools can too easily be discredited. If it merely describes the degree to which pupils achieve more at the end of their schooling than they could when they began it, the cynic will respond "and so they jolly well should!". The converse would indeed be calamitous. Value Added is thus in very real danger of being used as a sort of catch-all phrase to describe anything children achieve at school. In the climate of popular preoccupation with them, it will be readily assumed that this is assessed on the basis of league tables. So, a school achieving good results will claim to offer wonderful Value Added.

This fails to address what independent schools have always seen as true Value Added. Their concept has been shaped by the obvious misinterpretation that can be placed on league tables. The issue is simple. Schools which are selective, either by design or by virtue of competition arising from supply and demand, will recruit abnormally bright and high achieving pupils. Their results will, or at least should, be correspondingly glittering. Their standing in the tables will be high. The consequence is a prestige which makes them the aspiration of every hopeful family. Meanwhile, the schools which attract fewer high-flying pupils may enjoy a less glamorous league table position, which inevitably reflects their reputation. Yet is such a judgement fair or even accurate?

Value Added as a concept surely implies that a commodity has its worth not just held but positively increased. Those who come into the school as alpha performers must be expected to emerge as alpha performers. Anything less might well suggest a degree of Value Subtracted! But a child of good average beta or beta plus ability and maturity will surely have excelled if he or she emerges from a school career with a performance that is categorised as alpha. While nothing should be taken away from the virtues of schools that skilfully cater for the demanding needs of the very brightest, the achievements of those schools that inspire the less naturally endowed to excel are surely worthy of even greater commendation. Indeed, if one looks at Value Added in this, its proper sense, the ability of schools down the league table lists to achieve miracles is remarkable.

Yet, regardless of league table status, good schools add other priceless educational values on top of those purely academic ones which the tables measure. Conditioned as inevitably they are by the gruesome termly experience of paying the fees, independent school parents are understandably sensitive to the whole notion of value for money. Exam results alone are not enough. So they look for certain other qualities in the provision of the school of their choice. What those are may well vary from customer to customer. For many, the moral and spiritual element may be uppermost. Schools that focus their daily routine around the chapel and the inspiration provided directly or indirectly by a religious tradition will be the key. Other parents will require a genuine service of care, support, advice. Some will rate a cultural environment as crucial, with pupils sensitive to all aspects of the creative arts. Yet others will wish to see their children trained for the real world beyond school, competent and confident in 'life skills'. These are surely all added values, and good schools can guarantee an ample provision of them all.

So the discerning parent should perhaps see this concept of Value Added as a useful litmus test for the school selected for their child. Beware the possibly false message given by the league table. Ask the prospective head just how the school claims to offer Value Added, and listen closely to the reply.

Volunteering by young people

Roger Potter, *Director of Youth for Britain, outlines a scheme for harnessing an enormous reservoir of enthusiasm, idealism and practical skills*

Britain's failure to fill the vacuum left by the demise of national service in the early sixties diminished the fabric of community life in ways that we are only now beginning to recognise and regret. Overnight we became the only major European country not to demand of its young men a period of service. More significantly, we failed to replace compulsory military service with voluntary opportunities appropriate to the age and in tune with the wish of young men and women to contribute to the world in which they live.

In failing to expose young people to the notion and practice of civic responsibility we have failed ourselves as well as them. The 7 million 16-25 year olds in this country represent an enormous reservoir of enthusiasm, idealism and practical skill and we need to consider carefully how we can help to unleash this vast potential energy for good.

Youth for Britain is a recently founded charity dedicated to promoting volunteering. There is nothing novel in Youth for Britain's underlying belief that all young people should be encouraged to take up the opportunity of a period of voluntary service as an integral part of their education. There is some novelty in our approach to realising this aim. We are not in danger of reinventing the wheel. Rather we are putting a shoulder against the wheel in an attempt to give it greater momentum.

Historically, much of the debate about community service has centred on whether it should be compulsory or voluntary. Given sufficient funding and an appropriate number of suitable tasks it would in many ways be easier to implement a compulsory scheme. Such an obligatory programme would bring together people of every background in common tasks that none could avoid. It is often argued, furthermore, that voluntary schemes attract only the well-motivated, who are themselves in least need of the advantages to the volunteer that participation brings.

In practice, though, it is hard to imagine how any contemporary scheme for nationwide service by young people could be other than voluntary. The challenge is to make it the norm rather than the exception for young people to take part in significant periods of volunteering activity.

The programme envisaged by Youth For Britain embraces the voluntary principle and has a number of other prerequisites. It should not be the property of any one political party. There is among young people widespread disillusion both with politicians and, perhaps more disturbingly, with the political process itself: the taint of political party interest would be the kiss of death for any such scheme as we are considering. There must be no hidden agenda. Specifically, volunteering must not be workfare by another name and it must not be about massaging unemployment figures. It must not take jobs away from people who might reasonably expect to be paid for doing them. It should offer only jobs demonstrably worthwhile in themselves. Crucially, such a scheme must include projects that do not leave volunteers out of pocket though clearly they would receive less than a notional going rate for the job. The voluntary element lies in a willing contribution, not in an assumption that it has to be done for nothing, and to this end revision of the current tax and benefit system will be necessary.

These criteria are not as daunting as they may appear. In any society there are hundreds of things that its members would like to be done, which need to be done, but which they cannot reasonably expect the state (or anyone else) to pay for. Each one of us could rapidly produce a list of environmental, caring, teaching and other tasks that are not going to get done if volunteers do not do them. They are not essential but are in some way life-enhancing. They can be found in this country and overseas.

A crucial consideration for a successful voluntary service programme is that participation should be equally available and attractive to young people from every background, from the most privileged to the most disadvantaged. So the scheme needs flexibility in a variety of ways. The entry point and the duration of service must be sufficiently adaptable to satisfy individual circumstances. The range of opportunities available must appeal to widely differing interests and aspirations. No one approach can (or should) cater for every need and circumstance. Indeed it is desirable that there should be a great range of organisations each with its own autonomy and independence of action; each with its individual appeal to particular groups of young people.

One of the problems with our current provision for voluntary work by the young is that much of it is polarised. On the one hand there are glamorous and often expensive gap year projects which, because of the time and costs involved, are beyond the reach of many potentially excellent volunteers. On the other hand many existing organisations aim for the most part at involving and enabling the disadvantaged. Inspiring as the work of many of these organisations is, community service must not only be seen as a panacea for the perceived negative aspects of young people's lives. If it is there is a danger of an alienating effect, turning the vast majority of youngsters who are not particularly disadvantaged away from the idea of service.

More provision, though, must be made for the 80-90% of 16-25 year olds who are neither particularly privileged not particularly disadvantaged; that huge group that would undoubtedly put a great deal into and get a great deal out of participation in volunteer projects, but isn't yet being inspired by a sense of service and is not being encouraged to take up those opportunities that do exist.

Opportunities do, of course, already exist for this group - more of them, in fact, than many people realise. Youth for Britain has identified nearly 700 organisations with upwards of 250,000 volunteer placements a year between them - approximately one for every 35 of our 16-25 year olds. These organisations are the nucleus of what could become a national movement.

If all young people are to be given the opportunity of service, flexibility and variety are essential and existing assumptions will have to be challenged. Is there a danger, for instance, of longer-term volunteering being too closely associated with the 'gap' year which is taken by only a tiny percentage of that minority of students going to university? Why should a significant period of voluntary service not become a recognised part of everyone's education? Rather than expecting all to participate in the same way in a centralised, monolithic scheme, why not provide a menu of projects of varying length and nature to satisfy the widely differing interests, aspirations, circumstances and commitments of all young people?

A nationwide scheme of volunteering for young people will only succeed if it is introduced gradually and is based upon existing good practice in both public and private sectors, alongside the steady introduction of new projects as demand for them grows. To this end, Youth For Britain's most practical objective has been to create the UK's most comprehensive database of existing opportunities for young people. The database's search engine enables potential volunteers to access information through a range of criteria such as age; start date, type and location of voluntary work required; time available; financial considerations and so on. So, for example, a student with four weeks to spare in August, wanting to work with disabled young people in the North of England (or indeed any specified UK county or any country overseas) and unable to contribute to the cost of the project will have instant access to information about all those recorded organisations offering such projects.

This straightforward and instant provision of information eliminates the frustration for potential volunteers who would like to become involved but do not know how to do so. It nudges them in the direction of participation and is proving of great value to hard-pressed parents, careers teachers, and others who advise young people. Confirmation of Youth for Britain's appeal across the social spectrum can be seen in the enthusiastic reception it has received from inner city projects for disadvantaged young people as well as from leading state and independent schools.

The database is not, however, an end in itself. Youth for Britain's aim is to demonstrate that by giving young people the best possible information about volunteering more of them will participate. Evidence of improved take up of existing volunteering opportunities will be a powerful weapon for levering in new cash and new projects. By taking this gradualist approach it should be possible not only to increase the number of young people becoming involved in worthwhile volunteering projects but also to solve the delicate problem of ensuring that supply and demand march hand in hand.

None of this will be achieved unless young people themselves are enthused and excited by volunteering. One of the problems is that our education system has done little to emphasise the rewards as well as the sacrifices of service and civic duty. We now need to change the message that we send to young people about volunteering. Too often what is said is the patronising: "You should do something for other people because it is good for you" - true in part though that undoubtedly often is. How much more positive to turn the message around and say, "Society needs you; you have something very real to offer, will you help us?" Might we not in this way be able to harness more effectively the enthusiasm, idealism and practical skills of the younger generation?

The altruism and concern for others evinced by young people is plain to see. Every school notice-board and newsletter gives evidence of the fund-raising events that take place, the effort that goes into learning about the problems of others, the sympathy that there is with those less advantaged, the reaching out for a better world. It is high time that the older generation harnessed this vast reservoir of energy and talent - in our interests as well as theirs.

Youth For Britain's headquarters are at Higher Orchard, Sandford Orcas, Sherborne, Dorset DT9 4RP. Telephone and fax: 01963 220036.

Choosing a school initially

*Educational institutions often belong to organisations which guarantee their standards. A brief guide to what all the initials means starts with the **GSA** – The Girls' Schools Association*

The Girls' Schools Association represents 230 leading independent secondary schools for girls in the United Kingdom and overseas, educating over 113,000 girls. Schools in the Association offer a choice of day, boarding, weekly and flexi-boarding education and range from large urban schools of 1000 pupils to small rural schools of around 200. Many schools have junior and pre-prep departments and can offer a complete education from four to 18. A significant number of schools also have religious affiliations and all the schools in the Girls' Public Day School Trust are in membership of the GSA.

GSA schools offer their pupils high expectations irrespective of academic ability; an environment in which girls can learn to grow in confidence and ability; smaller classes and a high pupil:teacher ratio; dedicated teachers committed to, and experienced in, the teaching of girls; an emphasis on both participation and leadership in all activities; impressive cultural and sporting opportunities; and a strong emphasis on pastoral care and spiritual and moral values.

GSA schools are widely recognised for their exceptional record of examination achievements. However education is not only about success in exams. Girls' schools offer wider development opportunities and are special for a number of reasons. They provide an environment in which girls can learn to grow in confidence and ability.

In a girls' school, the needs and aspirations of girls are the main focus, and the staff are experts in teaching the girls. All the A level physicists are girls, all those using the computers are girls, and all those in the sports teams are girls. Girls hold all the senior positions in the school, and are encouraged by positive role models in the schools' teaching staff and management. Expectations are high. In GSA schools, girls do not just have equal opportunities; they have every opportunity.

We believe that the time for co-education is at university level, when girls are ready to enter a new world on equal terms. Socially, boys and girls mature at different rates. In a girls' school where the emphasis in the classroom is on work, there is less pressure to adopt a particular role or style for the benefit of male peers. Whilst all young people need to enjoy a social life and good relationships, we believe that in lesson time the focus should be on intellectual development.

Science and mathematics play a major part in the curriculum of GSA schools and girls are encouraged to think of themselves as good at these subjects. Both high fliers and average performers are more likely to take science subjects at A level. The climate of confidence and competence enhances girls' ambitions.

Girls' schools have a long tradition of serving generations of young women who are now well-established on the career ladder, with higher and more realistic aspirations than ever before. Their daughters deserve the same opportunity.

The Girls' Schools Association plays a vital role in advising and lobbying educational policy makers on issues relating to girls' schools and the education of girls. As the specialist organisation for the education of girls, the Association is regularly consulted by the Department for Education and Employment, the Office for Standards in Education, the School Curriculum and Assessment Authority and other bodies. However GSA is not only a 'single issue' organisation, and is a powerful and well respected voice within the educational establishment.

GSA membership is restricted to the Heads of independent secondary schools for girls whose schools meet the standards laid down by the Association. Schools must also belong to the Governing Bodies of Girls' Schools Association, and the Heads must be members of the Secondary Heads Association.

The GSA is a member of the Independent Schools' Joint Council, which also incorporates the other independent schools' representative bodies. The ISJC operates, on behalf of GSA, a strict accreditation scheme for schools wishing to join the Association. Once in membership, schools are required to undergo a regular cycle of inspections to ensure that these rigorous standards are being maintained. This inspection process, the Quality Management Audit, has been developed specifically for GSA in consultation with the government's Office for Standards in Education.

A programme of professional development for members ensures that the Heads of all GSA schools are highly trained and are fully up-to-date with all aspects of their profession. Courses are also regularly held for staff and opportunities are available for subject teachers to meet together on curriculum issues.

HMC

The Headmasters' and Headmistresses' Conference, to which the Heads of leading boys' and co-educational schools belong

Founded in 1869 the HMC exists to enable members to discuss matters of common interest and to influence important developments in education. It looks after the professional interests of members, central to which is their wish to provide the best possible educational opportunities for their pupils.

The Heads of 240 leading boys' and co-educational schools are members of The Headmasters' and Headmistresses' Conference. There are up to 20 additional members who are Heads of maintained schools. Overseas membership includes the Heads of around 75 schools.

The great variety of these schools is one of the strengths of HMC but all must exhibit high quality in the education provided. While day schools are the largest group, about a third of HMC schools consist mainly of boarders and others have a smaller boarding element including weekly boarders.

Most schools are noted for their academic excellence but some achieve good results with pupils from a broad ability band. All members believe that good education consists of more than academic results and schools provide a wide range of educational activities.

Only those schools which meet with the rigorous membership criteria are admitted and this helps ensure that HMC is synonymous with high quality in education. There is a Manual of Guidance and a Code of Practice to which members must subscribe.

Those who want the intimate atmosphere of a small school will find some with around 300 pupils. Others who want a wide range of facilities and specialisations will find these offered in large day or boarding schools. Some have over a thousand pupils. About 60 schools are for boys only, others are co-educational throughout or only in the Sixth Form.

Within HMC there are schools with continuous histories as long as any in the world and many others trace their origins to Tudor times, but HMC continues to admit to membership recently-founded schools which have achieved great success. The facilities in all HMC schools will be good but some have magnificent buildings and grounds which are the result of the generosity of benefactors over many years. Some have attractive rural settings, others are sited in the centres of cities.

Pupils come from all sorts of backgrounds. The Assisted Places Scheme and the bursaries and scholarships provided by the schools give well over a third of the 160,000 pupils in HMC schools help with their fees. These can be as high as £13,000 per annum in boarding schools or around £3500 in the least expensive day schools. About 120,000 are day pupils and 40,000 boarders.

Entry into some schools is highly selective but others are well suited to a wide ability range. Senior boarding schools usually admit pupils after the Common Entrance Examination taken when they are 13.

Most day schools select their pupils by 11+ examination. Many HMC schools have junior schools, some with nursery and pre-prep departments. The growing number of boarders from overseas is evidence of the high reputation of the schools worldwide.

The independent sector has always been fortunate in attracting very good teachers. Higher salary scales, excellent conditions of employment, exciting educational opportunities and good pupil/teacher ratios bring rewards commensurate with the demanding expectations. Schools expect teachers to have a good education culminating in a good honours degree and a professional qualification, though some do not insist on the latter especially if relevant experience is offered. Willingness to participate in the whole life of the school is essential.

Parents expect the school to provide not only good teaching which helps their children achieve the best possible examination results but also the dedicated pastoral care and valuable educational experiences outside the classroom in music, drama, games, outdoor pursuits and community service. Ninety per cent of pupils go on to Higher Education, many of them winning places on the most highly-subscribed university courses.

All members attend the Annual Meeting, usually held in a conference centre in a university city. There are seven divisions covering England, Wales, Scotland and Ireland.

The Chairman and Committee, with the advice of the Secretary and Membership Secretary, make decisions on matters referred by Sub-Committees (Academic Policy, Professional Development, Membership, Community Service, Sports) and working parties (Assisted Places, Boarding, Inspection, Transfer, University Entrance and those set up to deal with *ad hoc* issues).

Close links are maintained with other professional associations, especially the Girls' Schools Association and those in membership of the Independent Schools Joint Council and with the Secondary Heads Association.

IAPS

The Incorporated Association of Preparatory Schools maintains the standards of Independent Preparatory and Junior schools

The Incorporated Association of Preparatory Schools is a professional Association of headmasters and headmistresses of independent preparatory and junior schools throughout the British Isles and overseas.

There are more than 500 schools represented, in cities, towns and the countryside. They offer more than 100,000 boys and girls a choice of day, boarding, weekly and flexible boarding education, in both single sex and co-educational schools.

Some are wholly-independent prep schools, while others are junior schools linked to senior boys' and girls' schools. There are also choir schools, schools offering special educational provision or facilities, and schools with particular religious affiliations.

Parents are assured of high professional standards in IAPS schools, maintained by regular inspection and a comprehensive and up-to-date programme of in-service training and development.

Pupils, who may start as young as three and who may remain in IAPS schools until 14, are offered a rich and varied school life in which high academic standards and traditionally strong pastoral care have a firm moral and spiritual base. Cultural and sporting opportunities, from music, art and drama to more than 30 recreational games, are keenly fostered by IAPS.

In addition IAPS organises orchestra, choir and band courses, a history competition, holiday and term-time sporting competitions, games coaching courses, educational cruises, skiing activities at home and abroad, and a chess congress.

The targets of the National Curriculum are regarded as a basic foundation, which is greatly extended by the wider programmes of study offered in IAPS prep schools.

IAPS has well-established links with senior independent schools, and great experience in methods of transfer and entry to them. It also represents the views of independent primary and junior schools to the Department of Education and Employment, and plays an active part in national educational planning.

ISA

The Independent Schools Association, with membership across all types of school

The Independent Schools Association, which celebrated its centenary in 1979, is one of the oldest of the various organisations of independent schools. It differs from most of the others in that it is not confined to any one type of school, but includes Senior, Preparatory, Junior, Nursery, Co-educational, Single sex, Boarding and Day schools. The only criterion is that it should be good of its kind.

The Association began as the Association of Principals of Private Schools, and it was the first attempt to encourage high standards in private schools and to foster friendliness and co-operation among Heads who had previously worked in isolation. In 1895 it was incorporated as The Private Schools Association. In 1927 the word 'private' was replaced by 'independent', since by then many of the schools were no longer 'private' in the sense of being owned by private individuals. At present, although a number of the smaller schools are still privately owned, most are controlled by Boards of Governors constituted as Educational Trusts or Companies. The Association currently has 300 schools with approximately 60,000 pupils.

Membership is confined to Heads of schools which are not under the control of the DfEE or LEAs. Principals of such schools are eligible provided the Executive Council is satisfied as to their suitability and the efficiency of the school. In addition the school must fulfil the Accreditation requirements of the Independent Schools Joint Council. The ISA Executive Council monitors all developments through its national network of Area Co-ordinators and Committees and arranges for Accreditation of member schools to be reviewed at intervals of ten years.

The Association exists to:

promote fellowship and co-operation among Members both nationally and within ISA Areas through Area meetings and through inter-school and inter-Area competitions and festivals in Sport, Drama, Art and Music;

help and support individual Members by providing information and advice from the ISA office and from Area Co-ordinators;

foster high educational standards in the independent sector by providing training opportunities and conferences;

co-operate with other bodies which stand for professional freedom in education by maintaining due recognition for independent schools by Government and the public.

SHMIS

The Society of Headmasters and Headmistresses of Independent Schools, founded in 1961, represents the interests of the smaller independent schools

It has as its members 70 Heads of well-established secondary schools meeting a wide range of educational needs. All member schools provide education up to 18, with sixth forms offering both A and AS levels and vocational courses.

A number cater for pupils with special educational needs, whilst others offer places to gifted dancers and musicians. All the schools provide education appropriate to their pupils' individual requirements together with the best in pastoral care.

The average size of the schools is about 300, and all aim to provide small classes ensuring favourable pupil:teacher ratios. The majority are co-educational and offer facilities for both boarding and day pupils. Many of the schools are non-denominational, whilst others have specific religious foundations.

The Society believes that independent schools are an important part of Britain's national education system. Given their independence, the schools can either introduce new developments ahead of their state colleagues or maintain certain courses appropriate to the pupils in their schools. They are able to respond quickly to the needs of parents and pupils alike.

Schools are admitted to membership of the Society only after a strict inspection procedure carried out by experienced Heads and former HMIs. Regular visits thereafter ensure that standards are maintained.

The Society is a constituent member of the Independent Schools Joint Council and every school in the Society has been accredited to it.

All the Society's Heads belong to the Secondary Heads Association and their schools are members of the Governing Bodies Association.

The Society's policy is to maintain high standards of education, acting as a guarantee of quality to parents who choose a SHMIS school for their children; to ensure the genuine independence of member schools; to provide an opportunity for Heads to share ideas and common concerns for the benefit of the children in their care; to provide training opportunities for Heads and staff in order to keep them abreast of new educational initiatives; to promote links with higher and further education and the professions, so that pupils leaving the Society's schools are given the best advice and opportunities for their future careers; and to help Heads strengthen relations with their local committees.

The questions you should ask

However much a school may appeal on first sight, you still need sound information to form your judgement

Schools attract pupils by their reputations, so most go to considerable lengths to ensure that parents are presented with an attractive image.

Modern marketing techniques try to promote good points and play down (without totally obscuring) bad ones. But every Head knows that, however good the school prospectus is, it only serves to attract parents through the school gates. Thereafter the decision depends on what they see and hear.

When you choose a school for your son or daughter, the key factor is that it suits them. Many children and their parents are instinctively attracted (or otherwise) to a school on first sight. But even if it passes this test, and 'conforms' to what you are looking for in terms of location and academic, pastoral and extra-curricular aspects, you will need to satisfy yourself that the school does measure up to what your instincts tell you.

Research we have carried out over the years suggests that in many cases the most important factor in choosing a school is the impression given by the Head. As well as finding out what goes on in a school, parents need to be reassured by the aura of confidence which they expect from a Head. How they discover the former may help them form their opinion of the latter.

So how a Head answers questions is important. Based on our research, we have drawn up a list of 23 points on which you may need to be satisfied. The order in which they appear below does not necessarily reflect their degree of importance to each parent, but how the Head answers them may help you draw your own conclusions:

- How accessible is the Head, whose personality is seen by most parents as setting the 'tone' of the school?

- Will the child fit in? What is the overall atmosphere?

- To which organisations does the school belong? How has it been accredited?

- What is the ratio of teachers to pupils?

- What are the qualifications of the teaching staff?

- How often does the school communicate with parents through reports, parent/teacher meetings or other visits?

- What is the school's retention rate? Do larger lower classes and smaller upper classes reflect a school's inability to hang on to pupils?

- What are the school's exam results? What are the criteria for presenting them? Are they consistent over the years?

- How does the school cope with pupils' problems? What sort of academic and pastoral advice is available?

- What is the school's attitude to discipline?

- Have there been problems with drugs or sex? How have they been dealt with?

- What positive steps are taken to encourage good manners, behaviour and sportsmanship?

- Is progress accelerated for the academically bright?

- How does the school cope with pupils who do not work?

- What is the attitude to religion?

- What is the atitude to physical fitness and games?

- What sports are offered and what are the facilities?

- What are the extra-curricular activities? What cultural or other visits are arranged away from the school?

- What steps are taken to encourage specific talent in music, the arts or sport?

- Where do pupils go when they leave - are they channelled to a few selected destinations?

- What is the uniform? What steps are taken to ensure that pupils take pride in their personal appearance?

- What are the timetable and term dates?

- Is it possible to have the names and addresses of parents with children at the school to approach them for an opinion?

Scholarships

Clifton  Lodge

(Founded 1979)

8 Mattock Lane, Ealing, London W5 5BG
Tel: 0181 579 3662

Head: D.A.P. Blumlein, BA
Type: Boys' Preparatory School
Age range: 4-13.
No. of pupils enrolled as at 1.9.97:
Junior: 40 Boys; Senior/Sixth Form: 120 Boys
Fees per annum:
Day: £4100-£4600

Religious denomination: Christian

Choristerships: Boys who wish to join the choir
as full choristers are entitled to choristerships
on successful graduation. These choral
scholarships are awarded to the value of one
third of the basic fees, provided that parents
make a commitment to 13+ and undertake
to make the boy available when required.
A chorister's duties never encroach on his
academic programme or other essential
aspects of school life.

Further details available from the Headmaster.

Display Listings of
Schools in Central London

East London

City of London School for Girls

(Founded 1894)

Barbican,
London EC2Y 8BB
Tel: 0171 628 0841 Fax: 0171 638 3212

Head: Dr Y A Burne, BA, PhD, FRSA
Type: Independent School
Age range: 7-18
No. of pupils enrolled as at 19.1.97: 657
Junior: 106 Girls; Senior: 391 Girls; Sixth Form: 160 Girls
Fees per annum: Day £5427

Member of: GSA, SHA

Uniquely located in the Barbican, the City of London School for Girls benefits from proximity to museums, theatres and art galleries, historic buildings and modern institutions.

The school has enviable success in public examinations and the curriculum is designed for intellectual, creative and pastoral development. Careers advice is important, and wide contacts provide older girls with placements for work experience and 'shadowing'. The majority of girls go to University; medicine is popular, with girls encouraged by outstanding science and technology facilities.

Many girls learn a musical instrument and a full range of vocal and instrumental tuition is offered. There are several orchestras and choirs and girls are regularly invited to perform publicly and to make recordings.

Physical education is considered essential and the School has a superb swimming pool.

The School recognises the importance of foreign languages; French, German, Spanish, Russian, Latin and Greek are taught and girls' studies are complemented by trips abroad and exchange visits.

Contact the Admissions Secretary for details of entrance requirements, scholarships and Government Assisted Places.

St Paul's Cathedral Choir School

(Founded in the Twelfth Century)

2 New Change, London EC4M 9AD
Tel: 0171 248 5156 Fax: 0171 329 6568

Head: Mr S Sides, BEd (Oxon), CertEd
Type: Boys' Boarding and Day School
Age range: 7-13
No. of pupils enrolled as at 1.5.97:
100 Boys (40 Boarders)
Fees per annum: Day: £5100
Boarding: £3075 + Choir Scholarship

Religious denomination: Church of England, admits boys of all faiths

Member of: IAPS, CSA

Curriculum: A broad curriculum prepares boys for scholarship and Common Entrance examinations. There is a strong musical tradition and choristers' Cathedral choral training is outstanding. A wide variety of games is offered.

Entry requirements: Entry at 7+ years: Day boys interview and short test previous February; Choristers voice trials and tests in October, February and May for boys between $6^{3}/_{4}$-$8^{1}/_{2}$ years

Gatehouse School

(Founded 1948)

Sewardstone Road,
Victoria Park, London E2 9JG
Tel: 0181 980 2978/0181 981 5885
Fax: 0181 983 1642

Head: Miss Alexandra Eversole,
Montessori Teaching Diploma
Type: Independent Day School
Age range: 2½-11
No of pupils enrolled as at 1.1.97: 150
80 Boys 70 Girls
Fees per annum: From £3225-£4650

Religious affiliation: Christian basis but pupils of all races and creeds welcomed.

Curriculum: The National Curriculum is followed and from the age of seven teaching is by subject and by specialist teachers. Montessori methods are continued into the juniors from the Montessori nursery school. Classes are small, maximum 18. Strong learning support is provided, both through individual tuition and classroom support. Children with learning difficulties are fully integrated in lessons.

Entry requirements: For external candidates entry to junior school is by interview and test. Automatic progression to junior school from Montessori nursery school.

Examinations offered: Standard Assessment Tests at 7 and 11. Music exams.

Academic and leisure facilities: Preparation for entrance and scholarship exams to leading London day schools and public boarding schools, at 7, 10 and 11. Well-equipped IT department, library and Science laboratory. A strong programme of cultural visits. Swimming is a vital part of the curriculum and there is a range of sports clubs.

The objective of the School is that children of any race, colour, creed, background and intellect shall be accepted as students and work side by side, with the aim that each child shall develop his own uniqueness of personality to enable him to appreciate the world and the world to appreciate him.

The Gatehouse School is a registered charity and exists to provide high quality education for boys and girls.

South East London

Blackheath High School

SEC

(Founded 1880)

Senior School: Vanbrugh Park, London SE3 7AG
Tel: 0181 853 2929 Fax: 0181 853 3663

Headmistress: Miss R K Musgrave, MA (Oxon)
Type: Independent Day School for Girls
Age range: 4-18
No. of pupils enrolled as at 1.1.97: 641
Junior: 275 Girls; Senior: 366 Girls; Sixth Form: 66 Girls
Fees per annum: Day: £3765-£4920

Religious affiliation: Non-denominational

Member of: GPDST, GSA

Curriculum:
11-14: Art and Design, English, French, German, Spanish, Latin, Geography, History, Mathematics, Music, PE, RE, Science, Technology, Information Technology.
14-16: GCSEs in most of above.
16-18: A levels as above and History of Art, Economics and Business Studies.

Entry requirements: Examination (English, Mathematics, General) and interview.

Both Senior and Junior Schools occupy excellent and attractive premises where very good facilities are available to pupils. Girls also benefit from the school's proximity to London and its museums, theatres and art galleries. The curriculum is academic but care and attention are paid to creative and pastoral development and there is a strong careers department. Academic results are of a high standard and almost all girls go on to higher education. Each pupil is treated as an individual and the Headmistress welcomes enquiries from parents with whom she likes to discuss their daughter's particular needs.

The Girls' Public Day School Trust exists to provide high quality education for girls. (Registered Charity number 1026057)

St Dunstan's College

Stanstead Road, Catford,
London SE6 4TY
Tel: 0181 690 1274

Headmaster: Mr J D Moore, MA
Type: Independent Day Co-educational School
Fees per annum from 1.9.96: Day: £3810-£5745

Religious denomination: Church of England foundation, now inter-denominational

Member of: HMC, IAPS, SHA, GBA

Curriculum: In the Junior School emphasis is placed on literacy and numeracy as these provide the strongest basis for the best education. Other subject areas are introduced to the younger pupils (aged 4-6) by topic work and to older pupils using a combination of project work and class teaching. Pupils are encouraged to develop skills in IT, Music, Art, Physical Education and Drama by a variety of activities in and out of the classroom. The fine facilities of the College are extensively used by younger children to provide an excellent learning environment.

In the Senior School the wide initial curriculum allows pupils an excellent range of subjects at GCSE. Most students continue into the Sixth Form where they can choose from over 20 A level courses. Many pupils continue to Higher Education with several each year gaining places at Oxford and Cambridge Universities.

Extra Curricular activities: With playing fields, indoor swimming pool, sports hall and tennis and fives courts on site there are ample opportunities for a wide range of games. St Dunstan's also offers some fifty dramatic and musical performances a year for our pupils.

Location: Within a short walking distance of two railway stations and on main bus routes, the College serves principally the Boroughs of Bromley and Lewisham and metropolitan Kent. Coach services are being organised to assist pupils travelling from other areas.

St Dunstan's aims to develop the all-round talents of its pupils - academic, recreational and sporting, and cultura - providing a stable, stimulating environment and instilling sound moral and spiritual values.

The St Dunstan's Educational Foundation, a registered charity, exists to provide an academic education for children living in the locality of St Dunstan's College.

Dulwich College Preparatory School

(Founded 1885)

*42 Alleyn Park, Dulwich,
London SE21 7AA
Tel: 0181 670 3217 Fax: 0181 766 7586*

Head: Mr G Marsh, MA, CertEd
Type: Preparatory School
Age range: 3-13. Boarders from 8
No of pupils enrolled as at 1.1.97: 749
Boys (3-13): 737; Girls (3-4): 12
Fees per annum:
Day: £3801-£6156; Boarding: £9201

Religious affiliation: Church of England

Member of: IAPS

Founded in 1885, DCPS has a long history of academic success. Entry, which is at any age, is selective and boys are prepared for Common Entrance and for Scholarship examinations for a wide range of senior schools, including Dulwich College, Westminster, St Paul's, Eton and Tonbridge. Weekly boarding is offered in Brightlands, the school's boarding house, which is situated in 13 acres of grounds about ten minutes walk from the school.

Boys follow a broad curriculum which provides both a solid grounding in the traditional range of subjects and a broader education appropriate to the 1990s. The school has excellent facilities which include an indoor heated swimming pool, a fully equipped Design Technology workshop and, since 1989, a fine Music School. In September 1995 a new block was opened consisting of twelve form rooms, a computer suite and a studio theatre. New spacious, well equipped science laboratories were opened in September 1996. Languages taught include French, German, Latin and Greek. High standards are also maintained in Art, Music and Games.

The school has extensive playing fields and all major sports are taught as well as opportunities being provided for learning Judo, Squash and Golf. A large number of extra curricular activities take place each day ranging from Drama to Chess and Hockey to Ecology. Musical activities include orchestras, choirs and a jazz band.

Dulwich College Preparatory School Trust Ltd is a registered charity which aims to promote standards of excellence in education.

Dulwich College

SEU

(Founded 1619)

*London SE21 7LD
Tel: 0181 693 3601 Fax: 0181 693 6319*

The Master: G G Able MA, MA
Type: Independent selective
Age range: 7-18; Boarders 10-18
No. of pupils enrolled as at 1.1.97:
Junior: 447 Boys; Senior: 563 Boys; Sixth Form: 370 Boys
Fees per annum:
Day: £5985-£6318; Boarding: £12,636
Sixth Form Day: £6318; Boarding: £12,636

Religious denomination: Church of England

Member of: HMC, GBA, BSA, ISIS

Curriculum: Full range of subjects to GCSE. Sixth Form students follow a General Studies programme and study a wide range of A and A/S level subjects.

Dulwich has a fine record of academic, musical and sporting achievements, offering day, full and weekly boarding with easy access to rail, road and air links.

Entry requirements: Dulwich College Entrance and Scholarship Examination (ages 7-11, 13) or Common Entrance (age 13). Entry at age 16 is dependent on GCSE results.

Dulwich College, Registered Charity No. 312755, exists to provide education for children.

Rosemead Preparatory School

(Founded 1942)

*70 Thurlow Park Road,
London SE21 8HZ
Tel: 0181 670 5865 Fax: 0181 761 9159*

Head: Mrs R L Lait, BA, MBA(Ed), CertEd
Type: Independent Co-educational Preparatory
Age range: 3-11
No. of pupils enrolled as at 1.1.97:
135 Boys 135 Girls
Fees per annum: Day: £3150-£3750

Religious denomination: Non-denominational

Member of: ISA, ISIS

Boys and girls aged 3-11 years are prepared for entry to a range of independent secondary schools. Rosemead has a very successful academic record but ensures that there is a full and varied programme of activity. The School has a happy, caring atmosphere where children's individual needs are important.

The curriculum combines a traditional approach to Maths and English teaching with a busy and varied programme of cross-curricular studies including Science, History, Geography, Information and Design Technology, Art, Music and PE. French is taught throughout the school. Swimming is for all pupils aged 6+.

There is a wide range of extra-curricular activity which includes Sports, Ballet and Music. Tuition is available for most instruments and a number of music groups meet including the orchestra and choir.

Classes make frequent visits to places of interest. A residential field studies trip is arranged for pupils aged 7-8 years. School holidays are available for pupils aged 8+.

Rosemead Preparatory School (The Thurlow Educational Trust Ltd) is a registered charity which exists to provide a high standard of education in a happy, caring environment.

Alleyn's School

(Founded 1619)

*Townley Road, Dulwich,
London SE22 8SU
Tel: 0181 693 3422 Fax: 0181 299 3671
Junior School: 0181 693 3457*

Head: C H R Niven, MA(Cantab), DipEd(Oxon),
L ès L (Nancy), Dr de l'Univ (Lille)
Junior School Head: Mrs B E Weir
Type: Independent Co-educational School
Age range: Senior 11-18; Junior 5-10
No. of pupils enrolled as at 1.5.97: 1130
Junior: 97 Boys 110 Girls
Senior: 329 Boys 333 Girls
Sixth Form: 125 Boys 136 Girls
Fees per annum:
£4799 (5-8); £4974 (9-10); £6895 (11-18)

Religious denomination: Church of England

Member of: Headmasters' Conference

Curriculum: All students follow a wide curriculum in the first three years, including English, Mathematics, three Sciences, History, Geography, French, Latin/German/Spanish, Design and Technology, Art, Music, Religious Studies and Physical Education. In Years 10 and 11 pupils take nine or ten GCSE subjects which will include English, English Literature, Mathematics, Science, a Modern Language, and History or Geography. Sixth Formers take three or four A levels and a minority subject. Economics, Business Studies and Theatre Studies are introduced at this stage.

Entry requirements: Entry to the school is by competitive examination and interview at the ages of 5, 7, 11 and 13. There are also entries to the Upper School for those with good GCSE qualifications. Scholarships and APs are offered at 11, 13 and 16.

Alleyn's is a registered charity which offers boys and girls a high quality day school education balanced by a commitment to achievement in Music, Drama and Sport.

Sydenham High School GPDST

(Founded 1877)

19 Westwood Hill,
London SE26 6BL
Tel: 0181 778 8737 Fax: 0181 776 8830

Head: Mrs Geraldine Baker, BSc, FZS
Type: Girls' Independent Day School
Age range: 4-18
No. of pupils enrolled as at 1.9.96:
Junior: 225; Senior: 471; Sixth Form: 100
Fees per annum: Junior: £3864; Senior: £4920

Religious denomination: Non-denominational

Member of: GPDST, GSA, ISIS, GBGSA, SHA

Curriculum: The school provides a broad, balanced education that fosters confidence through success.

Academic standards are very high. Girls are able to make a free choice at GCSE and A level from a very full range of subjects on offer. Music and Drama are vital elements of the school curriculum and extra curricular plays and concerts are frequent. 93% of students proceed to degree courses.

An attractive blend of Victorian buildings and purpose-built accommodation, the School provides excellent facilities, which include separate Technology and Sixth Form centres. A Performing Arts Centre, opening in March 1997 will enhance Music and Drama facilities. A Sports Hall and all-weather pitch enable a full range of sport to be offered both at school and at the National Stadium at Crystal Palace. The School is conveniently reached by public transport.

Entry requirements: Entry is normally at 4, 7, 11 and 16. Occasional places become available at other levels.

Sydenham High School, as a member of the Girls' Public Day School Trust, provides an excellent education for pupils of a wide range of ability. Registered Charity No. 1026057.

South West London

Garden House School

(Founded 1951)

53 Sloane Gardens, London SW1W 8ED
Tel: 0171 730 1652 Fax: 0171 730 0470

Heads: Mrs R Whaley (Upper School)
Mrs W Challen (Lower School)
Type: Preparatory School
Age range: Girls 3-11; Boys 3-8
No of pupils enrolled as at 27.1.97: 72 Boys 270 Girls
Fees per annum: £2700-£6150

Religious affiliation: Church of England

Member of: IAPS, ISIS

Curriculum: English, Mathematics, Reading, Handwriting, Poetry, History, Geography, Nature Study, Science, Scripture, French, Computer, Current Events, Art, CDT, Drama, Singing and Music, Dancing, Fencing and Physical Education (netball, tennis, rounders, gym and swimming).

The aim of the School is to provide a sound education in a happy, caring environment for girls from 3-11 and boys from 3-8. Visits to museums and galleries form an essential part of the school curriculum as well as an annual field study in Suffolk for the older girls and a camping trip for boys. Girls are prepared for Entrance Examinations to top London Day and Boarding Schools at 11+. Boys are prepared for entry to Preparatory Schools at 8+. We achieve several scholarships each year.

Hill House International Junior School

(Founded 1951)

Hans Place,
Chelsea, London SW1X 0EP
Tel: 0171 584 1331 Fax: 0171 589 5925

Head: Lt Colonel H S Townend, OBE, MA(Oxon)
Type: Junior Co-educational School
Age range: 3-14 years
No of pupils enrolled as at 1.5.97: 1050
600 Boys 450 Girls
Fees per annum: £3510-£5148

Hill House was founded in 1951 and is fully co-educational, taking boys and girls from 3 to 13. It is an international school not only because it operates in two countries, England and Switzerland, but also because half the places in the school are given to English children and half to non-English children.

The Four Principles
The School works on four principles.
In order of priority these are:

1. Safety of the boy and girl

2. Happiness at work and games

3. Good manners and discipline

4. Preparation for the next school

Curriculum
The Curriculum is English, boys and girls being prepared not only for entry into the leading English public schools but also schools overseas. The main subjects in which each pupil has at least one lesson every day are: English, Maths, Science and French. The supporting subjects requiring fewer lessons are: Geography, History, Biology, Latin, Divinity, Carpentry, Computer Programming and (for girls) Ballet. Particular emphasis is given to Art and Music. (There is a music staff of 22 specialist teachers).

Swiss Annexe

Hill House has always had a permanent annexe in Switzerland.

The House in Glion was purpose built. The dormitory has French oak on the walls and a ceiling of polished Finnish Pine. Its view from 2,500 feet over the largest lake in Europe to the snow-capped mountains of Grammont and the 11,000 feet Dents du Midi is unique.

The courses in Switzerland are optional and parents pay no extra fees. The school pays the air fares and all expenses at Glion, and provides skis, boots *etc*.

More House School

(Founded 1953)

22-24 Pont Street, London SW1X 0AA
Tel: 0171 235 2855 Fax: 0171 259 6782

Headmistress: Miss Margaret Connell, MA(Oxon)
Type: Independent Girls' Day School
Age range: 11-18
No. of pupils enrolled as at 1.5.97: 230
Fees per annum: £5940

Religious affiliation: Roman Catholic (but all faiths welcome)

Member of: GSA, ISJC, GBGSA

Curriculum: More House offers an academic curriculum (A level pass rate 1996 was 91%) designed to avoid premature specialisation. Nine or ten subjects are taken at GCSE level and additional subjects at A level include Politics, Economics and History of Art. Each subject has its own specialist rooms including four laboratories, a computer network, art, music rooms, a gymnasium and a chapel. Girls also use the sport and leisure facilities available in the neighbourhood and benefit from the proximity of museums and galleries. Small classes, streamed as appropriate, and a generous teacher/pupil ratio give individual care and encouragement.

More House, a registered charity, exists to provide an academic education for girls aged 11 to 18 within the framework of a Catholic Day School.

In addition to the Scholarship Announcements, which appear at the start of this Section, there is up-to-date information on Bursaries, Assisted Places and Reserved Entrance Awards

Cameron House

(Founded 1980)

4 The Vale, London SW3 4AH
Tel: 0171 352 4040 Fax: 0171 352 2349

Principal: Mrs J M Ashcroft, BSc, DipEd, Member of IAPS
Headmistress: Miss F Stack, BA Hons PGCE, Member of IAPS
Type: London Day School

co-ed

Age range: 4-11
No. of pupils enrolled as at 1.5.97: 100
Fees per annum: Day: £5985-£6075
There are no compulsory extras and there is a 5% reduction
for a brother or sister whilst an older child remains in the school

Religious affiliation: Church of England

ISJC Accredited and member of BDA

Cameron House aims to produce pupils who appreciate the virtues of courtesy, good manners and kindness, are positive-minded and confident.

Our highly qualified and dedicated teaching staff create a stimulating environment in which initiative and individual objectives can flourish. The Principal and Headmistress are both members of the IAPS and the school is accredited by the ISJC.

Small classes and a high teacher pupil ratio are central to our approach, allowing children the necessary individual attention to reach their true potential. Special provision is made for the bright dyslexic.

The curriculum is broadly based and designed to cultivate a wide range of interests, although emphasis is placed on the Core Curriculum. Essential disciplines are balanced with other aesthetic and practical activities such as Speech and Drama, Debating and French. This provides a solid and well rounded education.

The School is well equipped with its own class libraries, audio visual equipment and computers. Excellent sports facilities are available locally and the School has its own safety surfaced playground.

We are keen for pupils to discover individual

Cameron House

talents at the earliest possible age by offering a wide variety of optional clubs after school. These currently include: French, Italian, art, ballet, judo, karate, fencing and tournament chess, as well as individual musical instruments.

The learning process necessarily focuses on public exams. For boys these can take place at any time after the age of seven. Girls are prepared for the entrance exam to independent London day or country boarding schools.

SWF

Kensington Preparatory School

(Founded 1873)

596 Fulham Road,
London SW6 5PA
Tel: 0171 731 9300 Fax: 0171 731 9301

Head: Mrs G M Lumsdon, BPharm, MEd
(Member of IAPS)
Type: Independent Day School for Girls
Age range: 4-11
No of pupils enrolled as at 1.5.97: 175 Girls
Fees per annum: £1616

Religious affiliation: Interdenominational

Member of: GPDST, IAPS

Curriculum: The school has recently moved from Kensington to spacious purpose-built premises in Fulham. The curriculum remains strongly academic and the excellent new facilities will enable already flourishing music, art and drama, as well as all PE activities, to expand.

Entry requirements: Entry at 4+ and 7+ is by individual and group assessment.

Kensington Preparatory School for Girls is one of the 26 schools of the Girls' Public Day School Trust, which is a Registered Charity, number 1026057. The aim of the Trust is to provide a fine academic education at a comparatively modest cost.

A special Section covering Nursery Schools in central London appears elsewhere in this guide

L'École des Petits

(Founded 1977)

2 Hazlebury Road, Fulham,
London SW6 2NB
Tel: 0171 371 8350

Head: Mrs Mirella Otten, CAP
Type: Independent Bilingual Pre-Primary School
Age range: 2½-6
No of pupils enrolled as at 1.5.97: 124
Fees per annum:
Full Day: £2880-£3120; Part Day: £2220

Religious affiliation: All denominations welcome.

L'Ecole des Petits aims to provide an education that enhances early learning skills in a controlled environment of small classes. It has a warm and friendly atmosphere that encourages its pupils to express themselves whilst following a structured curriculum.

The school caters for children who progress on

d English educational
bilingual atmosphere
flavour that prepares its
ds of today's modern
a sense of joy combined
........y values.

Entry requirements: Interview with parents.

Falkner House

SWG

(Founded 1954)

19 Brechin Place, London SW7 4QB
Tel: 0171 373 4501 Fax: 0171 835 0073

Headmistress: Mrs Jacina Bird, BA(Hons)
Type: Preparatory Girls' Day School
Age range: 2-11
No. of pupils enrolled as at 1.5.97: 140 Girls
Fees per annum: £5250

Religious affiliation: Christian
Member of: IAPS, ISIS

Curriculum: English, Mathematics, Science, Computers, Bible Studies, History, Geography, French, German, Latin and Classical Studies, Fine Art, Famous People, Art and Craft, Music (percussion, chimebars, violin, flute, piano, clarinet and recorders), Singing, Dancing, Drama, Ballet, Physical Education (netball, tennis, rounders, swimming, judo, athletics, gymnastics).

Entry requirements: Assessment and interview.

The aims and objectives of the School are to provide a sound education for girls aged 4-11 where academic standards are high, good manners viewed as important, first class tuition is given, the children are happy and enjoy school life, and kindness and consideration for others are regarded as essential. Great importance is attached to the maintenance of close co-operation between home and school, in order to foster self-confidence in a happy atmosphere.

Falkner House Nursery caters for boys and girls aged two and three years. The handsome premises, purpose built accommodation, private garden square and team of specialist staff, offer facilities that are ideal for toddlers. The School's specialist staff are on hand to enrich the Nursery School's curriculum.

SWG

Glendower School

(Founded 1899)

87 Queen's Gate, London SW7 5JX
Tel: 0171 370 1927

Headmistress: Mrs Barbara Humber, BSc
Type: Girls' Preparatory School
Age range: 4-12+
No. of pupils enrolled as at 1.1.97: 184 Girls
Fees per annum: Day: £4950

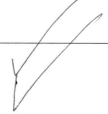

Religious affiliation: None

Member of: IAPS

Curriculum: In the Lower School, girls aged 4-8 years are taught General Subjects by a Class Teacher, who frequently has an assistant but Music, Drama, Swimming, Physical Education and French are taught by specialist staff.

Girls enter the Upper School at the age of 8 years where the average class size is approximately 15 girls, who are taught entirely by specialist teachers. Subjects included in the curriculum are: Mathematics, English, French, Science, History, Geography, Religious Education, Current Affairs, Latin (at 10 years), Computer Studies, Art, CDT, Music, Drama and Physical Education.

Entry requirements: Interviews at 4 years. Test and interview at 8 years or as vacancies occur at any other age.

Examinations offered: Girls are prepared for the Entrance Examinations for the London Independent Day Schools at 11+ and for various Boarding Schools at 11+ and 12+.

Academic and Leisure Facilities: The girls use

the excellent sports facilities at Imperial College but the School has its own ART/CDT Room, Music Room and a well-equipped Science Laboratory on site.

Visits to the museums, galleries, theatres, as well as ecology trips and visits to the Royal Institution form an essential part of the school curriculum. Various Club activities take place from 4-5pm most evenings.

Glendower School Trust Ltd is a Registered Charity which exists to provide high quality education for local girls.

SWG

The Hampshire Schools

(Founded 1928)

The Knightsbridge Upper School
63 Ennismore Gardens, London SW7 1NH
Tel: 0171 584 3297

The Knightsbridge Under School
5 Wetherby Place, London SW7 4NX
Tel: 0171 370 7081

The Kensington Gardens School
9 Queensborough Terrace, London W2 3TB
Tel: 0171 229 7065

Head: Mr A.G.Bray, CertEd
Type: Independent Day School
Knightsbridge: Co-educational to 8, Girls to 11
Kensington Gardens: Co-educational throughout
Age range:
Knightsbridge Upper School: 6-11
Knightsbridge Under School: 3-6
Kensington Gardens: 3-13
Maximum no of pupils:
Knightsbridge Upper School: 112
Knightsbridge Under School: 92;
Kensington Gardens: 146
Fees per annum: £2205-£6930

Religious denomination: Inter-denominational

Curriculum: A broad-based and balanced curriculum is provided. Children are given every opportunity to develop individual talents as fully as possible - standard academic subjects being supported by a high level of instruction in music, art, physical education and drama. Pupils are encouraged to study the history and development of their environment by means of regular visits to museums, art galleries, exhibitions and places of interest.

All pupils begin to learn French at the age of four. As an integral part of the syllabus, each form of pupils over the age of eight is accompanied by members of staff on an annual study visit to France where the staff combine with French teachers to provide a fully integrated programme of lessons and educational visits.

In the 11+, 12+ and 13+ examination classes, more advanced instruction is given in all subjects and extra opportunities are provided in further areas of study to reinforce maturity and readiness for the pupils' move into their next school. A more detailed and demanding approach is offered in subjects already introduced such as Information Technology, Current Affairs, Comparative Religion, Art (History and Appreciation), and Literary Appreciation (oral and written), including more detailed study of Shakespeare and other classics and participation in Experimental Drama.

The schools operate an Extended School Activities Programme, which includes: Door to door bus service; Early Bird Club from 08.00 hours; Stay and Study/Play until 18.00 hours; Multi Activity Camps during half terms and holidays.

Entry requirements: 3-5: Interview with the Headmaster. 5-8: Interview with the Headmaster, plus a report from previous school. 8+: Test, Interview with the Headmaster, plus possibly a day spent in the school.

Examinations offered:
Knightsbridge: Boys: 8+. Entry examinations to day and boarding Preparatory schools or transfer to the Kensington Gardens School. Girls: 11+. Scholarship plus Common Entrance and other entrance examinations to senior day and boarding schools or transfer to the Kensington Gardens School.
Kensington Gardens: Boys: Scholarship plus 13+ Common Entrance or other examinations to senior day and boarding schools. Girls: Scholarship plus 11+, 12+ and 13+ Common Entrance examinations to senior day and boarding schools.

Academic and leisure facilities:
On site: Form and school libraries, purpose built Science laboratory, purpose built Art/CDT studio, and Computer Room.
Off site: Extensive facilities for a full physical education curriculum, plus a wealth of cultural venues for educational visits.

The Hampshire Schools are a member of the Nord Anglia Education Group.

SW7

LYCEE FRANÇAIS CHARLES DE GAULLE

(Founded 1915)

35 Cromwell Road,
London SW7 2DG
Tel: 0171 584 6322 Fax: 0171 823 7684

Head: Dr H.L. Brusa, BA, MA, PhD (La Sorbonne)
Type: Independent Day School
Age range: 4-19
No. of pupils enrolled as at 1.1.97: 2900
Junior: 720 Boys 750 Girls
Senior: 525 Boys 550 Girls
Sixth Form: 168 Boys 187 Girls
Fees per annum:
Day £1779-£2916; Sixth Form Day £2169-£2916

Religious denomination: Non Confessional

Curriculum: French curriculum up to the Baccalauréat (French Baccalauréat) and an English section from Year 10 leading to GCSE and A level examinations (French is a compulsory subject).

Entry requirements: Interview and tests.

Montessori St Nicholas

(Founded 1970)

23/24 Princes Gate, London SW7 1PT
Tel: 0171 225 1277 Fax: 0171 823 7557

Head: Mrs Rosemary Hinde, Montessori Adv.Dip
Type: Nursery, Pre-Prep and Prep
Age range: 2.9 years to 9 years
No of pupils enrolled as at 1.9.97: 120
60 Boys 60 Girls
Fees per annum: £2850-£4350

Curriculum: Montessori: Maths, Language, Science, Sensorial, Cultural Subjects, French, IT, Music, Art, Gym, Games.

Entry requirements: Interview with Headteacher.

Montessori education uses a highly structured curriculum to enable each child's individual ability in each subject to be respected.

Children are encouraged to develop their creative imagination through art, craft, music and drama.

We are able to introduce non-English speaking pupils to a British education. Our pupils are prepared for entrance exams to London schools. French speaking pupils may enrol on our CNED programme.

The School is part of the Montessori St Nicholas Centre an educational trust, registered as a charity, established to encourage and promote education, particularly in accordance with the methods of Dr Maria Montessori.

Looking for a school outside London and the Home Counties?
John Catt Educational Ltd publish a range of regional *Which School?* guides

St James Independent Schools for Boys and for Girls

(Founded 1975)

Senior Boys: Pope's Villa, 19 Cross Deep,
Twickenham, Middlesex TW4 4QG
Tel: 0181 892 2002 Fax: 0181 892 4442

Junior Boys: 91 Queen's Gate, London SW7 5AB
Tel: 0171 373 5638 Fax: 0171 835 0771

Senior Girls: 19 Pembridge Villas, London W11 3EP
Tel: 0171 229 2253 Fax: 0171 792 1002

Junior Girls: 91 Queen's Gate, London SW7 5AB
Tel: 0171 373 5638 Fax: 0171 835 0771

Headmaster, Senior Boys: Mr Nicholas Debenham, MA(Cantab)
Headmaster, Junior Boys: Mr Paul Moss, CertEd
Headmistress, Senior Girls: Mrs Laura Hyde, CertEd
Headmaster, Junior Girls: Mr Paul Moss, CertEd
Type: Independent Day Schools for Boys and Girls
Age range: $4^1/_2$-18
No. of pupils enrolled as at 1.5.97:
Boys: Seniors 183; Sixth Form 34; Juniors 124
Girls: Seniors 150; Sixth Form 28; Juniors 122
Fees per annum: £3465-£4995

Religious denomination: All denominations welcome

Member of: ISA. Accredited by ISJC

Curriculum: The Schools aim to develop a strong, self-disciplined balance in their pupils which draws on a clear knowledge and understanding of fine principles of human conduct as expressed by the great Philosophies and Religions of mankind. Pupils are prepared to meet life in society with dignity, generosity and clarity of purpose.

The Schools strive to put into practice what are traditionally regarded as sound educational principles which establish firm foundations and nourish the growth and development of the whole person.

In addition to the best features of traditional English education, pupils are offered a Classical education through ancient Greek, Latin and Sanskrit. These languages provide a strong gramatical foundation. Sanskrit is introduced in the Junior School and Greek and Latin follow in the Secondary School. The Schools aim to provide the finest literature at all stages of education. Study of Shakespeare and the Scriptures are a strong feature. Writing is based on fine calligraphy and Mathematics begins with the learning of tables and the four rules of number at the age of five. Art, Singing, Speech, Drama and Physical Exercise are taught at all ages.

In the Senior Schools pupils take between eight and ten GCSEs, being introduced to the principles of their subjects as well as continuing their activities of Singing, Drama, Speech and Physical Activity. The Sixth Form offers a wide choice of A levels to which are added non-examination subjects such as Philosophy, Economics, 20th Century History, Law, Rhetoric and Debating.

Music plays an important part in the life of the Schools and there are regular dramatic productions and concerts. There are also regular school holidays for climbing, sailing and open-air projects as well as cultural visits abroad.

Each term a prominent member from public or business life is invited to deliver the Senior School Lecture.

Entry requirements: Interview and test.

Examinations offered: GCSE (Midland Board and ULEAC); A levels (Oxford and Cambridge Board and ULEAC).

Academic and sports facilities: The Schools are well equipped with libraries, laboratories and access to gymnasiums. There is daily physical exercise. Physical education for girls includes gymnastics, athletics, swimming, lacrosse, netball and tennis. The girls also have an Adventure Training Club and take part in the Duke of Edinburgh's Award Scheme. For the boys there are gymnastics, athletics, rugby, cricket and tennis. Team games are played at a fully equipped sports field at Chiswick. Boys have an ACF unit, sailing and climbing clubs. Being situated in London students have easy access to museums and galleries.

Religious activity: The Schools are open to all religious denominations. They teach philosophy which expresses the essential spiritual truths that are revealed through all religions. Children are introduced to the great scriptures of the world.

The Schools are owned by the Independent Educational Association Limited, a charitable trust which aims to make the education of St James Schools available to as many children as possible.

Newton PREP

(Founded 1991)

149 Battersea Park Road, London SW8 4BH
Tel: 0171 720 4091 Fax: 0171 498 9052

Head: Mr Richard Dell, MA(Oxon)
Type: Preparatory School
Age range: 3-13
No. of pupils enrolled as at 1.1.97: 254
132 Boys 122 Girls
Fees per annum: Pre-Prep: £4935; Prep: £5655

Religious denomination: Non-denominational

Member of: IAPS

Curriculum: Newton Prep is especially geared to the needs of bright children in the 3-13 age range, with a provision for the highly able.

With entry based upon cognitive ability, and special programmes to meet the individual needs of able children, it is possible to accelerate the learning process in its broadest sense without children feeling pressured.

The Newton curriculum has been set up to foster the physical, mental and spiritual well-being of our bright pupils. It aims for academic rigour, but is also designed to stimulate and awaken the mind. We aim to nurture well educated and well behaved children who are 'sparky' and who can think for themselves. The broad curriculum, which is centred around the three Rs during the early years,

provides an education that is excellent, exciting and ethical. Children from the age of seven are taught by specialist teachers in subject rooms. This ensures a depth of knowledge plus that all important enthusiasm which comes from teaching the subject that one loves.

Entry requirements: All entrants will be assessed by our educational psychologist. A report, where appropriate, will be required from the previous school.

Examinations offered, including Boards: Preparation is given for the entrance examinations to senior boys' and girls' schools both in London and nationally for the common entrance and scholarship examinations at 11, 12 and 13.

Academic and leisure facilities: There are extensive activities ranging from chess through Judo to debating. Central to the

...rs activities is its computerised Library. ...attersea Park, which is just five minutes from the School, offers excellent facilities for a wide range of sports. Full advantage is taken of the extensive resources of London's museums, galleries and theatres.

Redcliffe School

(Founded 1948)

47 Redcliffe Gardens, London SW10 9JH
Tel: 0171 352 9247 Fax: 0171 352 6936

Head: Miss Rosalind Cunnah, MA
Type: Co-educational School
Age range: 2½-11
No. of pupils enrolled as at 1.5.97:
Junior: 30 Boys 82 Girls
Fees per annum: £4950

Religious denomination: Interdenominational

Member of: IAPS

Curriculum: Redcliffe School is a small friendly school. It caters for a range of abilities and enables children to reach a high academic standard whilst developing the potential of each individual. Basic skills are accentuated within a broad and balanced curriculum incorporating creative and practical activities. The entire school meets each morning at assembly in which there is much child participation. Music plays an important part in school life and there are many outings to museums and theatres.

Entry requirements: Children are assessed at 3 years of age for entry at 4. Entry for subsequent years is by test. Some Scholarships available for girls at 7+.

Nursery class for children between the ages of 2½ and 4.

Redcliffe School Trust is a registered charity and provides a high standard of education for children within a caring environment.

Calder House School

(Founded 1987)

142 Battersea Park Road,
London SW11 4NB
Tel: 0171 720 8783 Fax: 0171 720 8783

Headmistress: Mrs Lesley Robertson, DipPrimEd, RSA dip in Teaching SLD
Type: Co-educational Day School
Age range: 6-13
No of pupils enrolled as at 1.5.97: 30
20 Boys 10 Girls
Fees per annum: £9660 inclusive

Religious affiliation: Interdenominational

Member of: Council for the Registration of Schools Teaching Dyslexic Pupils (CReSTeD), Corporate Member of British Dyslexia Association.

Curriculum: Calder House is a small preparatory school, suitable for children of average ability, but uneven achievement. Our structured timetable provides a happy and non-competitive environment and is tailored to meet each child's needs. Our pupils follow the National Curriculum, and enjoy a full range of school activities. They are taught in small classes with a high staff:pupil ratio. Any specialist remedial help required is incorporated into the school day. We have an established working relationship with other schools, and can advise parents on future schooling, when pupils are ready to leave Calder House.

Entry requirements: Interview and school assessment.

Center Academy

(Founded 1974)

*92 St John's Hill,
Battersea,
London SW11 1SH
Tel: 0171 821 5760 Fax: 0171 738 9862*

Head: Fintan J. O'Regan, MA
Type: School for Children with Learning Difficulties
Age range: 8-18
No. of pupils enrolled as at 1.1.97:
Lower: 8 Boys 2 Girls; Middle: 16 Boys 7 Girls
Upper: 16 Boys 7 Girls
Fees per annum: Day: £9500-£11,500

Religious denomination: None

Member of: European Council of International Schools, London International Schools Association, British Dyslexia Association, CReSTeD (A) Approved.

Curriculum: Center Academy is a full day school for children with learning difficulties such as dyslexia. Our students have normal or above intelligence, but they demonstrate specific deficiencies because of problems with motivation, maturing or learning. While teaching them how to overcome their learning difficulties we also teach standard curriculum content so that they can stay abreast of their peers. Older students are preparing for GCSEs or American high school graduation. There is a complete activities and athletic programme.

Entry requirements: Admission is by evaluation of ability, learning style and achievement levels done at the school. Information and Prospectus available upon request.

The Developmental Center Charitable Trust exists to provide high quality services for children with learning difficulties.

SWK

Emanuel School

(Founded 1594)

Battersea Rise, London SW11 1HS
Tel: 0181 870 4171 Fax: 0181 875 0267

Head: Mr Tristram Jones-Parry, MA
Type: Independent School
Age range: 10-18
No of pupils enrolled as at 1.1.97: 763
Junior: 201 Boys (19 girls admitted into the First Form from September 1996)
Senior: 365 Boys; Sixth Form: 166 Boys 12 Girls
Fees per annum: Day: £4650-£4950; Sixth Form: £4950

Religious affiliation: Church of England

Member of: HMC

Emanuel School, near Wandsworth Common, is an independent school for boys and girls aged 10-18. Assisted places and scholarships are available at 11+, 13+ and Sixth Form.

The recent introduction of girls is, in fact, a return to the co-educational origins of Emanuel School dating back to 1594. However, the new students will not find the school weighed down by tradition. A new Sixth Form Centre opened last year, new changing rooms have just been built for the school's swimming pool and the existing library was completely refurbished and computerised last year. A new Music Centre is planned.

Emanuel continues to produce impressive academic results, with last year's A level pass rate at 90% with 40% of grades at A or B.

There is also a wide range of extra-curricular activities on offer: December's production of an Alan Ayckbourn play was played to packed houses, the Emanuel rugby players returned undefeated from a tour of Canada and the Boat Club enjoyed similar success in South Africa.

Emanuel is a member of the United Westminster Schools (registered charity No 309267) and provides quality education for boys and girls.

South London Montessori School

(Founded September 1990)

Trott Street, Battersea, London SW11 3DS
Tel: 0171 738 9546 Fax: 0171 223 2904

Head: Mrs T M O'Regan-Byrnes, MontIntDip, DipAMI
Type: Montessori School
Age range: 2½-12
No of pupils enrolled as at 1.5.97: 36
Fees per annum: Day: (2-4): £590; (4-6): £1070; (6-12): £1360

Religious affiliation: Non-denominational

Member of: DFE and AMI Recommended Schools List

The South London Montessori School is unusual in the UK as it offers a co-educational

Montessori education for children from 2½ years up to the age of 12.

The curriculum is carefully planned having its basic structure rooted in the Montessori method. Great attention is taken to ensure full coverage of the requirements of the National Curriculum enabling children to adapt readily to mainstream education at any stage. Subjects included are Language, Arithmetic, Geometry, Geography, History, Science, Computer Studies, French, Music and Art and Crafts. Subjects are taught with specialised teaching materials designed to make abstract concepts easy to understand and which are unique to the Montessori method. Auto-education is encouraged as it aids the development of independence, responsibility and confidence.

The School offers a range of sporting activities including Swimming, Short Tennis, Basketball and Football. Optional extra-curricular activities include Violin and Guitartuition. There are regular educational excursions throughout the year. The school performs recitals and a play each year.

The South London Montessori Trust, a registered charity, exists to provide high quality Montessorian education for boys and girls from the age of 2½ up to 12.

Children may enter at any age. A Montessori background is preferred but not essential.

Broomwood Hall

(Founded 1984)

*74 Nightingale Lane,
London SW12 8NR
Tel: 0181 673 1616*

Headmistress: Mrs K A H Colquhoun, BEd, DipT
Type: Co-educational Day Pre-prep and Prep
Age range: Boys 4-8; Girls 4-13
No. of pupils enrolled as at 1.9.96:
118 Boys 186 Girls
Fees per term: £1600-£1890

Religious denomination: Church of England

Curriculum: Broomwood Hall is an Independent Pre-Prep and Preparatory School for boys and girls from the ages of 4-8 (boys) and 4-13 (girls). We aim specifically to prepare boys for entry to Preparatory schools and girls for the Common Entrance at 11+, 12+ and 13+ and London Day School examinations.

Entry requirements: Entry to the pre-Prep department is in the September next following a child's fourth birthday. Admission is by personal interview with both parents and the child at 3. Parents must live locally (Clapham/Wandsworth/Tooting) for children between the ages of 4-7. Entry to the Preparatory department is from 8 onwards, subject to space being available.

Examinations offered: Children are prepared for examinations to boys Prep schools, London Day Schools, and for girls Common Entrance and scholarship exams at 11+, 12+ and 13+. Pupils may also take Associated Board examinations (music), RAD exams (ballet), karate, speech and drama, Scottish dancing, BAGA and swimming.

Don't forget to read the articles which appear throughout this book. They may save you a lot of time and trouble

Hornsby House School

(Founded 1988)

*Hearnville Road,
London SW12 8RS
Tel: 0181 675 1255 Fax: 0181 877 9737*

Principal: Dr B Hornsby, PhD
Head: Mrs E Nightingale, BA
Type: Preparatory School
Age range: 3-11
No. of pupils enrolled as at 1.9.96: 180
99 Boys 81 Girls
Fees per term: £550-£1669

Religious affiliation: Christian but non-denominational

Curriculum: Hornsby House follows a full curriculum while at the same time offering specialist one-to-one tuition for a limited number of dyslexic children. A structured, phonetic, multisensory teaching method is adopted for all children, however, in tandem with a more traditional whole word approach. Sports, games, music, art, French and drama play their part in the development of the 'whole child'.

Entry requirements: There is no entry examination as such, children being accepted on interview and simple developmental tests. If a child enters the School at a later age and learning difficulties are suspected, a full educational psychology assessment, undertaken by the Hornsby International Dyslexia Centre, will be requested.

The Hornsby House Educational Trust, a registered charity, exists to provide education for boys and girls, and to supply such students with a sound religious, classical, mathematical, scientific and general education of the highest order.

Ibstock Place School

(Founded 1894)

Clarence Lane,
Roehampton,
London SW15 5PY
Tel: 0181 876 9991 Fax: 0181 878 4897
E-Mail: Ibstockplace@ukbusiness.com

Head: Mrs Franciska Bayliss, Froebel CertEd, FRSA
Type: Independent Co-educational Day School
Age range: 3-16
No of pupils enrolled as at 1.5.97: 524
Junior: 137 Boys 174 Girls
Senior: 100 Boys 113 Girls
Fees per annum: £1815-£5505

Religious affiliation: Non-denominational

Member of: ISIS, ISA, ISJC, FIS, NAHT

Ibstock Place School, founded in 1894, is located in spacious grounds adjacent to Richmond Park.

The philosophy of the school is to develop the whole child, offering a wide range of educational opportunities and challenges both inside and outside the classroom. Small classes (maximum 24 and often smaller) are taught by experienced and dedicated staff who ensure that the children achieve their potential. All school work is supported by a strong and effective pastoral system which both rewards and disciplines pupils, producing well balanced and socially accomplished young people.

Ibstock Place is undergoing a major expansion programme, including a large purpose built Science and Technology block with a 24 multi-media IT suite and a Sports Pavilion. In

September 1997 Priestman House, the Froebel Kindergarten, is opening its doors to a new teaching complex thereby doubling in size, which includes an assembly hall and additional IT suite for the primary school.

Entry to the Senior and Junior Schools is through examination and assessment in mathematics, English and science. This is to establish whether Ibstock Place is the right place for a child to flourish. Clearly, a level of academic ability is required but this is not the only criteria that the staff are looking for when a child is considered for a place.

Each department of the school is a close knit community, so the pupils have the advantages of large school facilities with the intimacy of a small school structure.

Senior School. Aged 11-16
In 1996, 97% of Ibstock pupils gained five or more GCSEs at grades A*-C, with an average number of subjects studied of 8.5. Full range of Arts, Science and Technology subjects are taught by experienced staff. Emphasis is placed on sports, drama and music in extra curricular activities, with recent expeditions to India, USA and Europe. Leavers are welcomed at a variety of independent and maintained Sixth Form schools and colleges, with places gained at Westminster, Lancing, Latymer Upper, Godolphin and Latymer, St Paul's, Bradfield College and Esher College where they achieve excellent A level results, with the majority going on to Universities and Higher Education.

Junior School, Macleod House. Aged 7-11
Macleod House is founded on Froebel's principles that each child is a unique and essential being, who develops by and through his own actions. The curriculum provides a rich and stimulating environment for all the children with a wide range of project based work carefully constructed to maximise each child's abilities and talents.

The Kindergarten, Priestman House. Aged 3-7
The Kindergarten, named after a former Headmistress who founded the school at Roehampton in 1946, is where the youngest start at Ibstock. Froebel's principle that the mother is the first teacher and links should be fostered between home and school is actively endorsed by an accomplished teaching staff who provide a stimulating environment for all the children.

Entry Procedure:
Prospective parents should apply to the Registrar.

The School, a registered charity, is part of the Incorporated Froebel Educational Institute and exists to provide high quality education.

Registered Charity No.312930R.

Putney High School

(Founded 1893)

35 Putney Hill, London SW15 6BH
Tel: 0181 788 4886 Fax: 0181 789 8068

Head: Mrs E Merchant, BSc
Type: Independent Girls' School
Age range: 4-18
No of pupils enrolled as at 1.1.97:
Junior: 280 Senior: 413 Sixth Form: 138
Fees per annum: Junior: £3864; Senior: £4920

Religious affiliation: Non-denominational

Member of: GPDST, GSA

Curriculum: Throughout the School girls follow a broad and varied curriculum in a happy, stimulating environment. In the Senior School most girls take nine subjects at GCSE and three at Advanced level. Additional courses cater for personal and social development. In the Sixth Form there are general courses to stimulate intellectual, cultural and sporting interests. Advice on universities, further education and careers is offered from an early stage. Private tuition is available in all musical instruments.

Entry requirements: 4+ and 7+ by assessment. Main entry at 11+ by competitive examination and interview. Sixth Form by interview and GCSE results. Scholarships and bursaries available at 11+ and Sixth Form. Music Scholarship.

Examinations offered, including Boards: GCSE and Advanced level. Examining Boards: ULEAC, MEG, NEAB, SEG, UCLES, O+C. Associated Boards Music Examinations.

Academic and leisure facilities: The Senior School includes seven well-equipped laboratories, a centre for craft, design and technology, a specialist music block, Sixth Form block and a three-storey classroom building for English, Mathematics and Geography. The school hall and library have recently been refurbished with the addition of a Learning Resources Centre to the library. The whole school is networked with powerful IBM compatible computers. The Junior Department has additional IT facilities in their buildings for integrated use within their curriculum. Sixth Formers enjoy the convenience of their own resources area to supplement those more widely available in the IT room and classrooms. The Junior Department has a spacious octagonal hall for Music and Drama and a new block opened in 1993 containing additional classrooms and a Science room. A new sports hall was opened in October 1996. There are netball and tennis courts and a rounders pitch. Nearby leisure facilities are fully used. Girls can choose from a range of sports, including swimming, trampolining, aerobics, badminton, fencing, rowing, touch rugby, soccer, rhythmic gymnastics, sports acrobatics.

The Girls Public Day School Trust, a charitable trust, provides a fine academic education at comparatively modest cost. Its schools achieve high academic standards, while cultural and sporting activities are an integral part of school life.

Bertrum House School

(Founded 1984)

*290 Balham High Road,
London SW17 7AL
Tel: 0181 767 4051
E-Mail: 101657,1017@compuserve.com.uk*

Head: Mrs Marie Cabourn-Smith
Type: Nursery and Pre-Preparatory
Age range: 2-8
No of pupils enrolled as at 1.5.97:
74 Boys 58 Girls
Fees per annum:
Day: £665 (Nursery), £1375 (Pre-Prep)

Bertrum House Pre-Prep and Nursery School provides a first-class education in a supportive family atmosphere. In 1996 children in Year 3 achieved a 100% success rate in entering the preparatory school of their choice. With dedicated teachers, small groups, individual attention and excellent equipment, Bertrum House maintains a happy balance between the children's enjoyment of school and their future educational success.

West London

Portland Place School

(Founded 1996)

*56-58 Portland Place,
London W1
Tel: 0171 307 8700 Fax: 0171 436 2676*

Principal: Richard Walker, BSc, CChem, MRSC
Type: Independent Day School
Age range: 11-18
No. of pupils enrolled as at 1.5.97: 120
Junior: 35 Boys 15 Girls; Senior: 50 Boys 20 Girls
Fees per annum: £5835, Sixth Form £6435

Religious denomination: None

Curriculum: Full range of academic subjects taught in small groups (maximum 16). GCSE and A level examination centre (MEG, ULEAC and SEG). Core curriculum of Mathematics, English and Science for all GCSE students.

Entry requirements: School reference, interview, written tests in English and Mathematics.

A belief in small classes and the success of the individual gives the School its lively atmosphere. Formerly known as Kensington Park School, Portland Place is a forward looking and rapidly expanding school which is flexible enough to accommodate the diverse requirements of its students, both boys and girls. Indeed, the school prides itself on the attention it gives to each individual student.

W1N

Queen's College, London

(Founded 1848)

Harley Street, London W1N 2BT
Tel: 0171 636 2446 (Registrar)
Fax: 0171 436 7607

Patron: HM The Queen Mother
Principal: The Hon Lady Goodhart, MA (Oxon)
Type: Independent Girls' Day School
Age range: 11-18
No. of pupils enrolled as at 1.9.96: 380
100 Girls in Senior College (Sixth Form)
Fees per annum: £6600

Member of: GSA, GBGSA

The curriculum is designed to meet the needs of the individual. We offer a wide range of A level subjects including Computing, and aim to provide almost any combination, including cross-curricular options. We prepare girls for entry to Oxford and Cambridge and other universities and colleges of Art and Music. Applicants should have five good GCSE grades for entry into the Sixth Form.

Academic and leisure facilites include two new science and computer laboratories, two language laboratories, excellent playing fields in Regent's Park and many and varied visits and outings to museums, art galleries, theatres and other places of interest as well as educational trips abroad.

Queen's College London was the pioneer institution for the academic education of women, providing the first ever qualifications. Started in 1848 by Professor F D Maurice, the Christian Socialist, it received the first charter for female education in 1853.

A registered charity, its aim is to promote self motivation and independence of mind within an academic framework.

Telephone the Registrar, Mrs Pearce on 0171 636 2446 for more information or to make an appointment to visit.

WC

International School of London

(Founded 1972)

139 Gunnersbury Avenue, London W3 8LG
Tel: 0181 992 5823 Fax: 0181 993 7012
E-Mail: 101635.1754@Compuserve.com

Headmaster: Mr Richard Hermon, MA
Type: International Co-educational Independent Day School
Age range: 4-18
No. of pupils enrolled as at 1.5.97:
Junior: 40 Boys 30 Girls; Senior: 50 Boys 42 Girls
Sixth Form: 18 Boys 9 Girls
Fees per annum:
Day: £5550-£8370; Sixth Form: £8760
School is registered for Nursery Vouchers

Member of: European Council of International Schools' Association, Association of Heads of Independent Schools.

Curriculum: The programme from reception to GCSE seeks to follow English National Curriculum, but special consideration is given to native languages other than English, such as Arabic, Danish, Turkish, French, Portuguese, Spanish, Japanese and Italian.

Where necessary, English is also taught as a second language (ESL). The International Baccalaureate programme is offered in the Sixth Form.

Entry requirements: Previous schools' reports plus tests where appropriate. Non-English speakers are assessed largely on reports and their language level is screened.

Examinations offered: GCSE (ULEAC, with some NEAB and MEG syllabuses), IGCSE, the International Baccalaureate, of which ISL is one of the pioneering schools in London.

The School has a spacious playground as well as a Nursery playground and is adjacent to Gunnersbury Park, whose sports fields it uses. Indoor sports facilities are in the building for younger children or at the nearby Brentford Leisure Centre for seniors. Though easily accessible from Central London, the School provides door-to-door transport for most London areas.

Articles in this guide include up-to-date information on Assisted Places, Bursaries and Reserved Entrance Awards

The Arts Educational School

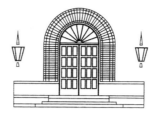

(Founded 1939)

14 Bath Road, Bedford Park, Chiswick, London W4 1LY
Tel: 0181 994 9366 Fax: 0181 994 9274

Head: Mrs Anna Sylvester-Johnson, BA (Hons), PGCE
Type: Independent Co-educational Day School
Age range: 8-16
No. of pupils enrolled as at 1.5.97: 118
Junior: 9 Boys 44 Girls
Senior: 18 Boys 44 Girls
Fees per annum: £3900-£5750

Religious affiliation: Non-denominational

Member of: ISA, SHA

Curriculum: All pupils take academic courses leading to KS2, KS3 and KS4. Pupils opt for eight or nine GCSE examinations but the curriculum also includes vocational training in music and drama and dance. Music and drama form an integrated performing arts course. Dance instruction includes ballet, tap, modern and character. Pupils go on to study for Advanced Levels at schools preparing for university entrance. Some pupils continue their vocational training at specialised colleges or at The Arts Educational Musical Theatre School.

Entry requirements: Entry is by tests in English and Mathematics, interview and audition.

Examinations offered, including Boards: GCSE (SEG, NEAB and EdExcel), ISTD, RAD. Music examinations are from a wide range of institutions.

Academic and leisure facilities: The School has numerous dance, drama and music rehearsal spaces. It shares a fully equipped proscenium arch theatre and a studio theatre with the Musical Theatre School and has all the facilities required to provide a rounded education for boys and girls.

The Arts Educational Schools are a registered charity Trust, no. 311087, and exists solely for educational purposes .

The Falcons Pre-Preparatory School

(Founded 1956)

*2 Burnaby Gardens,
London W4 3DT
Tel: 0181 747 8393 Fax: 0181 995 3903*

Head: Miss L Wall, CertEd
Type: Boys Pre-Preparatory School
No of pupils enrolled as at 1.1.97: 163
Fees per annum: £4920

curriculum provides a rich framework in which reading, writing and arithmetic are taught thoroughly. The curriculum also gives the breadth and variety in which an individual's creativity can be developed both in artistic work and academic skills. The school has its own playground and gymnasium.

Entry requirements: Registration order.

Religious affiliation: Inter-denominational

The Falcons is an independent pre-preparatory school for 3-8 year old boys. Our aim is for each child to reach his full potential in a happy, stimulating environment. The

WE

Beacon House School

(Founded 1946)

15 Gunnersbury Avenue, Ealing, London W5 3XD
Tel: 0181 992 5189

Headmistress: Mrs M Milner, BA Hons(Lond)
Type: Independent Day School taking both Boys and Girls
Age range: 3-11
No. of pupils enrolled as at 21.1.97: 144
25 Boys 119 Girls
Fees per annum (1996/97):
£1440 (Kindergarten); £2070 (Transition); £3210 (Forms I-V)

The School's aim is to provide a broad, well-balanced education for all. A warm, family atmosphere prevails in which pupils are encouraged to be self-motivated and realise their full potential.

Curriculum: Children in the Upper School are prepared for entrance into other schools, and special attention is paid to a sound grounding in English, Mathematics, and Junior Science. The National Curriculum is also covered. The syllabus includes Art, Design & Technology, History, Geography, Religious Education, French and Music. Computers are among the resources available. Physical Education takes place on two afternoons a week and children in Forms IV and V are taken swimming throughout the year. Every morning and lunchtime there is a twenty minute break in the garden.

Entry requirements: Entry is non-competitive, in order of registration.

Academic and leisure facilities: Clubs, headed by qualified staff, meet weekly to study choral singing and recorder. Elocution lessons are also available if required. All forms in the Senior School have an outing each term to a theatre or place of interest chosen to complement their studies, and entertain their parents annually. Liaison between home and school is supplemented by twice-yearly parents' form meetings and individual discussions with parents regarding progress. An after-school club (3.30-6.00pm) is available if required.

Clifton  Lodge

(Founded 1979)

8 Mattock Lane, Ealing, London W5 5BG
Tel: 0181 579 3662

Head: D.A.P. Blumlein, BA
Type: Boys' Preparatory School
Age range: 4-13. *No. of pupils enrolled as at 1.5.97:*
Junior: 40 Boys; Senior/Sixth Form: 120 boys
Fees per annum: Day: £4100-£4600

Religious denomination: Christian

Clifton Lodge is a school that stands for standards: standards of proper behaviour and all that that embraces in attitudes to others and standards of personal achievement of any sort and we believe that boys want to be a success in life. This they can only obtain by hard work, confidence in their own ability and a properly disciplined approach, whatever the activity. Clifton Lodge seeks at all times to impart these values.

The School is geared to give much individual attention, with boys being able to work at their own level, enabling them to realise their own potential.

The curriculum is based on the need to prepare boys for entry to Public School at 13+ through the Common Entrance Examination, Public School Scholarships or other equivalent examinations, and Clifton Lodge is justifiably proud of its excellent record of success in these. Whereas this provides the core of the academic programme, nevertheless we consider it essential to educate all pupils as broadly as possible and much time is also given to Music, Sport and Drama, these avenues providing boys with valuable opportunities to develop further talents and to build up their self-confidence.

The school is of Christian denomination and the daily assembly, attended by the whole community, is based around these ideals.

Choristerships to the value of one third of the basic fees are available for singing boys.

We believe that the combination of these values, the emphasis put on self-discipline, and the healthy encouragement to achieve success both within and without the classroom are essential ingredients for any boy's future happiness and fulfillment in life.

Latymer Upper School

(Founded 1624)

King Street, Hammersmith, London W6 9LR
Tel: 0181 741 1851 Fax: 0181 748 5212

Headmaster: Mr C Diggory, BSc, CMath, FIMA, FRSA
Type: Independent Boys' Grammar School with co-educational Sixth Form
Age range: 7-18
No. of pupils enrolled as at 1.5.97: 1045; Junior: 124 Senior: 631 Sixth Form: 290
Fees per annum: Day: £5424-£6180; Sixth Form: £6180

Religious denomination: Christian Non-denominational

Member of: HMC

Entry requirements: Applications must be registered by early December. Competitive examinations and interviews are held for entry at 7, 11 and 13. Entry at 16 for the Sixth Form is available to girls as well as boys and the first intake of 28 girls joined in 1996. Eight Academic Scholarships and three Music Scholarships are offered every year. The

School participates in the Assisted Places Scheme. The syllabus and past papers in mathematics and English are available from the Registrar, along with further details.

Curriculum: A full range of academic subjects is offered to GCSE and A level. Languages include Latin, Greek, French, German and Spanish (European Work experience and exchanges are run every year). Science is taught as separate subjects by subject specialists. Results are strong, and all pupils go to University. A school-wide computer network is used in many subjects. Form sizes of 22 and teaching group sizes often smaller than that ensure the personal attention of staff.

The preparatory department has just been developed as the independent Latymer Preparatory School for the 7-11 age range.

Pastoral Care: The School has a strong tradition of excellent pastoral care. The Upper School has three divisions (Lower School, Middle School, Sixth Form) led by a Head of Division. Teams of form tutors deliver a coherent programme promoting involvement in the community, charity work, and the personal, social and academic development of their form.

Music and Drama: These activities play a large part in the life of the School. There are several Orchestras and Choirs and two concerts each term.

There are five major drama productions each year, and opportunities for all pupils to perform in Gild events. Some orchestras and drama productions are run jointly with The Godolphin and Latymer School.

Sport: There are fine facilities for Sport. The School has a Boat House on site with direct river access, a large sports hall, a squash court and an indoor swimming pool on site. The playing fields are two miles away at Wood Lane. Emphasis is on involvement, participation and choice.

The School does well in the major sports of Rugby, Soccer, Rowing, Cricket and Athletics and runs more than one team per year group.

We also offer other sports such as fencing, swimming and golf to cater for individual interests. The School maintains excellent fixture lists in all major sports.

Outdoor Pursuits: Every pupil has the opportunity to have a residential experience and do outdoor pursuits as part of the Annual School Activities Week or with the Schools' Scouts. A very active Parents Gild ensures that no pupil is excluded from an activity for financial reasons.

The Duke of Edinburgh Award Scheme flourishes in the School with several pupils achieving the Gold Award each year.

The School, a Charitable Trust, exists to provide quality education to all, irrespective of their means, via Scholarships and bursaries. The School also operates the DFE Assisted Places Scheme.

Contact the Registrar for further details.

Ashbourne Middle School

WH

(Founded 1981)

17 Old Court Place, London W8 4PL
Tel: 0171 376 0360 Fax: 0171 937 2207

Head: Mr M J Hatchard-Kirby, MSc, BApSc
Type: Independent School
Age range: 10-16
No. of pupils enrolled as at 1.9.96: 50
Fees per annum: £8625

Wonderfully situated near Kensington Gardens and Hyde Park which provide facilities for games, the School is a few minutes away from the excellent museums of Natural History, Science and Geology and the Victoria and Albert Museum.

The curriculum is wide ranging and includes information technology, art, outings, trips abroad, and thinking skills. Students are prepared for Common Entrance and then the GCSE examinations. The School aims to unlock potential and in 1993 the Schools achieved the best GCSE results in the borough. Ashbourne offers the opportunity for change; many an academic career has been revitalized because of the individual attention offered by small groups, the insistence on aiming high and working hard.

Established in 1981 and co-educational, Ashbourne works in very small groups whose size never exceeds ten. Thus the School offers real opportunities for individual attention to those students who have previously lacked motivation and need a closely supervised, structured approach to work.

WH

Lady Eden's School

(Founded 1947)

*39-41 Victoria Road,
Kensington, London W8 5RJ
Tel: 0171 937 0583 Fax: 0171 376 0515*

Head: Mrs. J A Davies, BA, CertEd
Type: Independent Pre-Preparatory and Preparatory
Day School for Girls
Age range: 3½-11
No of pupils enrolled as at 1.5.97: 155 Girls
Fees per annum: £2595-£5910

Religious affiliation: Christian, non-denominational

Member of: IAPS, ISIS

Curriculum: Lady Eden's has a proven record of academic achievement. The broad curriculum combines traditional values with modern methods, including a wide provision for IT. Girls secure places in the leading boarding and London day schools. With thorough groundwork girls develop an enthusiasm for learning and an eager sense of enquiry. Music, art and drama are valued. Specialist teaching, generous provision for physical education and a variety of extra-curricular activities. Girls are encouraged to think independently and to show consideration for others.

Entry requirements: Early registration essential. Main entry (non-selective) at three years. Written examination and/or interview for later occasional vacancies.

**For further information about
Special Needs Schools consult
Which School? for Special Needs
also published by
John Catt Educational Ltd**

WM

Avenue House School

(Founded January 1995)

70 The Avenue,
Ealing, London W13 8LS
Tel: 0181 998 9981 Fax: 0181 991 1533

Head: Carolyn Barber, CertEd (Bristol University)
Type: Co-educational Pre-preparatory
and Preparatory School
Age range: 2¹/₂-11
Fees per annum: £1890-£3780

Religious affiliation: Non denominational

Avenue House is a small, happy, caring, academic school situated in a quiet leafy area of Ealing.

Founded in January 1995, the aim of this Co-educational Pre-preparatory and Preparatory School is to provide an environment where each child can realise his or her educational potential to the full. Pupils are encouraged to develop their own individual talents and personalities, enabling them to become self-confident, enthusiastic and caring children who learn to value the importance of diligent work from an early age.

Pupils are taught in small classes where they can achieve their full potential in academic subjects, music, drama, sport and public examinations. A broad curriculum is taught where the emphasis is on understanding concepts so pupils can convey the fruits of their skills. All pupils are monitored individually and frequent meetings with parents and the School are actively encouraged. We believe, a positive approach to learning leads to excellence.

Children in the Nursery are taught in a stimulating environment. Apart from being introduced to their numbers and a variety of initial reading schemes, French, Computers, Cooking, Drama, PE, Art, Craft, Music and Movement form a vital part of the Nursery sessions. Weekly swimming lessons are given at the Gurnell Swimming Pool by specialist instructors.

The Preparatory School Curriculum, whilst aware of the National Curriculum, is based on the need to prepare pupils for the relevant public examination of the parents' choice. In conjunction with the traditional academic subjects Computers, Music, Art, Craft, Drama, Swimming, Gymnastics and Games are taught. Although the emphasis is still on developing all the childrens' talents, we also believe in the traditional values of courtesy, kindness and consideration for others.

In addition to its own Library and purpose-built Gymnasium, the School has the use of a purpose-built Science Laboratory. The School also offers a pre- and after school care service for parental convenience.

Educational visits play an important role in helping children relate their class work to the real world. For this reason pupils are taken on outings where they can benefit from having first-hand knowledge of London and its surrounding area.

At Avenue House we believe a happy child is most likely to succeed.

North West London

The Cavendish School

(Founded 1875)

*179 Arlington Road,
London NW1 7EY
Tel: 0171 485 1958 Fax: 0171 267 0098*

Head: Mrs L J Harris, BA
Type: Catholic Day Preparatory School for Girls;
Pre-preparatory School for Boys
Age range: 3-11
No. of pupils enrolled as at 1.5.97:
9 Boys 156 Girls
Fees per annum (1996/97): £3870-£4131

Religious denomination: Catholic

Member of: IAPS

The Cavendish School is a small friendly school with over a century's experience in providing a well-balanced academic education in a caring Christian environment.

The School is housed in spacious Victorian school buildings with three secluded playgrounds. Particular attention is given at The Cavendish School to each child's individual needs. Throughout the School a pupil's progress is carefully monitored so that, in consultation with parents, talents may be encouraged or difficulties overcome with supplementary specialist teaching. In addition to the usual range of subjects, French is taught from four years and there is an enrichment programme in mathematics and science. Spanish conversation and specialist dyslexia tuition are also offered. The recent acquisition of additional land and premises adjacent to the School has enabled The Cavendish to provide enhanced facilities for art and science.

An extensive programme of extra-curricular activities is offered including ballet, gymnastics, jazz dancing, CDT and cookery. The School operates an after-school care service.

Senior pupils are prepared in small tutorial groups for entry to independent day and boarding schools. The highly experienced and dedicated staff aim to enable pupils to make a self-confident and happy progression to the senior school of their parents' choice. The School attaches great importance to maintaining strong yet informal links between home and school. The Head Mistress and her staff are available weekly for consultation. There are also termly written reports and an annual Parent-Teacher meeting. There is a Parents' Association to which all parents belong.

The school aims to stimulate the children's attainment of sound academic standards whilst encouraging the development of their creative skills, confidence and happiness.

The Cavendish School Charitable Trust Ltd exists to promote education for girls and boys.

Don't forget to use the Reader Enquiry Card and John Catt Schools Advisory Service, details of which appear at the back of this guide

Francis Holland School

(Founded 1878)

*Clarence Gate, Ivor Place,
Regent's Park, London NW1 6XR
Tel: 0171 723 0176 Fax: 0171 706 1522*

Headmistress: Mrs Pamela Parsonson, MA(Oxon)
Type: Independent Girls' Day School
Age range: 11-18
No. of pupils enrolled as at 20.1.97:
Senior: 366 Girls; Sixth Form: 87 Girls
Fees per annum: £5295

Religious affiliation: Church of England

Member of: GSA, GBA, ISJC, ISIS, ISCO

Curriculum: Girls on arrival are placed in one of two parallel forms and taught a wide range of subjects. In the third year they start a second language - Italian, German, Spanish or Classical Greek. Girls usually take nine subjects for GCSE. Nearly all girls take three subjects for Advanced Level, some taking a combination of A and A/S levels, and then proceed to University, Art or Music College. The curriculum is kept under constant review, and there is regular consultation with parents about each girl's programme of study.

Entry: Entry at 11 is by means of written tests in English and Mathematics, together with an interview. A number of girls are accepted into the Sixth Form each year and into other years as vacancies occur.

Examinations: Examination Boards include ULEAC, OCEAC, NEAB, MEG. GCSE subjects offered are: Art, Classical Civilisation, English, English Literature, French, German, Geography, Greek, History, Italian, Latin, Mathematics, Music, Religious Studies, Spanish, Science (Combined). Additional subjects for A level include History of Art, Economics and Politics. GCSE Drama as a one year course is offered in the Sixth Form.

Leisure and facilities: The School's own gymnasium, swimming pool and nearby Regent's Park offer the opportunity for a full programme of sport. Four choirs, two orchestras and many clubs run in the lunch hours.

Music, Drama and Art play an important part in the school. Individual instrumental lessons and lessons in speech and drama, pottery, self-defence and fencing are popular.

Francis Holland School Charitable Trust exists to provide high quality education for girls and religious instruction in accordance with the principles of the Church of England.

Devonshire House Preparatory School

(Founded 1989)

2 Arkwright Road, Hampstead, London NW3 6AD
Tel: 0171 435 1916

Principals: Sir John Loveridge, MA(Cantab), JP;
Lady Loveridge; M W Loveridge, MA(Cantab)
Headmistress: Mrs S Donovan, BEd(Hons)
Type: Preparatory, Pre-Preparatory and Nursery Day School
Age range: 2¹/₂-13
Fees per annum: Day £3765-£4980

Religious denomination: Non denominational

Curriculum: The central themes of the curriculum are the traditional subjects of literacy and numeracy. Specialist teaching of subjects and the combined sciences form an increasingly important part of the curriculum as the children grow older. Expression in all forms of communication is encouraged with classes having lessons in Art, Music, Drama, Information and Design Technology, Physical Exercise and Games. Much encouragement is given to pupils to help to widen their horizons and broaden their interests. The School fosters a sense of personal responsibility amongst the pupils.

Entry requirements: The offer of places is subject to availability and to an interview with the Head. Children wishing to enter the School over the age of six will be required to sit a more formal test.

Academic and leisure facilities: The School is situated in lovely premises in the heart of Hampstead with its own walled grounds. The aim is to achieve high academic standards whilst developing enthusiasm and initiative throughout a wide range of interests. It is considered essential to encourage pupils to develop their own individual personalities and a good sense of personal responsibility.

NWC

Hampstead Hill School

Nursery School Branch
*St Stephen's Hall,
Pond Street, Hampstead,
London NW3 2PP*

Pre-Preparatory School Branch
*All Hallows Hall,
53 Courthope Road,
Hampstead, London NW3 2LE*

All Enquiries: *Tel/Fax: 0171 435 6262*

Headmistress: Mrs Andrea Taylor
Type: Pre-preparatory & Nursery School
Age range: Pre-prep: 5-8+; Nursery: 2+-5+
No. of pupils enrolled as at 1.5.97:
Pre-Prep: 90; Nursery: 120
Fees per annum: On application

Hampstead Hill School was founded in 1949 and has remained in the hands of the same family ever since. This much valued continuity means that the School has a wealth of experience in providing a sound, traditional and happy education for children aged 2+ to 8+ years of age. The School offers a full academic syllabus, a comprehensive artistic and creative programme, a variety of music and singing activities and French and swimming from 4 years of age.

The Nursery School Branch offers part or full time education and care, 52 weeks a year or term times only. The Pre-Preparatory School Branch prepares children for entrance examinations to Junior Public and Preparatory Schools at 7+ or 8+.

Extended hours are open to all pupils and Holiday Schemes are available for Pre-Preparatory pupils. Fees at both branches are payable weekly, monthly or termly.

NWC

The Royal School, Hampstead

(Founded 1855)

*65 Rosslyn Hill,
London NW3 5UD
Tel: 0171 794 7707*

Principal: Mrs C A Sibson, BA(Oxon)
Type: Girls' Independent
Boarding and Day School
Age range: 4-18. Boarders from 7
No. of pupils enrolled as at 1.5.97:
Junior: 80 Girls; Senior: 100 Girls
Fees per annum:
Day: £3450-£4050; Boarding: £7500-£9300;
Weekly Boarding: £5760-£7500

Religious affiliation: Anglican (other religions welcome)

The School was founded on its present site in 1855. The patron is HRH Princess Alexandra, the Hon Lady Ogilvy, GVCO. Today, the School is a small independent boarding and day school for girls. The School's curriculum includes the core subjects leading to GCSE, AS and A level examinations and is compatible with the National School Curriculum. It also includes two foreign languages and the combined sciences. There is a well qualified staff with a low pupil to teacher ratio.

Entry requirements: Entry to both the Senior and Junior departments is by interview and previous school reports. An entrance test is taken when applicable. Scholarships are available at 11 years, and for the Sixth Form.

Examinations offered: GCSE, AS, A levels, and RSA.

The School is situated in pleasant and spacious surroundings. It has comfortable modern boarding accommodation and a large garden. There are excellent sports facilities. The School is close to London's major educational, cultural and recreational centres which are visited regularly. There is a large car park which facilitates the arrival and departure of pupils. The School was founded in the Christian tradition but girls of all faiths are welcome. An assembly is held most mornings.

The Royal School Hampstead is a registered charity which exists to provide a sound and broad-based education which prepares girls both to meet and cope with the challenges of the 1990s.

St Margaret's School

(Founded 1884)

18 Kidderpore Gardens,
Hampstead,
London NW3 7SR
Tel: 0171 435 2439 Fax: 0171 431 1308

Head: Mrs Suzanne Meaden,
BA(Hons), MBA, PGCE
Type: Girls Day School
Age range: 5-16
No of pupils enrolled as at 1.1.97: 142
Junior: 64 Girls, Senior: 78 Girls
Fees per annum: £3690-£4365

Religious affiliation: Church of England

Member of: ISA

Curriculum: Girls follow a curriculum based on the National Curriculum. French, Music and Drama are taught by specialists in the Reception Class. The girls are taught increasingly by specialist teachers as they progress through the Junior School. In the Senior School Spanish and Classical Civilisation are taught in addition to the National Curriculum subjects. Individual instrumental and Speech and Drama lessons are available.

Entry requirements: 5 and 6 years, interview; from 7 years, test and interview.

St Margaret's School is a registered charity which exists to provide an education tailored to individual needs.

St Mary's School Hampstead

(Founded 1926)

47 Fitzjohn's Avenue,
Hampstead, London NW3 6PG
Tel: 0171 435 1868 Fax: 0171 794 7922

Head: Mrs Wanda Nash, BA (Cert Ed), FCollP
Type: Preparatory School
Age range: 3-11
No of pupils enrolled as at 1.1.97: 257
40 Boys 217 Girls
Fees per annum: £4425

Religious denomination: Roman Catholic

Member of: IAPS, ISJC

We have a thriving Nursery. The boys are prepared for transference to popular London boys preparatory schools at the age of 7-8 years.

The girls are prepared for the Common Entrance and the entrance examinations for the London Senior Schools at the age of 11 years. In addition to a broad curriculum a wider range of activities is seen as essential to the rounded development of a healthy child. Importance is attached to physical education, drama and the arts. Extra curriculum classes include Speech and Drama, Italian, Ballet, Tap, Violin, Recorder and Piano. School trips abroad are arranged for older children.

ST MARY'S SCHOOL HAMPSTEAD

St Mary's School, Hampstead is an Educational Charity managed by a majority of lay Trustees and Governors, Registered Charity No.1006411.

South Hampstead High School GPDST

(Founded 1876)

3 Maresfield Gardens,
London NW3 5SS
Tel: 0171 435 2899 Fax: 0171 431 8022

Head: Mrs J G Scott, BSc
Type: Independent Girls' Day School
Age range: 4-18
No. of pupils enrolled as at 1.5.97:
Junior: 288 Girls; Senior: 624 Girls
Fees per annum: £4044-£4920

Religious denomination: Non denominational

Member of: GPDST

Curriculum: In the Junior School is broadly based, in sympathy with the National Curriculum. In the Senior School all usual subjects plus four modern and two classical languages offered to GCSE and Advanced Level. Purpose built theatre and sports hall. Outstanding art, music and drama. Academic standards are extremely high, A Level pass rate in 1996 99.5% and GCSE 100%, (School with the largest entry in the country, 94 candidates, to gain 100% pass rate). School is a lively, caring and creative community of individuals.

Entry requirements: Entry is at 4+ (24 places), 11+ (48 places) and 16+ (20 places). There are Assisted Places and Scholarships at 11+ and 16+.

The Girls' Public Day School Trust is of Charitable Status and exists solely to provide educational facilities.

The Village School

(Founded 1985)

2 Parkhill Road,
Belsize Park,
London NW3 2YN
Tel: 0171 485 4673

Headmistress: Mrs F M Prior, BA Hons(Cantab)
Type: Girls Preparatory Day School
Age range: 4-11
No. of pupils enrolled as at 1.5.97: 130 Girls
Fees per annum: £4290-£5310

Religious denomination: Non-denominational

Curriculum: We offer an education based on traditional standards of literacy and numeracy which includes a good grounding in science. We offer all the usual academic subjects as well as French, History of Art, Music, Art, Drama, Dance and various sports.

Thanks to small classes, selective entry and specialist subject teaching, our girls have established an enviable reputation for success in the entrance examinations to independent secondary schools, whilst enjoying the benefits of an unusually wide curriculum. We also place a high value on enterprise, individuality and good manners.

Goodwyn School

(Founded 1938)

Hammers Lane,
Mill Hill,
London NW7 4DB
Tel: 0181 959 3756 Fax: 0181 906 8961

Head Master: Struan Robertson
Age range: 3-8
No of pupils enrolled as at 1.5.97: 200
Fees per annum: £2070-£4140

Religious affiliation: Non-denominational

Curriculum: The School teaches along traditional lines. Various activities are designed to provide the opportunity for each child to mature under our guidance on lines appropriate to his or her ability. During their school career each child will receive instruction in all aspects of the curriculum including French, an appreciation of music is taught throughout the school and children can express themselves through their ability to sing, play musical instruments and in movement.

Entry requirements: Early registration is required and there is an interview with the Head prior to entry. Exam for 7+ entry.

The Mount School

(Founded 1925)

Accredited as efficient by ISJC in March 1994

Milespit Hill, Mill Hill,
London NW7 2RX
Tel: 0181 959 3403 Fax: 0181 959 1503

Headmistress: Mrs M Pond, BSc(Lon), MI Biol
Type: Independent Girls' Day School
Age range: 4-18
No. of pupils enrolled as at 8.1.97:
Junior: 60 Senior: 235 Sixth Form: 45
Fees per annum:
Pre-Prep: £3240;Junior: £3345; Senior: £3900

Religious denomination: None

Member of: ISA, ISIS

The school has five acres of grounds within the green belt, which are attractively arranged with a hockey pitch, tennis courts and a large well-equipped gymnasium containing a badminton court. A new Laboratory building was completed in 1994 and there are good facilities for Art, CDT, Music, Information Technology and Business Studies.

Curriculum: The Junior school follows the National Curriculum and is a sound foundation for entrance to the Senior school. Sports, Music and Art also play a large part in their activities. Pupils take up to ten GCSE subjects which include core subjects - Single, Double Certificated or Separate Sciences together with a range of optional subjects are offered.

A wide range of Advanced Level subjects is offered and most combinations can be arranged.

English for overseas students is provided.

Entry requirements: Interview for 4, 5, 6 year olds and VIth form. Examination and interview at 7+, 11+ and 13+. Places are sometimes available at other age groups.

The school is a charitable company which provides individual care in a supportive environment so that each student works to achieve her own full potential.

NWH

Abercorn Place School

(Founded 1987)

28 Abercorn Place, London NW8 9XP
Tel: 0171 286 4785 Fax:0171 286 4785

Headmistress: Mrs Andrea Greystoke, BA (Hons)
Interim member of ISAI
Type: Co-educational Nursery, Pre-Preparatory
and Preparatory School
Age range: 2¹/2-13 years
No. of pupils enrolled as at 1.5.97:
Junior: 50 Boys 50 Girls; Senior: 50 Boys 40 Girls
Fees per annum: Day: £3150-£5850

Religious denomination: None

Curriculum: A happy atmosphere, traditional values and modern equipment prepare pupils for entrance to London's leading schools. A wide curriculum is followed with specialist facilities for science, computing, art and CDT. French is taught from age three and Latin from age ten. Abercorn is unusual in that it provides specialist subject teaching from the age of six. Younger children learn the basic skills through project work and practical experience. A full schedule of outings, sport and musical activities complement the academic programme for all ages from nursery up.

The School offers a pre and after school care

service including clubs, *eg* science, football, jewellery making, art, dance, French and German.

The American School in London

(Founded 1951)

2-8 Loudoun Road, London NW8 0NP
Tel: 0171 722 0101 Fax: 0171 586 6885
WWW Site: http: www.asl.org

Head: Judith Glickman, PhD
Type: Co-educational Day School
Age range:
Lower School: 4-10; Middle School: 11-13; High School: 14-18
No of pupils enrolled as at 20.1.97: 1241
Lower School: 265 Boys 231 Girls
Middle School: 160 Boys 136 Girls
High School: 218 Boys 231 Girls
Fees per annum (inc VAT) as at 20.1.97:
Lower School: £8835-£9020; Middle School: £10,195 High School: £10,410

Member of: National Association of Independent Schools (US), Middle States Association of Colleges and Schools (US), Secondary Schools Admission Test Board (US), European Council of International Schools

The American School in London is a co-educational, college preparatory day school enrolling an international student body aged 4-18. Founded in 1951, ASL is the oldest American-curriculum school in the UK and remains the only non-profit independent school in England with an American curriculum. At graduation, students receive the universally recognised American high school diploma; they also have the option to prepare for the Advanced Placement International Diploma, which involves following a program of study through which students complete university-level work and sit specified AP exams. ASL graduates enter the most selective universities in the US, the UK and other countries.

The core program of English, math, science, modern languages and social studies or history is enriched with classes in fine arts, computer and physical education. Small classes foster close teacher-student relationships, and students are encouraged to take an active role in learning in order to develop the skills necessary for independent critical thinking and expression. Numerous extra-curricular activities, including athletics, community service and an after-school program, round out a student's experience.

ASL welcomes students of all nationalities, including non-English speakers below the age of 12, who meet the entry requirements. Entry is at any age and at any time throughout the school year depending on availability of places. Previous school records and teacher recommendations are required for entry.

The American School in London Educational Trust Limited, a registered charity, exists to provide an American education of the highest quality.

The King Alfred School

(Founded 1898)

Manor Wood, North End Road,
London NW11 7HY
Tel: 0181 457 5200 Fax: 0181 457 5249

Head: Mr Francis Moran, MA(Cantab), PGCE
Type: Independent School
Age range: 4-18
No. of pupils enrolled as at 13.1.97:
Junior: 119 Boys 120 Girls; Senior: 94 Boys 115 Girls
Sixth Form: 17 Boys 22 Girls
Fees per annum: £3780-£6450

Religious affiliation: Non-denominational

Member of: GBA, ISA

KAS remains distinctive among its many independent school neighbours in North London: it remains determinedly small; it accepts a wide range of ability; it has no religious affiliation; and it is cautious about over-ready acceptance of educational dogma, whatever the source.

It sees the child - each and every individual - as being at the heart of the curriculum, and the School's role as supporting that child's growth and development to healthy independence and maturity.

Curriculum: At primary level (4-11) standard good primary practice, including Computing, Woodwork, Art and Music. Middle School (11-14) offers a common curriculum, including Drama and CDT; wide range of GCSEs (including Photography, Theory and Practice of Physical Education; but English Language, French, Science and Mathematics are 'core' subjects). Sixth Form offers A levels only (including Theatre Studies, Spanish, CDT, Music, Music Technology, Computing, Technology, Photography and standard subjects). At all levels, curriculum includes elements which are non-examinable. Assisted places available at Sixth Form only.

Entry requirements: Two-day visit. Some evidence of literacy and numeracy: previous school report(s). At Sixth Form, good results at GCSE required.

The King Alfred School Society is a registered charity which exists to educate children.

North London

The Montessori House

(Founded 1984)

5 Princes Avenue, Muswell Hill, London N10 3LS
Tel: 0181 444 4399

Head: Mrs Nicola Forsyth, AMI Dip
Type: Montessori School
Age range: 2-5; Pre-Prep 5-7
No of pupils enrolled as at 1.5.97: 30 Boys 33 Girls
Fees per annum: £1467-£3417

Religious affiliation: None

Member of: Registered AMI Montessori School

The Montessori House, Muswell Hill, is a high quality Montessori school. All the classrooms are equipped to the highest standard and there are no correspondence or part-time trained teachers.

At two years old children can join a class especially designed for such young children and continue on to a full morning. Later, they can stay for a home-cooked lunch followed by play in the large, secure garden. Eventually, at around four years, children stay until 3pm, when afternoon activities include cookery, ballet, art, craft and woodwork.

A proper Montessori environment gives children confidence in themselves and their abilities and, even more importantly, self motivation. As a result, children leaving at five are expected to reach a good standard of reading, writing and basic maths.

The school has a small pre-prep department for children from 5-7 years.

The Princes Avenue School

(Founded: Nursery Dept 1984, Pre-Prep 1990)

*5 Prince's Avenue,
Muswell Hill, London N10 3LS
Tel: 0181 444 4399*

Head: Mrs N Forsyth, AMI Dip
Type: Montessori Nursery to 5 years,
traditional Pre-Prep for 5-7 years
Age range: 2-7
No. of pupils enrolled as at 1.5.97: 35 Girls 40 Boys
Fees per annum: £1600-£4950

Religious affiliation: None

The Princes Avenue School is in a converted house and offers the benefit of small classes and a friendly atmosphere.

There are 12 children in each class, allowing each to be treated as an individual and to progress according to their ability.

Pupils are given an in-depth foundation in the 3R's, as well as in science, history, geography, French and social studies. Music too forms an important part of the curriculum and sports include football, tennis, swimming and dance.

Preparation for entrance exams and interviews is given in a positive way and incorporated as part of the curriculum.

Nursery children are taught in a high quality, fully equipped Montessori class. (See The Montessori House for details.)

Lists of schools which accept pupils at 16+ to study A Levels or Vocational Courses appear elsewhere in this guide

Woodside Park School

(Founded 1988)

Frien Barnet Road,London N11 3DR
Tel: 0181 368 3777 Fax: 0181 368 3220

88 Woodside Park Road,
North Finchley, London N12 8SH

Woodside Lane,
North Finchley, London N12 8SY
Tel: 0181 445 2333 Fax: 0181 445 0835

Headmaster: R F Metters
Type: A co-educational Day School for
between the ages of $2^{3}/_{4}$ and 18
No. of pupils enrolled as at 1.9.96: 480
Pre-Prep: 105 Boys 59 Girls; Prep: 130 Boys 44 Girls
Senior: 137 Boys 5 Girls
Fees per annum: Day: £820-£7500

Religious denomination: Inter-denominational

Member of: IAPS, ECIS

Curriculum: The curriculum in the Pre-preparatory Department is designed to give a sound training in the basic skills of literacy and numeracy, and to stimulate interest and participation in a variety of other activities including games, music and the arts. In the Preparatory Department the usual subjects are taught plus Art, Craft, Design and Technology, Health, Drama, Music, PE and Games.

The Secondary Department prepares children for GCSE and the International Baccalaureate examinations in a wide range of subjects and offers an extensive programme of after-school activities.

Entry requirements: Entrance into the Secondary Department is automatic for children who already attend the School. Tests

and interviews are held for those children wishing to enter the School aged 11 for the limited number of places available. Boys and girls entering the Preparatory Department ("St Albans") (aged 7 upwards) are required to take informal tests and attend an interview. Children wishing to enter the Pre-Preparatory Department ("Holmewood") are interviewed at the School with their parents, and the younger boys and girls (aged 3 and 4) normally spend a morning at the school during the term before entry.

Examinations offered: GCSE, International Baccalaureate.

Academic and leisure facilities: All departments have their own well equipped classrooms, halls and playgrounds. Nearby games fields and swimming pools offer a wide range of sports facilities which include soccer, cricket, athletics, netball, rounders, tennis, cross-country running, hockey, golf and badminton. A great variety of clubs and activities are organised after school each day.

Religious activities: There are regular assemblies each day, and at the end of the Winter term an annual Carol Service is held.

Nursery Schools in Central London

E1

ORANGES AND LEMONS DAY NURSERY
Shoreditch Parish Church, London E1 6JN
Tel: 0171 729 4192 *Head:* Paula Cadogan
Type: Co-educational Day

EB

Gatehouse School

(Founded 1948)

*Sewardstone Road,
Victoria Park, London E2 9JG
Tel: 0181 980 2978/0181 981 5885
Fax: 0181 983 1642*

Head: Miss Alexandra Eversole,
Montessori Teaching Diploma
Type: Independent Day School
Age range: 2-11
No of pupils enrolled as at 1.1.97: 150.
80 Boys 70 Girls
Fees per annum: From £3225-£4650

See Main Section for full details. Page 29

E2

HAPPY NEST NURSERY
Fellows Court Community Centre, London E2
Tel: 0171 739 3193 *Type:* Co-educational Day

PEBBLE CENTRE MONTESSORI SCHOOL
66 Warner Place, London E2
Tel: 0171 739 4343 *Type:* Co-educational Day

E3

PILLAR BOX MONTESSORI NURSING SCHOOL
City House, 107 Bow Road, London E3
Tel: 0181 980 0700 *Head:* Ms Lorraine Redknapp
Type: Co-educational Day

E4

AMHURST NURSERY
13 The Avenue, London E4
Tel: 0181 527 1614 *Head:* Mrs Mills
Type: Co-educational Day

BILLETS CORNER NURSERY
11 Walthamstow Avenue, London E4 8TA
Tel: 0181 523 3823 *Head:* B Harmsworth
Type: Co-educational Day

MERRYFIELD MONTESSORI PRE-SCHOOL
76 Station Road, London E4 7BA
Tel: 0181 524 7697 *Head:* G Wilson
Type: Co-educational Day

MARLBOROUGH DAY NURSERY
22 Marlborough Road, London E4 9AL
Tel: 0181 527 2902 *Head:* Ms J Crowe NNEB
Type: Co-educational Day B0-5 G0-5
Fees: DAY £4680-£5980

ROCKING HORSE NURSERY
1 Hatch Lane, London E4 6LP
Tel: 0181 523 7030 *Head:* Valerie Smith
Type: Co-educational Day

E5

DOWNS SIDE NURSERY SCHOOL
Rendlesham Road, London E5
Tel: 0181 985 5937 *Type:* Co-educational Day

FAMILY CARE DAY NURSERY
51 Mayola Road, London E5
Tel: 0181 985 6486 *Head:* Mrs Juliet Marcano
Type: Co-educational Day

LEAVIEW COMMUNITY NURSERY
Leaview House, Springfield, London E5 9EJ
Tel: 0181 806 9012 *Head:* Leticia Adu AdvMontDip
Type: Co-educational Day B0-5 G0-5
No of pupils: B12 G14 *Fees:* DAY £3000-£6250

E6

FELLOWSHIP HOUSE DAY NURSERY
St Barts Centre, London E6
Tel: 0181 503 5278 *Head:* Mrs Pat Bradley
Type: Co-educational Day

E7

FIRST STEPS (MONTESSORI) DAY NURSERY
5 Sebert Road, London E7
Tel: 0181 555 0125 *Head:* Mrs Maria Adeseqha
Type: Co-educational Day

E8

136 NURSERY
c/o Ann Taylor Centre, London E8
Tel: 0171 249 9826 *Type:* Co-educational Day

BARNARDOS FERNCLIFF CENTRE
4 Ferncliff Road, London E8
Tel: 0171 254 1906 *Type:* Co-educational Day

MARKET NURSERY
Wilde Close, off Pownall Road, London E8 4JS
Tel: 0171 241 0978 *Head:* Mrs Flor Frampton
Type: Co-educational Day

E9

GET ALONG GANG PLAYGROUP
St Mary of Eton Church Hall, Eastway, London E9
Tel: 0181 533 0926 *Head:* Miss Karen Niazi
Type: Co-educational Day

E10

BARCLAY INFANT SCHOOL (NURSERY)
Essex Road, London E10
Tel: 0181 539 1299 *Type:* Co-educational Day

BEAUMONT NURSERY UNIT
192 Vicarage Road, London E10
Tel: 0181 518 7203 *Type:* Co-educational Day

CHESTERFIELD DAY NURSERY
38 Chesterfield Road, London E10
Tel: 0181 539 5541 *Head:* Karen James
Type: Co-educational Day

MULBERRY DAY NURSERY
70 Canterbury Road, London E10
Tel: 0181 558 4639 *Head:* Marcia McCollin
Type: Co-educational Day

ROSEBANK NURSERY
56 Leyton Park Road, London E10
Tel: 0181 558 8573 *Head:* Ms Downer
Type: Co-educational Day

E11

BUSHWOOD DAY NURSERY
10 Bushwood, London E11
Tel: 0181 530 2784 *Head:* Kim Swiftbury
Type: Co-educational Day

FOREST GLADE NURSERY
15 Dyson Road, London E11 1NA
Tel: 0181 989 9684 *Head:* Mrs Starmer-Jones
Type: Co-educational Day

HAPPY DAYS NURSERY
39 Fillebrook Road, London E11
Tel: 0181 556 5085 *Head:* Mrs Mehmuda Ahmed
Type: Co-educational Day

Humpty Dumpty Nursery

(Established 1972)

24/26 Fairlop Road, London E11 8BL
Tel: 0181 539 3810

Head: Ms Maryanne Gregory, NNEB
Type: Co-Educational Day
Age range: 1-5
No of pupils enrolled as at 1.1.97: 17 Boys 15 Girls
Hours: 8.00-6.00
Fees per week: £52-£92

Member of: PLA, NEYN

Open between 8.00am and 6.00pm, we offer a cosy yet stimulating environment in which children learn to socialise with their peers and develop new skills through free and structured play.

Our qualified, experienced staff provide a balanced early years curriculum paying careful attention to the individual development of each child. Both nurseries are purpose built, well-equipped and have large outdoor playgrounds.

Fresh, wholesome food is prepared daily in our own kitchens. Special diets are catered for and a vegetarian option is always available.

LITTLE CHERUBS DAY NURSERY
167 Wallward Road, London E11 1AQ
Tel: 0181 556 6889 *Head:* Miss Cher Tully
Type: Co-educational Day

LITTLE GREEN MAN NURSERY
15 Lemna Road, London E11
Tel: 0181 539 7228
Head: Mrs Philippa Carr NNEB
Type: Co-educational Day B0-5 G0-5
No of pupils: B22 G24

PETER PAN DAY NURSERY
1 Ashbridge Road, London E11
Tel: 0181 989 3346 *Head:* Mrs A Dwarika
Type: Co-educational Day

E13

FIRST FRIENDS CHILDREN'S CENTRE
Memorial Baptist Church, London E13
Tel: 0171 474 5625
Type: Co-educational Day

OOPS-A-DAISY DAY NURSERY
St Phillips/St James Church, London E13
Tel: 0171 474 8737 *Head:* Sharon McNicholas
Type: Co-educational Day

SMARTY PANTS DAY NURSERY
1 Plashet Road, London E13
Tel: 0181 471 2620
Heads: Jennifer Lewis & Sylvia Lewis
Type: Co-educational Day

STEP BY STEP CHILDREN'S CENTRE
Lawrence Hall, London E13
Tel: 0171 511 2916 *Head:* Mrs Irene Langford
Type: Co-educational Day B0-5 G0-5

STEPPING STONES DAY NURSERY
Woodside School, Woodside Road, London E13
Tel: 0171 474 0121 Ext 214
Type: Co-educational Day

E14

BUSHYTAILS DAY NURSERY AND NURSERY SCHOOL
591 Manchester Road, London E14
Tel: 0171 537 7776 *Head:* Christine G Bush NNEB
Type: Co-educational Day B0-5 G0-5

LANTERNS NURSERY AND PRESCHOOL
F4-F6 Lanterns Court, London E14
Tel: 0171 363 0951 *Type:* Co-educational Day

E17

DOROTHY MATILDA DAY NURSERY
Green Pond Road, London E17
Tel: 0181 531 7204 *Head:* Rebecca O'Brien
Type: Co-educational Day

FIRST NEIGHBOURHOOD CO-OP NURSERY
34 Verulam Avenue, London E17 8ER
Tel: 0181 520 2417 *Head:* F Beregovoi
Type: Co-educational Day

HAPPY CHILD PRE SCHOOL NURSERY
The Old Town Hall, 14B Orford Road, London E17 9LN
Tel: 0181 520 8880 *Head:* Mrs Margaret Murphy
Type: Co-educational Day

LOW HALL NURSERY
Low Hall Lane, London E17
Tel: 0181 520 1689 *Type:* Co-educational Day

MAGIC ROUNDABOUT NURSERY
London E17 4UH
Tel: 0181 523 5551 *Head:* Mr Iqbal
Type: Co-educational Day

RASCALS EDUCATIONAL PRESCHOOL DAY NURSERY
8 Downsfield Road, London E17
Tel: 0181 520 7359 *Head:* Mrs Aguda
Type: Co-educational Day

E17

Tom Thumb Nursery

(Established 1980)

20 Shirley Close, 1-7 Beulah Road, London E17 9LZ

Heads: Ms Kerry Sprackling, NNEB
and Mrs Helen Redhead, NNEB
Age range: 2-5
No. of pupils enrolled as at 1.5.97: 22 Boys 21 Girls
Hours: 8.00-6.00
Fees per week: £52-£92

Member of: PLA, NEYN

Open between 8.00am and 6.00pm, we offer a cosy yet stimulating environment in which children learn to socialise with their peers and develop new skills through free and structured play.

Our qualified, experienced staff provide a balanced early years curriculum paying careful attention to the individual development of each child. Both nurseries are purpose built, well-equipped and have large outdoor playgrounds.

Fresh, wholesome food is prepared daily in our own kitchens. Special diets are catered for and a vegetarian option is always available.

We are accredited by the Pre-School Learning Alliance and are validated to accept nursery vouchers from April 1997.

Nina West Nurseries is a registered charity which exists to provide daycare and education for pre-school children.

Registered Charity No.27274R

TINKERBELLS NURSERY
185 Coppermill Lane, London E17 7HU
Tel: 0181 520 8338 *Head:* Sue Walker
Type: Co-educational Day

E18

CLEVELANDS PARK
71 Cleveland Road, London E18
Tel: 0181 518 8855 *Type:* Co-educational Day

TREE HOUSE NURSERY SCHOOL
2 Malmsbury Road, London E18
Tel: 0181 504 1036 *Type:* Co-educational Day

EC2

BROADGATE DAY NURSERY
27/31 Earl Street, London EC2
Tel: 0171 247 3491 *Head:* Jacky Roberts NNEB
Type: Co-educational Day B0-5 G0-5

SE1

ST PATRICKS MONTESSORI NURSERY SCHOOL
91 Cornwall Road, London SE1
Tel: 0171 928 5557 *Head:* Gillian Wright
Type: Co-educational Day

SE2

PARKWAY NURSERY
Parkway Primary School, Alsike Road, London SE2
Tel: 0181 311 9799 *Head:* Mrs L Lanham
Type: Co-educational Day

SE3

BLACKHEATH & BLUECOATS DAY NURSERY
Old Dover Road, London SE3
Tel: 0181 858 8221 Ext 147 *Head:* Tracy Malyon
Type: Co-educational Day

BLACKHEATH DAY NURSERY
The Rectory Field, London SE3
Tel: 0181 305 2526 *Head:* Mrs Shipley
Type: Co-educational Day

BLACKHEATH MONTESSORI CENTRE
Independents Road, London SE3 9LF
Tel: 0181 852 6765 *Head:* Jane Skillen
Type: Co-educational Day

FRIENDS MEETINGHOUSE PLAYGROUP PPA
Independents Road, London SE3 9LS
Tel: 0181 297 1014 *Head:* Mrs Mandy Sauthion
Type: Co-educational Day

KIDS & CO DAY NURSERY
41 Westcombe Park Road, London SE3
Tel: 0181 858 6222 *Head:* Mrs Lawrence
Type: Co-educational Day

LINGFIELD DAY NURSERY
37 Kidbrooke Grove, London SE3
Tel: 0181 858 1388 *Head:* Mrs D L Smith
Type: Co-educational Day

LOLLIPOPS 2 DAY NURSERY
69 Charlton Road, London SE3
Tel: 0181 305 2014 *Head:* Mrs Thompson
Type: Co-educational Day

NEW BROOKLANDS PARK PLAY GROUP
Community Hall, London SE3
Tel: 0181 297 1816
Type: Co-educational Day

PARAGON NURSERY
29 Wemyss Road, London SE3 0TG
Tel: 0181 297 2395
Type: Co-educational Day

SE4

HILLYFIELDS DAY NURSERY
41 Harcourt Road, London SE4
Tel: 0181 694 1069 *Head:* Ms Elaine Dalton
Type: Co-educational Day

MYATT GARDEN NURSERY SCHOOL
Rokeby Road, London SE4 1DF
Tel: 0181 691 6919 *Type:* Co-educational Day

SE6

BROADFIELDS NURSERY
96 Broadfields Road, London SE6 1NG
Tel: 0181 697 1488
Type: Co-educational Day

MRS TREBLE CLEF'S SCHOOL OF MUSIC
10 Westdown Road, London SE6 4RL
Tel: 0181 690 7243 *Head:* Mrs Julia Bentham
Type: Co-educational Day

THE PAVILION NURSERY
Catford Cricket Club Pavilion, London SE6
Tel: 0181 698 0878 *Head:* Miss Corinna Wilson
Type: Co-educational Day

THORNSBEACH DAY NURSERY
10 Thornsbeach Road, London SE6 1DX
Tel: 0181 697 7699 *Head:* Mrs M Jones
Type: Co-educational Day

SE7

POUND PARK NURSERY SCHOOL
Pound Park Road, London SE7
Tel: 0181 858 1791 *Head:* Ms Pat Whittaker
Type: Co-educational Day

SE9

ELTHAM GREEN DAY NURSERY
Eltham Green School, London SE9
Tel: 0181 850 4720 *Type:* Co-educational Day

LOLLYPOP DAY NURSERY
27 Southwood Road, London SE9 3QE
Tel: 0181 859 5832 *Head:* Mrs Thompson
Type: Co-educational Day

LOLLIPOPS
88 Southwood Road, London SE9 3QT
Tel: 0181 305 2014 *Head:* Miss L Thompson
Type: Co-educational Day

NEW ELTHAM PRE SCHOOL
699 Sidcup Road, London SE9 3AQ
Tel: 0181 851 5057
Head: Lesley Watkins CertEd, NNEB
Type: Co-educational Day B0-5 G0-5
No of pupils: B89 G67

NIKKI'S DAY NURSERY
164 Footscray Road, London SE9 2TD
Tel: 0181 265 1584 *Head:* Mrs Dervish
Type: Co-educational Day

TINY TOTS DAY NURSERY
467 Footscray Road, London SE9 3UH
Tel: 0181 850 4445 *Head:* Mrs J Pool
Type: Co-educational Day

WILLOW PARK
19 Glenlyon Road, London SE9
Tel: 0181 850 8753 *Head:* Mrs McMahon
Type: Co-educational Day

SE10

ROBERT OWEN NURSERY SCHOOL
Conley Street, London SE10
Tel: 0181 858 0529 *Head:* Judith Stephenson
Type: Co-educational Day

SE11

TOAD HALL NURSERY SCHOOL (MONTESSORI)
37 St Mary's Gardens, London SE11 4UF
Tel: 0171 735 5087
Head: Mrs V K Rees NNEB, MontDip
Type: Co-educational Day B2-5 G2-5 *Fees:* DAY £1950

SE13

THE VILLAGE NURSERY
St Mary's Centre, Ladywell Road, London SE13
Tel: 0181 690 6766 *Head:* Frances Rogers
Type: Co-educational Day

SE13

The Village Montessori

*Kingswood Hall, Kingswood Place,
London SE13 5BU
Tel: 0181 318 6720*

Directress: Catherine Westlake,
Montessori Nursery Teaching Diploma
Type: Co-educational Day School
Age range: 3-5
No of pupils enrolled as at 1.1.97: 30
15 Boys 15 Girls
Fees per annum: £1491 (per term: £497)
The School is sessional: Morning Times: 9.15am to
12.00pm Afternoon Times: 1.15pm to 4.00pm

Member of: Montessori

Curriculum: Montessori is not simply a teaching method, it is a full bodied approach to develop in each child through love and understanding a belief in themselves and all things around them.

SE14

ANNABEL'S MONTESSORI NURSERY
Adj. 37 Kitto Road, London SE14
Tel: 0171 277 6414 *Type:* Co-educational Day

SE15

BELLENDEN DAY NURSERY
Faith Chapel, London SE15
Tel: 0171 639 4896 *Type:* Co-educational Day

COLOURBOX NURSERY
385 Ivydale Road, London SE15
Tel: 0171 277 9662 *Type:* Co-educational Day

THE GARDEN NURSERY
Studley Villa, London SE15
Tel: 0171 701 5411 *Head:* Mrs Gillian Leigh
Type: Co-educational Day

HEADSTART MONTESSORI
24 Waveney Avenue, London SE15 3UE
Tel: 0171 635 5501 *Type:* Co-educational Day

MOTHER GOOSE NURSERY SCHOOL
34 Wavevey Avenue, London SE15
Tel: 0171 277 5951 *Type:* Co-educational Day

MOTHER GOOSE TWO
54 Lindon Grove, London SE15
Tel: 0171 277 5956 *Type:* Co-educational Day

NEIL GWYNN NURSERY
Meeting House Lane, London SE15
Tel: 0171 252 8265 *Type:* Co-educational Day

IVYDALE ADVENTIST
149 Ivydale Road, London SE15
Tel: 0171 639 9790/635 9878 *Type:* Co-educational Day

SE16

SCALLYWAGS DAY NURSERY
St Crispin's Church Hall, London SE16
Tel: 0171 252 3225 *Head:* Miss Alison Armstrong
Type: Co-educational Day

SILWOOD FAMILY CENTRE
31-32 Alpine Road, London SE16
Tel: 0171 237 2376 *Head:* Miss Jean Williams
Type: Co-educational Day

TRINITY CHILD CARE
Holy Trinity Church Hall, Bryan Road, London SE16
Tel: 0171 231 5842 *Head:* Sharon Spice
Type: Co-educational Day

SE18

ACCESS DAY NURSERY
International House, Brook Hill Road, London SE18
Tel: 0181 316 8123 *Head:* Claudia Padfield

MOLLYZAC DAY NURSERY
60 Spray Street, London SE18 6AG
Tel: 0181 316 7591 *Type:* Co-educational Day

SIMBA DAY NURSERY
48-50 Artillery Place, London SE18 4AB
Tel: 0181 317 0451 Exts 72/74
Head: Eileen Green *Type:* Co-educational Day

SE20

ANERLEY MONTESSORI NURSERY
45 Anerley Park, London SE20 8NQ
Tel: 0181 778 2810 *Head:* Mrs P Bhatia
Type: Co-educational Day

THE CHILDRENS CENTRE
9a Stembridge Road, London SE20
Tel: 0181 778 2135 *Type:* Co-educational Day

SE21

THE BURRELL GROUP
87 Park Hall Road, London SE21
Tel: 0181 670 4736 *Type:* Co-educational Day

Dulwich College Preparatory School
(Founded 1885)

42 Alleyn Park, Dulwich,
London SE21 7AA
Tel: 0181 670 3217 Fax: 0181 766 7586

Head: Mr G Marsh, MA, CertEd
Type: Preparatory School
Age range: 3-13. Boarders from 8
No of pupils enrolled as at 1.1.97: 749
Boys (3-13): 737; Girls (3-4): 12
Fees per annum:
Day: £3801-£6156; Boarding: £9201

See Main Section for full details. Page 32

DULWICH MONTESSORI NURSERY SCHOOL
All Saints Church, London SE21 8LN
Tel: 0181 761 9560/673 7930 *Head:* Mrs E Irwin
Type: Co-educational Day B2-6 G2-6
No of pupils: B15 G15 *Fees:* DAY £1425-£1530

Rosemead Preparatory School
(Founded 1942)

70 Thurlow Park Road,
London SE21 8HZ
Tel: 0181 670 5865 Fax: 0181 761 9159

Head: Mrs R L Lait, BA, MBA(Ed), CertEd
Type: Independent Co-educational Preparatory
Age range: 3-11
No. of pupils enrolled as at 1.1.97:
135 Boys 135 Girls
Fees per annum: Day: £3150-£3750

See Main Section for full details. Page 33

SE22

FIRST STEPS MONTESSORI NURSERY
254 Upland Road, London SE22
Tel: 0181 299 6897 *Head:* Mrs Heather Benyayer
Type: Co-educational Day

GREENDALE PRE SCHOOL NURSERY
The Pavilion, Greendale, London SE22 8IX
Tel: 0171 274 1955 *Head:* Miss Sarah Legalle
Type: Co-educational Day

MONTESSORI FIRST STEPS
254 Upland Road, London SE22
Tel: 0181 299 6897 *Type:* Co-educational Day

MOTHER GOOSE NURSERIES
248 Upland Road, London SE22 0DN
Tel: 0181 693 9429 *Head:* Mrs K Chandra
Type: Co-educational Day

WAVERLEY NURSERY
Waverley School, London SE22 ONR
Tel: 0171 732 1142 *Head:* Mrs M Burrell
Type: Co-educational Day

SE24

HALF MOON MONTESSORI NURSERY
Methodist Church Hall, London SE24
Tel: 0171 326 5300 *Head:* Mrs Lucy Brignall
Type: Co-educational Day

HERON COMMUNITY CENTRE
Heron Road, London SE24
Tel: 0171 274 2894 *Heads:* Mr & Mrs Youngs
Type: Co-educational Day

KESTREL MONTESSORI NURSERY
27 Kestrel Avenue, London SE24 0ED
Tel: 0171 274 8072 *Type:* Co-educational Day

THE WHITEHOUSE
331 Norwood Road, London SE24
Tel: 0181 671 7362
Head: Mrs S Mitchell AdvDipChildcare & Edu, NNEB
Type: Co-educational Day

SE25

CHILDRENS PARADISE
4 Crowther Road, London SE25
Tel: 0181 654 1737 *Type:* Co-educational Day

SE26

SYDENHAM MONTESSORI
Wells Park Hall, London SE26
Tel: 0181 291 3947 *Type:* Co-educational Day

SE27

ABC CHILDRENS CENTRE
48 Chapel Road, London SE27
Tel: 0181 766 0246/Eves 761 8985 *Head:* Ms E Carr
Type: Co-educational Day

I

) ...oad, London SE27 0RL
Tel: ... 0 3511 *Head:* Ms C Jones
Type: Co-educational Day

SW1

LITTLE ACORNS NURSERY SCHOOL
Church of St James The Less, London SW1V
Tel: 0171 931 0898 *Type:* Co-educational Day

SWA

Garden House School

(Founded 1951)

53 Sloane Gardens,
London SW1W 8ED
Tel: 0171 730 1652 Fax: 0171 730 0470

Head: Mrs W Challen (Lower School)
Type: Preparatory School
Age range: Girls 3-11; Boys 3-8
No of pupils enrolled as at 27.1.97: 72 Boys 270 Girls
Fees per annum: £2700-£6150

See Main Section for full details. Page 35

SWA

Hill House International Junior School

(Founded 1951)

Hans Place, Chelsea,
London SW1X 0EP
Tel: 0171 584 1331 Fax: 0171 589 5925

Head: Lt Colonel H S Townend, OBE, MA(Oxon)
Type: Junior Co-educational School
Age range: 3-14 years
No of pupils enrolled as at 1.5.97: 1050
600 Boys 450 Girls
Fees per annum: £3510-£5148

See Main Section for full details. Page 36

LONDON PRE-SCHOOL PLAYGROUPS ASSOCIATION
314-316 Vauxhall Bridge Road, London SW1V
Tel: 0171 828 2417/1401 *Type:* Co-educational Day

MISS MORLEYS NURSERY SCHOOL
Fountain Court Club Room, London SW1
Tel: 0171 730 5797 *Head:* Mrs C Spence
Type: Co-educational Day B2-5 G2-5
No of pupils: B20 G25 *Fees:* DAY £1560-£1950

MORLEY'S NURSERY SCHOOL
Club Room, Fountain Court, London SW1W
Tel: 0171 730 5797 *Head:* Mrs Susan Spence
Type: Co-educational Day B2-5 G2-5
No of pupils: B13 G15 *Fees:* DAY £575-£700

THOMAS'S KINDERGARTEN
14 Ranelagh Grove, London SW1W 8PD
Tel: 0171 730 3596 *Head:* Mrs A Grant
Type: Co-educational Day B2-5 G2-5
No of pupils: B30 G30 *Fees:* DAY £1365-£2100

RINGROSE KINDERGARTEN (PIMLICO)
32a Lupus Street, London SW1V
Tel: 0171 976 6511 *Head:* Mrs Stark
Type: Co-educational Day

YOUNG ENGLAND KINDERGARTEN
St Saviour's Hall, London SW1V 3QW
Tel: 0171 834 3171 *Head:* Mrs Kay C King MontDip
Type: Co-educational Day B2-5 G2-5
No of pupils: B40 G30 *Fees:* DAY £1470-£2265

SW2

ABACUS
St Margaret's, Cricklade Avenue, London SW2
Tel: 0181 674 9333 *Head:* Ms J Chidgey
Type: Co-educational Day

ELM PARK NURSERY SCHOOL
Brixton Methodist Church, London SW2
Tel: 0181 678 1990 *Heads:* Mr & Mrs Taylor
Type: Co-educational Day

GARDEN OF EDEN
Gospel Tabernacle, London SW2
Tel: 0181 674 9462 *Head:* Mrs B Adetona
Type: Co-educational Day

STREATHAM MONTESSORI NURSERY SCHOOL
66 Blairderry Road, London SW2 4SB
Tel: 0181 674 2208 *Head:* Mrs Gangi
Type: Co-educational Day

WOODENTOPS
Telford Park Tennis Club, London SW2
Tel: 0181 674 9514 *Head:* Mrs M McCahery
Type: Co-educational Day

SW3

KNIGHTSBRIDGE KINDERGARTEN ONE
British Red Cross Hall, London SW3 5BS
Tel: 0171 581 4242
Head: Mrs J Ewing-Hoy CertEd(Oxon)
Type: Co-educational Day B2-5 G2-5 *Fees:* DAY £2250

RINGROSE KINDERGARTEN (CHELSEA)

St Lukes Church Hall, London SW3
Tel: 0171 352 8784 *Type:* Co-educational Day

SW4

ABACUS
Clapham United Church, London SW4 0DE
Tel: 0171 720 7290 *Head:* Ms J Chidgey
Type: Co-educational Day

DAISY CHAIN MONTESSORI NURSERY
Stockwell Methodist Church, London SW4
Tel: 0171 738 8606 *Head:* Lucy Gordon Lennox MontDip
Type: Co-educational Day B2-5 G2-5
No of pupils: B20 G26 *Fees:* DAY £1860

MONTESSORI SCHOOL
St Pauls Community Hall, London SW4
Tel: 0171 498 8324 Head: Mrs R Bowles

SW5

LADYBIRD NURSERY SCHOOL
24 Collingham Road, London SW5
Tel: 0171 244 7771 *Head:* Miss Fanny Ward

SW6

LANGFORD PLAY CENTRE
Langford School, London SW6
Tel: 0181 766 6750 *Type:* Co-educational Day

MELROSE HOUSE NURSERY SCHOOL
55 Finlay Street, London SW6
Tel: 0171 763 9296 *Type:* Co-educational Day

RISING STAR MONTESSORI SCHOOL
St Clement Church Hall, London SW6
Tel: 0171 381 3511 *Head:* Mrs H Casson
Type: Co-educational Day B2-5 G2-5 *Fees:* DAY £1560

STUDIO DAY NURSERY
93 Moore Park Road, London SW6 2DA
Tel: 0171 736 9256
Head: Miss Jenny M R Williams NNEB, RSH
Type: Co-educational Day B2-5 G2-5
No of pupils: B30 G35

TWICE TIMES MONTESSORI NURSERY SCHOOL
The Cricket Pavilion, London SW6 3AF
Tel: 0171 731 4929
Heads: Mrs A Welch MontDip &
          Mrs S Henderson MontDip
Type: Co-educational Day B2-5 G2-5
Fees: DAY £1650-£2100

THE ZEBEDEE NURSERY SCHOOL
Sulivan Hall, London SW6
Tel: 0171 371 9224 *Head:* Miss Noemi Young
Type: Co-educational Day

SWG

Falkner House

(Founded 1954)

19 Brechin Place, London SW7 4QB
Tel: 0171 373 4501 Fax: 0171 835 0073

Headmistress: Mrs Jacina Bird, BA(Hons)
Type: Preparatory Girls' Day School
Age range: 2-11
No. of pupils enrolled as at 1.5.97: 140 Girls
Fees per annum: £5250

See Main Section for full details. Page 40

SWG

The Hampshire Schools

(Founded 1928)

The Knightsbridge Under School
5 Wetherby Place, London SW7 4NX
Tel: 0171 370 7081

Head: Mr A.G.Bray, CertEd
Type: Independent Day School
Knightsbridge: Co-educational to 8, Girls to 11
Age range: 3-6
Maximum no of pupils: 92;
Fees per annum: £2205-£6930

See Main Section for full details. Page 42

SW7

KNIGHTSBRIDGE NURSERY SCHOOL
51 Thurloe Square, London SW7
Tel: 0171 823 9771 *Type:* Co-educational Day

SWG

Montessori St Nicholas

(Founded 1970)

23/24 Princes Gate,
London SW7 1PT
Tel: 0171 225 1277 Fax: 0171 823 7557

Head: Mrs Rosemary Hinde, Montessori Adv.Dip
Type: Nursery, Pre-Prep and Prep
Age range: 2.9 years to 9 years
No of pupils enrolled as at 1.9.97: 120
60 Boys 60 Girls
Fees per annum: £2850-£4350

See Main Section for full details. Page 44

TINY TOTS OF KENSINGTON
48 St Stephens House, London SW7
Tel: 0171 373 6111 *Head:* Mrs M Christiano
Type: Co-educational Day

THE ZEBEDEE NURSERY SCHOOL
St Pauls Hall, London SW7
Tel: 0171 584 7660 *Head:* Susan Gahan
Type: Co-educational Day

SW8

NINE ELMS NURSERY
Savona Club-room, Ascalon Street,
London SW8 4DL
Tel: 0171 627 5191 *Head:* Pauline Khoo
Type: Co-educational Day

ST CECILIA'S
Christchurch Hall, London SW8
Tel: 0171 720 0827 Head: Mrs D Farley
Type: Co-educational Day

THE WILLOW NURSERY SCHOOL
Clapham Baptist Church, London SW8
Tel: 0171 498 0319 *Type:* Co-educational Day

THE WILLOW SCHOOL
c/o Clapham Baptist Church, London SW8 3JX
Tel: 0171 498 0319 *Head:* Mrs C Kane
Type: Co-educational Day B2-5 G2-5
No of pupils: B17 G18 *Fees:* DAY £1725-£1875

Newton Preparatory School

(Founded 1991)

*149 Battersea Park Road,
London SW8 4BH
Tel: 0171 720 4091 Fax: 0171 498 9052*

Head: Mr Richard Dell, MA(Oxon)
Type: Preparatory School
Age range: 3-13
No. of pupils enrolled as at 1.1.97: 254
132 Boys 122 Girls

See Main Section for full details. Page 47

SW9

BUNNYSHAPES
United Reform Church, London SW9
Tel: 0171 738 4795
Heads: Ms B Stovell & Ms G Walters
Type: Co-educational Day

WILTSHIRE NURSERY
85 Wiltshire Road, London SW9
Tel: 0171 274 4446 *Type:* Co-educational Day

SW10

THE BOLTONS NURSERY SCHOOL
262 Fulham Road, London SW10
Tel: 0171 351 6993 *Head:* Mrs V Heine
Type: Co-educational Day B2-5 G2-5
No of pupils: B19 G21 *Fees:* DAY £1650-£3783

BUSY BEE NURSERY
St Lukes Hall, Adrian Mews, London SW10
Tel: 0171 373 3628 *Head:* Miss J Hicks
Type: Co-educational Day

THE CHELSEA NURSERY SCHOOL
The Chelsea Centre, Worlds End Place, London SW10
Tel: 0171 351 0993 *Head:* Sheila Ochugbojau
Type: Co-educational Day B2-5 G2-5
Fees: DAY £356-£1800

KNIGHTSBRIDGE KINDERGARTEN TWO
St Andrews Church, London SW10 0AU
Tel: 0171 352 4856/229 5194
Head: Mrs Suzanne Stevens CertEd
Type: Co-educational Day B2-5 G2-5
Fees: DAY £2250-£4035

PAINT POTS MONTESSORI SCHOOL, CHELSEA
Chelsea Christian Centre, London SW10 0LB
Tel: 0171 376 5780 *Head:* Miss G Hood MontDip
Type: Co-educational Day B2-5 G2-5
No of pupils: B15 G15 *Fees:* DAY £1053-£3561

PARK WALK PRIMARY SCHOOL
Park Walk, King's Road, London SW10 0AY
Tel: 0171 352 8700 *Head:* Ms N Ostwald
Type: Co-educational Day

TADPOLES NURSERY SCHOOL
Park Walk Play Centre, London SW10 0AY
Tel: 0171 352 9757 *Head:* Mrs C Dimpsl
Type: Co-educational Day

SW11

ALPHABET NURSERY SCHOOL
Chatham Hall, Northcote Road, London SW11 6DY
Tel: 0181 871 7473 *Head:* Mrs A McKenzie-Lewis
Type: Co-educational Day *Fees:* DAY £1500-£1800

BLUNDELLS DAY NURSERY
The Old Court, 194-196 Sheepcote Lane, London SW11
Tel: 0171 924 4204 *Type:* Co-educational Day

South London Montessori School

(Founded September 1990)

*Trott Street, Battersea, London SW11 3DS
Tel: 0171 738 9546 Fax: 0171 223 2904*

Head: Mrs T M O'Regan-Byrnes, MontIntDip, DipAMI
Type: Montessori School
Age range: 2-12
No of pupils enrolled as at 1.5.97: 36
Fees per annum:
Day: (2-4): £590; (4-6): £1070; (6-12): £1360

See Main Section for full details. Page 51

LITTLE RED ENGINE
Church of the Nazarene, London SW11
Tel: 0171 738 0321 *Head:* Miss Annie Richardson
Type: Co-educational Day

THE MOUSE HOUSE NURSERY SCHOOL
27 Mallinson Road, London SW11
Tel: 0171 924 1893/5325
Head: Mrs Barney White-Spunner
Type: Co-educational Day
No of pupils: B80 G80 *Fees:* DAY £780-£2040

THOMAS'S KINDERGARTEN, BATTERSEA
The Crypt, St Mary's Church, London SW11 3NA
Tel: 0171 738 0400 *Head:* Mrs B Angus
Type: Co-educational Day B2-5 G2-5
No of pupils: B25 G25 s*Fees:* DAY £1365-£2100

SW12

ABACUS EARLY LEARNING NURSERY SCHOOL
135 Laitwood Road, London SW12 9QH
Tel: 0181 675 8093 *Type:* Co-educational Day

BALHAM NURSERY SCHOOL
72 Endlesham Road, London SW12
Tel: 0181 673 4055 *Head:* Mrs Ann Douglas
Type: Co-educational Day

CATERPILLAR NURSERY SCHOOL
74 Endlesham Road, London SW12 8JL
Tel: 0181 673 6058 *Head:* Marilyn Hassell
Type: Co-educational Day

CRESSET KINDERGARTEN
Waldorf School of S W London, London SW12 8DR
Tel: 0181 673 4881 *Head:* Pat Hague
Type: Co-educational Day

GATEWAY HOUSE NURSERY SCHOOL
St Judes Church Hall, London SW12 8EG
Tel: 0181 675 8258 *Head:* Miss Elizabeth Marshall
Type: Co-educational Day *Fees:* DAY £1800-£1980

KNIGHTINGALES NURSERY
St Francis Xavier College, London SW12
Tel: 0181 673 2208 *Head:* Miss Justine Lucey
Type: Co-educational Day

SWK

Hornsby House School
(Founded 1988)

*Hearnville Road,
London SW12 8RS
Tel: 0181 675 1255 Fax: 0181 877 9737*

Principal: Dr B Hornsby, PhD
Head: Mrs E Nightingale BA
Type: Preparatory School
Age range: 3-11
No. of pupils enrolled as at 1.9.96: 180
99 Boys 81 Girls
Fees per term: £550-£1669

See Main Section for full details. Page 52

MONTESSORI NIGHTINGALE NURSERY
St Lukes Church Hall, London SW12
Tel: 0181 675 4387 *Type:* Co-educational Day

NOAH'S ARK NURSERY SCHOOL
Endlesham Church Hall, London SW12
Tel: 0181 673 8227 *Type:* Co-educational Day
Fees: DAY £1935

THE OAK TREE NURSERY SCHOOL
21 Ramsden Road, London SW12 8QX
Tel: 0181 870 5760 *Head:* Mrs Jill Gould
Type: Co-educational Day B2-5 G2-5
No of pupils: B14 G20 *Fees:* DAY £1740

SW13

THE ARK NURSERY SCHOOL
Kitson Hall, London SW13
Tel: 0181 741 4751
Heads: Lorraine Ladbon & Victoria Brown
Type: Co-educational Day

LOWTHER NURSERY
Stillingfleet Road, London SW13
Type: Co-educational Day

ST MICHAELS NURSERY SCHOOL
St Michaels Church Hall, London SW13
Tel: 0181 878 0116 *Head:* Mrs J L Gould
Type: Co-educational Day B2-5 G2-5

SW14

PARKSIDE SCHOOL
459 Upper Richmond Road West, London SW14
Tel: 0181 876 8144 *Head:* Ms Claire Wilson
Type: Co-educational Day

SW15

BUSY BEE NURSERY SCHOOL
106 Felsham Road, London SW15
Tel: 0181 780 1615 *Type:* Co-educational Day

BUSY BEE NURSERY SCHOOL
19 Lytton Grove, London SW15 2EZ
Tel: 0181 789 0132 *Head:* Mrs Lucy Lindsay
Type: Co-educational Day

BEES KNEES NURSERY SCHOOL
12 Priory Lane, London SW15 5JQ
Tel: 0181 876 1149 *Head:* Mrs Sarah Ramsay
Type: Co-educational Day

MISS GRAYS NURSERY SCHOOL
St Margarets Church Hall, London SW15
Tel: 0181 788 4809 *Head:* Mrs M Gray
Type: Co-educational Day B2-5 G2-5 *Fees:* DAY £1140

PUTNEY COMMON MONTESSORI NURSERY SCHOOL
All Saints Hall, Putney Common, London SW15
Tel: 0181 780 1029 *Head:* Anna Wood
Type: Co-educational Day

PUTNEY VALE TINY TOTS
Newlands Community Centre, London SW15
Tel: 0181 780 5050 *Type:* Co-educational Day

RIVERSIDE MONTESSORI NURSERY SCHOOL
95 Lacy Road, London SW15 1NR
Tel: 0181 780 9345 *Head:* Miss Barbara Ladden
Type: Co-educational Day

SQUARE ONE
12 Ravenna Road, London SW15
Tel: 0181 788 1546 *Type:* Co-educational Day

SUNFLOWER NURSERY SCHOOL
Rosslyn Park Rugby Football Club, London SW15
Tel: 0181 947 8097 *Head:* Mrs Lucy Ennis
Type: Co-educational Day

TIGGERS NURSERY SCHOOL LTD
87 Putney Bridge Road, London SW15 2PA
Tel: 0181 874 4668 *Head:* Natasha Green
Type: Co-educational Day *Fees:* DAY £1575

SW16

ABACUS EARLY LEARNING NURSERY SCHOOL
7 Drewstead Road, London SW16 1LY
Tel: 0181 677 9117
Heads: Mrs M Taylor BEd & Ms S Petgrave
Type: Co-educational Day

CARMENA CHRISTIAN DAY NURSERIES
38 Mitcham Lane, London SW16
Tel: 0181 677 1376 *Type:* Co-educational Day

CARMENA CHRISTIAN DAY NURSERIES
47 Thrale Road, London SW16
Tel: 0181 677 8231 *Type:* Co-educational Day

CROYDON MONTESSORI NURSERY SCHOOL
Next to 55 Ederline Avenue, London SW16 4RZ
Tel: 0181 764 2531/660 0282
Head: Mrs A McConway
        PGCE, BA(Hons), MontDip, SpLDDip
Type: Co-educational Day B2-5 G2-5
No of pupils: B30 G30 *Fees:* DAY £474-£2400

FATEMAH DAY NURSERY
53 Buckleigh Road, London SW16 5RY
Tel: 0181 764 8657 *Head:* Ms S Ismail
Type: Co-educational Day

FIRST STEPS
48 Barrow Road, London SW16 5PF
Tel: 0181 769 9677 *Head:* Mrs N Abbas
Type: Co-educational Day

FISHER HOUSE DAY NURSERY
32 Mitcham Lane, London SW16 6NP
Tel: 0181 696 9642/3 *Head:* Mrs Carol Edwards
Type: Co-educational Day

NORBURY NURSERY SCHOOL
Fairholme Dunbar Avenue, London SW16
Tel: 0181 764 2564 *Type:* Co-educational Day

RAINBOW DAY NURSERY (STREATHAM COMMON)
34 Kempshott Road, London SW16
Tel: 0181 679 4235 *Head:* Mrs Azra Siddique
Type: Co-educational Day

ST LEONARD'S
38 Mitcham Lane, London SW16 6NP
Tel: 0181 677 1376 *Type:* Co-educational Day

SW17

THE CHILDREN'S HOUSE MONTESSORI
St Mary's Church Hall, London SW17 0UQ
Tel: 0181 947 7359 *Head:* Mrs S Gmaj MontDip
Type: Co-educational Day B2-5 G2-5 *Fees:* DAY £1440

THE CRESCENT KINDERGARTEN
Flat 1, 10 Trinity Crescent, London SW17 7AE
Tel: 0181 767 5882 *Head:* Philip Evelegh
Type: Co-educational Day

THE EVELINE DAY NURSERY SCHOOLS LTD
30 Ritherdon Road, London SW17 8QD
Tel: 0181 672 7549/7259 *Head:* Mrs T Larche
Type: Co-educational Day

IN LOCO PARENTIS
272 Balham High Road, London SW17
Tel: 0181 767 7109
Head: Ms Emily Dexter MontDip, NNEB
Type: Co-educational Day

JACK IN THE BOX NURSERY SCHOOL
Seacadets Hall, Mellison Road, London SW17
Tel: 0171 622 1106 *Head:* Miss J Clarke
Type: Co-educational Day

SW17

Little Wandsworth Nursery

290 Balham High Road,
London SW17 7AL
Tel/Fax: 0181 767 4051

Head: Mrs Marie Cabourn-Smith
Age range: 2-4+
No of pupils enrolled as at 1.1.97: 80
43 Boys 37 Girls
Fees per 5 am Sessions: £655

We teach the children in small informal groups which allows them the individual attention they need. The curriculum, even at this early stage, is carefully structured to provide for each child's intellectual, social, emotional and physical needs. The foundation for the more formal teaching they will receive later is laid here.

THE MONTESSORI NURSERY-CHILDREN'S HOUSE
St Mary's Church Hall, London SW17
Tel: 0181 947 7359 *Head:* Samantha Gmaj
Type: Co-educational Day

RED BALLOON NURSERY SCHOOL
St Mary Magdalene Church Hall, London SW17 7SD
Tel: 0181 672 4711/228 4447
Head: Ms T Millington-Drake MontDip
Type: Co-educational Day B2-5 G2-5
Fees: DAY £620-£640

SW18

345 NURSERY SCHOOL
Fitzhugh Community Clubroom, London SW18 4AA
Tel: 0181 870 8441/877 0437 *Head:* Mrs Annabel Dixon
Type: Co-educational Day

CROSSFIELD KINDERGARTEN
United Reform Church, Earlsfield Road, London SW18 *Tel:*
0181 875 0898 *Type:* Co-educational Day

MELROSE HOUSE NURSERY SCHOOL
39 Melrose Road, London SW18 1LX
Tel: 0181 874 7769 *Head:* Mrs Ruth Oates NNEB
Type: Co-educational Day B2-5 G2-5
No of pupils: B15 G15

THE PUTNEY KINDERGARTEN
176 Sutherland Grove, London SW18
Tel: 0181 877 3555 *Type:* Co-educational Day

SQUARE ONE NURSERY SCHOOL
17B Amerland Road, London SW18 1PX
Tel: 0181 871 3377/947 8497 *Head:* Mrs S J Stewart
Type: Co-educational Day

WANDLE HOUSE NURSERY SCHOOL
25-27 West Hill, London SW18
Tel: 0181 875 0752
Head: Mrs Shirley Stewart MontDip, BEd(Hons)
Type: Co-educational Day

WIMBLEDON PARK MONTESSORI SCHOOL
206 Heythorp Street, London SW18
Tel: 0181 944 8584 *Head:* Mrs Wilberforce Ritchie
Type: Co-educational Day B2-5 G2-5 *Fees:* DAY £1620

SW19

THE CASTLE KINDERGARTEN
20 Henfield Road, London SW19
Tel: 0181 544 0089 *Head:* Mrs Beverley Davis DipEd
Type: Co-educational Day B2-5 G2-5
No of pupils: B34 G34

COSMOPOLITAN DAY NURSERY
65/67 High Street, London SW19
Tel: 0181 544 0758
Type: Co-educational Day

THE GROVE NURSERY
28 Wilton Grove, London SW19
Tel: 0181 540 2388 *Head:* V Kimber
Type: Co-educational Day *Fees:* DAY £1575

HERBERT DAY NURSERY
Park House Hall, London SW19
Tel: 0181 542 7416 *Head:* Mrs V I Bedford
Type: Co-educational Day

THE HILL KINDERGARTEN
65 Wimbledon Hill Road, London SW19
Tel: 0181 946 7467 *Heads:* Mrs Dobbs TechCertFroebel
& Mrs Fox BA(Hons)Soc
Type: Co-educational Day B3-5 G3-5
No of pupils: B51 G44 *Fees:* DAY £1320-£1560

MONTESSORI 3-5 NURSERY
58 Queens Road, London SW19 8LR
Tel: 0181 946 8139 *Head:* Mrs I Hodgson
Type: Co-educational Day B2-6 G2-6
Fees: DAY £1431-£2694

TRINITY NURSERY SCHOOL
The Holy Trinity Church Centre, London SW19
Tel: 0181 540 3868 *Head:* Miss A Turpin
Type: Co-educational Day

THE WIMBLEDON VILLAGE MONTESSORI SCHOOL
26 Lingfield Road, London SW19 4QD
Tel: 0181 944 0772 *Head:* Paul Nolan
Type: Co-educational Day

W1

JUMBO MONTESSORI NURSERY SCHOOL
St James Church Hall, London W1H
Tel: 0171 935 2441 *Head:* Miss J Barnical
Type: Co-educational Day B2-5 G2-5
No of pupils: B13 G22 *Fees:* DAY £1785

LONDON MONTESSORI CENTRE LTD
18 Balderton Street, London W1Y 1TG
Tel: 0171 493 0165
Head: Lauren Joffe BA, MontDip, AdDip
Type: Co-educational Day B17-60 G17-60
No of pupils: B10 G290 *Fees:* DAY £3600

W2

CREME DE LA CREME (UK) LTD
32 Edgeware Road, London W2
Tel: 0171 286 6544 *Type:* Co-educational Day

DR ROLFE'S MONTESSORI SCHOOL
10 Pembridge Square, London W2 4ED
Tel: 0171 727 8300
Head: Miss A Arnold NNEB (Dyslexia Therapist)
Type: Co-educational Day B2-5 G2-5
No of pupils: B30 G30 *Fees:* DAY £2190-£3753

KINDERLAND MONTESSORI NURSERY SCHOOL
47 Palace Court, London W2 4LF
Tel: 0171 792 1964 *Head:* Ms Elaine Quigley
Type: Co-educational Day

PAINT POTS MONTESSORI SCHOOL, BAYSWATER
Bayswater United Reform Church, London W2 5LS
Tel: 0171 792 0433 *Head:* Miss G Hood MontDip
Type: Co-educational Day B2-5 G2-5
No of pupils: B12 G12 *Fees:* DAY £2085-£3618

MONTESSORI KINDERLAND NURSERY SCHOOL
47 Palace Court, London W2
Tel: 0171 792 1964 *Type:* Co-educational Day

ST JOHNS NURSERY SCHOOL
St Johns Church, London W2 2QD
Tel: 0171 402 2529 *Head:* Ms Nukki Cosh
Type: Co-educational Day B2-5 G2-5
No of pupils: B17 G14 *Fees:* DAY £2530-£5450

W3

EALING MONTESSORI SCHOOL
St Martins Church Hall, London W3
Tel: 0181 992 4513/998 0249 *Head:* Mrs P Jaffer
Type: Co-educational Day B2-6 G2-6
Fees: DAY £1730-£2595

THE VILLAGE MONTESSORI NURSERY
All Saints Church, Bollo Bridge Road, London W3
Tel: 0181 993 3540 *Head:* Miss Kay Bingham
Type: Co-educational Day

W4

THE CATERPILLAR MONTESSORI LTD
St Albans Church Hall, London W4
Tel: 0181 747 8531 *Type:* Co-educational Day

CATERPILLAR MONTESSORI NURSERY SCHOOL
St Albans Church Hall, South Parade, London W4 3HY
Tel: 0181 747 8531 *Head:* Mrs M Ward-Niblett
Type: Co-educational Day B2-5 G2-5
Fees: DAY £1560-£1830

ELMWOOD MONTESSORI SCHOOL
St Michaels Church Hall, London W4 3DY
Tel: 0181 994 8177 *Head:* Mrs S Herbert BA
Type: Co-educational Day B2-5 G2-5
No of pupils: B20 G20 *Fees:* DAY £2025

HOMEFIELDS UNDER FIVES CENTRE
Homefields, London W4
Tel: 0181 995 4648 *Head:* Mrs Sandra Lane
Type: Co-educational Day

THE MEADOWS MONTESSORI SCHOOL
Dukes Meadows Community Centre, London W4 2TD
Tel: 0181 742 1327/995 2621 *Head:* Mrs S Herbert BA
Type: Co-educational Day B2-5 G2-5
No of pupils: B20 G20 *Fees:* DAY £2010

ORCHID HOUSE SCHOOL
16 Newton Grove, London W4 1LB
Tel: 0181 742 8544 *Type:* Co-educational Day

W5

BUTTERCUPS NURSERY SCHOOL
Ealing Dance Centre, Pitshanger Lane, London W5
Tel: 0181 998 2774 *Head:* Mrs C Whitehouse
Type: Co-educational Day

JUMPERS! NURSERY SCHOOL
25 St Mary's Road, London W5 5RE
Tel: 0181 579 6946 *Head:* Ann Babb
Type: Co-educational Day

KITE OF EALING MONTESSORI NURSERY
45 Queens Walk, London W5 1TL
Tel: 0181 566 7962 *Type:* Co-educational Day

WE

Beacon House School
(Founded 1946)

15 Gunnersbury Avenue, Ealing,
London W5 3XD
Tel: 0181 992 5189

Headmistress: Mrs M Milner, BA Hons(Lond)
Type: Independent Day School taking
both Boys and Girls
Age range: 3-11
No. of pupils enrolled as at 21.1.97: 144
25 Boys 119 Girls
Fees per annum (1996/97): £1440 (Kindergarten)

See Main Section for full details. Page 61

LA PETITE FRANCE
Ealing YMCA, 25 St Mary's Road, London W5 5RE
Tel: 0181 579 5076 *Head:* Miss Beatrice Saison
Type: Co-educational Day

NURSERY LAND
Ninth Ealing Scouts Hall, London W5
Tel: 0181 566 5962 *Type:* Co-educational Day

PARK VIEW NURSERY SHOOL
Methodist Church Hall, Rooms 1, 2 & 3,
London W5 1LY
Tel: 0181 575 2199 *Head:* Mrs Marilyn Blackledge
Type: Co-educational Day B2-5 G2-5

PITSHANGER BUSY BEES NURSERY
181 Pitshanger Lane, London W5 1RQ
Tel: 0181 997 5078 *Head:* Mrs Marysia Maryniak
Type: Co-educational Day B3-5 G3-5

ST MATTHEWS MONTESSORI SCHOOL
North Common Road, London W5 2QA
Tel: 0181 579 2304 *Head:* Mrs Y Abdulrahman
Type: Co-educational Day

TORTOISE GREEN NURSERY SCHOOL
43 Castlebar Road, London W5 2DJ
Tel: 0181 998 0638 *Head:* Mrs Olivia Woodward
Type: Co-educational Day

W6

THE JORDANS NURSERY SCHOOL 2
Holy Innocents Church, London W6
Tel: 0181 746 3144
Head: Mrs S Jordan MontDip, NNEB, RSHDip
Type: Co-educational Day B2-5 G2-5
Fees: DAY £1680-£2016

W7

BUTTONS NURSERY SCHOOL
99 Oaklands Road, London W7
Tel: 0181 840 3355
Heads: Jane Loukes SRN, RMN &
          Anthony Loukes MA(Oxon)
Type: Co-educational Day B2-5 G2-5
No of pupils: B22 G26 Fees: DAY £300-£3378

W8

POOH CORNER MONTESSORI NURSERY SCHOOL
Christ Church Vestry, London W8
Tel: 0171 937 1364 *Type:* Co-educational Day

Lady Eden's School

(Founded 1947)

39-41 Victoria Road,
Kensington,
London W8 5RJ
Tel: 0171 937 0583 Fax: 0171 376 0515

Head: Mrs. J A Davies, BA, CertEd
Type: Independent Pre-Preparatory and Preparatory
Day School for Girls
Age range: 3-11
No of pupils enrolled as at 1.5.97: 155 Girls
Fees per annum: £2595-£5910

See Main Section for full details. Page 66

W9

LITTLE SWEETHEARTS NURSERY SCHOOL LTD
St Saviours Church, London W9
Tel: 0171 266 1616 *Head:* Mrs Ulker Eaton
Type: Co-educational Day

WINDMILL MONTESSORI NURSERY SCHOOL
Former Caretaker's Cottage, London W9
Tel: 0171 289 3410
Heads: Miss M H Leoni & Miss J Davidson
Type: Co-educational Day *Fees:* DAY £2400-£4800

W11

ACORN NURSERY SCHOOL
2 Lansdowne Crescent, London W11
Tel: 0171 727 2122
Head: Mrs Jane Cameron BEd(Hons)
Type: Co-educational Day B2-5 G2-5 *Fees:* DAY £2250

DENBIGH UNDER FIVES GROUP
5/7 Denbigh Road, London W11
Tel: 0171 221 5318 *Type:* Co-educational Day

KENLEY MONTESSORI SCHOOL
Kenley Walk, London W11 4BA
Tel: 0171 229 2740/0181 876 5021
Head: Isabel Aljovin MontDipAdv
Type: Co-educational Day B2-6 G2-6
No of pupils: B10 G10 *Fees:* DAY £1560-£1920

LADBROKE SQUARE MONTESSORI SC
43 Ladbroke Square, London W11 3ND
Tel: 0171 229 0125
Head: Mrs Sophia Russell-Cobb MontDip
Type: Co-educational Day B2-5 G2-5
No of pupils: B60 G40
Fees: DAY £2100-£3750

SQUARE MONTESSORI SCHOOL
18 Holland Park Avenue, London W11 3QU
Tel: 0171 221 6004 *Head:* Mrs V Lawson-Tancred
Type: Co-educational Day *Fees:* DAY £2220

ST PETERS NURSERY SCHOOL
59a Portobello Road, London W11
Tel: 0171 243 2617 *Head:* Beverley Gibbs
Type: Co-educational Day

W12

BRINGING UP BABY
101 Frithville Gardens, London W12
Tel: 0181 749 1255/6 *Type:* Co-educational Day

THE JORDANS NURSERY SCHOOL 1
Kelmscott Gdns Community Centre, London W12
Tel: 0181 749 1984
Head: Mrs S Jordan MontDip, NNEB, RSHDip
Type: Co-educational Day B2-5 G2-5
Fees: DAY £1680-£2016

LITTLE PEOPLE OF WILLOW VALE
9 Willow Vale, London W12 0PA
Tel: 0181 749 2877 *Head:* Miss Jane Gleasure
Type: Co-educational Day

Avenue House School

(Founded January 1995)

70 The Avenue, Ealing,
London W13 8LS
Tel: 0181 998 9981 Fax: 0181 991 1533

Head: Carolyn Barber, CertEd (Bristol University)
Type: Co-educational Pre-preparatory
and Preparatory School
Age range: 2-11
Fees per annum: £1890-£3780

See Main Section for full details. Page 67

13

HOLISTIC EARLY LEARNING SCHOOL
2 Amherst Road, London W13
Tel: 0181 998 2723 *Head:* Teri Farrar
Type: Co-educational Day

JIGSAW NURSERY & MONTESSORI SCHOOL
1 Courtfield Gardens, London W13
Tel: 0181 997 8330 *Head:* Debbie Clements
Type: Co-educational Day

MIDHURST NURSERY SCHOOL
146 Midhurst Road, London W13 9TP
Tel: 0181 579 4028 *Head:* Mrs Hawes
Type: Co-educational Day

W14

BRAMBER NURSERY
Bramber Road, London W14
Tel: 0171 385 5489
Type: Co-educational Day

BRIGHT SPARKS MONTESSORI SCHOOL
25 Minford Gardens, London W14 0AP
Tel: 0171 371 4697 *Head:* Matilda D'Angelo
Type: Co-educational Day B2-5 G2-5

BUSY BEE NURSERY SCHOOL
Addison Boys Club, London W14
Tel: 0171 602 8905
Type: Co-educational Day

JAMES LEE NURSERY SCHOOL
Gliddon Road, London W14
Tel: 0181 741 8877
Type: Co-educational Day

HOLLAND PARK DAY NURSERY
9 Holland Road, London W14 8HJ
Tel: 0171 602 9266 *Head:* Audrey Bryant
Type: Co-educational Day B0-3 G0-3

HOLLAND PARK DAY NURSERY'S SCHOOL HOUSE
5 Holland Road, London W14
Tel: 0171 602 9066 *Head:* Sophie Bashall
Type: Co-educational Day

WC2

CHERUBS NURSERY
48 The Market, London WC2E 8RF
Tel: 0171 240 4686 *Type:* Co-educational Day

KINGSWAY CHILDREN'S CENTRE
70 Great Queen Street, London WC2B
Tel: 0171 831 7460 *Type:* Co-educational Day

NW1

THE CAMDEN DAY NURSERY
123-127 St Pancras Way, London NW1 0SY
Tel: 0171 284 3600 *Head:* Sue Timms
Type: Co-educational Day B0-3 G0-3
Fees: DAY £1955

NW1

St Marks Square Nursery School

St Marks Church,
London NW1
Tel: 0171 586 8383

Head: Dr Sheema Parsons, BEd
Age range: 2-5 years
No of pupils enrolled as at 1.1.97: 28 per session
14 Boys 14 Girls
Fees: Term £800; Year £2400

Member of: Jungian Society

St Marks is a school run largely on Jungian principles. The children spend a high proportion of time partaking in their own choice of play activities which are all educational and designed to stimulate them. They also all have maths, reading and writing books, which they work in every day at their own rate. The children's individual needs are catered to, so that even children with disabilities such as Cerebral Palsy thrive in the caring environment. The staff are all highly dedicated to the ideal, with 2/3 having degrees. They all meditate. We are in the *Good Nursery Guide*, and teach French, Ballet, Martial Arts, Violin and Meditation.

NW2

ABBEY NURSERY SCHOOL LTD
The Scout Hut, London NW2
Tel: 0181 208 2202
Type: Co-educational Day

The Little Ark Montessori

*80 Westbere Road,
London NW2 3RU
Tel: 0171 794 6359 Fax: 0171 431 7059*

Principal: Angela Coyne, MontDip
Age range: 2-5 years
No of pupils enrolled as at 1.1.97: 24
12 Boys 12 Girls
Fees per annum:
Part-time: £3360; Full-time: £6000

The school is open 48 weeks of the year from 8am-6pm. All qualified staff. There are a range of times your child may attend. The Little Ark is a small private Nursery within the ground floor of a house. The Principal lives above. A high standard of care and education in a kind and caring environment.

NW3

ANNABEL'S MONTESSORI NURSERY SCHOOL
Recreation Club, Royal Free Hospital, London NW3
Tel: 0171 431 6158 *Type:* Co-educational Day

CHALCOT MONTESSORI SCHOOL AMI
9 Chalcot Gardens, London NW3 4YB
Tel: 0171 722 1386 *Head:* J Morfey AMI Dip
Type: Co-educational Day B2-6 G2-6
No of pupils: B12 G12 *Fees:* DAY £2235

CHERRYFIELDS NURSERY SCHOOL
523 Finchley Road, London NW3
Tel: 0181 905 3350 *Type:* Co-educational Day

CHURCH ROW NURSERY
Hampstead Parish Church, Church Row, London NW3
Tel: 0171 431 2603 *Type:* Co-educational Day

ETON NURSERY MONTESSORI SCHOOL
45 Buckland Crescent, London NW3
Tel: 0171 722 1532 *Type:* Co-educational Day

FRIENDS PRE-SCHOOL
120 Heath Street, London NW3 1DR
Tel: 0171 433 3195
Heads: Mrs Charmain Hunt & Mrs Carmen Tan
Type: Co-educational Day

MARIA MONTESSORI CHILDREN'S HOUSE
26 Lyndhurst Gardens, London NW3 5NW
Tel: 0171 435 3646 *Head:* Mrs L Lawrence
Type: Co-educational Day B2-6 G2-6
Fees: DAY £3300-£3800

NORTH BRIDGE HOUSE SCHOOL
33 Fitzjohns Avenue, London NW3 5JY
Tel: 0171 435 9641 *Head:* Ms R Allsopp BEd
Type: Co-educational Day B2-5 G2-5
No of pupils: B115 G103 *Fees:* DAY £5616

THE OAK TREE NURSERY
2 Arkwright Road, London NW3 6AD
Tel: 0171435 1916 *Head:* Mrs S P T Donovan
Type: Co-educational Day
No of pupils: B15 G15 *Fees:* DAY £4035

OCTAGON NURSERY SCHOOL
St Saviour's Church Hall, London NW3
Tel: 0171 586 3206
Type: Co-educational Day

OLIVER'S NURSERY SCHOOL
52 Belsize Square, London NW3
Tel: 0171 435 5898
Type: Co-educational Day

PETER PIPER NURSERY SCHOOL
St Lukes Church Hall, London NW3 7SR
Tel: 0171 431 7402/0181 441 8189 *Head:* Mrs T Vickers
Type: Co-educational Day B2-5 G2-5
No of pupils: B20 G10

READY STEADY GO
12a King Henrys Road, London NW3 3RP
Tel: 0171 586 6289/5862
Head: Jennifer Silverton BA(Hons), PGTC
Type: Co-educational Day B2-5 G2-5 *Fees:* DAY £3600

NW5

BLUEBELLS NURSERY
Church Hall, London NW5
Tel: 0171 284 3952 *Head:* A Pearson
Type: Co-educational Day

CAMDEN COMMUNITY NURSERIES
99 Leighton Road, London NW5
Tel: 0171 485 2105 *Type:* Co-educational Day

CRESSWOOD NURSERY
215 Queens Crescent, London NW5
Tel: 0171 485 1551 *Type:* Co-educational Day

ROOFTOPS NURSERY
Preistly House, Athlone Street, London NW5 4LL
Tel: 0171 267 7949 *Head:* Mrs Elaine Walton
Type: Co-educational Day

TADPOLE NURSERY
Highgate Road Baptist Chapel, London NW5 1BS
Tel: 0171 267 4465 *Head:* Anni McTavish
Type: Co-educational Day B2-5 G2-5
No of pupils: B5 G5

YORK RISE NURSERY
St Mary Brookfield Hall, London NW5 1SB
Tel: 0171 485 7962 *Head:* Miss Becca Coles
Type: Co-educational Day B2-5 G2-5
No of pupils: B10 G10

NW6

BEEHIVE MONTESSORI SCHOOL
Christchurch Hall, Christchurch Avenue, London NW6
Tel: 0181 451 5477 *Head:* Ms Lucilla Baj
Type: Co-educational Day B2-5 G2-5
No of pupils: B8 G9 *Fees:* DAY £2550

THE BEEHIVE ON QUEEN'S PARK
147 Chevening Road, London NW6
Tel: 0181 969 2235 *Head:* Ms Lucilla Baj
Type: Co-educational Day B2-5 G2-5
No of pupils: B10 G12 *Fees:* DAY £3900-£4300

CCCR NURSERY
160 Mill Lane, London NW6
Tel: 0171 431 1279 *Head:* Margaret Connolly
Type: Co-educational Day

CHASTON NURSERY SCHOOL
30 Palmerston Road, London NW6
Tel: 0171 372 2120 *Type:* Co-educational Day

RAINBOW MONTESSORI SCHOOL
St James's Hall, Sherriff Road, London NW6 2AP
Tel: 0171 328 8986
Head: Mrs Linda Madden MontDipAdv
Type: Co-educational Day B2-5 G2-5
No of pupils: B15 G15 *Fees:* DAY £1956-£2559

SOUTH KILBURN RESIDENTS UNDER 5 NURSERY
19 Malvern Road, London NW6
Tel: 0171 625 4014 *Head:* Miss L Wilson*T*
Type: Co-educational Day

WEST HAMPSTEAD PRE SCHOOL
11 Woodchurch Road, London NW6 3PL
Tel: 0171 328 4787 *Head:* Tarja Haikdnen
Type: Co-educational Day B2-5 G2-5 *Fees:* DAY £6480

NW7

LITTLE CHERUBS KINDERGARTEN
2 Accommodation Road, London NW7
Tel: 0181 959 2420 *Head:* Mrs P Nixon
Type: Co-educational Day

NW8

TODDLERS INN NURSERY SCHOOL
Cicely Davis Hall, London NW8
Tel: 0171 586 0520 *Head:* Laura McCole
Type: Co-educational Day

NW10

BRIDGE PARK KINDER CARE LTD
Bridge Park, Harrow Road, London NW10
Tel: 0181 838 1688 *Type:* Co-educational Day

THE CHILDREN'S CENTRE
Christ Church, London NW10
Tel: 0181 961 9250 *Head:* Denise Lepore
Type: Co-educational Day

THE CHILDREN'S CENTRE
40 Nicoll Road, London NW10
Tel: 0181 961 6648 *Head:* Denise Lepore
Type: Co-educational Day

DOYLE NURSERY SCHOOL
College Road, London NW10
Tel: 0181 969 2179 *Type:* Co-educational Day

NW11

GOLDERS HILL SCHOOL NURSERY
678 Finchly Road, London NW11
Tel: 0181 455 0063 *Type:* Co-educational Day

MONTESSORI SCHOOL
31 Hoop Lane, London NW11
Tel: 0181 209 0813 *Type:* Co-educational Day

SPEEDWELL MONTESSORI NURSERY SCHOOL
St Albans Church Hall, London NW11
Tel: 0181 209 0281 *Head:* Mrs Benedict
Type: Co-educational Day

N1

THE CHILDREN'S HOUSE SCHOOL
77 Elmore Street, London N1
Tel: 0171 354 2113 *Head:* Jane Gibberd DipEd
Type: Co-educational Day B2-5 G2-5
No of pupils: B45 G48 *Fees:* DAY £2310-£3495

THE COMET NURSERY SCHOOL
20 Halcombe Street, London N1
Tel: 0171 729 0936 *Type:* Co-educational Day

FLORAL PLACE NURSERY
1 Floral Place, London N1 2PL
Tel: 0171 354 9945 *Head:* Mrs Susan Haye
Type: Co-educational Day

St Andrew's Montessori

St Andrew's Church,
Thornhill Square,
London N1 1BQ
Tel: 0171 700 2961

Principal: Charlotte Biss, Mont.Dip
Type: Co-educational Day School
Age range: 2¹/₂-5+
No of pupils enrolled as at 1.5.97: 32
15 Boys 17 Girls
Fees per annum: £1950–£3180

Curriculum: At St Andrew's Montessori we provide a safe, happy and caring environment in which each child learns and develops at their optimum pace. As well as learning mathematics, language, science and cultural subjects the children are encouraged to express themselves freely using art and crafts, dance and music, percussion and singing. We also have visiting teachers for Ballet, French and Computing. We take full advantage of our wonderful gardens for play, nature study and organised games. The staff are highly qualified and experienced Montessori teachers and we have an excellent success record in sending children to the school of their parents choice.

GOODWILL NURSERY
Hoxton Youth Community Centre, London N1
Tel: 0171 739 3313 Head: Mrs Muriel McClenahan
Type: Co-educational Day

ISLINGTON GREEN NURSERY
327 Upper Street, London N1
Tel: 0171 704 0756 *Head:* Miss Christina Clayton
Type: Co-educational Day

SPRIGS & SPROGS DAY NURSERY
Unit 3, Shepperton House, London N1
Tel: 0171 704 6204 *Type:* Co-educational Day

N2

KEREM HOUSE
18 Kingsley Way, London N2 0ER
Tel: 0181 455 7524 *Head:* Mrs D Rose CertEd
Type: Co-educational Day B3-5 G3-5

SUNFLOWER PLAYGROUP
43 Linden Lea, London N2
Tel: 0181 201 8386 *Type:* Co-educational Day

N4

CARIBBEAN COMMUNITY CENTRE NURSERY
416 Seven Sisters Road, London N4
Tel: 0181 802 0550 *Type:* Co-educational Day

ST ANGELA DAY NURSERY
34 & 36 Adolphus Road, London N4 2AY
Tel: 0181 800 5228 *Type:* Co-educational Day

N6

THE HIGHGATE ACTIVITY NURSERY
1 Church Road, London N6 4QH
Tel: 0181 348 9248 *Head:* Ms J Crowe NNEB
Type: Co-educational Day B2-5 G2-5 *Fees:* DAY £6500

N7

NORTH CALEDONIAN PRE-SCHOOL CENTRE
577 Caledonian Road, London N7
Tel: 0171 609 7302 *Head:* Ms Bernadette Doherty
Type: Co-educational Day

THE SAM MORRIS CENTRE
Parkside Crescent, London N7 7JG
Tel: 0171 6091735 *Head:* Linda Singh
Type: Co-educational Day

NJ

The Montessori House

(Founded 1984)

5 Princes Avenue,
Muswell Hill,
London N10 3LS
Tel: 0181 444 4399

Head: Mrs Nicola Forsyth, AMI Dip
Type: Montessori School
Age range: 2-5; Pre-Prep 5-7
No of pupils enrolled as at 1.5.97:
30 Boys 33 Girls
Fees per annum: £1467-£3417

Religious affiliation: None

Member of: Registered AMI Montessori School

The Montessori House, Muswell Hill, is a high quality Montessori school. All the classrooms are equipped to the highest standard and there are no correspondence or part-time trained teachers.

At two years old children can join a class especially designed for such young children and continue on to a full morning. Later, they can stay for a home-cooked lunch followed by play in the large, secure garden. Eventually, at around four years, children stay until 3pm, when afternoon activities include cookery, ballet, art, craft and woodwork.

A proper Montessori environment gives children confidence in themselves and their abilities and, even more importantly, self motivation. As a result, children leaving at five are expected to reach a good standard of reading, writing and basic maths.

The school has a small pre-prep department for children from 5-7 years.

N8

THE ARK MONTESSORI NURSERY SCHOOL
42 Turnpike Lane, London N8
Tel: 0181 881 6556 *Type:* Co-educational Day

LITTLE TREE MONTESSORI NURSERY SCHOOL
143 Ferme Park Road, London N8
Tel: 0181 342 9231 *Head:* Mrs Kathy Twomey-Brenner
Type: Co-educational Day

N10

THE MONTESSORI HOUSE SCHOOL
5 Princes Avenue, London N10 3LS
Tel: 0181 444 4399 *Head:* Mrs N Forsyth AMIDip
Type: Co-educational Day B2-5 G2-5
No of pupils: B43 G27 *Fees:* DAY £1653-£3900

THE NURSERY MONTESSORI MUSWELL HILL
24 Tetherdown, London N10 1NB
Tel: 0181 883 7958 *Head:* Mrs E Sweby
Type: Co-educational Day

N12

LAUREL WAY PLAYGROUP
Union Church Hall, London N12 7ET
Tel: 0181 445 7514 *Head:* Mrs Susan Farber
Type: Co-educational Day

N14

SALCOMBE PRE-SCHOOL
33 The Green, London N14
Tel: 0181 882 2136 *Head:* Mrs G Dinner
Type: Co-educational Day

N16

APPLETREE NURSERY
59A Osbaldeston Road, London N16
Tel: 0181 806 3525 *Type:* Co-educational Day

BEATTY ROAD NURSERY
162 Albion Road, London N16
Tel: 0171 254 7309 *Head:* Phylis Seymour
Type: Co-educational Day

COCONUT NURSERY
133 Stoke Newington Church Street, London N16
Tel: 0171 923 0720 *Type:* Co-educational Day

HACKNEY CARE FOR KIDS
61 Evering Road, London N16
Tel: 0171 923 3471 *Head:* Mrs Sandra Dowdy
Type: Co-educational Day

LUBAVITCH ORTHODOX JEWISH NURSERY
Unit 1, 109-115 Stamford Hill, London N16 5RP
Tel: 0181 800 0022 *Head:* Mrs F Sudak
Type: Co-educational Day

THE METHODIST CHURCH MISSION MONTESSORI
Day Nursery, London N16
Tel: 0171 254 6218 *Type:* Co-educational Day

PHOENIX HOUSE NURSERY SCHOOL
27 Stamford Hill, London N16
Tel: 0181 880 2550 *Head:* Mrs Barbara MacIntosh
Type: Co-educational Day

RAINBOW NURSERY
Nevill Road, London N16
Tel: 0171 254 7930 *Type:* Co-educational Day

SMALL STEPS PLAY CENTRE
Scout Hall, London N16
Tel: 0181 809 3518 *Type:* Co-educational Day

STOKE NEWINGTON DAY NURSERY
104 Stoke Newington High Street, London N16
Tel: 0171 254 8028 *Type:* Co-educational Day

SUNRISE DAY NURSERY
1 Cazenove Road, London N16
Tel: 0181 806 6279 *Head:* Miss D D Carmody
Type: Co-educational Day

N17

MONTESSORI PLAYSKOOL
Unit 16, 2 Somerset Road, London N17
Tel: 0181 808 1149 *Type:* Co-educational Day

PEMBURY HOUSE NURSERY SCHOOL
Lansdowne Road, London N17
Tel: 0181 801 9914 *Head:* Mrs Anne Jones
Type: Co-educational Day

N20

PRE-SCHOOL PLAYGROUPS ASSOCIATION
Biboard House, London N20
Tel: 0181 446 4684 *Type:* Co-educational Day

N21

SUPER TOT NURSERY
Highlands Hospital, London N21
Tel: 0181 360 6655 *Head:* Miss Louise Eden
Type: Co-educational Day

N22

KIDS BUSINESS
New River Sports Centre, London N22
Tel: 0181 881 5738 *Head:* Miss Jurina Ikoloh
Type: Co-educational Day

Display Listings of
Schools in Greater London

Essex

ESS

Cranbrook College
(Founded 1896)

Mansfield Road,
Ilford, Essex IG1 3BD
Tel: 0181 554 1757 Fax: 0181 518 0317

Headmaster: G T Reading, MA, CertEd(Oxon), FRSA
(Member of ISA, ISIS)
Type: Primary and Secondary Boys Day School
Age range: 4-16+
No of pupils enrolled as at 1.1.97: 221
Junior: 95; Senior: 126
Fees per annum: £3030-£3885

Religious affiliation: Non denominational

Member of: ISA, ISIS

Curriculum: In the Lower School boys follow a general primary course, and in the Upper School they prepare for GCSE.

Entry requirements: Entry at age 4, or at higher ages when vacancies exist.
Under 8: informal test.
8 and over: entrance examination.

General information: The School aims to provide a happy, ordered and secure environment giving every boy an opportunity to reach the highest standards within his capability. The past six years have seen the opening of a new classroom block, an enlarged science department and a new computer room.

Cranbrook College Educational Trust Limited is a registered charity, and aims to provide 'general instruction of the highest class' for pupils from Ilford and the surrounding area.

Hertfordshire

Lyonsdown School Trust Ltd

(Founded 1906)

3 Richmond Road,
New Barnet, Herts EN5 1SA
Tel: 0181 449 0225 Fax: 0181 441 4690

Headmistress: Mrs R Miller, BA
Type: Independent Primary School
Age range: 4-11 years
No. of pupils enrolled as at 1.5.97: 189
Juniors: 38 Boys 151 Girls
Fees per annum: £2970-£3285

Religious affiliation: Church of England

Curriculum: The School has a tradition of high academic standards and achievements. The experienced, qualified staff follow a varied curriculum which is the subject of continual evaluation and review. Extra curricular activities include Recorders, Country Dancing, Diction, Netball, Chess, Violin and Choir. A number of outings to places of interest are offered. A five day Field Trip for the eleven year old girls is arranged during the summer term.

Entry requirements: Entry at the age of 4 is for all abilities and is from a waiting list. There are a few places available for girls at 7+, when entry is by assessment and interview.

Lyonsdown School Trust Ltd, a registered charity, aims to keep fees low in order to make Independent education available to a wider spectrum of children.

St Martha's Senior School

(Founded 1947)

Camlet Way, Hadley, Barnet, Hertfordshire EN5 5PX
Tel: 0181 449 6889

Head: Sister M Cecile Archer, BA(Hons), (PGCE), (Member of Congregation of St Martha)
Type: Independent Girls' Day School
Age range: 11-18
No. of pupils enrolled as at 1.5.97: Seniors: 304 Girls; Sixth Form: 50
Fees per annum: Day: £3150

Religious affiliation: Roman Catholic

Curriculum: The School is divided into two classes per year. During the first three years pupils follow a basic course in academic and craft subjects, including computer studies and CDT. During the third year girls, in consultation with staff and parents, choose the course for which they are best suited.

English Language, English Literature, French, Mathematics and Science are compulsory subjects to GCSE level. There are fifteen further subjects from which choice may be made for GCSE.

There is an expanding Sixth Form and a wide range of courses available. Sixth Form girls are given every opportunity to become responsible adults. They have their own common and study rooms and are taught in small tutorials.

There is a lively careers department under the guidance of a senior member of staff. A wide range of information is available, and the School holds Careers Conventions from time to time.

Entry requirements: The School holds its own entrance examination in the Spring term before entry.

Examinations offered: GCSE with Midland, Southern and London Groups. A level with AEB, Oxford and London Boards.

Academic and leisure facilities: The Mount House (18th Century) has become the centre of a large complex, including Science Labs, Music/Drama Studio, dining hall, Gymnasium, Home Economics, Art & Crafts Centre and a CDT centre.

Physical education forms an important part of the curriculum. There are four tennis/netball courts on the School premises. Older girls may participate in swimming, squash and golf. Matches are arranged with schools in the area.

There is a school choir, chamber orchestra and recorder group. There are regular concerts and productions.

Religious activities: We have a part-time School Chaplain. There is Mass for the whole School at the end of each term, and Mass is celebrated regularly with attendance on a voluntary basis. Every morning begins with prayer, either in a General Assembly, or in form units.

St Martha's motto is Servite Domino in Laetitia - Serve the Lord with Joy - and a happy friendly atmosphere prevails. The aim of the School is to help girls to feel known, valued, loved and respected as individuals, to help them grow into responsible human beings capable of independence, hard work, and unselfish and caring relationships, and all this within the context of the Christian faith which with Christ as their model helps them realise that life has a purpose and a meaning.

Kent

Bromley High School GPDST

(Founded 1883)

*Blackbrook Lane, Bickley,
Bromley, Kent BR1 2TW
Tel: 0181 468 7981 Fax: 0181 295 1062
(15 minutes BR Victoria - Bromley South)*

Headmistress: Mrs E J Hancock, BA
Type: Independent Day School for Girls (GPDST)
Age range: 4-18
No. of pupils enrolled as at 1.5.97: 861
Junior: 302 Girls; Senior: 427 Girls; Sixth Form: 132 Girls
Fees per annum:
Juniors: £3864; Seniors: £4920; Sixth Form Day: £4920

Religious affiliation: Christian: Non-denominational
Member of: GSA, GPDST

Curriculum: The Senior curriculum is designed to combine the best of academic tradition, with its emphasis on depth and rigour of learning, with cross-curricular skills such as Information Technology. Sport, Music, Drama and Art are also highly valued. At GCSE all girls take English Language and Literature, Mathematics, a modern language and Double or Triple Award Science, with a choice of at least three more subjects. A wide programme of Advanced level subjects is available supplemented by a broad choice of minority studies: together these equip the large Sixth Form for higher education, including Oxbridge entry.

Bursaries and Scholarships are available at 11+ and 16+.
"Successful ... happy ... effective ... excellent facilities" *Daily Telegraph Good Schools Guide.*
The GPDST aims to provide a fine academic education at comparatively modest cost.
Registered Charity No: 1026057.

Farringtons & Stratford House

(Founded 1911)

*Perry Street,
Chislehurst, Kent BR7 6LR
Tel: 0181 467 0256 Fax: 0181 467 5442
Internet: http://www.darch.co.uk.*

Headmistress: Mrs Barbara J Stock, BA(Hons)
Type: Girls' Independent Day and Boarding School
Age range: 2^1/2-18. Boarders from 7
No. of pupils enrolled as at 1.5.97: 487
Junior: 208; Senior: 205 (inc Sixth Form: 75)
Fees per annum:
Day: £3698-£5205; Boarding: £8916-£10,278

Religious affiliation: Methodist (but all denominations welcomed)

Member of: GSA, GBSA, BSA

Curriculum: At Farringtons & Stratford House every girl is special because everyone is gifted in something, be it sport, the arts or academically. It is our job to find that gift in all our pupils and to build the confidence in each girl, to reach her maximum potential in all things. We accept girls from a wide range of abilities and yet our 1996 A*-C pass rate was 91%, with 74% of all candidates achieving eight or more A*-C grades. A level passes ran at 89%. Our success, we feel, speaks for itself!

Farringtons & Stratford House, a registered charity, exists solely to provide a high quality, caring education for girls. Registered Charity No.307916.

St David's College

(Founded 1926)

Beckenham Road,
West Wickham
Kent BR4 0QS
Tel: 0181 777 5852 Fax: 0181 777 9549
E-mail: StDavids@dial.pipex.com
www site: http://dspace.dial.pipex.
com/st-davids/

Principals: Mrs P A Johnson, CertEd, FRGS (Member of
NAHT) Mrs F V Schove (ISAI); Mrs A Wagstaff,
BA(Hons)Lond
Type: Co-educational Day School
Age range: 4-11
No of pupils enrolled as at 1.5.97: 195
Junior: 104 Boys 93 Girls
Fees per annum: £2655-£2805

Religious affiliation: Inter-denominational

Member of: ISA, ISIS

Curriculum: St David's College offers a wide
and varied academic and sporting curriculum.
At the age of 11 pupils are entered for the
independent schools' entrance examinations,
as well as for the London Boroughs of Bexley,
Bromley and Sutton selective examinations,
with outstanding results. Kent Grammar
School places are also achieved each year.

After-school activities include Ballet and
French Club. Pupils also have the opportunity
to learn Speech and Drama, Clarinet, Piano,
Recorder and Violin.

St David's is situated in five acres of beautiful
playing fields and grounds. The main sports
are athletics, cricket, football and netball.

Entry requirements: Entrance is by test and
interview.

Middlesex

The American Community School

Hillingdon Court, 108 Vine Lane, Hillingdon,
Uxbridge, Middlesex UB10 0BE
Tel: 01895 259771 Fax: 01895 256974

Head: Mr Paul Berg
Type: Co-educational Day School
Age range: Lower School: 4-9; Middle School: 10-13; High School: 14-18
No. of pupils enrolled as at 1.1.97: Boys 290 Girls 288
Fees per annum: On application

The American Community School Hillingdon campus provides a non-sectarian co-educational education for students aged 4-18 covering grades Pre-Kindergarten through the 12th grade. Situated less than 15 miles from central London and accessible by the London Underground, the School's door-to-door bus service covers a great deal of West London - east into central London and west as far as High Wycombe.

STUDENT BODY. Approximately 44% of the 578 students are American, 11% are Canadian, and the remaining 45% represent 31 other nationalities.

ACADEMIC PROGRAM. The School follows a

standard American curriculum with Advanced Placement (AP) courses and the International Baccalaureate (IB), a diploma sought by colleges and universities in the US and world-wide. The School has an outstanding pass rate for the International Baccalaureate and, in 1995, Hillingdon IB diplomates averaged 35 points.

The traditional American curriculum leads to an American High School Diploma. The School administers all examinations required for admission to American universities. Supported by specialized university counselling, Hillingdon students attend universities in the US and their home countries including Oxford, Cambridge and the London School of Economic in the UK; MIT, McGill University and University of Chicago in North America, and Keio University in Japan.

ENGLISH AS A SECOND LANGUAGE. The School follows a "total immersion" policy, whereby students attend most classes with their peer group and receive English as a Second Language (ESL) support once or twice a day. While it is not necessary to have previous knowledge of English in the lower grades, an intermediate level of English is required for students in the 9th Grade (age 14).

The School is accredited in the US by the New England Association of Schools and Colleges and in the UK by ISJC. The School is recognised by the International Baccalaureate office to offer its program.

FACULTY. There are 74 full-time teachers on the faculty, all holding a university degree. The student faculty ratio is 8:1.

THE CAMPUS. Situated on an 11-acre site, the Hillingdon campus combines a restored 19th century mansion which is the setting for school classes, concerts, art exhibitions and receptions, with a purpose-built addition housing classrooms, computer room, gymnasium and library. Limited five or seven day boarding space for Hillingdon students is available in the family-style residential facility on the new Woodlee campus.

OTHER CAMPUSES. The 128-acre campus at Cobham features an Olympic standard running track, nature-trail, arboretum, golf course and extensive woodlands. The Egham campus provides modern teaching blocks, recreation rooms and two floodlit tennis courts, set against the original Victorian mansion and beautiful gardens. Both of these campuses offer 5 and 7 day boarding facilities.

STUDENT ACTIVITES. A full range of sports are offered including basketball, tennis, soccer, rugby, swimming, baseball, track and field, cross country, softball and volleyball. Other activities available are Student Council, yearbook, music, computers, drama, scouting, Model United Nations, art clubs, Latin club and recycling.

ADMISSION. On a space available basis, new students are accepted in all grades throughout the year. To apply for admission, submit a completed application form and previous school records. Diagnostic testing may be necessary prior to grade replacement.

Halliford School

(Founded 1921)

Russell Road,
Shepperton, Middlesex TW17 9HX
Tel: 01932 223593 Fax: 01932 229781

Head: Mr. John R Crook, CertEd(Lond), BA(Wales), (Member of SHMIS)
Type: Independent Boys Day School
Age range: 11-19
No of pupils enrolled as at 1.5.97:
Senior: 231 Boys; Sixth Form: 53 Boys
Fees per annum:
Day: £4680; Sixth Form: £2580-£4680

Religious affiliation: Non-denominational

Member of: GBA

The administrative centre of Halliford School is a fine Georgian House set in six acres beside the Thames. Passers-by may think the old house is the school, but behind the house are modern buildings housing light and airy classrooms, Laboratories, a well-equipped Information Technology Centre, Art Rooms, a Design and Technology Workshop, a Gymnasium, Multi-Gym, Swimming Pool and four acres of playing fields. There is also a well appointed Sixth Form centre.

Halliford accepts on to its roll at 11+ and 13+ boys with a wider range of ability than many independent schools, so a pass rate of 96.2 at A level (with a choice of 20 subjects) and 86.8 per cent with five or more passes A-C at GCSE is a clear indication of Halliford's commitment to its pupils.

The Sixth Form at Halliford is co-educational. There are consortium arrangements with St David's School for Girls, Ashford and girls are encouraged into Halliford's own Sixth Form. Sixth-formers automatically become prefects,

giving them the responsibility of being in authority and the experience of making decisions which directly affect others.

Halliford is a small selective school based on the grammar school tradition where, unusually in this day and age, staff can respond to each pupil as an individual. Within this atmosphere of security and imaginative response every child can flourish.

Halliford School, a registered charity, exists to provide high quality education. Registered Charity No.312090.

Hampton School

(Founded 1557)

Hanworth Road,
Hampton,
Middlesex TW12 3HD
Tel: 0181 979 5526 Fax: 0181 941 7368

Headmaster: B R Martin, MA(Cantab), MBA, MIMgt
Type: Independent Boys' Day School
Age range: 11-18
No. of pupils enrolled as at 12.1.97:
Senior: 930 Boys; Sixth Form: 280 Boys
Fees per annum: £5280

Religious affiliation: Non-denominational

Member of: HMC, GBA

Curriculum: Hampton offers a challenging and broad-based academic education within a friendly and supportive community. All boys take at least 10 GCSE subjects, including Sciences, French, Mathematics and English, and go on to three specialist A levels together with one A/S subject and A level General Studies. Classical music, drama, sport and the Adventure Society are some of the many extra-curricular activities balancing boys' academic work.

Entry requirements: At 11: by the School's own examination; at 13: by Common Entrance (65%); at 16: by interview and conditional on GCSE grades. Academic and Music Scholarships, Government Assisted Places.

The Hampton School Foundation, a registered charity, exists to provide high quality education for boys from the surrounding area.

A special Section covering Nursery Schools in central London appears elsewhere in this guide

Heathfield School

(Founded 1900)

Beaulieu Drive,
Pinner, Middlesex HA5 1NB
Tel: 0181 868 2346 Fax: 0181 868 4405

Head: Miss C M Juett, BSc(Member of SHA)
Type: Girls' Independent Day School
Age range: 3-18
No of pupils enrolled as at 1.5.97: 486
Junior: 178 Girls, Senior: 240 Girls
Sixth Form: 68 Girls
Fees per annum:
£3444-£4920; Sixth Form: £4920

Religious affiliation: Non-denominational

Member of: GPDST, GSA, GBGSA, ISIS, ACE, ISCO, ISDTA, ISJC

Heathfield is a long-established school which joined the Girls' Public Day School Trust in 1987. It is situated in a quiet residential area close to stations and bus routes. The accommodation includes specialist rooms, a Music School and a new Junior wing. There are extensive playing fields and an indoor swimming pool is planned.

The school has a reputation as a friendly, caring and close-knit community, with a strong emphasis on pastoral care. Personal and social development has a high profile, with the acquisition of a sense of responsibility and self-confidence considered important.

Girls are assessed before entry and scholarships, bursaries and assisted places are available. The curriculum promotes the pursuit of academic excellence and personal potential. The Juniors follow the National Curriculum subjects. Senior girls take nine GCSEs, followed by three A levels, with nearly 20 subjects offered. A Sixth Form General Studies programme runs in conjunction with local boys' schools. Pass rates average 96% at GCSE and 95% at A level. Virtually all girls continue to university.

A strength of the School is its range of extra-curricular activities and visits in Britain and abroad.

The Girls' Public Day School Trust exists to provide a fine academic education at a comparatively modest cost. Registered Charity No.1026057.

MDX

The John Lyon School

(Founded 1876)

*Middle Road,
Harrow,
Middlesex HA2 0HN
Tel: 0181 422 2046
Fax: 0181 422 5008*

Head: The Revd T J Wright, BD, AKC
Type: Independent Boys Day School
Age range: 11-18
No. of pupils enrolled as at 8.1.97: 525
Sixth Form: 136 Boys
Fees per annum: £5790

Religious affiliation: Non-denominational

Member of: HMC, GBA, ISCO

Situated on the hill at Harrow near its famous brother, the John Lyon School offers a strongly academic education for day boys from the surrounding area. It is easily accessible from many parts of North and West London via the Piccadilly and Metropolitan lines and numerous bus routes.

Compared often to a grammar school it has traditionally possessed an atmosphere of purposefulness, excellence and friendliness.

Entry is mainly at 11+ but there are also some places at 13+ - both by examination and interview. At 16+ a few places are available conditional on good grades at GCSE. Academic and music scholarships are offered at 11+ and 13+ and 15 Government Assisted Places in each year group.

Almost every boy who leaves the Sixth Form normally goes on to university with a steady flow of boys to Oxford and Cambridge.

Music, sport and drama have a high profile in the school. There are two orchestras, a wind band, a jazz group and two choirs. At least fourteen sports are available including soccer and cricket as major games and a wide variety of dramatic productions are staged each term.

An ambitious development plan has just been completed and there is now a new science school, sports centre, swimming pool and library.

There is an Open Day once a year in October but parents are also invited to meet the Headmaster and tour the school by appointment.

The Keepers and Governors of the Free Grammar School of John Lyon is a registered charity which exists for the independent secondary education of boys aged 11-18.

Northwood College
(Founded 1878)

Maxwell Road,
Northwood,
Middlesex HA6 2YE
Tel: 01923 825446 Fax: 01923 836526

Head: Mrs Ann Mayou, MA
Type: Girls' Independent Day School
Age range: 3-18
No of pupils enrolled as at 1.5.97: 714
plus 11 Nursery School girls
Pre-Prep: 105; Junior: 162; Senior: 341 Sixth Form: 106
Fees per annum: £3420-£5172

Religious affiliation: Non-denominational

Member of: GSA, SHA

Curriculum: We have recently opened Redington, the Northwood College Nursery School, which provides nursery education for girls aged 3-4 years. The five sections of Northwood College, Nursery, Pre-Prep, Junior School, Senior School and Sixth Form are all on the same site, although the Nursery, Pre-Prep and Junior School each occupy their own self-contained buildings. The Junior School pupils are housed in a brand new building adjoining the Pre-Prep department. All parts of the School are equipped with specialist subject facilities. The sporting facilities include a Sports Hall and a 25 metre swimming pool.

The aims of the College are to foster a love of learning, to develop creative and sporting talents, to encourage initiative and to promote traditional values.

In addition to all National Curriculum subjects, German, Spanish, Classics and Drama are offered. Girls are prepared for GCSE and A level examinations and for university entrance.

Entry requirements: Examination/interview.

Scholarships: Two academic scholarships and a music scholarship are awarded annually to Senior School girls and three academic scholarships to Sixth Form girls.

Assisted Places: Available at 7+, 11+ and 16+.

The Northwood College Educational Trust is a registered charity which exists to provide high quality education for girls.

St Helen's School

(Founded 1899)

Eastbury Road, Northwood, Middlesex HA6 3AS
Tel: 01923 828511 Fax: 01923 835824

Head: Mrs D.M. Jefkins, MA (Cantab), CPhys (Member of GSA)
Type: Girls' Day and Boarding School
Age range: 4-18. Boarders from 8
No of pupils enrolled as at 1.5.97: 965 Girls
Fees per annum:
Day: £3294-£5082; Boarding: £8103-£9576; Sixth Form: Day £5082, Boarding £9576

Religious denomination: Church of England

Member of: GSA, GBGSA

Founded in 1899 St Helen's is a flourishing school with over 960 girls. The school has three departments - Pre-Preparatory, Junior and Senior - with excellent boarding accommodation. Pleasantly located in a 22 acre green site, we offer a wide range of sporting facilities, including a heated swimming pool.

The ethos of St Helen's is to foster excellence within a friendly and supportive community. All girls are encouraged to succeed and there is a wide range of extra-curricular activities to complement the academic curriculum which is broad and progressive. Girls acquire skills in both Information and Design Technology and there is a strong emphasis on Science, Mathematics and Modern Foreign Languages. Music, drama and art play a significant role in school life. An ongoing building programme

ensures that our facilities and accommodation are of the highest standard.

We have an excellent record of academic success and almost all our Sixth Formers enter Higher Education, many gaining Oxbridge places. In 1996, St Helen's achieved a 100% pass rate at A Level, 68% gaining an A or B grade, and our GCSE pass rate was 99.9%, with 68% gaining A* or A grades. The dedicated staff maintain excellent standards of teaching and our girls emerge as highly qualified young women. The opportunities for European work experience and our substantial links with industry give St Helen's girls the self confidence and experience necessary to succeed in the modern competitive world.

The close links between St Helen's and Merchant Taylors' School for Boys enable our pupils to receive all the benefits of single-sex education with the advantage of contact with a highly successful boys' school.

We are a Christian foundation and seek to promote mutual understanding and respect for all traditions and beliefs. We warmly welcome girls of all faiths.

Entry to St Helen's is competitive by examination and interview. Scholarships and Assisted Places are available.

St Helen's School is a registered charity (No 312762) which exists to provide high quality education for girls.

MDX

Staines Preparatory School Trust

(Founded 1935)
Charity No. 296691

*3 Gresham Road,
Staines,
Middlesex TW18 2BT
Tel: 01784 450909/452916 Fax: 01784 464424*

Head: P A Monger, MA, PGCE
Type: Preparatory School
Age range: 3-12
No of pupils enrolled as at 1.1.97:
3-7: 148 Boys 102 Girls
8-12: 100 Boys 70 Girls
Fees per annum: £2730-£3255 (inc lunch)

Religious affiliation: Non denominational

Member of: ISA (in process)

Entry requirements: Boys and girls normally enter in September after their third or fourth birthday year. Pupils are accepted at other ages if there are vacancies. The School is not a nursery, and from the beginning pupils have lessons in the early stages of regular school work.

Curriculum: All normal preparatory school curriculum subjects are taught, including French from six and Latin from nine years. A small special needs unit exists. Extras offered include judo, aerobics, tennis, ballet, swimming, speech training, drama club.

Staines Preparatory School Charitable Trust exists to provide education to a high level and within a family environment for local boys and girls from the ages 3 to 12 years.

Five assisted places available from ages 7/8.

MDX

Sunflower Montessori School

(Founded 1990)

*8 Victoria Road,
Twickenham,
Middlesex TW1 3HW
Tel: 0181 891 2675 Fax: 0181 891 1204*

Principal: Mr Peter Colbert
Head Teacher: Mrs Janet Yandell
Type: Montessori Elementary School
Age range: 2$\frac{1}{2}$-8 (will be up to 12)
No of pupils enrolled as at 1.5.97:
33 Boys 41 Girls
Fees per annum: Day: £1755-£3255

Religious affiliation: Christian

Member of: Montessori Association of Teachers and Schools

Curriculum: We follow the Montessori Elementary curriculum (up to 12) in this Christian school, giving a rich education in Arts, Science, all general academic subjects and Scripture. We note and fulfil the National Curriculum requirements, and prepare children for entrance examinations to the school of their choice.

Our aim is to impart academic or creative excellence, and to instil hope, confidence and self-assurance so that the child grows up a responsible, intelligent and useful member of society caring for people. The happiness and fulfilment of each child is our most important endeavour.

Entry requirements: Entry is subject to interview. Children are admitted when vacancies exist.

**Looking for a school outside London and the Home Counties?
John Catt Educational Ltd publish a range of regional *Which School?* guides**

MDX

Twickenham Preparatory School

(Founded 1932)

*Beveree, 43 High Street,
Hampton, Middlesex TW12 2SA
Tel: 0181 979 6216 Fax: 0181 979 1596*

Headmaster: N D Flynn, MA(Oxon)
Member of IAPS
Type: Co-educational Day Preparatory School
Age range: Boys 4-13 Girls 4-11
No of pupils enrolled as at 1.5.97:
Junior: 50 Boys 31 Girls; Senior: 30 Boys 38 Girls
Fees per annum: £2670-£4260

Religious affiliation: Non-denominational

Member of: IAPS

Twickenham Preparatory School Trust aims to give children a good academic start to their education in a quiet, settled atmosphere in our delightful surroundings.

Curriculum: Boys are prepared for Common Entrance and Scholarship examinations to Independent Secondary Schools. Girls take entry examinations to local Independent Day Schools at 11. Academic Scholarships offered.

Music and drama are actively encouraged, as are many extra-curricular activities. Main team games are Netball, Rounders, Soccer nd Cricket which are played on the adjacent sports field. Children are taught to swim.

Entry requirements: Details are set out in our Prospectus.

Twickenham Preparatory School Trust, a registered charity, exists to provide quality education for local children.

Registered Charity No.5318/6067A.

Surrey

SUR

Croham Hurst School

(Founded 1899)

*79 Croham Road,
South Croydon,
Surrey CR2 7YN
Tel: 0181 680 3064 Fax: 0181 688 1142*

Head: Miss S.C. Budgen, BA
Type: Independent Girls' Day School
Age range: 3+-18
No. of pupils enrolled as at 1.9.96:
Junior: 181; Senior: 314; Sixth Form: 63
Fees per annum: £2370-£4890

Religious denomination: Christian Foundation, but all faiths welcome

Member of: GSA

The School, which is on a main bus route and within walking distance of South Croydon station, lies on the verge of woods and green

belt. The extensive facilities include a modern Science block, Information Technology and Technology rooms, Art and Drama studios, a fine Music suite, large gymnasia and on site playing fields and swimming pool.

Curriculum: The Senior School curriculum caters for a comprehensive range of GCSE and A level subjects while keeping abreast of National Curriculum developments. The first three years include Latin or Classical Civilisation, Spanish, German, Art, Textiles, Drama and Information Technology. The remaining years contain a core of English, Mathematics, Science and French together with a wide range of options. Sixth Formers can choose from a selection of twenty A level courses including Economics, Theatre Studies and Latin, supplemented by a programme of General Studies. In addition they may study for GCSE in Spanish, Media Studies or Physical Education. Girls are encouraged to develop their full potential in artistic, musical and sporting directions and achieve consistently high standards.

Housed within its own building, the Junior School, known as 'The Limes', offers a caring, disciplined environment where children enjoy sound, structured teaching, stimulating creative opportunities and a range of sporting activities.

The School combines an excellent all-round education in a friendly atmosphere with consistently high public examination results. Most girls go on to higher education, the majority to universities including Oxford and Cambridge.

Entry requirements: 3+-11: Entrance test and interview. 11+: Entrance examination and interview. Sixth Form: Entry conditional on interview and GCSE results.

Nursery Vouchers, Government Assisted Places at 8+ and 11+, Bursaries and Scholarships. Additional Sixth Form Scholarships.

Croham Hurst School is a registered charity and its sole purpose is to provide an excellent education for girls.

Cumnor House Preparatory School

(Founded 1931)

168 Pampisford Road,
South Croydon,
Surrey CR2 6DA
Tel: 0181 660 3445 Fax: 0181 660 3445

Headmaster: J T Jenkins, MA (Cantab)
Type: Boys' Preparatory School
Age range: 4-13
No. of pupils enrolled as at 1.5.97:
330 Boys
Fees per annum: Day: £3885-£4425

Religious denomination: Church of England

Member of: IAPS

Curriculum: Cumnor House is one of Surrey's leading Preparatory Schools. Pleasantly and conveniently situated, the School prepares boys for scholarships and common entrance examinations to leading public schools and local grammar schools.

Scholarships have been won recently to Dulwich, Epsom, Lancing, Millfield and the local senior independent schools, Whitgift, Trinity and Caterham.

Music, Art, Drama and Games play a large part in the life of the School and all contribute to the busy, happy atmosphere.

Choir, Sports Tours and matches, ski trips, regular stage productions and a broad spectrum of clubs and options, give the boys the opportunity to pursue a wide range of interests.

Entry requirements: Assessment test and interview.

Holy Cross Preparatory School

(Founded 1929)

George Road,
Kingston upon Thames,
Surrey KT2 7NU
Tel: 0181 942 0729 Fax: 0181 336 0764

Head: Mrs M K Hayes, MA
Member of ISIS, IAPS
Type: Independent Girls (4-11) Preparatory School
Age range: 4-11
No of pupils enrolled as at 1.5.97:
245 Girls
Fees per annum: £3390

Religious affiliation: Roman Catholic but all faiths welcome

Curriculum: Founded by the Sisters of the Holy Cross, an International teaching order, who have been engaged in the work of education since 1844. A sound Christian education is given and we are well known for our high academic standard, our happy and caring atmosphere together with an excellent record of success in Common Entrance and preparing children for the Public, High and Grammar schools. A broad and relevant curriculum is offered with specialist teaching in Physical Education, Music, French and Technology. Excellent facilities in eight picturesque acres (featured in the *Sunday*

Times 29 Top Preparatory Schools, August 1996).

Entry requirements: Entry at 4 to Infant Department. Assessment and interview for entrants at 6+, 7+, 8+ and 9+.

The Holy Cross Convent Charitable Trust exists to provide excellence in Christian education for local children.

Trinity School

(Founded 1596)

Shirley Park,
Croydon,
Surrey CR9 7AT
Tel: 0181 656 9541 Fax: 0181 655 0522

Head: Mr B J Lenon, MA
Type: Independent Day School for Boys
Age range: 10-18
No of pupils enrolled as at 14.1.97:
Senior: 675 Sixth Form: 215
Fees per annum 1996-97: £5622

Religious affiliation: Church of England

Member of: HMC, SHA, ISIS

Curriculum: A full range of subjects is taught at GCSE, 21 are taken at A or AS level, and there is an ambitious General Studies programme.

The facilities are outstanding, with all teaching and activities in appropriately designed areas. The school has a nationally famous reputation for music, and is very strong in sport and drama. Outdoor Activities, CCF, the Duke of Edinburgh scheme and Community Service all thrive, and there is a wide range of clubs and many travel opportunities.

Entry requirements: Written tests and interview. Main ages of entry: 10, 11, 12, 13 and Sixth Form.

Scholarships and Bursaries: Scholarships are awarded to approximately 40 pupils on entry each year. Generous Bursaries are given to all parents with an income of less than £30,000 on a means-tested basis. 45 government assisted places are awarded annually.

The school is a registered charity (The Whitgift Foundation, Registered Charity No. 312612) which exists to provide a high standard of education for children aged 10 to 18 years.

Display Listings of
Schools in the South East

Berkshire

Cheam  Hawtreys

(Founded 1645)

Headley, Newbury, Berkshire RG19 8LD
Tel: 01635 268242 Fax: 01635 269345 Registrar: 01635 268381

Headmaster: Mr C C Evers, BA (Member of IAPS)
Type: Preparatory School
Age range: 7-13. Boarders from 8
No. of pupils enrolled as at 1.5.97: 132
Fees per annum: Day: £6780; Boarding: £9600

Religious affiliation: Church of England

Member of: ISIS

Curriculum: The Public Schools Scholarship and Common Entrance syllabus which complies with and exceeds National Curriculum requirements.

Examinations offered: Scholarship and Common Entrance to public schools.

Religious activities: Regular morning prayers. Sunday Services.

Scholarships, Exhibitions and Bursaries: Two Scholarships offered annually for up to 30% of fees. The Haughey Scholarship is for a boarder, the Governors' Scholarship is for either a boarder or a day pupil. Examinations held late February or early March.

Location: Located in 80 acres of parkland on the borders of Berkshire and Hampshire, the School is easily accessible from both the M3 and M4. Ten minutes from Newbury and 15 minutes from Basingstoke, it is just over an hour from West London and Bristol, and less from Oxford and Portsmouth. A coach service to London is provided at the beginning and

end of half-term and exeats.

Academic, sports, games and leisure facilities:
Academic: Small classes following the curriculum in all major subjects (including Latin). Up to three streams in the last three years. Most classrooms enjoy dedicated video facilities. Quiet library. Additional support unit available for those with learning difficulties. Thriving Music department (orchestra and two choirs, sound-proofed [almost!] percussion room), networked 30 station computer centre; good Art and Design centre.
Sports: Extensive playing fields. Large dedicated Sports Hall, heated outdoor pool,

four all-weather hard tennis courts, golf course, squash court. Rugby, soccer, hockey and cross-country in winter terms; lacrosse and netball for girls; cricket, tennis, athletics and swimming in summer term. Basketball, judo, rifle shooting (including matches), badminton, short tennis, canoeing training and instruction.

Games and Leisure Facilities: Climbing wall, adventure slide and obstacle course. Camping ground (summer term). 'Camps' - a wooded part of the 80 acre parkland site. Croquet lawn (summer term, 1st Form). Four separate play rooms/TV rooms for different year groups. Pool room. Modelling room. Tuck shop.

Activities: Once a week, instead of games, there is a formal 'activities' period. Activities are also offered during an extended lunch break and in the evenings. Activities include cooking, craft, motor cycle maintenance, bridge, chess and fly-tying among other things.

Boarding (approximately 80%). Comfortable, carpeted and curtained dormitories, separate first year boarding area. Three resident matrons and four resident tutors look after the welfare of the boarders upstairs in a disciplined but relaxed atmosphere. Day Pupils: day boys arrive in time for morning assembly (8.20 am) and are fully integrated into all school events. They return home after prep (approximately 6.30 pm). A mini-bus service is operated locally.

Cheam School Educational Trust, a registered charity, exists to foster excellence in education, awareness of others and development of the whole being.

From September 1997 the school will become co-educational. There will be a separate girls' Boarding House.

Traditional Values
Modern Thinking
Education for the 21st Century

Heathfield School

(Founded 1899)

London Road,
Ascot,
Berkshire SL5 8BQ
Tel: 01344 882955 Fax: 01344 890689

Head: Mrs J M Benammar, BA, MèsL
(Member of GSA, SHA, RSA)
Type: Senior Independent School
Age range: 11-18; Boarders from 11
No of pupils enrolled as at 1.5.97: 215
Junior: 100 Girls (form I-III)
Senior: 58 Girls (form IV-V)
Sixth Form: 57 Girls
Fees per annum:
Boarding: £4375; Sixth Form (Boarding): £4375

Religious affiliation: Church of England

Member of: GSA, ISIS

Curriculum: The broad curriculum of the first three years includes Latin, French and Spanish and lays solid foundations for GCSE when 19 subjects are offered, including separate Sciences, four languages and practical subjects. 97% A*-C grades in 1996, 90% A*-B, 69% A*-A. At A Level 23 subjects are offered, results are excellent - 99% pass rate in 1996, 78% A and B grades - and nearly all girls go on to University. Small classes, streaming in core subjects and a highly qualified staff mean individual potential is reached.

Entry requirements: Entry, usually at 11+, is through our own Assessment Papers and the Common Entrance Examination. A few girls also join at 12+ and 13+, others come to us for the Sixth Form.

Heathfield School Ascot, registered charity No. 309086, exists to provide an excellent all-round education for girls aged 11-18 within a Christian framework and in an all-boarding environment.

Buckinghamshire

Maltman's Green School

(Founded 1918)

Maltmans Lane,
Gerrards Cross,
Buckinghamshire SL9 8RR
Tel: 01753 883022 Fax: 01753 891237

Head: Mrs Madeleine Evans, BA(Hons), PGCE
Type: Girls Day Preparatory School
Age range: 3 to 13.
No. of pupils enrolled as at 1.9.96: 370 Girls
Fees per annum: £1545 (Nursery) to £5028

Religious denomination: Non-denominational

Member of: IAPS

Curriculum: Mathematics, English, French, History, Geography, Scripture, Chemistry, Physics, Biology and Combined Sciences, Computer Studies, Singing, Music, Art Craft and Design, Technology, Gymnastics, Netball, Hockey, Tennis, Swimming, Athletics and Short Tennis. Extra Subjects include, Ballet, Fencing, Riding, Speech and Drama, Spanish and German.

Entry requirements: Scholarships at 8 and 9 years. Day (or morning for younger girls) in School for interviews and testing with standardised tests, and/or the School's own tests.

Maltman's Green School Trust Ltd, a registered charity, is a non-profit making preparatory school.

Hampshire

Farnborough Hill
(Founded 1889)

Farnborough Road,
Farnborough,
Hampshire GU14 8AT
Tel: 01252 545197

Head: Miss R McGeoch, MA, MLitt, PGCE
Type: Independent Day School for Girls
Age range: 11-18
No of pupils enrolled as at 1.3.97: 526
Senior: 415; Sixth Form: 111
Fees per annum: £4782

Religious affiliation: Roman Catholic

Member of: GSA, SHA

Farnborough Hill is committed to the education of the whole person within a Christian environment. It is housed in the former home of the Empress Eugenie to which has been added purpose-built school accommodation. Facilities include a library, Sixth Form suite, chapel, gymnasium, indoor swimming pool, laboratories, technology workshops and extensive playing fields.

The School participates in the Government Assisted Places Scheme and offers academic scholarships at 11+ and for girls entering the Sixth Form.

Farnborough Hill was founded in 1889 and is now an educational trust. As a registered charity, the school aims to educate the whole person through academic achievement, personal development and values based in Catholic Christian tradition.

The Grey House School
(Founded 1949)

Mount Pleasant,
Hartley Wintney,
Hampshire RG27 8PW
Tel: 01252 842353 Fax: 01252 845527

Head: Mrs E.M. Purse, CertEd
Type: Preparatory School
Age range: 4-11+
No. of pupils enrolled as at 1.5.97:
75 Boys 72 Girls
Fees per annum: Day: £3168-£3900

Religious denomination: Church of England

Curriculum: The usual academic subjects are taught to 11+ Common Entrance, plus Computer Studies, Science, French, Geography, History, RE, Environmental Studies, Art, Craft, CDT, Music, Speech, Drama, Ballet, PE and Games.

HAM

St Swithun's Junior School

(Founded May 1884)

Alresford Road,
Winchester,
Hampshire SO21 1HA
Tel: 01962 852634 Fax: 01962 841874

Head: Mrs V A M Lewis, MA, MSc, DipEd
Type: Preparatory School
Age range: 3-11
No of pupils enrolled as at 1.5.97: 208
42 Boys 166 Girls
Fees per annum: £1875-£4725

Religious denomination: Church of England

Member of: IAPS

Curriculum: The usual preparatory curriculum is offered with due regard to the requirements of the National Curriculum.

Entry requirements: The School is non-selective but children are usually invited to spend a day in school before being offered a place.

Examinations offered: Boys are prepared for entry to prep schools at 7 or 8. Girls are prepared for Common Entrance at 11.

Academic and leisure facilities: A stimulating environment and a broad curriculum provide opportunities for those who are academically able and for those whose abilities are of a creative, practical or sporting nature. Music is a special strength, with a Choir, Orchestra and Recorder Consort. Activities include various clubs and societies, catering for a wide range of interests.

The St Swithun's School Charitable Trust exists to provide a high quality education for girls and boys.

St Swithun's School

(Founded 1844)

Alresford Road, Winchester, Hampshire SO21 1HA
Tel: 01962 861316 Fax: 01962 841874

Headmistress: Dr H L Harvey, BSc, PhD (London)
Type: Girls' Independent School
Age range: 11-18. Boarders from 11
No. of pupils enrolled as at 1.9.96:
450 (including Sixth Form: 115 Girls)
Fees per annum: Day: £6720; Boarding: £11,130

Religious denomination: Church of England

Member of: GBGSA, GSA, BSA

The School was founded in 1884 in the city of Winchester and moved in 1931 to its present fine site on the Downs to the east of the city, about a mile from its centre.

The majority of girls enter the Senior School between the ages of 11 and 13 years by means of the Common Entrance Examination for Independent Schools, but girls are accepted at other ages, including the Sixth Form, subject to satisfactory tests.

A flexible, broadly-based education is offered, enabling girls to develop their potential to the full. 19 subjects are available at GCSE of which English Language and Literature, a modern Foreign Language, Mathematics and at least one Science subject are compulsory. The selection of others is made on an individual basis with an emphasis on breadth of course as well as future career prospects. In the Sixth Form, girls are offered a free choice of 24 subjects and all follow to A level a challenging and wide-ranging General Course.

The School flourishes in a way appropriate to the present day, but is glad to be firmly rooted in its fine traditions. In attitude it largely reflects the changes and relaxations found in any modern institution or community. Within a framework of easier discipline, there is a remarkably friendly and caring atmosphere in the School.

St Swithun's School (Winchester), a Registered Charity, exists to provide education for girls, both Day and Boarding, aged 11-18 years.

Hertfordshire

HER

Abbot's Hill School

Bunkers Lane, Hemel Hempstead,
Hertfordshire HP3 8RP
Tel: 01442 240333/5 Fax: 01442 69981

Headmistress: Mrs K Lewis, MA (Cantab), BSc (Open), PGCE, FRSA, MIMgt

School foundation: 1912

Independent Full/Weekly Boarding and Day School

Religious affiliation: Church of England

Age range of pupils: 11-16

No. of students enrolled as at 1.9.96: 165

Range of fees per annum as at 1.9.96:
  Full Boarders: £10,710
  Weekly Boarders: £10,635
  Day Girls: £6330

Abbot's Hill is an Independent Full/Weekly Boarding and Day School for girls aged 11-16 years. There are 165 pupils. The School is situated in parkland which extends to over 70 acres, under three miles from M1/M25, all major road/rail networks and international airports. The main accommodation is located in a spacious and comfortable late Georgian House. The teaching blocks are in the grounds with a new Science and IT and Technology building recently completed.

There is a modern and well equipped gymnasium, lacrosse pitches, a heated swimming pool, four grass and five hard tennis courts with the use of two indoor courts.

The main sports are lacrosse and netball in winter and tennis, athletics and swimming during the summer. Tennis coaching is available throughout the year and there is a strong competitive Ski Team. Other sports include badminton, squash and riding. A wide range of extra curricular activities is offered, which is enhanced by the School's easy proximity to London.

With a staff ratio of 1:8, girls are taught in small subject classes to GCSE. Outstanding results are achieved commensurate with pupils' ability. At Abbot's Hill, girls are encouraged to consider their future prospects and are very well prepared to choose from a wide range of A level and GNVQ courses offered to them when they leave. There is a comprehensive careers programme available in the Fifth Year to further enhance their decisions. Girls are individually coached for music, dance, speech and drama examinations. Details of Scholarships and Bursaries are available on request.

Religious denomination: The School follows the principles of the Church of England and has a daily service in the Chapel. Abbot's Hill also welcomes girls of other religious beliefs.

THE ARTS EDUCATIONAL SCHOOL

TRING PARK

(Founded 1919)

Tring, Hertfordshire HP23 5LX
Tel: 01442 824255 Fax: 01442 891069

Principal: Mrs J D Billing, GGSM(London), CertEd, FRSA
Type: Boarding and Day School
Age range: 8-18
No. of pupils enrolled as at 1.1.97: Boarders: 160, Day: 60
Average size of class: 17
Fees per annum:
Day: £5253-£7353; Boarding: £9108-£11,901

Religious affiliation: Inter-denominational

Member of: ISA, BSA, SHA

The Arts Educational School is one of the major performing arts schools in the United Kingdom and is housed in a magnificent Rothschild Mansion set in 17 acres of beautiful parkland.

It is an Independent School for boys and girls between the ages of eight and 18 and entry is by audition and academic examination where the principal criterion is artistic talent. A few part scholarships are available for which every applicant is assessed at audition.

Its specialist subjects of Dance, Drama and Music are complemented by a fine academic education to GCSE and A level thereby preparing pupils for a wide choice of routes into Further Education.

A Preparatory Department was opened in

September 1993 and there has been extensive development of Sixth Form Courses during the past two years. The artistic curriculum in the Lower School has been refined during the past year to introduce the Theatre Arts Course alongside the Dance Course making the School very much at the forefront of artistic education.

Students in the Fourth to Sixth Forms study one of the following two-year vocational courses while taking their examinations in Dance, Drama and Music.

The *Dance Course* is for those who wish to specialise in dance as performers, teachers or in other related areas.

The *Drama Course* is designed for pupils who are interested in theatre in a variety of ways: as potential actors, actresses or singers or from a more technical or academic point of view.

The *Musical Theatre Course* is for all rounders and places an equal emphasis on dance, drama and music.

There is a strong tutorial system in the School and as we are small in comparison to many schools, there is a family atmosphere.

Whatever the career or course chosen, the fusion of natural talent, creativity and personality with sound teaching and direction produces young communicators, well-equipped to grasp the many opportunities that lie ahead.

Aided places are available under the Government's Music and Ballet Scheme.

The Trust exists as a Registered Charity to provide vocational and academic education.

The Princess Helena College

(Founded 1820)

Temple Dinsley,
Preston, Hitchin,
Hertfordshire SC14 7RT
Tel: 01462 432100 Fax: 01462 431497

Head: John F Jarvis, OBE, BA, MSc, FIPD, FIMgt, FRGS
Type: Independent Girls School
Age range: 10-18 Boarders from 10
No of pupils enrolled as at 1.5.97: 140
Senior: 97 Girls; Sixth Form: 43 Girls
Fees per term:
Day: £1932-£2415; Boarding: £2776-£3470;
Sixth Form: Day: £2415; Boarding: £3470

The Princess Helena College is a well established girls' school, committed to single-sex education. We believe that this offers a girl the greatest chance to fulfil her potential, academically and personally, and to prepare for the combination of career and family life which the 21st-century is likely to demand of her.

We are a small school by choice, accommodating day girls and boarders and believe that in this environment all our pupils can flourish and be significant members of a close-knit community in which every individual is noticed, respected and valued. All are able to gain confidence, accept responsibility, not only for themselves, but for their friends and colleagues.

Although we are privileged to be in a beautiful setting in a safe rural environment, we believe in developing in our pupils an understanding of the wider world and a proper understanding of their place in it. We are therefore outward looking and we value our contacts with the local community, with the parent body and past students.

If you would like to receive further information about The Princess Helena College please request a copy of our prospectus which will give you an insight into the life and work of the College, but to fully appreciate its excellent facilities, exceptional residential accommodation and caring atmosphere, we would recommend a visit. We are always pleased to welcome visitors and would be proud to show you our beautiful and historic school.

The Princess Helena College is a registered charity which exists to provide high quality education for girls. Charity No. 311064.

St Christopher School

(Founded 1915)

Letchworth,
Hertfordshire SG6 3JZ
Tel: 01462 679301 Fax: 01462 481578

Headmaster: Mr Colin Reid, MA
Type: Co-educational Boarding and Day School
Age range: 2^{1}/$_{2}$-18. Boarders from 7:
Half of the senior school are boarders
No. of pupils enrolled as at 6.1.97:
Junior: 69 Boys 39 Girls; Senior: 194 Boys 119 Girls;
Sixth Form: 47 Boys 48 Girls
Average size of class: 16; Teacher/Pupil ratio: 1: 7

Location: One mile from A1(M) and 35 minutes from Kings Cross.

Religious affiliation: Non-denominational

Member of: SHMIS, GBA

Curriculum: The core areas of the National Curriculum are covered with all pupils continuing with Physics, Chemistry and Biology to Double Certificate Level at the GCSE. Foreign Languages have a strongly practical emphasis with all pupils paying at least one visit to our exchange schools in France and/or Germany in years II, III and IV. The creative arts and technology are particularly encouraged and the facilities are available and staffed at weekends. Internationalist and green values are fostered. The diet is vegetarian.

Entry requirements: Entry for boarders is usually at age 11 with some joining at 9 and others at 13. Decisions are made in the light of interview, school reports and informal tests, usually conducted on the day of interview. We look for an ability to respond to the spirit and opportunities of St Christopher. Direct entrants to the 100 strong Sixth Form have to show that they are ready to follow a 3 A/AS level programme. The School provides for children of average to outstanding ability

aiming to help everyone achieve their full potential.

Examinations offered: GCSE (MEG, NEG, SEG); GCE A and AS levels (Oxford & Cambridge, JMB, AEB) in 19 subjects.

Destination and career prospects of leavers: Almost all leavers go on to a course in further or higher education.

Boarding: Half the pupils aged over 11 are boarders. The younger ones live with houseparents in a warm domestic setting while Sixth formers have student style rooms.

Academic and sports facilities: The School has all the usual specialist rooms and science laboratories with particularly fine Theatre, Music, Art and Technology Centres added in recent years. As one of the pilot schools of Education 2000 it has pioneered major

developments in information technology, and two computer networks link the library and all the teaching areas. We complement academic study with learning through experience. There is a strong emphasis on Outdoor Pursuits (with all pupils learning to canoe, sail and rock climb), on service to the whole community and on self-government through which pupils learn both how to put forward their own ideas and listen to those of others.

Values: The School is an unusually tolerant community, recognising and caring for all as individuals. There is no compulsory worship so people of different religions and of none feel equally at home. There is a significant period of silence in every assembly.

Long-term aims: St Christopher has long been noted for its success in developing lifelong self-confidence. The School is informal (there is no uniform and all children and adults are called by their first names); at the same time it is purposeful and challenging of mind, body and spirit. We aim for our young people to develop an effective competence, a social conscience, moral courage, a sense of initiative, the capacity for friendship and a true zest for life.

St Christopher School is a registered charity providing education for 3 to 18 year olds, with boarders from age 7

.HER

St Edmund's College

(Founded 1568)

Old Hall Green, Nr Ware,
Hertfordshire SG11 1DS
Tel: 01920 821504 Fax: 01920 823011
Email: registrar@secware.demon.co.uk

Head: Mr D J J McEwen, MA(Oxon), FRSA
Member of HMC
Age range: 3-18. Boarders from 7
No. of pupils enrolled as at 1.5.97: 520
Junior: 40 Boys 25 Girls
Senior: 195 Boys 130 Girls; Sixth Form: 80 Boys 50 Girls
Fees per annum 1996/97:
Day: £4050-£6480; Boarding: £8340-£10,320
Sixth Form Day: £6480; Boarding: £10,320

Religious denomination: Roman Catholic, all welcome

Member of: HMC

The College is in 400 acres of private parkland, only 50 minutes from central London or Cambridge by road. Nearest railway station Ware is only 30 minutes from London's Liverpool Street Station.

Computer rooms, science laboratories, art and technology workshops and multi-sports hall. Dedicated Sixth Form Centre. GNVQ courses in Business, and Art and Design alongside traditional range of A levels. In 1995 92% of our A level candidates took up university places. Full boarder, day pupils or weekly boarders accepted. High level of pastoral care. Wide range of extra-curricular sports and activities. Indoor heated swimming pool on campus.

St Edmund's College, a registered charity, exists to provide a Catholic education for children.

St Margaret's School

(Founded 1749)

*Merryhill Road, Bushey,
Hertfordshire WD2 1DT
Tel: 0181 950 1548 Fax: 0181 950 1677*

Headmistress: Miss Marlene de Villiers, BA
(Member of GSA, SHA)
Type: Independent Girls' School
Age range: 4-18. Boarders from 9
No. of pupils enrolled as at 1.2.97: 438
Infant & Prep: 105; Junior: 100; Senior: 167
Sixth Form: 66
Fees per annum:
Day: £3675-£5925; Boarding: £8685-£9885
Sixth Form Day: £5925; Boarding: £9885

Religious affiliation: Anglican

Member of: GSA, GBSA, BSA

The school has a broad balanced curriculum and strong academic tradition with a very good GCSE, A level and Oxbridge record. Each year girls proceed to a wide range of courses at University and Colleges of Further Education. Education takes place in small classes in a caring and supportive community. Enrolment to St Margaret's is via assessment and interview at 4+ to 6+ and via the school's own Entrance Examination and interview at 7+, 11+ and 13+. Sixth Form places are conditional on GCSE results. Scholarships and Bursaries are available.

St Margaret's School Bushey, a registered charity, exists to provide high quality education for girls.

Kent

Combe Bank School

(Founded 1972)

*Sundridge,
Sevenoaks, Kent TN14 6AE
Tel: 01959 563720 Fax: 01959 561997*

Heads: Miss Nina Spurr, BSc and
Mrs E. Marsden, BA
Member of FRSA
Type: Independent Day School
Age range: 3-18
No. of pupils enrolled as at 1.9.96:
Junior: 17 Boys 189 Girls; Seniors: 153 Sixth Form: 47
Fees per annum: Day: £1950-£6030

Religious denomination: (Catholic foundation) Ecumenical

Member of: GSA, GBGSA, FSIS

Curriculum: Our curriculum is broadly based. We offer A levels and GNVQ Group 3. Scholarships.

Entry requirements: School's own exam at 11+. Common entrance at 13+. Sixth Form Scholarship by interview.

Combe Bank School, a registered charity, provides quality education for boys 3-5 years and girls 3-18 years.

Looking for a school outside London and the Home Counties? John Catt Educational Ltd publish a range of regional *Which School?* guides

Dulwich Preparatory School

(Founded 1939)

Coursehorn, Cranbrook,
Kent TN17 3NP
Tel: 01580 712179 Fax: 01580 715322

Headmaster: M C Wagstaffe, BA(Hons), PGCE
Type: Independent Co-educational Preparatory School
Age range: 3-13. Boarders from 8
No. of pupils enrolled as at 1.2.97: 533
Junior: 138 Boys 127 Girls
Senior: 138 Boys 130 Girls
(Including Sixth Form: 62 Boys 68 Girls)
Fees per annum:
Day: £2025-£5850; Boarding: £8775-£8985

Religious affiliation: Church of England

Member of: IAPS, ISIS

Environment: The School is situated in countryside one mile outside Cranbrook. There are extensive grounds including a sports hall, swimming pool, all-weather hockey pitch and new teaching block incorporating Science, DT and IT, classrooms and resource centre.

Entry is mainly at 3, 4 and 7, and at 8 and 9 for boarders.

Curriculum: Common Entrance and scholarship subjects are taught, following the National Curriculum.

Reports and Consultation: Half-term and end-of-term reports. There is ample consultation. Every effort is made to establish close and friendly contact between the School and parents.

Boarding: Three boarding houses.

Sports include cricket, rugby, football, hockey, athletics, tennis, rounders, netball, swimming, gymnastics, lacrosse and cross-country.

Comments: The School is under the same Governing Body as Dulwich College Preparatory School, London. The link with Dulwich College is historical only. The School is fully co-educational taking pupils on a first come, first served, basis. There is a wide range of ability, with special needs for those with learning difficulties yet with a strong academic tradition enabling children to achieve scholarships to top senior schools. There is an emphasis on up to date teaching and the School has achieved notable successes in Music and Art. There is a pre-prep department. There is a wide range of extra-curricular activities.

The Dulwich College Preparatory School Trust exists to provide a high quality education in a caring environment for boys and girls aged 3-13. Registered Charity No. 312715.

King's School, Rochester

(Founded 604 AD)

Satis House,
Boley Hill, Rochester,
Kent ME1 1TE
Tel: 01634 843913 Fax: 01634 832493

Head: Dr I R Walker, BA, PhD, LTh, ABIA, FCollP, FRSA
Type: Independent School
Age range: 4-18. Boarders from 8
No of pupils enrolled as at 1.5.97: 691
Pre-Prep: 86 Boys 41 Girls
Prep: 179 Boys 66 Girls
Senior: 152 Boys 50 Girls
Sixth Form: 94 Boys 23 Girls
Fees per annum:
Day: £3510-£7110; Boarding £9735-£12,375
Sixth Form Day: £7110; Boarding: £12,375

Religious affiliation: Church of England

Member of: HMC, CSA, IAPS, ESHA, SHA

Curriculum: Broadly based up to 14, and not tied to the National Curriculum. German taught by native speakers from 4 to develop bi-lingualism by 13. Links with German and French schools for exchanges of up to one term. Five core GCSEs, and four options from choice of 15. Broad A and A/S opportunities in the Sixth Form with General Studies programme. Separate sciences from 11. Flourishing tradition in Classics. Significant Oxbridge record. Computer literacy for all pupils.

Entry requirements: Normal entry at 4, 8, 11 and 13 by means of test, interview, school report and Common Entrance. Sixth Form places for pupils with suitable GCSE results.

King's School, Rochester, is a registered charity for the purposes of educating children.

Somerhill Pre-Prep, Derwent Lodge, Yardley Court

Somerhill, Tonbridge,
Kent TN11 ONJ
Tel: 01732 352124 Fax: 01732 363381

Principal: J S M Morris
Type: Co-educational Day Pre-Prep, Single Sex Prep School
Age range: 3-13
No of pupils enrolled as at 1.5.97: 400
236 Boys 164 Girls
Fees per annum: £1620-£6225

Religious affiliation: Christian

Member of: IAPS, ISA

The Schools at Somerhill comprise a Preparatory School for boys, Yardley Court, a Preparatory School for girls, Derwent Lodge and a co-educational School for young children, Somerhill Pre-Prep. Emphasis is placed on academic potential. Each child is encouraged to enjoy the process of learning. Children are prepared for Common Entrance and Scholarship examinations; they can also participate in the Kent selection tests. Somerhill, a Grade I Jacobean mansion is surrounded by 150 acres of parkland and purpose built playing fields, yet is within a mile of the centre of Tonbridge and easily accessed from the motorways.

Surrey

American Community Schools

Heywood, Portsmouth Road,
Cobham, Surrey KT11 1BL
Tel: 01932 867251 Fax: 01932 869789

Headmaster: Mr T Lehman
Type: Co-educational Day and Boarding School
Age range: Lower School: 3-9; Middle School: 10-13; High School 14-18
No. of pupils enrolled as at 1.1.97: 666 Boys 584 Girls
Fees per annum: On application

The three American Community Schools, founded in 1967, are non-sectarian co-educational schools for students between the ages of 3 and 18. The Surrey School is located in Cobham, 25 miles from London and accessible by British Rail. A door-to-door bus service is provided by the School. The boarding school division accepts students in grades 7 to 13.

STUDENT BODY. Approximately 60% of the 1250 students are American, 7% are Canadian, and the remaining 33% represent 47 other nationalities.

ACADEMIC PROGRAM. The traditional American curriculum, offering a wide range of subjects is designed to lead to an American High School Diploma. Experienced university counselling is provided by the Academic Dean and all examinations required for admission to American universities are administered by the School.

The School provides courses leading to the International Baccalaureate Diploma, a recognised qualification for entry to universities in Britain, Europe and for advanced standing in American universities. Students may also pursue college-level studies through the American-based Advanced Placement (AP) Program.

An English as a Second Language Program is available for non-English speaking applicants between the ages of 6 and 15.

The School is accredited by the new England Association of Schools and Colleges, ISJC, and holds membership in the International Baccalaureate Organisation.

FACULTY. There are 119 full-time teachers on the faculty, all holding a university degree. The student faculty ratio is 10:1.

THE CAMPUS. Recent years have seen the advancement of the 128 acre campus by the building of a High School, Middle School, boarding dormitory and cafetorium/ gymnasium complex, providing pleasant and efficient libraries, media centre, language, computer and science laboratories, music room, art studios and sports facilities. A new purpose built Lower School was opened in September 1995 and there are plans for a state-of-the-art auditorium/theatre complex and swimming pool facility in the future.

OTHER CAMPUSES. The Hillingdon campus, with its superb landscaped gardens and classical period mansion, includes an impressive sports complex, barbecue area and delightful architectural features. The Egham campus provides modern teaching blocks and recreational facilities, set against the original Victorian mansion and beautiful gardens. 5 and 7 day boarding facilities are also available at Egham.

STUDENT ACTIVITIES. A full range of sports is offered as well as other activities including Student Council, yearbook, music, computers, drama, video, cheerleading and scouting.

ADMISSION. New students are accepted in all grades throughout the year on the basis of a completed application form and previous school records (with a provision prior to grade placement when necessary). Financial aid is available on the basis of need.

American Community Schools, England

(New School - opened August 1995)

Woodlee, London Road (A30), Egham, Surrey TW20 0HS
Tel: 01784 430611 Fax: 01784 430626

Head Principal: Mrs K. Alderdice
Type: Co-educational School
Age range: 3-14
No. of pupils enrolled as at 1.1.97: 260; 105 Girls 155 Boys
Fees: On application

The three American Community Schools, founded in 1967, are non-sectarian co-educational schools for students between the ages of three and eighteen. The Woodlee campus is located in Egham, Surrey and is 18 miles from London and is accessible by British Rail. The School is conveniently placed in relation to Heathrow Airport and the M25 motorway. A door-to-door bus service is provided by the School.

STUDENT BODY
Approximately 60 per cent of the 260 students are American, the remaining 40 per cent representing 20 other nationalities.

ACADEMIC PROGRAM
The traditional American curriculum offering a wide range of subjects is available. Learning support and programs for gifted students are also provided, with specialists included on the staff. Class sizes are small with individual support and guidance being provided. Modern language instruction is offered beginning in Grade I. Computers are used throughout the school as a learning tool.

FACULTY
There are 37 full-time teachers on the faculty, all holding a university degree. The student ratio is 7:1.

THE CAMPUS
The school is situated on a 20 acre campus which provides the students with a purpose-built environment, including gymnasium, all-

149

weather, floodlit tennis courts, dining hall, laboratory and playing fields. The library is fully computerised with CD-ROM materials available.

STUDENT ACTIVITIES

A full range of sports are offered, including basketball, tennis, track and field, soccer, softball and volleyball. Other activities available are Student Council, yearbook, after school clubs, music, computers, scouting and intra-mural sports.

BOARDING

There is provision for boarding on the campus. Modern purpose-built facilities are available with single room accommodation for students being offered.

ADMISSION

New students are accepted subject to space being available in all grades throughout the year and on the basis of a completed application form and previous school records (with a provision for testing prior to grade placement when necessary).

Caterham School

(Founded 1811)

Harestone Valley, Caterham, Surrey CR3 6YA
Tel: 01883 343028 Fax: 01883 347795

Headmaster: Mr R A E Davey, MA(Dublin)
Type: Independent Co-educational Day and Boarding School
Age range: 3-18 *No of pupils enrolled as at 10.1.97:*
Senior School (11-18): 710; and 220 in Sixth Form; Preparatory School (3-11): 170
Fees per annum: Day: £1740-£6090; Boarding: £11,130-£11,730

Entry requirements: Tests in Maths, English and Reasoning for candidates aged 7-12; Common Entrance at 13; Sixth Form candidates: minimum of 5 good passes with high grades in GCSE in the proposed A level subjects.

Continuity of education is provided at Caterham. Pupils move from the Preparatory School (3-11) to the Senior School where they stay until 18+. Caterham has a fine record of academic, musical and dramatic achievements offering day, full and flexi-boarding. Situated in 80 acres of the North Downs with easy access to the M25 (2 miles), Gatwick (20 minutes), Heathrow (50 minutes) and London, by rail, is 40 minutes.

Caterham School's facilities have been enhanced impressively in the 1990s through a £4 million development programme - new 24 room teaching block, new sports hall and swimming pool, two new rooms for

Information Technology and a new all-weather sports pitch.

Caterham School aims to provide a high quality all-round education in a caring Christian context.

A Charitable Trust which exists to provide a first-class education to boys and girls from a wide range of social, economic and cultural backgrounds.

Cranleigh Preparatory School

(Founded 1881)

Horseshoe Lane,
Cranleigh, Surrey GU6 8QH
Tel: 01483 274199 Fax: 01483 277136

Head: Mr M R Keppie, MA, PGCE (St Catharine's College, Cambridge)
Type: Boys' Boarding and Day Preparatory School
Age range: 7-13. Boarders from 7
No of pupils enrolled as at 1.5.97: 185 Boys
Fees per annum:
Day: £6465; Boarding: £8700

Religious affiliation: Church of England

Member of: IAPS

The School stands in its own 35 acres of beautiful Surrey countryside, across the road from Cranleigh (senior) School. Mr and Mrs Keppie live in the main building with the boarders, matron, and other residential staff.

The School operates essentially as a boarding school, the benefits of which are available to the day boys. Boarding life is busy and fun, with committed staff, full weekends, and regular exeats. Parents are most welcome at matches and on Sundays. Regular outings are offered to the South Coast, the countryside and London.

The boys enter at seven or eight after an entry test, and are prepared for Common Entrance or Scholarships. The School has a high academic reputation, where Scholarships are won annually to Cranleigh and other prestigious schools, along with a 100% success rate in the Common Entrance examination.

A broad, balanced but academic curriculum includes computing, art and design, pottery, woodwork, metalwork and music, and many timetabled activities. The science labs, music school and sports hall are recently built.

Sport is strong and varied. Rugby, soccer, hockey, cricket, tennis, swimming and athletics are the main sports, among many others such as golf and basket-ball. Musical life includes three choirs and an orchestra.

New classrooms, changing rooms and a computer centre were opened in September 1996.

Cranleigh Preparatory School is a charitable trust for the purpose of educating children.

SUR

Cranleigh School

(Founded 1865)

Horseshoe Lane,
Cranleigh,
Surrey GU6 8QQ
Tel: 01483 273997
Fax: 01483 267398

Headmaster: Mr T A A Hart, MA (New College, Oxford)
From 1.9.97: Mr G de W Waller, MA MSc
FRSA (Worcester College, Oxford)
Type: Independent Boys' Boarding and Day School
with Girls in the Sixth Form
Age range: 13-18. Boarders from 13
No. of pupils enrolled as at 1.1.97: 486
Senior: 415 Boys; Sixth Form: 176 Boys 71 Girls
Fees per annum:
Day: £9615; Boarding: £12,990

Religious denomination: Church of England

Member of: HMC

Cranleigh is an energetic School, with a warm atmosphere. Pupils are encouraged to make the most of their varied potential, to relish challenge, to feel they are known as individuals and to become talented and wise adults in a fast-changing world.

Cranleigh has high standards, but is not elitist. Over the last five years, more than 95%, on average, have gone on to University, including one in ten to Oxbridge.

A great strength is drawn from the fact that the School operates as a strong boarding community, where both day and boarding members play a full part in House activities, and its style incorporates a close relationship between staff and pupils. Open boarding is a policy, encouraging parents to visit as often as they can. There is a strong focus on pastoral care and personal development, and individual tutoring ensures that each pupil's potential is fulfilled.

Only eight miles from Guildford, and less than an hour from Central London, Gatwick, Heathrow, and the South Coast, Cranleigh is attractively located in 200 acres of rolling Surrey, with tremendous facilities such as three theatres, a golf course, and horse-riding facilities.

Recent developments include a total refurbishment of computing facilities, right in the centre of the School to encourage its use in any subject; more flexible arrangements for day pupils; a major reconstruction of East House; and a second Astroturf (floodlit).

Cranleigh School is a charitable trust for the purpose of educating children.

SUR

Hoe Bridge & Trees Schools

(Founded 1871)

Hoe Place,
Old Woking Road,
Woking, Surrey GU22 8JE
Tel: 01483 760018 & 01483 772194
Fax: 01483 757560

Heads: R W K Barr, BEd(Oxon) Mrs L Renfrew
Type: Nursery, Pre-prep and Preparatory
for boys and girls
Age range: 2¹/2-14 Boarders from 7 years
No of pupils enrolled as at 1.1.97:
Junior: 323 Boys 82 Girls
Fees per annum:
Day: £750-£6075; Boarding £7890-£8715

Religious affiliation: Non-denominational

Member of: IAPS

Curriculum: The curriculum ranges from Latin to Computing, covering requirements for Common Entrance and incorporating the demands of the National Curriculum. This provides opportunities for those who are academically able and also for those whose abilities are of a creative, practical or sporting nature.

Entry requirements: Entry to the Kindergarten, Nursery, and Pre-prep is by interview. Entry to the Prep School is by assessment and interview.

The aim of the Charitable Trust is to provide a well-rounded education for boys and girls aged 2fi-14.

The Hoe Bridge and Trees Charitable Trust exists to provide high quality education for boys and girls.

SUR

King Edward's School

(Founded 1553)

Witley,
Wormley, Godalming,
Surrey GU8 5SG
Tel: 01428 682572 Fax: 01428 682850

Headmaster: Mr R J Fox, MA, CMath, FIMA
Type: Co-educational Independent School
Age range: 11-18. Boarders from 11
No. of pupils enrolled as at 1.5.97: 458
Junior: 49 Boys 52 Girls Senior: 110 Boys 101 Girls
Sixth Form: 82 Boys 64 Girls
Fees per annum:
Day: £6240; Boarding: £8970

Religious affiliation: Church of England

Member of: HMC, BSA

Curriculum: Art, Biology, Business Studies, Classics, German, English, Economics, French, Geography, History, Latin, Mathematics, Physics, Chemistry, Information Technology, Religious Studies, Drama, CDT, Home Technology, Music.

Entry requirements: Own entrance examination at 11, 12 or 13, or Common Entrance. Good GCSE results and school report for Sixth Form entrance.

King Edward's School, which is a registered charity, provides a structured approach to education and offers a substantial number of bursaries to children whose home circumstances make boarding a real need.

A list of schools offering Learning Support appears elsewhere in this guide

Prior's Field, Godalming

(Founded 1902)

Godalming, Surrey GU7 2RH
Tel: 01483 810 551 Fax: 01483 810 180

Head: Mrs J M McCallum, BA
Type: Independent
Age range: 11-18. Boarders from 11
No of pupils enrolled as at 1.1.97: 228, Sixth Form: 45
Fees per annum: Day: £2289; Boarding £3429
Sixth Form Day: £2289; Boarding: £3429

Religious affiliation: Inter-denominational

Member of: GSA

Prior's Field is situated within half a mile of the A3 and Charterhouse, and is close to Heathrow and Gatwick airports.

Founded by the Huxley Family in 1902, Prior's Field was unusual in offering a full science and mathematics curriculum for girls, a tradition it has continued to this day with a high pass rate at A level and GCSE in 1995 and an excellent 'Times' League Table rating. Most Sixth Formers proceed to University. Special coaching is available for Oxbridge candidates. Nineteen subjects are offered at Advanced level in addition to a business skills programme.

Junior boarders are accommodated in bedrooms for about six girls and senior and Sixth Formers have single study bedrooms, the Sixth Form in a separate house on campus.

The school is surrounded by playing fields. The major sports are lacrosse and tennis though a wide range of sports is offered in addition to these and horse riding is available nearby.

The school choirs and instrumentalists are successful in local festivals, and the school mounts several drama productions annually. Visits to Florence and Venice have recently complemented the History of Art course. Extra curricular activities include Australian football, a Japanese club, the Duke of Edinburgh Award Scheme and Young Enterprise.

Entry requirements: Entry to the school is by common entrance at 11+ or 12+ or by special arrangement for girls from abroad. Details of academic, music, drama and art scholarships are available on request and fee reductions are offered to service families.

Prior's Field School Trust is a registered charity which provides care and education for the young people in its charge. (Charity No.312038).

St Andrew's School, Woking

(Founded 1937)

Church Hill House, Horsell, Woking,
Surrey GU21 4QW
Tel: 01483 760943 Fax: 01483 740314

Head: Mr Barry Pretorius, BEd
Type: Co-educational Day Preparatory School
Age range: 3-13+
No. of pupils enrolled as at 1.5.97: 180
Junior: 85 Boys 15 Girls Senior: 80 Boys
Fees per annum: £2340-£6285

Religious denomination: Church of England

Member of: IAPS, ISIS

Curriculum: The children are prepared for Common Entrance and Scholarships to a wide range of Senior Schools. Music, Art, Drama, IT and DT form part of the general curriculum. A wide range of sports are played and these are coached to a high standard.

Entry requirements: Test and interview for entry into Prep School (7+). No formal entry requirement for the Pre-Preparatory department.

The School is situated on the outskirts of Woking near Horsell Common. Modern classroom blocks supplement the original brick house. There are excellent playing fields, a sports hall, two hard tennis courts and a

heated swimming pool. Activities are offered on three evenings a week at no extra charge.

The St Andrew's (Woking) School charitable trust exists to provide high quality education for boys and girls aged 3 to 14 years.

Registered Charity No.297580.

TASIS England American School

(Founded 1976)

Coldharbour Lane, Thorpe, Surrey TW20 8TE
Tel: +44 (0) 1932 565252 Fax: +44 (0) 1932 564644
E-mail: ukadmissions@tasis.com; uksummer@tasis.com
Internet: http://www.tasis.com

"The American School in a Class by Itself"

TASIS England, frequently cited as the premier American school in the United Kingdom, is now into its third decade of offering an American college-preparatory curriculum to day students from grades Pre-K through to 12 and to boarding students from grades 9-12. Mrs M Crist Fleming, who established The American School in Switzerland in 1955, founded TASIS England in 1976. Located on a stunningly beautiful historic estate of Georgian mansions and 17th century cottages some 18 miles southwest of London, TASIS combines an excellent academic program with exceptional facilities for art, drama, music, computers, and sports. Small classes and a dedicated, experienced faculty numbering in excess of 100 provide highly individualised attention and an outstanding environment for learning.

TASIS England embraces three divisions: Lower (grades PK-5; ages 4-10), Middle (grades 6-8; ages 11-13), and Upper (grades 9-12; ages 14-18). Students in each division regularly benefit from the opportunity to work closely with visiting artists, actors, musicians,

and sports professionals. The comprehensive athletics program includes intramurals in the Lower School and interschool games for Middle School, JV, and Varsity teams. Throughout the year, students enjoy numerous field trips, weekend activities, and in-program travel to London, elsewhere within the UK, and abroad.

TASIS' ongoing effort to provide its students with the very best educational experience was recently underscored with the opening of the Early Childhood Center. Linked to the Lower School's Thorpe House, a Grade II listed building, the Center adds five classrooms and a multi-purpose room for dining, assemblies, and physical education. The three-storey Georgian-style building represents the latest stage in the School's on-going development plan, which has also included the inauguration of the 400-seat Fleming Theatre, the scene of student and professional productions throughout the year.

Admissions decisions for the academic school year are made on a rolling basis upon receipt of a completed application form together with the application fee, three teachers' recommendations, and three years of transcripts. Standardised test scores and a student questionnaire are requested, but are not required. An interview is recommended unless distance is a prohibiting factor.

For additional information please contact Dr Duncan J Rollo, Director of Admissions.

The TASIS England Summer Program, open to students ages 12-18 from the UK and around the world, is both rigorous and exciting. Intensive summer programs include high school credit and enrichment courses, theatre workshops, ESL, TOEFL, and SAT Review. Students also enjoy a full range of sports, activities, and travel, both international and within the UK. For admission to the summer program, a completed application, deposit, and teacher recommendation form are required.

For additional information please contact Faie Gilbert, Director of Summer Admissions.

TASIS England is accredited by the European Council of International Schools (ECIS) and the New England Association of Schools and Colleges (NEASC) and is a member of the National Association of Independent Schools (NAIS).

Wispers School for Girls, Haslemere

50th Anniversary Year

1 9 4 7   1 9 9 7

(Founded 1947)

High Lane, Haslemere, Surrey GU27 1AD
Station: Haslemere (Portsmouth Line)
Tel: 01428 643646 Fax: 01428 641120

Wispers School is an independent boarding, weekly and day School for 130 girls aged between 11 and 18. The School is administered by a Board of Governors and is registered as an Educational Charitable Trust, formed for the purpose of excellence in education

Chairman of the Board of Governors: Mr John Parker
Head: Mr L H Beltran, BA Hons (Exeter), PGCE (Leeds)
Deputy Headmistress: Mrs G M Eaves, BSc Hons (Leicester), PGCE (Nottingham), MA (Reading)
Bursar: Mr M Smith
Admissions Secretary: Mrs D R Siddons

Why choose Wispers?
Wispers School is the only small independent school for girls aged 11 to 18 in and around Haslemere, Surrey. This means that we know every girl and her parents extremely well.

Our GCSE and A level timetables are tailor made to suit each girl's requirements. Our pupils obtain sound results (Summer 1996 A and AS 100 per cent pass rate, GCSE 95.5 per cent). We expect our bright pupils to excel. Our less gifted pupils often do extremely well to the delight of their parents and their preparatory school. Our size allows more girls to represent the school in sports, public speaking, school productions, concerts, charity and general activities.

We welcome girls from abroad and from counties all across the United Kingdom. Many of our pupils live in Surrey and many in London are weekly boarders going home on weekends.

We are a few miles from Guildford, conveniently equidistant from Heathrow and Gatwick airports, and also within easy reach of Chichester, Portsmouth and London.

Wispers has always been a small school and we have maintained our unique identity in times of change and school mergers. Our school's security lies in its rich assets, it has wonderful facilities and is set in 26 acres of outstanding natural beauty.

We provide a caring, responsible and forward looking approach to education in partnership with you. We welcome discussion about your daughter and we will keep in touch with you every step of the way.

The school puts on an equal footing with academic sucess and university entrance, moral awareness and a wide ecumenical experience of Christian witness. In particular we expect all our pupils to willingly accept their school and local community responsibilities and to develop adult life skills needed for employment and marriage in the 21st century.

With the guidance offered by our specialist staff and the support you provide, our pupils distinguish themselves with academic success and by being decent, trustworthy people.

Their readiness to serve others is widely known and respected. The girls develop lifelong loyalties to their friends and school. The proof of this loyalty and of the school's success is that so many of them continue to keep in touch with us, often helping current pupils with work experience, and decide to send their own daughters to Wispers.

We are particularly interested in encouraging specialised vocal potential through our

voice/choral scholarships. Successful applicants study singing under our Director of Music who is head of junior voice at the Royal Academy of Music, London. Several former pupils have entered both the Royal Academy of Music and the Royal Northern College of Music, Manchester. Further details can be gained from the admissions secretary.

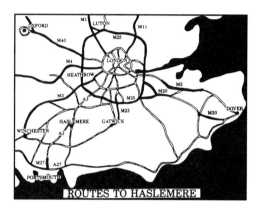

ROUTES TO HASLEMERE

We look forward to welcoming you at Wispers.

East Sussex

Bellerbys College,
Mayfield and Wadhurst

(Founded 1868)

(Central Admissions) Mayfield Lane, Wadhurst, East Sussex TN5 6JA
Tel: 01892 782000 Fax: 01892 784323

Heads: Mr Jörg Müller, MA and Mr Eric Reynolds, BA(Hons), PGCE
Type: International Boarding School
Age range: 11-18 Boarders from: 11
No of pupils enrolled as at 1.5.97: 317
Junior: 39 Boys 53 Girls, Senior: 65 Boys 89 Girls; Sixth Form: 29 Boys 42 Girls
Fees per term: Day: £1000; Boarding: £4200; Sixth Form Day: £2140; Boarding: £4200

Religious affiliation: Inter-denominational

Member of: ISA, GSA, BSA

At Bellerbys College Mayfield and Bellerbys College Wadhurst we have created a successful international community within the best traditions of British education. The Colleges, set in the beautiful countryside of South East England and yet just 8 km apart,

offer a combination of single sex boarding with co-educational teaching.

Students aged 11-14 follow the National Curriculum. International students who do not have sufficient English/Study skills to study in the mainstream are given intensive EFL preparation and an introduction to the main subjects taught. There are two types of GCSE programme, the traditional 8/9 subject course and the Intensive course focusing on six subjects in two streams, Business Studies or Art and Design. The Intensive course comprises two terms of GCSE preparation and four terms of GCSE study.

At Sixth Form students can opt for the extensive A level programme or follow a two year Diploma Course in either Business Studies or Art and Design. All students wishing to join the Sixth Form whose English is not of a sufficient standard are required to complete an English Preparation Course. GCSEs in Russian, Mandarin, German and other languages for International students.

Entry requirements: School transcripts, interview, EFL and Maths test. Validated/equivalent overseas qualifications for GCSE/Sixth Form entry.

West Sussex

Cottesmore School
(Founded 1894)

Buchan Hill, Pease Pottage,
West Sussex RH11 9AU
Tel: 01293 520648 Fax: 01293 614784

Headmaster: M A Rogerson, MA(Cantab),
(Member of IAPS)
Type: Independent Co-educational Boarding School
Age range: 7-13
No. of pupils enrolled as at 1.5.97: 100 Boys 45 Girls
Fees per annum: £9150

Curriculum: Work: Boys and Girls are taught together in classes averaging 14 in number. The teacher/pupil ratio is 1:9. All subjects necessary for CE and scholarship examinations are taught.

Recent Developments: There is a 20m indoor heated Swimming Pool, a Computer Room, an

Religious affiliation: Church of England

Member of: IAPS, ISIS

Founded in 1894, the School moved from Hove in 1946 to its present site at Buchan Hill. It lies a mile from Exit 11 of the M23, 10 minutes from Gatwick Airport, and within one hour from central London.

Cottesmore is a co-educational boarding school with 110 boys and 45 girls. There are no day children.

Art Studio and a new building containing six classrooms including a Science laboratory and a specially equipped Language Room. A new Technology Centre is to be completed in the course of 1998.

Hobbies and Activities: These include Pottery, Stamp Collecting, Chess, Bridge, Model-Making, Model Railway, Tenpin Bowling, Gardening, Ballet, Modern Dancing, Drama, Craft, Photography, Carpentry, Printing, Cooking and Debating.

The boys and girls share most activities with the exception of the major games. They lead a busy and varied life and are all encouraged to take part in as wide a variety of activities as possible. Through learning to use their time usefully, the children build up self-reliance and confidence, thus preparing them for the fullest possible life at Public School and beyond.

Entry requirements: Entry is by Headmaster's interview and report from previous school.

WSX

Great Ballard School

(Founded 1924)

Eartham, Nr Chichester, West Sussex PO18 0LR
Tel: 01243 814236 Fax: 01243 814586

Headmaster: Mr Richard E T Jennings, CertEd
Type: Co-educational Preparatory and Pre-Preparatory School
Age range: 2-13. Boarders from 7
No. of pupils enrolled as at 1.5.97: 155
Fees per annum:
Day: 3-7: £3025; 1/2 Day: £1620; 7-13: £4800-£5418
Boarding: £7176-£7677

Religious affiliation: Church of England

Member of: IAPS

Curriculum: The curriculum covers the normal range of subjects and includes Computing, Design Technology, PE, Music, Drama and Current Affairs. Children are prepared for Common Entrance and Scholarship Examinations to appropriate Senior Schools, the particular emphasis being to help each and every child to fulfil their potential.

Entry requirements: Entrance is by interview and testing or through the annual Scholarship in January/February.

Great Ballard: The Pre-prep department in its own walled garden inspires children aged 3-7 to achieve high standards while enjoying their very happy and busy schooldays. Music and movement, drama, PE, swimming, computing and cooking are all introduced in these early years.

The Main School starts at age seven; approximately half of the children board, but there is no compulsion to do so at any stage. Boarding may be done on a full, weekly or occasional basis. We are used to arranging travel for children stationed overseas and ensure that, with outings each weekend, there is life outside the School.

New facilities include music practice rooms, tennis courts, computer room housing a networked system of PCs, all with CD rom, computer aided reference library and an extensive new sports field complex.

At Great Ballard we believe that school must provide a stable, caring environment, a place where children are genuinely happy and are involved in a very wide range of activities, where their interest is constantly being stimulated. Exam results are obviously important, but a happy, busy life in which all achieve their maximum potential, must be the main objective.

Handcross Park School

(Founded 1887)

*Handcross,
Haywards Heath,
West Sussex RH17 6HF
Tel: 01444 400526 Fax: 01444 400527*

Head: Mr W J Hilton, BA, CertEd
(Member of IAPS)
Type: Independent Co-educational Weekly Boarding and Day School
Age range: $2^1/_2$-13. Boarders from 7
No. of pupils enrolled as at 1.5.96:
132 Boys 106 Girls
Fees per annum: Day: £5250-£6105 Boarding: £7380

Religious denomination: Church of England

Member of: IAPS

Curriculum: The School maintains high academic standards and prepares children for Public School scholarships and Common Entrance. Handcross Park is a busy school with good musical, artistic and sporting traditions and is situated on a beautiful 57 acre country estate, close to the major (Sussex) towns of Horsham, Crawley and Haywards Heath. Facilities include golf course, new Music School (1987), Nursery, Pre-Preparatory School (1990), new Sports Hall, Science and Technology Centre.

Entry requirements: By interview with the Headmaster. Scholarship Examinations take place each January/February.

The School is a Charitable Trust (Newells School Trust Ltd) which aims to provide a high quality education for each individual child.

Don't forget to use the Reader Enquiry Card and John Catt Schools Advisory Service, details of which appear at the back of this guide

Windlesham House School

(Founded 1837)

Washington, Pulborough, West Sussex RH20 4AY
Tel: 01903 873207 Fax: 01903 873017
E-mail: windleshamhouse.pulborough@campus.bt.com

Head: Philip Lough MA (Oxon), PGCE (Dunelm)
Member of IAPS
Type: Co-educational Boarding Preparatory School
Age range: 4-13. Boarders from 8
No. of pupils enrolled as at 1.5.97: 261 155 Boys 106 Girls
Fees per annum: Boarding: £9435

Ask any child at Windlesham what they like best about the school and their reply will be, almost without exception, the very wide range of activities available here. Ask the children's parents what makes Windlesham such a very special school and they would probably say its strong family feeling and the knowledge that the children's happiness comes top of our priorities.

This year Windlesham House celebrates 160 years and for all that time we have been at the forefront of educational development and innovation.

We are a boarding prep school lying in the heart of the South Downs in West Sussex, within easy reach of both Gatwick and Heathrow Airports. Worthing lies 5 miles to the South and Horsham 15 miles to the North.

In September 1997 we are opening a Pre prep. Department for children between the ages of 4 to 7 years within a specially designed and converted area of the school, with a specially created play area. The school also has a new Animal Corner.

One of Windlesham's great strengths is that we have been offering a genuine co-educational environment for over 30 years. The girls and boys all have classes and activities together in a broad curriculum which allows us to place a great emphasis on the individual development of every child - academically, socially and emotionally. Our average class size is 17, while the ratio of staff - children is 1:9. Our experienced staff are all specialists in their own field which allows us to help the children to fulfil their potential.

We have high academic standards and we gain many scholarships to Public Schools. In the past 4 years over 55 children have been awarded scholarships and almost every child has gained entry to their first choice public school. We teach all the subjects required by the Common Entrance board including Latin. Children may also study Greek. Information Technology plays a vital part in all subjects at Windlesham and when the children leave at 13 they have all experienced a wide range of IT. throughout the Curriculum. We have many computers which are available to the children, and the computer room is always busy whether in lessons or free time.

Children with Specific Learning Difficulties are welcomed at Windlesham where, with individual or small group teaching and specialist teachers, the children are given the best possible teaching to allow them to overcome their problems. Dyslexia and dyspraxia are not perceived as problems at Windlesham. The children flourish and grow in the knowledge that help is near at hand.

Windlesham possesses excellent facilities. We have a beautiful theatre which converts into an open space for sport and two further halls for games, gymnastics and dance. There is also a chapel, two libraries, two newly converted Science laboratories and a recently refurbished Language department. The Design Centre and Art Department are always full of children working on their own projects and in the Textile Department the children are able to silk paint and fabric design. The walls are full of the children's pictures and paintings.

Outside we have some of the finest sporting fields in the area. There are 3 hockey pitches, 5 football pitches and 4 rugby pitches, an athletics track, as well as floodlit tennis and netball courts.

Whilst we are a boarding school, our weekend boarding arrangements are flexible with some children going home, but with large numbers remaining at school and participating in our full action-packed weekend activity programme. We have regular weekend visits to local attractions and all the children become involved in the activities available to them.

School finishes at 12 noon on Saturday and we have a bus which runs from Putney back to Windlesham on a Sunday evening. Those children who travel to school from abroad are taken and collected from the airports at the beginning and end of term where the children are delivered safely to the correct terminus and are collected from the airport on arrival in the UK.

Windlesham has an excellent pastoral system with every child belonging to a House wherein they have a close relationship with both their House parents. They maintain regular and close contact with the parents and write home weekly by means of post, fax, or E-mail. We encourage parents to come to the school and often the major meeting place is the front hall of the school following matches!

The school is a Charitable Trust (Malden Trust Ltd) which exists to provide high quality boarding education for boys and girls between the ages of 7 and 13 years.

Display Listings of
International Schools

SUR

TASIS England American School

(Founded 1976)

Coldharbour Lane, Thorpe, Surrey TW20 8TE
Tel: +44 (0) 1932 565252 Fax: +44 (0) 1932 564644
E-mail: ukadmissions@tasis.com; uksummer@tasis.com
Internet: http://www.tasis.com

"The American School in a Class by Itself"

TASIS England, frequently cited as the premier American school in the United Kingdom, is now into its third decade of offering an American college-preparatory curriculum to day students from grades Pre-K through to 12 and to boarding students from grades 9-12. Mrs M Crist Fleming, who established The American School in Switzerland in 1955, founded TASIS England in 1976. Located on a stunningly beautiful historic estate of Georgian mansions and 17th century cottages some 18 miles southwest of London, TASIS combines an excellent academic program with exceptional facilities for art, drama, music, computers, and sports. Small classes and a dedicated, experienced faculty numbering in excess of 100 provide highly individualised attention and an outstanding environment for learning.

TASIS England embraces three divisions: Lower (grades PK-5; ages 4-10), Middle (grades 6-8; ages 11-13), and Upper (grades 9-12; ages 14-18). Students in each division regularly benefit from the opportunity to work closely with visiting artists, actors, musicians,

and sports professionals. The comprehensive athletics program includes intramurals in the Lower School and interschool games for Middle School, JV, and Varsity teams. Throughout the year, students enjoy numerous field trips, weekend activities, and in-program travel to London, elsewhere within the UK, and abroad.

TASIS' ongoing effort to provide its students with the very best educational experience was recently underscored with the opening of the Early Childhood Center. Linked to the Lower School's Thorpe House, a Grade II listed building, the Center adds five classrooms and a multi-purpose room for dining, assemblies, and physical education. The three-storey Georgian-style building represents the latest stage in the School's on-going development plan, which has also included the inauguration of the 400-seat Fleming Theatre, the scene of student and professional productions throughout the year.

Admissions decisions for the academic school year are made on a rolling basis upon receipt of a completed application form together with the application fee, three teachers' recommendations, and three years of transcripts. Standardised test scores and a student questionnaire are requested, but are not required. An interview is recommended unless distance is a prohibiting factor.

For additional information please contact Dr Duncan J Rollo, Director of Admissions.

The TASIS England Summer Program, open to students ages 12-18 from the UK and around the world, is both rigorous and exciting. Intensive summer programs include high school credit and enrichment courses, theatre workshops, ESL, TOEFL, and SAT Review. Students also enjoy a full range of sports, activities, and travel, both international and within the UK. For admission to the summer program, a completed application, deposit, and teacher recommendation form are required.

For additional information please contact Faie Gilbert, Director of Summer Admissions.

TASIS England is accredited by the European Council of International Schools (ECIS) and the New England Association of Schools and Colleges (NEASC) and is a member of the National Association of Independent Schools (NAIS).

Display Listings of Tutorial Colleges and Colleges of Further Education

South West London

Inchbald School of Design

(Founded 1960)

Interior Design Faculty

7 Eaton Gate, London SW1W 9BA
Tel: 0171 730 5508 Fax: 0171 730 4937

**Garden Design Faculty and
Design History Faculty**

32 eccleston Square, London SW1V 1PB
Tel: 0171 630 9011 Fax: 0171 976 5979
E-mail:design@inchbald.demon.co.uk
Internet: www.inchbald.demon.co.uk

Principal: Mrs Jacqueline Duncan, IIDA, FIDDA
No. of students enrolled as at 1.6.96: Male 20 Female 100
Range of fees (including VAT): from £11,000
Other courses (from 3-day to 10-week): range from £585 to £3850

Diploma Courses:
Environmental Design (2-year)
Interior Design (1-year; 1-year with
Advanced Studies)
Garden Design (1-year)
Design History (1-year)

Certificate Courses:
Design & Decoration (10-week)
Design History (3 x 10-week)
Garden Design (3 x 10-week)
Design & Drawing Foundation (6-week)

Short Courses: Selection varying in length
from 3-day to 3-week courses in interior
design, design history, garden design,
computer aided design, colour, business
management for designers, design drawing,
design of furniture and built-in fitments,
and decorative paint finishes.

Nature of tuition: Lectures, classes, small
groups, one-to-one, practical projects and
visits.

Average class or group: 20

Teacher/Student ratio: 1: 8

The School provides an assistance service
for accommodation. A non-residential adult
education school situated in Belgravia and
Pimlico with excellent access to London
museums, exhibitions and leading designers.

Correspondence Course started March 1997.

FE

London Study Centre

(Founded 1975)

Munster House, 676 Fulham Road,
London SW6 5SA
Tel: 44 171 731 3549 or 736 4990
Fax: 44 171 731 6060
E-Mail: 106153.2344@compuserve.com

Principal: Colin D Gordon, MA(Oxon)
(Founder of the EFL Gazette)
Type: Language School
Age range: 16+
No. of pupils enrolled as at 10.1.97:
400 Male, 450 Female
Fees: Tuition: Approx £25 for 15 hours per week;
(including 25 minutes break daily)
Accommodation: From £80 to £120
depending on type of accommodation

Member of: ARELS

Courses offered: General English Courses. All levels from basic beginners to advanced. Open all year except Christmas and Easter vacations. Summer courses: mid-June to mid-September. Special pronunciation and Introduction to Business English and English for Tourism classes (depending on demand). Full and part-time Teacher Training Courses (Trinity College TESOL Cert).

Accommodation arrangements: Self-catering or with local family approved by institution.

Near Kings Road and Central London. Student common room, satellite TV, patio, garden, library, listening centre/language laboratory, video games, facilities for private study. Excursions and social activities.

West London

Abbey Tutorial College

(Founded 1985)

*28A Hereford Road,
London W2 5AJ
Tel: 0171 229 5928 Fax: 0171 727 4382*

Principal: James Burnett, BSc
Type: Independent
Age range: 18-20+
No. of pupils enrolled as at 1.1.97: 90
Senior: 45 Boys 45 Girls
Fees per annum: Day: £1700-£8000

Curriculum: Mathematics (Pure, Applied, Statistics and Further), Physics, Chemistry, Biology at Advanced Level only.

Abbey is London's leading tutorial centre for A level Mathematics and Science. Founded in 1985, it has an impressive reputation for university entrance and A level results. New colleges have opened in Manchester, Birmingham and Cambridge.

Most of the 90 students enrolled at Abbey this year are taking A levels in order to gain grades required for medicine, dentistry, law and other subjects requiring A and B grades. We have been particularly successful at placing students at medical school (more than 100 over the last four years). We also have a number of graduate students who are taking A levels in the sciences in order to gain entry into medical or veterinary schools.

In the January 1996 examinations 85% of grades were at A and B, and 97% at C or above (75 students).

Tuition takes place in small groups and students follow a highly structured programme which is exclusively examination orientated. By restricting the size of the College it is possible to monitor each student very thoroughly over their short course as well as carefully guiding them through their UCAS applications.

Lists of schools which accept pupils at 16+ to study A Levels or Vocational Courses appear elsewhere in this guide

FE

Ashbourne Independent Sixth Form College

(Founded 1981)

17 Old Court Place, London W8 4PL
Tel: 0171 937 3858 Fax: 0171 937 2207

Head: Mr M J Hatchard-Kirby, MSc, BApSc
Type: Independent Sixth Form College
Age range: 16-19
No. of pupils enrolled as at 1.9.96: 150
Fees per annum: £8625-£10,050

Established in 1981 Ashbourne is now regarded as one of the best schools of its type in the UK. Wonderfully situated near Kensington Gardens and Hyde Park, the School is a few minutes away from the excellent museums of Natural History, Science and Geology and the Victoria and Albert Museum.

The atmosphere is adult, friendly and informal and unencumbered by petty restrictions. Working in very small groups which never exceed ten, the college has helped students of all abilities achieve their academic goals. Ashbourne recognizes the importance of communication, individual attention and motivation, and has been particularly successful with those students who need a closely supervised, structure approach to work. A wide-ranging curriculum includes Media Studies and Psychology and the programme for two year students includes thinking skills, trips abroad and participation in an award programme for the Cambridge Diploma of Achievement.

At Ashbourne students are encouraged to work hard and the College stays open until 8.00 pm during the week and all day Saturday. The College aims to offer the opportunity for change; many an academic career has been revitalized because of the individual attention offered by small groups, the insistence to aiming high and working hard.

Geographical Directory of Schools in Central London

E1

THE ACADEMY DRAMA SCHOOL
189 Whitechaple Road, London E1 1DN
Tel: 0171 377 8735
Head: T Reynolds RADA
Type: Co-educational Day B17-40 G17-40
Fees: DAY £2220-£3900

EUROPEAN COLLEGE
Neil House, London E1 1DU
Tel: 0171 377 8962
Head: S Ahmad
Type: Co-educational Day

ISLAMIC COLLEGE LONDON
16 Settles Street, London E1 1JP
Tel: 0171 377 1595
Head: A Sayeed BA, MM
Type: Boys Day B11-16
No of pupils: B32
Fees: DAY £1000-£1500

MADNI GIRLS SCHOOL
15/17 Rampart Street, London E1 2LA
Tel: 0171 791 3531
Head: S F R Liyawdeen
Type: Co-educational Day

ORANGES AND LEMONS DAY NURSERY
Shoreditch Parish Church, London E1 6JN
Tel: 0171 729 4192
Head: Paula Cadogan
Type: Co-educational Day

E2

★ GATEHOUSE SCHOOL
Sewardstone Road, London E2 9JG
Tel: 0181 980 2978
Head: Miss Alexandra Eversole MontDip
Type: Co-educational Day B2-11 G2-11
No of pupils: B80 G70
Fees: DAY £3225-£4650

HAPPY NEST NURSERY
Fellows Court Community Centre, London E2
Tel: 0171 739 3193
Type: Co-educational Day

PEBBLE CENTRE MONTESSORI SCHOOL
66 Warner Place, London E2
Tel: 0171 739 4343
Type: Co-educational Day

RIVER HOUSE MONTESSORI SCHOOL
c/o 46 Quilter Street, London E2 7BT
Tel: 0171 6801288
Head: Miss S Greenwood
Type: Co-educational Day & Boarding

E3

PILLAR BOX MONTESSORI NURSING SCHOOL
City House, 107 Bow Road, London E3
Tel: 0181 980 0700
Head: Ms Lorraine Redknapp
Type: Co-educational Day

E4

AMHURST NURSERY
13 The Avenue, London E4
Tel: 0181 527 1614
Head: Mrs Mills
Type: Co-educational Day

BILLETS CORNER NURSERY
11 Walthamstow Avenue, London E4 8TA
Tel: 0181 523 3823
Head: B Harmsworth
Type: Co-educational Day

MARLBOROUGH DAY NURSERY
22 Marlborough Road, London E4 9AL
Tel: 0181 527 2902
Head: Ms J Crowe NNEB
Type: Co-educational Day B0-5 G0-5
Fees: DAY £4680-£5980

MERRYFIELD MONTESSORI PRE-SCHOOL
76 Station Road, London E4 7BA
Tel: 0181 524 7697
Head: G Wilson
Type: Co-educational Day

NORMANHURST SCHOOL
68-74 Station Road, London E4 7BA
Tel: 0181 529 4307
Head: J Leyland ACP, FRGS, FRSA
Type: Co-educational Day B3-16 G3-16
No of pupils: B90 G60
Fees: DAY £3600-£4600

ROCKING HORSE NURSERY
1 Hatch Lane, London E4 6LP
Tel: 0181 523 7030
Head: Valerie Smith
Type: Co-educational Day

E5

BEIS CHINUCH LEBONOS
139 Clapton Common, London E5 9EA
Tel: 0181 802 1425
Head: Mrs Bertha Schneck
Type: Co-educational Day

DOWNS SIDE NURSERY SCHOOL
Rendlesham Road, London E5
Tel: 0181 985 5937
Type: Co-educational Day

FAMILY CARE DAY NURSERY
51 Mayola Road, London E5
Tel: 0181 985 6486
Head: Mrs Juliet Marcano
Type: Co-educational Day

LEAVIEW COMMUNITY NURSERY
Leaview House, Springfield, London E5 9EJ
Tel: 0181 806 9012
Head: Leticia Adu AdvMontDip
Type: Co-educational Day B0-5 G0-5
No of pupils: B12 G14
Fees: DAY £3000-£6250

LENNOX LEWIS COLLEGE
Theydon Road, London E5 9NA
Tel: 0181 806 8700
Head: Liz Jones
Type: Co-educational Day

PARAGON CHRISTIAN ACADEMY
233-241 Glyn Road, London E5 0JP
Tel: 0181 985 1119
Head: G W Olson
Type: Co-educational Day

TALMUD TORAH MACHZIKEI HADASS
The Woodlands, London E5 9AL
Tel: 0181 800 6070
Type: Co-educational Day & Boarding

E6

FELLOWSHIP HOUSE DAY NURSERY
St Barts Centre, London E6
Tel: 0181 503 5278
Head: Mrs Pat Bradley
Type: Co-educational Day

E7

THE CEDAR SCHOOL
5-7 Stafford Road, London E7 8NL
Tel: 0181 472 5723
Head: S J Sherwood BSc(Hons), DipEd
Type: Co-educational Day B4-11 G4-11
No of pupils: B18 G12
Fees: DAY £2550

FIRST STEPS (MONTESSORI) DAY NURSERY
5 Sebert Road, London E7
Tel: 0181 555 0125
Head: Mrs Maria Adeseqha
Type: Co-educational Day

GRANGEWOOD INDEPENDENT SCHOOL
Chester Road, London E7 8QT
Tel: 0181 472 3552
Head: B Davies BA(Hons), DipEd
Type: Co-educational Day B4-11 G4-11
No of pupils: B57 G63
Fees: DAY £2805

E8

136 NURSERY
c/o Ann Taylor Centre, London E8
Tel: 0171 249 9826
Type: Co-educational Day

BARNARDOS FERNCLIFF CENTRE
4 Ferncliff Road, London E8
Tel: 0171 254 1906
Type: Co-educational Day

INDEPENDENT PLACE NURSERY
26/27 Independent Place, London E8 2HD
Tel: 0171 275 9499
Head: Ms Louise Hodgson NNEB
Type: Co-educational Day B0-5 G0-5

MARKET NURSERY
Wilde Close, off Pownall Road, London E8 4JS
Tel: 0171 241 0978
Head: Mrs Flor Frampton
Type: Co-educational Day

E9

GET ALONG GANG PLAYGROUP
St Mary of Eton Church Hall, Eastway, London E9
Tel: 0181 533 0926
Head: Miss Karen Niazi
Type: Co-educational Day

E10

BARCLAY INFANT SCHOOL (NURSERY)
Essex Road, London E10
Tel: 0181 539 1299
Type: Co-educational Day

BEAUMONT NURSERY UNIT
192 Vicarage Road, London E10
Tel: 0181 518 7203
Type: Co-educational Day

CHESTERFIELD DAY NURSERY
38 Chesterfield Road, London E10
Tel: 0181 539 5541
Head: Karen James
Type: Co-educational Day

MULBERRY DAY NURSERY
70 Canterbury Road, London E10
Tel: 0181 558 4639
Head: Marcia McCollin
Type: Co-educational Day

ROSEBANK NURSERY
56 Leyton Park Road, London E10
Tel: 0181 558 8573
Head: Ms Downer
Type: Co-educational Day

E11

BUSHWOOD DAY NURSERY
10 Bushwood, London E11
Tel: 0181 530 2784
Head: Kim Swiftbury
Type: Co-educational Day

FOREST GLADE NURSERY
15 Dyson Road, London E11 1NA
Tel: 0181 989 9684
Head: Mrs Starmer-Jones
Type: Co-educational Day

HAPPY DAYS NURSERY
39 Fillebrook Road, London E11
Tel: 0181 556 5085
Head: Mrs Mehmuda Ahmed
Type: Co-educational Day

HUMPTY DUMPTY NURSERY
24/26 Fairlop Road, London E11 8BL
Tel: 0181 539 3810
Head: Ms M Gregory NNEB
Type: Co-educational Day B1-5 G1-5
No of pupils: B17 G15
Fees per week: £52-£92

LITTLE CHERUBS DAY NURSERY
167 Wallward Road, London E11 1AQ
Tel: 0181 556 6889
Head: Miss Cher Tully
Type: Co-educational Day

LITTLE GREEN MAN NURSERY
15 Lemna Road, London E11
Tel: 0181 539 7228
Head: Mrs Philippa Carr NNEB
Type: Co-educational Day B0-5 G0-5
No of pupils: B22 G24

PETER PAN DAY NURSERY
1 Ashbridge Road, London E11
Tel: 0181 989 3346
Head: Mrs A Dwarika
Type: Co-educational Day

ST JOSEPH'S CONVENT SCHOOL FOR GIRLS
59 Cambridge Park, London E11 2PR
Tel: 0181 989 4700
Head: Mrs C D Youle
Type: Girls Day G4-11
No of pupils: G186
Fees: DAY £2085

E13

FIRST FRIENDS CHILDREN'S CENTRE
Memorial Baptist Church, London E13
Tel: 0171 474 5625
Type: Co-educational Day

OOPS-A-DAISY DAY NURSERY
St Phillips/St James Church, London E13
Tel: 0171 474 8737
Head: Sharon McNicholas
Type: Co-educational Day

SMARTY PANTS DAY NURSERY
1 Plashet Road, London E13
Tel: 0181 471 2620
Heads: Jennifer Lewis & Sylvia Lewis
Type: Co-educational Day

STEP BY STEP CHILDREN'S CENTRE
Lawrence Hall, London E13
Tel: 0171 511 2916
Head: Mrs Irene Langford
Type: Co-educational Day B0-5 G0-5

STEPPING STONES DAY NURSERY
Woodside School, Woodside Road, London E13
Tel: 0171 474 0121 (Ext 214)
Type: Co-educational Day

E14

BUSHYTAILS DAY NURSERY AND NURSERY SCHOOL
591 Manchester Road, London E14
Tel: 0171 537 7776
Head: Christine G Bush NNEB
Type: Co-educational Day B0-5 G0-5

LANTERNS NURSERY AND PRESCHOOL
F4-F6 Lanterns Court, London E14
Tel: 0171 363 0951
Type: Co-educational Day

WESTERN INTERNATIONAL UNIVERSITY
18 Ensign House, London E14 9RN
Tel: 0171 537 3388
Type: Co-educational Day

E15

ALPHABET HOUSE DAY (MONTESSORI) NURSERY
Methodist Church, Windmill Lane, London E15 1PG
Tel: 0181 519 2023
Head: Ms Kemi Balogun
Type: Co-educational Day

STEPPING STONES DAY NURSERY
Brickfield Church, Welfare Road, London E15
Tel: 0181 534 8777
Type: Co-educational Day

E17

DOROTHY MATILDA DAY NURSERY
Green Pond Road, London E17
Tel: 0181 531 7204
Head: Rebecca O'Brien
Type: Co-educational Day

FIRST NEIGHBOURHOOD CO-OP NURSERY
34 Verulam Avenue, London E17 8ER
Tel: 0181 520 2417
Head: F Beregovoi
Type: Co-educational Day

FOREST BOYS SCHOOL
College Place, London E17 3PY
Head: A G Boggis MA(Oxon)
Type: Co-educational Boarding & Day B7-18 G7-18
No of pupils: B807 FB23
Fees: FB £9087 DAY £5790

FOREST GIRLS SCHOOL
London E17 3PY
Tel: 0181 520 1744
Head: A G Boggis MA(Oxon)
Type: Girls Day G11-18
No of pupils: G360
Fees: DAY £5790

FOREST PREP SCHOOL
London E17 3PY
Tel: 0181 520 1744
Head: R T Cryer MEd
Type: Boys Day & Boarding B7-13 G7-11
No of pupils: B350 G50 FB2
Fees: FB £6366-£9087 WB £6051-£9087
DAY £3960-£5790

HAPPY CHILD PRE SCHOOL NURSERY
The Old Town Hall, 14B Orford Road, London E17 9LN
Tel: 0181 520 8880
Head: Mrs Margaret Murphy
Type: Co-educational Day

HYLAND HOUSE
896 Forest Road, London E17 4AE
Tel: 0181 520 4186
Head: Mrs T Thorpe
Type: Co-educational Day B3-11 G3-11
Fees: DAY £1290

LOW HALL NURSERY
Low Hall Lane, London E17
Tel: 0181 520 1689
Type: Co-educational Day

MAGIC ROUNDABOUT NURSERY
London E17 4UH
Tel: 0181 523 5551
Head: Mr Iqbal
Type: Co-educational Day

RASCALS EDUCATIONAL PRESCHOOL DAY NURSERY
8 Downsfield Road, London E17
Tel: 0181 520 7359
Head: Mrs Aguda
Type: Co-educational Day

TINKERBELLS NURSERY
185 Coppermill Lane, London E17 7HU
Tel: 0181 520 8338
Head: Sue Walker
Type: Co-educational Day

★ **TOM THUMB NURSERY**
20 Shirley Close, 1-7 Beulah Road, London E17 9LZ
Tel: 0181 520 1329
Heads: Ms K Sprackling NNEB & Mrs H Redhead NNEB
Type: Co-educational Day B2-5 G2-5
No of pupils: B22 G21
Fees per week: £52-£92

E18

CLEVELANDS PARK
71 Cleveland Road, London E18
Tel: 0181 518 8855
Type: Co-educational Day

SNARESBROOK COLLEGE
75 Woodford Road, London E18 2EA
Tel: 0181 989 2394
Head: Mrs L J Chiverrell CertEd
Type: Co-educational Day B3-11 G3-11
No of pupils: B71 G91
Fees: DAY £2946-£4014

TREE HOUSE NURSERY SCHOOL
2 Malmsbury Road, London E18
Tel: 0181 504 1036
Type: Co-educational Day

EC1

THE CHARTERHOUSE SQUARE SCHOOL
40 Charterhouse Square, London EC1M 6EA
Tel: 0171 600 3805
Head: Mrs J Malden MA, BEd(Hons)
Type: Co-educational Day B4-11 G4-11
No of pupils: B88 G72
Fees: DAY £4500

DALLINGTON SCHOOL
8 Dallington Street, London EC1V OBQ
Tel: 0171 251 2284
Head: Mrs M C Hercules BA, BEd
Type: Co-educational Day B3-11 G3-11
No of pupils: B80 G90
Fees: DAY £3200-£4155

ITALIA CONTI ACADEMY OF THEATRE ART
23 Goswell Road, London EC1M 7AJ
Tel: 0171 608 0047
Head: C K Vote BA, DipEd
Type: Co-educational Day B10-21 G10-21
No of pupils: B35 G125
Fees: DAY £4650-£6900

EC2

BROADGATE DAY NURSERY
27/31 Earl Street, London EC2
Tel: 0171 247 3491
Head: Jacky Roberts NNEB
Type: Co-educational Day B0-5 G0-5

★ CITY OF LONDON SCHOOL FOR GIRLS
London EC2Y 8BB
Tel: 0171 628 0841
Head: Dr Y A Burne BA, PhD, FRSA
Type: Girls Day G7-18
No of pupils: G657 VIth160
Fees: DAY £5427

EC4

CITY OF LONDON SCHOOL
Queen Victoria Street, London EC4V 3AL
Tel: 0171 489 0291
Head: R M Dancey MA
Type: Boys Day B10-18
No of pupils: B616 VIth252
Fees: DAY £6120

★ ST PAUL'S CATHEDRAL CHOIR SCHOOL
2 New Change, London EC4M 9AD
Tel: 0171 248 5156
Head: Stephen A Sides BEd(Oxon), CertEd
Type: Boys Boarding & Day B7-13
No of pupils: B100 FB40
Fees: FB £3075 DAY £5100

SE1

CHRYSOLYTE INDEPENDENT CHRISTIAN SCHOOL
155 Old Kent Road, London SE1 5UT
Tel: 0171 237 3339
Type: Co-educational Day B2-11 G2-11
No of pupils: B25 G30
Fees: DAY £2400

HIGHWAY CHRISTIAN SCHOOL
Union Chapel, 255 Tooley Street, London SE1 2LA
Tel: 0171 403 6192
Head: K R W Dilliway CertEd
Type: Co-educational Day B5-11 G5-11
No of pupils: B27 G27

LONDON CITY COLLEGE
Royal Waterloo House, London SE1 8TX
Tel: 0171 928 0029/0938/0901
Head: N Kyritsis MA, DMS, MCIM
Type: Co-educational Day

MORLEY COLLEGE
61 Westminster Bridge Road, London SE1 7HT
Tel: 0171 928 8501
Type: Co-educational Day

SCHILLER INTERNATIONAL UNIVERSITY
Royal Waterloo House, London SE1 8TX
Tel: 0171 928 1372
Head: Dr Richard Taylor PhD
Type: Co-educational Day

ST PATRICKS MONTESSORI NURSERY SCHOOL
91 Cornwall Road, London SE1
Tel: 0171 928 5557
Head: Gillian Wright
Type: Co-educational Day

SE2

ABBEY WOOD NURSERY SCHOOL
Dahlia Road, London SE2 0SX
Tel: 0181 311 0619
Type: Co-educational Day

PARKWAY NURSERY
Parkway Primary School, Alsike Road, London SE2
Tel: 0181 311 9799
Head: Mrs L Lanham
Type: Co-educational Day

SE3

BLACKHEATH & BLUECOATS DAY NURSERY
Old Dover Road, London SE3
Tel: 0181 858 8221 Ext 147
Head: Tracy Malyon
Type: Co-educational Day

BLACKHEATH DAY NURSERY
The Rectory Field, London SE3
Tel: 0181 305 2526
Head: Mrs Shipley
Type: Co-educational Day

★ BLACKHEATH HIGH SCHOOL GPDST
Vanbrugh Park, London SE3 7AG
Tel: 0181 853 2929
Head: Miss R K Musgrave MA(Oxon)
Type: Girls Day G4-18
No of pupils: G641 VIth66
Fees: DAY £3765-£4920

BLACKHEATH MONTESSORI CENTRE
Independents Road, London SE3 9LF
Tel: 0181 852 6765
Head: Jane Skillen
Type: Co-educational Day

CHRIST'S COLLEGE
4 St Germans Place, London SE3 ONJ
Tel: 0181 858 0692
Head: R Bellerby MA, BSc, FInstM, FBIS, GradCertEd
Type: Co-educational Day & Boarding B4-19 G4-19
No of pupils: B100 G28 VIth29
Fees: FB £7125-£8925 WB £6645-£8445
DAY £2685-£4485

FRIENDS MEETINGHOUSE PLAYGROUP PPA
Independents Road, London SE3 9LS
Tel: 0181 297 1014
Head: Mrs Mandy Sauthion
Type: Co-educational Day

HEATH HOUSE PREPARATORY SCHOOL
37 Wemyss Road, London SE3 0TG
Tel: 0181 297 1900
Head: Ian Laslett MA, FRGS
Type: Co-educational Day B4-11 G4-11
No of pupils: B20 G20
Fees: DAY £3750-£4350

KIDS & CO DAY NURSERY
41 Westcombe Park Road, London SE3
Tel: 0181 858 6222
Head: Mrs Lawrence
Type: Co-educational Day

LINGFIELD DAY NURSERY
37 Kidbrooke Grove, London SE3
Tel: 0181 858 1388
Head: Mrs D L Smith
Type: Co-educational Day

LOLLIPOPS 2 DAY NURSERY
69 Charlton Road, London SE3
Tel: 0181 305 2014
Head: Mrs Thompson
Type: Co-educational Day

NEW BROOKLANDS PARK PLAY GROUP
Community Hall, London SE3
Tel: 0181 297 1816
Type: Co-educational Day

PARAGON NURSERY
29 Wemyss Road, London SE3 0TG
Tel: 0181 297 2395
Type: Co-educational Day

THE POINTER SCHOOL
19 Stratheden Road, London SE3 7TH
Tel: 0181 2931331
Head: R J S Higgins MA, BEd, CertEd
Type: Co-educational Day B3-12 G3-12
No of pupils: B45 G45
Fees: DAY £1890-£3660

SE4

HILLYFIELDS DAY NURSERY
41 Harcourt Road, London SE4
Tel: 0181 694 1069
Head: Ms Elaine Dalton
Type: Co-educational Day

MYATT GARDEN NURSERY SCHOOL
Rokeby Road, London SE4 1DF
Tel: 0181 691 6919
Type: Co-educational Day

SE5

ICHTHUS PRIMARY SCHOOL
Wells Way Church Hall, Wells Way, London SE5 7SY
Tel: 0171 703 0924
Head: Mrs H Pears BA
Type: Co-educational Day B4-11 G4-11
Fees: DAY £1040

SOUTHWARK SMALL SCHOOL
47A Grove Lane, London SE5 8SP
Tel: 0171 277 1220
Head: Dr Peter Rundell
Type: Co-educational Day & Boarding

SE6

BROADFIELDS NURSERY
96 Broadfields Road, London SE6 1NG
Tel: 0181 697 1488
Type: Co-educational Day

MRS TREBLE CLEF'S SCHOOL OF MUSIC
10 Westdown Road, London SE6 4RL
Tel: 0181 690 7243
Head: Mrs Julia Bentham
Type: Co-educational Day

THE PAVILION NURSERY
Catford Cricket Club Pavilion, London SE6
Tel: 0181 698 0878
Head: Miss Corinna Wilson
Type: Co-educational Day

PRIORY HOUSE SCHOOL
61 Bromley Road, London SE6 2UA
Tel: 0181 697 4518
Head: Mrs H Thomas
Type: Co-educational Day B3-11 G3-11
No of pupils: B50 G50

★ **ST DUNSTAN'S COLLEGE**
Stanstead Road, Catford, London SE6 4TY
Tel: 0181 690 1274
Head: J D Moore MA
Type: Co-educational Day B4-18 G4-18
No of pupils: B155 G26
Fees: DAY £3810-£5745

THORNSBEACH DAY NURSERY
10 Thornsbeach Road, London SE6 1DX
Tel: 0181 697 7699
Head: Mrs M Jones
Type: Co-educational Day

SE7

POUND PARK NURSERY SCHOOL
Pound Park Road, London SE7
Tel: 0181 858 1791
Head: Ms Pat Whittaker
Type: Co-educational Day

SE9

ELTHAM COLLEGE
Grove Park Road, London SE9 4QF
Tel: 0181 857 1455
Head: D M Green MA, FRSA
Type: Boys Day & Boarding B7-18 G16-18
No of pupils: B705 G50 VIth183 FB9
Fees: FB £11,481-£12,801 DAY £4410-£5724

ELTHAM GREEN DAY NURSERY
Eltham Green School, London SE9
Tel: 0181 850 4720
Type: Co-educational Day

LOLLIPOPS
88 Southwood Road, London SE9 3QT
Tel: 0181 305 2014
Head: Miss L Thompson
Type: Co-educational Day

LOLLYPOP DAY NURSERY
27 Southwood Road, London SE9 3QE
Tel: 0181 859 5832
Head: Mrs Thompson
Type: Co-educational Day

NIKKI'S DAY NURSERY
164 Footscray Road, London SE9 2TD
Tel: 0181 265 1584
Head: Mrs Dervish
Type: Co-educational Day

NEW ELTHAM PREPARATORY SCHOOL
699 Sidcup Road, London SE9 3AQ
Tel: 0181 851 5057
Head: Lesley Watkins CertEd, NNEB
Type: Co-educational Day B0-5 G0-5
No of pupils: B89 G67

ST OLAVE'S PREPARATORY SCHOOL
106 Southwood Road, London SE9 3QS
Tel: 0181 850 9175
Head: P D Stradling BA(Hons), CertEd
Type: Co-educational Day B3-11 G3-11
No of pupils: B125 G85
Fees: DAY £1608-£3900

TINY TOTS DAY NURSERY
467 Footscray Road, London SE9 3UH
Tel: 0181 850 4445
Head: Mrs J Pool
Type: Co-educational Day

WILLOW PARK
19 Glenlyon Road, London SE9
Tel: 0181 850 8753
Head: Mrs McMahon
Type: Co-educational Day

SE10

ROBERT OWEN NURSERY SCHOOL
Conley Street, London SE10
Tel: 0181 858 0529
Head: Judith Stephenson
Type: Co-educational Day

SE11

TOAD HALL NURSERY SCHOOL (MONTESSORI)
37 St Mary's Gardens, London SE11 4UF
Tel: 0171 735 5087
Head: Mrs V K Rees NNEB, MontDip
Type: Co-educational Day B2-5 G2-5
Fees: DAY £1950

SE12

COLFE'S SCHOOL
Horn Park Lane, London SE12 8AW
Tel: 0181 852 2283
Head: Dr D Richardson PhD, BA, FRSA
Type: Boys Day B3-18 G16-18
No of pupils: B896 G39 VIth206
Fees: DAY £3465-£5370

RIVERSTON SCHOOL
63-69 Eltham Road, London SE12 8UF
Tel: 0181 318 4327
Head: D M Lewis
Type: Co-educational Day B2-16 G2-16
No of pupils: B210 G180
Fees: DAY £3177-£4197

SE13

★ THE VILLAGE MONTESSORI
Kingswood Hall, Kingswood Place, London SE13 5BU
Tel: 0181 318 6720
Head: Catherine Westlake MontDip
Type: Co-educational Day B3-5 G3-5
No of pupils: B15 G15
Fees: DAY £1491

THE VILLAGE NURSERY
St Mary's Centre, Ladywell Road, London SE13
Tel: 0181 690 6766
Head: Frances Rogers
Type: Co-educational Day

SE14

ANNABEL'S MONTESSORI NURSERY
Adj. 37 Kitto Road, London SE14
Tel: 0171 277 6414
Type: Co-educational Day

SE15

BELLENDEN DAY NURSERY
Faith Chapel, London SE15
Tel: 0171 639 4896
Type: Co-educational Day

COLOURBOX NURSERY
385 Ivydale Road, London SE15
Tel: 0171 277 9662
Type: Co-educational Day

THE GARDEN NURSERY
Studley Villa, London SE15
Tel: 0171 701 5411
Head: Mrs Gillian Leigh
Type: Co-educational Day

HEADSTART MONTESSORI
24 Waveney Avenue, London SE15 3UE
Tel: 0171 635 5501
Type: Co-educational Day

IVYDALE ADVENTIST
149 Ivydale Road, London SE15
Tel: 0171 639 9790/635 9878
Type: Co-educational Day

MOTHER GOOSE NURSERY SCHOOL
34 Wavevey Avenue, London SE15
Tel: 0171 277 5951
Type: Co-educational Day

MOTHER GOOSE TWO
54 Lindon Grove, London SE15
Tel: 0171 277 5956
Type: Co-educational Day

NEIL GWYNN NURSERY
Meeting House Lane, London SE15
Tel: 0171 252 8265
Type: Co-educational Day

SE16

SCALLYWAGS DAY NURSERY
St Crispin's Church Hall, London SE16
Tel: 0171 252 3225
Head: Miss Alison Armstrong
Type: Co-educational Day

SILWOOD FAMILY CENTRE
31-32 Alpine Road, London SE16
Tel: 0171 237 2376
Head: Miss Jean Williams
Type: Co-educational Day

TRINITY CHILD CARE
Holy Trinity Church Hall, Bryan Road, London SE16 1HB
Tel: 0171 231 5842
Head: Sharon Spice
Type: Co-educational Day

SE18

ACCESS DAY NURSERY
International House, Brook Hill Road, London SE18
Tel: 0181 316 8123
Head: Claudia Padfield
Type: Co-educational Day

MOLLYZAC DAY NURSERY
60 Spray Street, London SE18 6AG
Tel: 0181 316 7591
Type: Co-educational Day

SIMBA DAY NURSERY
48-50 Artillery Place, London SE18 4AB
Tel: 0181 317 0451 (Exts 72/74)
Head: Eileen Green
Type: Co-educational Day

SE19

VIRGO FIDELIS CONVENT
Central Hill, London SE19 1RS
Tel: 0181 670 6917
Head: Sr Bernadette
Type: Girls Day G11-18
No of pupils: G150
Fees: DAY £1200-£4275

VIRGO FIDELIS PREPARATORY SCHOOL
Central Hill, London SE19 1RS
Tel: 0181 653 2169
Head: Sr Renata
Type: Co-educational Day B2-8 G2-11
No of pupils: B24 G198
Fees: DAY £1110-£3150

SE20

ANERLEY MONTESSORI NURSERY
45 Anerley Park, London SE20 8NQ
Tel: 0181 778 2810
Head: Mrs P Bhatia
Type: Co-educational Day

THE CHILDRENS CENTRE
9a Stembridge Road, London SE20
Tel: 0181 778 2135
Type: Co-educational Day

SE21

THE BURRELL GROUP
87 Park Hall Road, London SE21
Tel: 0181 6704736
Type: Co-educational Day

★ **DULWICH COLLEGE KINDERGARTEN &
INFANT SCHOOL**
Eller Bank, 87 College Road, London SE21 7HN
Tel: 0181 693 1538
Principal: Mrs A C Anderson BA, RPP
Type: Co-educational Day B0-7 G0-7
No of pupils: B59 G52
Fees: DAY £770-£4530

★ **DULWICH COLLEGE**
London SE21 7LD
Tel: 0181 693 3601
Head: G G Able MA, MA
Type: Boys Day & Boarding B7-18
No of pupils: B1380 VIth370
Fees: FB £12,636 DAY £5985-£6318

★ **DULWICH COLLEGE PREPARATORY SCHOOL**
42 Alleyn Park, Dulwich, London SE21 7AA
Tel: 0181 670 3217
Head: G Marsh MA(Oxon), CertEd
Type: Boys Boarding & Day B3-13 G3-4
No of pupils: B737 G12
Fees: FB £9201 DAY £3801-£6156

DULWICH MONTESSORI NURSERY SCHOOL
All Saints Church, London SE21 8LN
Tel: 0181 761 9560/673 7930
Head: Mrs E Irwin
Type: Co-educational Day B2-6 G2-6
No of pupils: B15 G15
Fees: DAY £1425-£1530

OAKFIELD PREPARATORY SCHOOL
125-128 Thurlow Park Road, London SE21 8HP
Tel: 0181 670 4206
Head: Mrs Anne Tomkins
Type: Co-educational Day B2-11 G2-11
No of pupils: B267 G229
Fees: DAY £3750

★ **ROSEMEAD PREPARATORY SCHOOL**
70 Thurlow Park Road, London SE21 8HZ
Tel: 0181 670 5865
Head: Mrs R L Lait BA, MBA(Ed), CertEd
Type: Co-educational Day B3-11 G3-11
No of pupils: B135 G135
Fees: DAY £3150-£3750

SE22

★ **ALLEYN'S SCHOOL**
Townley Road, Dulwich, London SE22 8SU
Tel: 0181 693 3422
Head: Dr C H R Niven MA, DipEd, L ès L(Nancy),
    Dr de l'Univ(Lille)
Type: Co-educational Day B5-18 G5-18
No of pupils: B551 G579 VIth261
Fees: DAY £4799-£6895

FIRST STEPS MONTESSORI NURSERY
254 Upland Road, London SE22
Tel: 0181 299 6897
Head: Mrs Heather Benyayer
Type: Co-educational Day

GREENDALE PRE SCHOOL NURSERY
The Pavilion, Greendale, London SE22 8IX
Tel: 0171 274 1955
Head: Miss Sarah Legalle
Type: Co-educational Day

JAMES ALLEN'S GIRLS' SCHOOL
East Dulwich Grove, London SE22 8TE
Tel: 0181 693 1181
Head: Mrs M Gibbs BA, MLitt
Type: Girls Day G11-18
No of pupils: G543 VIth207
Fees: DAY £5970-£6150

JAMES ALLEN'S PREPARATORY SCHOOL
East Dulwich Grove, London SE22 8TE
Tel: 0181 693 0374
Head: Piers Heyworth MA(Oxon), PGCE
Type: Co-educational Day B4-7 G4-11
No of pupils: B56 G239
Fees: DAY £4770-£4950

MONTESSORI FIRST STEPS
254 Upland Road, London SE22
Tel: 0181 299 6897
Type: Co-educational Day

MOTHER GOOSE NURSERIES
248 Upland Road, London SE22 0DN
Tel: 0181 693 9429
Head: Mrs K Chandra
Type: Co-educational Day

TINY TOTS NURSERY SCHOOL
United Reformed Church Hall, London SE22
Tel: 0181 693 4404
Head: Mrs Sandra Brown
Type: Co-educational Day B2-5 G2-5
No of pupils: B14 G10
Fees: DAY £2880

WAVERLEY NURSERY
Waverley School, London SE22 0NR
Tel: 0171 732 1142
Head: Mrs M Burrell
Type: Co-educational Day

SE24

HALF MOON MONTESSORI NURSERY
Methodist Church Hall, London SE24
Tel: 0171 326 5300
Head: Mrs Lucy Brignall
Type: Co-educational Day

HERNE HILL SCHOOL
127 Herne Hill, London SE24 9LY
Tel: 0171 274 6336
Heads: Mrs C Ratsey and Mrs P J Bennett
Type: Co-educational Day

HERON COMMUNITY CENTRE
Heron Road, London SE24
Tel: 0171 274 2894
Heads: Mr & Mrs Youngs
Type: Co-educational Day

KESTREL MONTESSORI NURSERY
27 Kestrel Avenue, London SE24 0ED
Tel: 0171 274 8072
Type: Co-educational Day

THE WHITEHOUSE
331 Norwood Road, London SE24
Tel: 0181 671 7362
Head: Mrs S Mitchell AdvDipChildcare & Edu, NNEB
Type: Co-educational Day

SE25

CHILDRENS PARADISE
4 Crowther Road, London SE25
Tel: 0181 654 1737
Type: Co-educational Day

SE26

★ **SYDENHAM HIGH SCHOOL GPDST**
19 Westwood Hill, London SE26 6BL
Tel: 0181 778 8737
Head: Mrs G Baker BSc, FZS
Type: Girls Day G4-18
No of pupils: G796 VIth100
Fees: DAY £3864-£4920

SYDENHAM MONTESSORI
Wells Park Hall, London SE26
Tel: 0181 291 3947
Type: Co-educational Day

SE27

ABC CHILDRENS CENTRE
48 Chapel Road, London SE27
Tel: 0181 766 0246/(eves) 761 8985
Head: Ms E Carr
Type: Co-educational Day

ONE WORLD
11 Thurlby Road, London SE27 0RL
Tel: 0181 670 3511
Head: Ms C Jones
Type: Co-educational Day

NOAH'S ARK
St Cuthberts Church, London SE27 9BZ
Tel: 0181 761 1307
Head: Mrs C M C McCulloch
Type: Co-educational Day

SW1

EATON HOUSE SCHOOL
3-5 Eaton Gate, London SW1W 9BA
Tel: 0171 730 9343
Head: Mrs J Aviss GTCL (Hons)
Type: Boys Day B4-9
No of pupils: B250
Fees: DAY £5100

 EATON SQUARE NURSERY & PRE-PREP SCHOOL
30 Eccleston Street, London SW1W 9PY
Tel: 0171 823 6217
Head: Miss Y Cuthbert
Type: Co-educational Day B4-11 G4-11
No of pupils: B75 G75
Fees: DAY £2125-£5895

EATON SQUARE PREPARATORY SCHOOL
79 Eccleston Square, London SW1V 1PP
Tel: 0171 931 9469
Head: Miss Y Cuthbert
Type: Co-educational Day B4-11 G4-11
No of pupils: B75 G75
Fees: DAY £2125-£5895

 FRANCIS HOLLAND SCHOOL
39 Graham Terrace, London SW1W 8JF
Tel: 0171 730 2971
Head: Mrs J A Anderson MA(Cantab), MA(London)
Type: Girls Day G4-18
No of pupils: G310 VIth48
Fees: DAY £6330

 ★ **GARDEN HOUSE SCHOOL**
53 Sloane Gardens, London SW1W 8ED
Tel: 0171 730 1652
Heads: Mrs R Whaley & Mrs W Challen
Type: Girls Day B3-8 G3-11
No of pupils: B72 G270
Fees: DAY £2700-£6150

HELLENIC COLLEGE OF LONDON
67 Pont Street, London SW1X 0BD
Tel: 0171 581 5044
Head: J Wardrobe MA
Type: Co-educational Day B2-18 G2-18
No of pupils: B108 G100
Fees: DAY £3885-£5070

HOUSE INTERNATIONAL JUNIOR SCHOOL
ans Place, London SW1X 0EP
Tel: 0171 584 1331
Head: Col H S Townend OBE, MA(Oxon)
Type: Co-educational Day B3-14 G3-14
No of pupils: B600 G450
Fees: DAY £3510-£5148

INCHBALD SCHOOL OF DESIGN
7 Eaton Gate, London SW1 9BA
Tel: 0171 730 5508
Head: Mrs Jacqueline Duncan FIDDA, IIDA
Type: Co-educational Day B18-50 G18-50
No of pupils: B20 G100
Fees: DAY £585-£11,000

LITTLE ACORNS NURSERY SCHOOL
Church of St James The Less, London SW1V
Tel: 0171 931 0898
Type: Co-educational Day

LONDON PRE-SCHOOL PLAYGROUPS ASSOCIATION
314-316 Vauxhall Bridge Road, London SW1V
Tel: 0171 828 2417/1401
Type: Co-educational Day

MISS MORLEYS NURSERY SCHOOL
Fountain Court Club Room, London SW1
Tel: 0171 730 5797
Head: Mrs C Spence
Type: Co-educational Day B2-5 G2-5
No of pupils: B20 G25
Fees: DAY £1560-£1950

★ **MORE HOUSE SCHOOL**
22-24 Pont Street, London SW1X 0AA
Tel: 0171 235 2855
Head: Miss M Connell MA(Oxon)
Type: Girls Day G11-18
No of pupils: G230 VIth36
Fees: DAY £5940

MORLEY'S NURSERY SCHOOL
Club Room, Fountain Court, London SW1W
Tel: 0171 730 5797
Head: Mrs Susan Spence
Type: Co-educational Day B2-5 G2-5
No of pupils: B13 G15
Fees: DAY £575-£700

RINGROSE KINDERGARTEN (PIMLICO)
32a Lupus Street, London SW1V
Tel: 0171 976 6511
Head: Mrs Stark
Type: Co-educational Day

SUSSEX HOUSE SCHOOL
68 Cadogan Square, London SW1X 0EA
Tel: 0171 584 1741
Head: N P Kaye MA(Cantab), ACP, FRSA
Type: Boys Day B8-13
No of pupils: B175
Fees: DAY £2015

THOMAS'S KINDERGARTEN
14 Ranelagh Grove, London SW1W 8PD
Tel: 0171 730 3596
Head: Mrs A Grant
Type: Co-educational Day B2-5 G2-5
No of pupils: B30 G30
Fees: DAY £1365-£2100

WESTMINSTER SCHOOL
17 Dean's Yard, London SW1P 3PB
Tel: 0171 963 1003
Head: D M Summerscale MA
Type: Boys Boarding & Day B13-18 G16-18
No of pupils: B320 VIth361 FB185
Fees: FB/WB £13,530 DAY £9300-£10,125

WESTMINSTER ABBEY CHOIR SCHOOL
Deans Yard, London SW1P 3NY
Tel: 0171 222 6151
Head: G Roland-Adams BMus, CertEd
Type: Boys Boarding B7-13
No of pupils: B38 FB38
Fees: FB £2619

WESTMINSTER CATHEDRAL CHOIR SCHOOL
Ambrosden Avenue, London SW1P 1QH
Tel: 0171 798 9081
Head: C Foulds BA
Type: Boys Day & Boarding B8-13
No of pupils: B96 FB27
Fees: FB £3030-£3372 DAY £6120

WESTMINSTER UNDER SCHOOL
Adrian House, London SW1P 2NN
Tel: 0171 821 5788
Head: G Ashton MA
Type: Boys Day B8-13
No of pupils: B270
Fees: DAY £6165

YOUNG ENGLAND KINDERGARTEN
St Saviour's Hall, London SW1V 3QW
Tel: 0171 834 3171
Head: Mrs Kay C King MontDip
Type: Co-educational Day B2-5 G2-5
No of pupils: B40 G30
Fees: DAY £1470-£2265

SW2

ABACUS
St Margaret's, Cricklade Avenue, London SW2
Tel: 0181 674 9333
Head: Ms J Chidgey
Type: Co-educational Day

ELM PARK NURSERY SCHOOL
Brixton Methodist Church, London SW2
Tel: 0181 678 1990
Heads: Mr & Mrs Taylor
Type: Co-educational Day

GARDEN OF EDEN
Gospel Tabernacle, London SW2
Tel: 0181 674 9462
Head: Mrs B Adetona
Type: Co-educational Day

SOMERVILLE SCHOOL
12 Wavertree Road, London SW2 3SJ
Tel: 0181 674 5495
Head: Mrs E A Tye
Type: Co-educational Day B3-7 G3-7
No of pupils: B34 G31
Fees: DAY £2100

STREATHAM MONTESSORI NURSERY SCHOOL
66 Blairderry Road, London SW2 4SB
Tel: 0181 674 2208
Head: Mrs Gangi
Type: Co-educational Day

WOODENTOPS
Telford Park Tennis Club, London SW2
Tel: 0181 674 9514
Head: Mrs M McCahery
Type: Co-educational Day

SW3

★ **CAMERON HOUSE**
4 The Vale, London SW3 4AH
Tel: 0171 352 4040
Heads: Mrs J M Ashcroft BSc, DipEd &
        Mrs F N Stack BA, PGCE
Type: Co-educational Day B4-11 G4-11
No of pupils: 100
Fees: DAY £5985-£6075

JAMAHIRIYA SCHOOL
Glebe Place, London SW3 5JP
Tel: 0171 352 3015
Head: Mr Mohammed
Type: Co-educational Day

KNIGHTSBRIDGE KINDERGARTEN ONE
British Red Cross Hall, London SW3 5BS
Tel: 0171 581 4242
Head: Mrs J Ewing-Hoy CertEd(Oxon)
Type: Co-educational Day B2-5 G2-5
Fees: DAY £2250

RINGROSE KINDERGARTEN (CHELSEA)
St Lukes Church Hall, London SW3
Tel: 0171 352 8784
Type: Co-educational Day

SW4

BEECHWOOD SCHOOL
Aristotle Road, London SW4 7UY
Tel: 0181 677 8778
Head: Mrs M Marshall
Type: Co-educational Day

CLAPHAM MONTESSORI
St Paul's Community Centre, London SW4 0DX
Tel: 0171 498 8324/0181 674 0559
Head: Mrs R Bowles BSc, IntMontDip
Type: Co-educational Day B2-5 G2-5

CLAPHAM PARK MONTESSORI
St James' Church House, London SW4 7DN
Tel: 0171 498 8324/0181 674 0559
Head: Mrs R Bowles BSc, IntMontDip
Type: Co-educational Day B2-5 G2-5

EATON HOUSE THE MANOR
58 Clapham Common, London SW4 9RU
Tel: 0171 924 6000
Heads: S Hepher BEd(Hons) & Miss P de Giles TCert
Type: Boys Day B4-13
No of pupils: B320
Fees: DAY £5100-£5700

DAISY CHAIN MONTESSORI NURSERY
Stockwell Methodist Church, London SW4
Tel: 0171 738 8606
Head: Lucy Gordon Lennox MontDip
Type: Co-educational Day B2-5 G2-5
No of pupils: B20 G26
Fees: DAY £1860

MONTESSORI SCHOOL
St Pauls Community Hall, London SW4
Tel: 0171 498 8324
Head: Mrs R Bowles
Type: Co-educational Day

PARKGATE HOUSE SCHOOL
80 Clapham Common Northside, London SW4 9SD
Tel: 0171 350 2452
Head: Miss C M Shanley AMI
Type: Co-educational Day B2-11 G2-11
No of pupils: B65 G65
Fees: DAY £2385-£4650

THEODORE MCLEARY PRIMARY SCHOOL
Ducie Street, London SW4 7QG
Tel: 0171 7374688
Head: Mrs J M Thompson
Type: Co-educational Day & Boarding

SW5

COLLINGHAM
23 Collingham Gardens, London SW5 0HL
Tel: 0171 244 7414
Heads: G Hattee MA(Oxon), DipEd & Mrs G Green MSc
Type: Co-educational Day B14-19 G14-19
No of pupils: B126 G120
Fees: DAY £2940-£7560

LADYBIRD NURSERY SCHOOL
24 Collingham Road, London SW5
Tel: 0171 244 7771
Head: Miss Fanny Ward
Type: Co-educational Day

ST JAMES'S SECRETARIAL COLLEGE
4 Wetherby Gardens, London SW5 0JN
Tel: 0171 373 3852
Head: N C E Knight
Type: Co-educational Day B17-45 G17-45
No of pupils: B5 G130
Fees: DAY £7725

SW6

AL-MUNTADA ISLAMIC SCHOOL
7 Bridges Place, London SW6 4HW
Tel: 0171 371 7308
Head: Z Chehimi MBA
Type: Co-educational Day B4-11 G4-11
Fees: DAY £1450

BLOOMSBURY COLLEGE
52A Walham Grove, London SW6 1QR
Tel: 0171 381 0213
Head: S Howse BSc, MSc
Type: Co-educational Day B14-19 G14-19
No of pupils: B25 G20
Fees: DAY £4500-£6500

BOBBY'S PLAYHOUSE
57 Marville Road, London SW6 7BB
Tel: 0171 386 5265
Head: Mrs Emma Hannay
Type: Co-educational Day
No of pupils: B10 G12

DAWMOUSE MONTESSORI NURSERY
Brunswick Club, London SW6 7EU
Tel: 0171 381 9385
Head: Emma V Woodcock
Type: Co-educational Day B2-5 G2-5
Fees: DAY £1515-£1755

★ **KENSINGTON PREPARATORY SCHOOL GPDST**
596 Fulham Road, London SW6 5PA
Tel: 0171 731 9300
Head: Mrs G M Lumsdon BPharm, MEd
Type: Girls Day G4-11
No of pupils: G175
Fees: DAY £1616

LANGFORD PLAY CENTRE
Langford School, London SW6
Tel: 0181 766 6750
Type: Co-educational Day

★ **L'ECOLE DES PETITS**
2 Hazlebury Road, London SW6 2NB
Tel: 0171 371 8350
Head: Mrs M Otten CAP
Type: Co-educational Day B2fi-6 G2fi-6
Fees: DAY £2220-£3120

LE HERISSON
St Peter's Church Hall, London SW6
Tel: 0171 381 6758
Head: B Rios
Type: Co-educational Day B2-6 G2-6
Fees: DAY £1740-£2535

MELROSE HOUSE NURSERY SCHOOL
55 Finlay Street, London SW6
Tel: 0171 763 9296
Type: Co-educational Day

RISING STAR MONTESSORI SCHOOL
St Clement Church Hall, London SW6
Tel: 0171 381 3511
Head: Mrs H Casson
Type: Co-educational Day B2-5 G2-5
Fees: DAY £1560

SINCLAIR HOUSE SCHOOL
159 Munster Road, London SW6 6DA
Tel: 0171 736 9182
Head: Mrs E A Sinclair House BA, CertEdPsy, PGCEd, CertPsychol
Type: Co-educational Day B2-8 G2-8
No of pupils: B25 G25
Fees: DAY £2025-£4200

★ **THE STUDIO DAY NURSERY**
93 Moore Park Road, London SW6 2DA
Tel: 0171 736 9256
Head: Miss Jenny M R Williams NNEB, RSH
Type: Co-educational Day B2-5 G2-5
No of pupils: B30 G35
Fees: AM £13 PM £12

TWICE TIMES MONTESSORI NURSERY SCHOOL
The Cricket Pavilion, London SW6 3AF
Tel: 0171 731 4929
Heads: Mrs A Welch MontDip &
Mrs S Henderson MontDip
Type: Co-educational Day B2-5 G2-5
Fees: DAY £1650-£2100

THE ZEBEDEE NURSERY SCHOOL
Sulivan Hall, London SW6
Tel: 0171 371 9224
Head: Miss Noemi Young
Type: Co-educational Day

SW7

DAVID GAME TUTORIAL COLLEGE
86 Old Brompton Road, London SW7 3LQ
Tel: 0171 584 9097/7580
Head: D T P Game MA, MPhil
Type: Co-educational Day

★ **FALKNER HOUSE**
19 Brechin Place, London SW7 4QB
Tel: 0171 373 4501
Head: Mrs J Bird BA(Hons)
Type: Girls Day G2-11
No of pupils: G140
Fees: DAY £5250

★ **GLENDOWER SCHOOL**
87 Queen's Gate, London SW7 5JX
Tel: 0171 370 1927
Head: Mrs B Humber BSc
Type: Girls Day G4-12
No of pupils: G184
Fees: DAY £4950

★ **THE HAMPSHIRE SCHOOL, KNIGHTSBRIDGE**
63 Ennismore Gardens, London SW7 1NH
Tel: 0171 584 3297
Head: A G Bray CertEd
Type: Co-educational Day B3-8 G3-11
No of pupils: B32 G80
Fees: DAY £2205-£6930

HURON UNIVERSITY USA IN LONDON
58 Prince's Gate, London SW7 2PG
Tel: 0171 584 9696
Head: Ms Fay Poosti
Type: Co-educational Day B17-60 G17-60

KNIGHTSBRIDGE NURSERY SCHOOL
51 Thurloe Square, London SW7
Tel: 0171 823 9771
Type: Co-educational Day

LUCIE CLAYTON SECRETARIAL COLLEGE
4 Cornwall Gardens, London SW7 4AJ
Tel: 0171 581 0024
Head: Mrs Denise Perry
Type: Girls Boarding & Day G16-21
No of pupils: G100
Fees: FB £6300 DAY £3000

★ **LYCEE FRANCAIS CHARLES DE GAULLE**
35 Cromwell Road, London SW7 2DG
Tel: 0171 584 6322
Head: Dr H L Brusa BA, MA, PhD(La Sorbonne)
Type: Co-educational Day B4-19 G4-19
No of pupils: B1413 G1487 VIth355
Fees: DAY £1779-£2916

MANDER PORTMAN WOODWARD
108 Cromwell Road, London SW7 4ES
Tel: 0171 835 1355
Heads: Dr Nigel Stout MA, DPhil &
    Miss Fiona Dowding MA
Type: Co-educational Day B15-18 G15-18
No of pupils: B193 G136
Fees: DAY £8190-£8289

MANDER PORTMAN WOODWARD
24 Elvaston Place, London SW7 5NL
Tel: 0171 584 8555
Heads: Miss Fiona Dowding & Dr Nigel Stout
Type: Co-educational Day B14-19 G14-19
Fees: DAY £8661

★ **MONTESSORI ST NICHOLAS SCHOOL**
23-24 Princes Gate, London SW7 1PT
Tel: 0171 225 1277
Head: Mrs R Hinde MontAdvDip
Type: Co-educational Day B2-9 G2-9
No of pupils: B60 G60
Fees: DAY £2805-£4350

QUEEN'S GATE SCHOOL
133 Queen's Gate, London SW7 5LE
Tel: 0171 589 3587
Head: Mrs A M Holyoak CertEd
Type: Girls Day G4-18
No of pupils: G310 VIth46
Fees: DAY £3480-£5400

★ **ST JAMES INDEPENDENT SCHOOLS**
91 Queen's Gate, London SW7 5AB
Tel: 0171 373 5638
Head: P Moss CertEd
Type: Co-educational Day B4-18 G4-18
No of pupils: B124 G122 VIth62
Fees: DAY £3465-£4995

ST PHILIP'S SCHOOL
6 Wetherby Place, London SW7 4ND
Tel: 0171 373 3944
Head: H Biggs-Davison MA(Cantab)
Type: Boys Day B7-13
No of pupils: B98
Fees: DAY £4860

TINY TOTS OF KENSINGTON
48 St Stephens House, London SW7
Tel: 0171 373 6111
Head: Mrs M Christiano
Type: Co-educational Day

THE VALE SCHOOL
2 Elvaston Place, London SW7 5QH
Tel: 0171 584 9515
Head: Miss S Calder TCertEd
Type: Co-educational Day B4-11 G4-11
No of pupils: B40 G60
Fees: DAY £5100

WESTMINSTER INDEPENDENT SIXTH FORM COLLEGE
82 Old Brompton Road, London SW7 3LQ
Tel: 0171 584 1288
Head: Mrs Jane Darwin MA, BLit
Type: Co-educational Day

THE ZEBEDEE NURSERY SCHOOL
St Pauls Hall, London SW7
Tel: 0171 584 7660
Head: Susan Gahan
Type: Co-educational Day

SW8

★ **NEWTON PREPARATORY SCHOOL**
149 Battersea Park Road, London SW8 4BH
Tel: 0171 720 4091
Head: R G Dell MA(Oxon)
Type: Co-educational Day B3-13 G3-13
No of pupils: B132 G122
Fees: DAY £4935-£5655

NINE ELMS NURSERY
Savona Club-room, Ascalon Street, London SW8 4DL
Tel: 0171 627 5191
Head: Pauline Khoo
Type: Co-educational Day

THE OVAL MONTESSORI NURSERY SCHOOL
88 Fentiman Road, London SW8 1LA
Tel: 0171 735 4816
Head: Mrs Rebecca Grainzevelles
Type: Co-educational Day B2-5 G2-5
Fees: DAY £530

ST CECILIA'S
Christchurch Hall, London SW8
Tel: 0171 720 0827
Head: Mrs D Farley
Type: Co-educational Day

THE WILLOW SCHOOL
c/o Clapham Baptist Church, London SW8 3JX
Tel: 0171 498 0319
Head: Mrs C Kane
Type: Co-educational Day B2-5 G2-5
No of pupils: B17 G18
Fees: DAY £1725-£1875

THE WILLOW NURSERY SCHOOL
Clapham Baptist Church, London SW8
Tel: 0171 498 0319
Type: Co-educational Day

SW9

BUNNYSHAPES
United Reform Church, London SW9
Tel: 0171 738 4795
Heads: Ms B Stovell & Ms G Walters
Type: Co-educational Day

THOMAS FRANCIS INDEPENDENT SCHOOL
143-145 Brixton Road, London SW9 6EL
Tel: 0171 820 8429
Head: Miss K Thomas
Type: Co-educational Day

WILTSHIRE NURSERY
85 Wiltshire Road, London SW9
Tel: 0171 274 4446
Type: Co-educational Day

SW10

THE BOLTONS NURSERY SCHOOL
262 Fulham Road, London SW10
Tel: 0171 351 6993
Head: Mrs V Heine
Type: Co-educational Day B2-5 G2-5
No of pupils: B19 G21
Fees: DAY £1650-£3783

BUSY BEE NURSERY
St Lukes Hall, Adrian Mews, London SW10
Tel: 0171 373 3628
Head: Miss J Hicks
Type: Co-educational Day

THE CHELSEA NURSERY SCHOOL
The Chelsea Centre, Worlds End Place,
London SW10 ODR
Tel: 0171 351 0993
Head: Sheila Ochugbojau
Type: Co-educational Day B2-5 G2-5
Fees: DAY £356-£1800

KNIGHTSBRIDGE KINDERGARTEN TWO
St Andrews Church, London SW10 0AU
Tel: 0171 352 4856/229 5194
Head: Mrs Suzanne Stevens CertEd
Type: Co-educational Day B2-5 G2-5
Fees: DAY £2250-£4035

THE OCTAGON SCHOOL
459A Fulham Road, London SW10 9UZ
Tel: 0171 351 4142
Head: Mrs B E Davies
Type: Co-educational Day B3-13 G3-13
No of pupils: B100 G71
Fees: DAY £2580-£5850

PARAYHOUSE SCHOOL
St Johns, Worlds End, London SW10 0LU
Tel: 0171 352 2882
Head: Mrs S L Jackson CertEd, DipEd
Type: Co-educational Day B6-16 G6-16
No of pupils: B20 G16
Fees: DAY £9750

PAINT POTS MONTESSORI SCHOOL, CHELSEA
Chelsea Christian Centre, London SW10 0LB
Tel: 0171 376 5780
Head: Miss G Hood MontDip
Type: Co-educational Day B2-5 G2-5
No of pupils: B15 G15
Fees: DAY £1053-£3561

PARK WALK PRIMARY SCHOOL
Park Walk, King's Road, London SW10 0AY
Tel: 0171 352 8700
Head: Ms N Ostwald
Type: Co-educational Day

★ **REDCLIFFE SCHOOL**
47 Redcliffe Gardens, London SW10 9JH
Tel: 0171 352 9247
Head: Miss R E Cunnah MA
Type: Co-educational Day B2fi-11 G2fi-11
No of pupils: B30 G82
Fees: DAY £4950

TADPOLES NURSERY SCHOOL
Park Walk Play Centre, London SW10 OAY
Tel: 0171 352 9757
Head: Mrs C Dimpsl
Type: Co-educational Day

SW11

ALPHABET NURSERY SCHOOL
Chatham Hall, Northcote Road, London SW11 6DY
Tel: 0181 871 7473
Head: Mrs A McKenzie-Lewis
Type: Co-educational Day
Fees: DAY £1500-£1800

BLUNDELLS DAY NURSERY
The Old Court, 194-196 Sheepcote Lane, London SW11
Tel: 0171 924 4204
Type: Co-educational Day

BRIDGE LANE MONTESSORI SCHOOL
23 Bridge Lane, London SW11 3AD
Tel: 0171 228 9403
Head: Mrs J Brittain BA(Hons), AMI MontDip
Type: Co-educational Day B2-5 G2-5
Fees: DAY £1100-£3000

★ **CALDER HOUSE SCHOOL**
142 Battersea Park Road, London SW11 4NB
Tel: 0171 720 8783
Head: Mrs L Robertson RSA, DipPrimEd
Type: Co-educational Day B6-13 G6-13
No of pupils: B20 G10
Fees: DAY £9660

★ **CENTER ACADEMY**
92 St John's Hill, London SW11 1SH
Tel: 0171 821 5760
Head: Finton J O'Regan MA
Type: Co-educational Day B8-18 G8-18
No of pupils: B40 G16
Fees: DAY £9500-£11,500

DOLPHIN SCHOOL
Northcote Road Baptist Church, London SW11 6QP
Tel: 0171 924 3472
Head: Miss Ruth Martin BA(Hons)
Type: Co-educational Day B5-11 G5-11
No of pupils: B37 G44
Fees: DAY £1350-£1450

★ **EMANUEL SCHOOL**
Battersea Rise, London SW11 1HS
Tel: 0181 870 4171
Head: T Jones-Parry MA
Type: Co-educational Day B10-18 G10-18
No of pupils: B732 G31 VIth178
Fees: DAY £4650-£4950

LITTLE RED ENGINE
Church of the Nazarene, London SW11
Tel: 0171 738 0321
Head: Miss Annie Richardson
Type: Co-educational Day

THE MOUSE HOUSE NURSERY SCHOOL
27 Mallinson Road, London SW11
Tel: 0171 924 1893/5325
Head: Mrs Barney White-Spunner
Type: Co-educational Day
No of pupils: B80 G80
Fees: DAY £780-£2040

NORTHCOTE LODGE
26 Bolingbroke Grove, London SW11 6EL
Tel: 0171 924 7170
Head: D G U Bain CertEd
Type: Boys Day B7-13
No of pupils: B105
Fees: DAY £5985

THE PARK NURSERY SCHOOL
St Saviour's Church, London SW11 4LH
Tel: 0171 627 5125
Head: Mrs Lena Pattenden MontDip
Type: Co-educational Day B2-5 G2-5
No of pupils: B14 G16
Fees: DAY £2100-£3780

★ **SOUTH LONDON MONTESSORI SCHOOL**
Trott Street, Battersea, London SW11 3DS
Tel: 0171 738 9546
Head: Mrs Teresa O'Regan-Byrnes MontIntDip, DipAMI
Type: Co-educational Day B2fi-12 G2fi-12
No of pupils: 36
Fees: DAY £590-£1360

THOMAS'S KINDERGARTEN, BATTERSEA
The Crypt, St Mary's Church, London SW11 3NA
Tel: 0171 738 0400
Head: Mrs B Angus
Type: Co-educational Day B2-5 G2-5
No of pupils: B25 G25
Fees: DAY £1365-£2100

THOMAS'S PREPARATORY SCHOOL, BATTERSEA
28-40 Battersea High Street, London SW11 3JB
Tel: 0171 978 4224
Head: Rev A Sangster MA, BD, AKC, MPhil
Type: Co-educational Day B4-13 G4-13
No of pupils: B245 G208
Fees: DAY £1820-£2120

THOMAS'S PREPARATORY SCHOOL CLAPHAM
Broomwood Road, London SW11 6JZ
Tel: 0171 924 5006
Head: Mrs P Evelegh
Type: Co-educational Day B4-13 G4-13
No of pupils: B175 G175
Fees: DAY £4740-£6150

SW12

ABACUS EARLY LEARNING NURSERY SCHOOL
135 Laitwood Road, London SW12 9QH
Tel: 0181 675 8093
Type: Co-educational Day

BALHAM NURSERY SCHOOL
72 Endlesham Road, London SW12
Tel: 0181 673 4055
Head: Mrs Ann Douglas
Type: Co-educational Day

BALHAM PREPARATORY SCHOOL
47A Balham High Road, London SW12 9DW
Tel: 0181 675 7747
Head: M I Abrahams
Type: Co-educational Day

★ **BROOMWOOD HALL SCHOOL**
74 Nightingale Lane, London SW12 8NR
Tel: 0181 673 1616
Head: Mrs K A H Colquhoun BEd, DipT
Type: Co-educational Day B4-8 G4-13
No of pupils: B118 G186
Fees: DAY £4800-£5670

CATERPILLAR NURSERY SCHOOL
74 Endlesham Road, London SW12 8JL
Tel: 0181 673 6058
Head: Marilyn Hassell
Type: Co-educational Day

CRESSET KINDERGARTEN
Waldorf School of South West London,
London SW12 8DR
Tel: 0181 673 4881
Head: Pat Hague
Type: Co-educational Day

GATEWAY HOUSE NURSERY SCHOOL
St Judes Church Hall, London SW12 8EG
Tel: 0181 675 8258
Head: Miss Elizabeth Marshall
Type: Co-educational Day
Fees: DAY £1800-£1980

★ **HORNSBY HOUSE SCHOOL**
Hearnville Road, London SW12 8RS
Tel: 0181 675 1255
Head: Mrs E M Nightingale, BA
Type: Co-educational Day B3-11 G3-11
No of pupils: B99 G81
Fees: DAY £1650-£5007

KNIGHTINGALES NURSERY
St Francis Xavier College, London SW12
Tel: 0181 673 2208
Head: Miss Justine Lucey
Type: Co-educational Day

MONTESSORI NIGHTINGALE NURSERY
St Lukes Church Hall, London SW12
Tel: 0181 675 4387
Type: Co-educational Day

NOAH'S ARK NURSERY SCHOOL
Endlesham Church Hall, London SW12
Tel: 0181 673 8227
Type: Co-educational Day
Fees: DAY £1935

THE OAK TREE NURSERY SCHOOL
21 Ramsden Road, London SW12 8QX
Tel: 0181 870 5760
Head: Mrs Jill Gould
Type: Co-educational Day B2-5 G2-5
No of pupils: B14 G20
Fees: DAY £1740

**WOODENTOPS PRE-PREPARATORY SCHOOL &
KINDERGARTEN**
72 Thornton Road, London SW12 0LF
Tel: 0181 674 9514
Head: Mrs M McCahery CertEd
Type: Co-educational Day B2-8 G2-8
No of pupils: B35 G35
Fees: DAY £1495-£3300

SW13

THE ARK NURSERY SCHOOL
Kitson Hall, London SW13
Tel: 0181 741 4751
Heads: Lorraine Ladbon & Victoria Brown
Type: Co-educational Day

THE HARRODIAN SCHOOL
Lonsdale Road, London SW13 9QN
Tel: 0181 748 6117
Head: Mr Peter Thomson
Type: Co-educational Day B5-13 G5-13
No of pupils: B80 G50
Fees: DAY £4950-£5700

LOWTHER NURSERY
Stillingfleet Road, London SW13
Type: Co-educational Day

MONTESSORI PAVILION SCHOOL
Vine Road, Recreation Ground, London SW13 0NE
Tel: 0181 8789695
Head: Georgina Dashwood
Type: Co-educational Day & Boarding

ST MICHAELS NURSERY SCHOOL
St Michaels Church Hall, London SW13
Tel: 0181 878 0116
Head: Mrs J L Gould
Type: Co-educational Day B2-5 G2-5

ST PAUL'S SCHOOL
Lonsdale Road, London SW13 9JT
Tel: 0181 748 9162
Head: R S Baldock MA(Cantab)
Type: Boys Day & Boarding B13-18
No of pupils: B467 VIth318 WB100
Fees: FB /WB £12,765 DAY £8490

ST PAUL'S PREPARATORY SCHOOL
Colet Court, London SW13 9JT
Tel: 0181 748 3461
Head: G J Thompson BA, CertEd(Newcastle), MEd,
    CBid, MIBid, FLS, FCP, FRSA
Type: Boys Day & Boarding B7-13
No of pupils: B425 FB6
Fees: FB/WB £9855 DAY £6510

SWEDISH SCHOOL SOCIETY LTD
82 Lonsdale Road, London SW13 9JS
Tel: 0181 741 1751
Head: Asa Lena Loof
Type: Co-educational Day & Boarding

SW14

PARKSIDE SCHOOL
459 Upper Richmond Road West, London SW14
Tel: 0181 876 8144
Head: Ms Claire Wilson
Type: Co-educational Day

TOWER HOUSE SCHOOL
188 Sheen Lane, London SW14 8LF
Tel: 0181 876 3323
Head: J D T Wall BA(Bristol), PGCE
Type: Boys Day B4-13
No of pupils: B174
Fees: DAY £1695

SW15

BEES KNEES NURSERY SCHOOL
12 Priory Lane, London SW15 5JQ
Tel: 0181 876 1149
Head: Mrs Sarah Ramsay
Type: Co-educational Day

BUSY BEE NURSERY SCHOOL
106 Felsham Road, London SW15
Tel: 0181 780 1615
Type: Co-educational Day

BUSY BEE NURSERY SCHOOL
19 Lytton Grove, London SW15 2EZ
Tel: 0181 789 0132
Head: Mrs Lucy Lindsay
Type: Co-educational Day

THE HALL SCHOOL WIMBLEDON
Beavers Holt, Stroud Crescent, London SW15 3EQ
Tel: 0181 788 2370
Head: T J Hobbs
Type: Co-educational Day B3-13 G3-13
Fees: DAY £945-£4770

HURLINGHAM SCHOOL
95/97 Deodar Road, London SW15 2NU
Tel: 0181 874 1673
Head: Mrs M L Hamilton
Type: Co-educational Day B4-8 G4-11
No of pupils: B40 G50
Fees: DAY £3000-£3750

★ IBSTOCK PLACE
Clarence Lane, Roehampton, London SW15 5PY
Tel: 0181 876 9991
Head: Mrs F Bayliss CertEd(Froebel), FRSA
Type: Co-educational Day B3-16 G3-16
No of pupils: B237 G287
Fees: DAY £1815-£5505

LION HOUSE SCHOOL
The Old Methodist Hall, London SW15 6EH
Tel: 0181 780 9446
Head: Miss H J Luard MontDip
Type: Co-educational Day B3-8 G3-8
No of pupils: B48 G52
Fees: DAY £400-£1450

THE MERLIN SCHOOL
4 Carlton Drive, London SW15 2BZ
Tel: 0181 788 2769
Head: Mrs J Addis
Type: Co-educational Day B4-8 G4-8

MISS GRAYS NURSERY SCHOOL
St Margarets Church Hall, London SW15
Tel: 0181 788 4809
Head: Mrs M Gray
Type: Co-educational Day B2-5 G2-5
Fees: DAY £1140

NODDY'S NURSERY SCHOOL
2 Gwendolen Avenue, London SW15
Tel: 0181 785 9191
Head: Mrs Sarah Edwards NNEB, MontDip
Type: Co-educational Day B2-5 G2-5
No of pupils: B50 G50

PROSPECT HOUSE SCHOOL
75 Putney Hill, London SW15 3NT
Tel: 0181 780 0456
Heads: Mrs S Eley BEd & Mrs H Gerry SRN, MSc
Type: Co-educational Day B3-11 G3-11
No of pupils: B80 G100
Fees: DAY £2295-£5100

PUTNEY COMMON MONTESSORI NURSERY SCHOOL
All Saints Hall, Putney Common, London SW15
Tel: 0181 780 1029
Head: Anna Wood
Type: Co-educational Day

★ **PUTNEY HIGH SCHOOL**
35 Putney Hill, London SW15 6BH
Tel: 0181 788 4886
Head: Mrs E Merchant BSc
Type: Girls Day G4-18
No of pupils: G831 VIth138
Fees: DAY £3864-£4920

PUTNEY PARK SCHOOL
Woodborough Road, London SW15 6PY
Tel: 0181 788 8316
Head: Mrs Ruth Mann BSc(Hons), PGCE
Type: Co-educational Day B4-8 G4-16
No of pupils: B89 G211
Fees: DAY £3810-£4380

PUTNEY VALE TINY TOTS
Newlands Community Centre, London SW15
Tel: 0181 780 5050
Type: Co-educational Day

RIVERSIDE MONTESSORI NURSERY SCHOOL
95 Lacy Road, London SW15 1NR
Tel: 0181 780 9345
Head: Miss Barbara Ladden
Type: Co-educational Day.

SQUARE ONE
12 Ravenna Road, London SW15
Tel: 0181 788 1546
Type: Co-educational Day

SUNFLOWER NURSERY SCHOOL
Rosslyn Park Rugby Football Club, London SW15
Tel: 0181 947 8097
Head: Mrs Lucy Ennis
Type: Co-educational Day

TIGGERS NURSERY SCHOOL LTD
87 Putney Bridge Road, London SW15 2PA
Tel: 0181 874 4668
Head: Natasha Green
Type: Co-educational Day
Fees: DAY £1575

SW16

ABACUS EARLY LEARNING NURSERY SCHOOL
7 Drewstead Road, London SW16 1LY
Tel: 0181 677 9117
Heads: Mrs M Taylor BEd & Ms S Petgrave
Type: Co-educational Day

BRIGHT HORIZON PREPARATORY SCHOOL
St James Hall, Welham Road, London SW16 6NT
Tel: 0181 677 3947
Head: Mrs L W Timmerman
Type: Co-educational Day

BRIGHT SPARKS THEATRE SCHOOL
16-16A Wellfield Road, London SW16 2BP
Tel: 0181 769 3500
Head: Mrs E Martin
Type: Co-educational Day

CARMENA CHRISTIAN DAY NURSERIES
38 Mitcham Lane, London SW16
Tel: 0181 677 1376
Type: Co-educational Day

CARMENA CHRISTIAN DAY NURSERIES
47 Thrale Road, London SW16
Tel: 0181 677 8231
Type: Co-educational Day

CROYDON MONTESSORI NURSERY SCHOOL
Next to 55 Ederline Avenue, London SW16 4RZ
Tel: 0181 764 2531/660 0282
Head: Mrs A McConway PGCE, BA(Hons), MontDip,
   SpLDDip
Type: Co-educational Day B2-5 G2-5
No of pupils: B30 G30
Fees: DAY £474-£2400

FATEMAH DAY NURSERY
53 Buckleigh Road, London SW16 5RY
Tel: 0181 764 8657
Head: Ms S Ismail
Type: Co-educational Day

FIRST STEPS
48 Barrow Road, London SW16 5PF
Tel: 0181 769 9677
Head: Mrs N Abbas
Type: Co-educational Day

FISHER HOUSE DAY NURSERY
Church Walk, London SW16 5JH
Tel: 0181 679 0222
Head: Mrs Carol Edwards
Type: Co-educational Day

NORBURY NURSERY SCHOOL
Fairholme Dunbar Avenue, London SW16
Tel: 0181 764 2564
Type: Co-educational Day

RAINBOW DAY NURSERY (STREATHAM COMMON)
34 Kempshott Road, London SW16
Tel: 0181 679 4235
Head: Mrs Azra Siddique
Type: Co-educational Day

ST LEONARD'S
38 Mitcham Lane, London SW16 6NP
Tel: 0181 677 1376
Type: Co-educational Day

STREATHAM HILL & CLAPHAM HIGH SCHOOL
42 Abbotswood Road, London SW16 1AW
Tel: 0181 677 8400
Head: Miss G M Ellis BSc(Hons)(Glasgow)
Type: Girls Day G4-18
No of pupils: G581 VIth95
Fees: DAY £3864-£4920

STREATHAM MODERN SCHOOL
508 Streatham High Road, London SW16 3QB
Tel: 0181 764 7232
Head: B Russell-Owen
Type: Boys Day B3-12
No of pupils: B110
Fees: DAY £2265

WALDORF SCHOOL OF SOUTH WEST LONDON
A Rudolf Steiner School, London SW16 1AP
Tel: 0181 769 6587
Type: Co-educational Day B4-14 G4-14
No of pupils: B60 G60
Fees: DAY £1350-£1500

SW17

★ BERTRUM HOUSE SCHOOL
Little Wandsworth Nursery, 290 Balham High Road,
London SW17 7AL
Tel: 0181 767 4051
Head: Mrs Marie Cabourn-Smith
Type: Co-educational Day B2-8 G2-8
No of pupils: B74 G58
Fees: DAY £665-£1375

THE CHILDREN'S HOUSE MONTESSORI
St Mary's Church Hall, London SW17 0UQ
Tel: 0181 947 7359
Head: Mrs S Gmaj MontDip
Type: Co-educational Day B2-5 G2-5
Fees: DAY £1440

THE CRESCENT KINDERGARTEN
Flat 1, 10 Trinity Crescent, London SW17 7AE
Tel: 0181 767 5882
Head: Philip Evelegh
Type: Co-educational Day

EVELINE DAY SCHOOL
14 Trinity Crescent, London SW17 7AE
Tel: 0181 672 4673
Head: Eveline Brut
Type: Co-educational Day

THE EVELINE DAY NURSERY SCHOOLS LTD
30 Ritherdon Road, London SW17 8QD
Tel: 0181 672 7549/7259
Head: Mrs T Larche
Type: Co-educational Day

FINTON HOUSE SCHOOL
171 Trinity Road, London SW17 7HL
Tel: 0181 682 0921
Head: Miss Emma Thornton MA
Type: Co-educational Day B4-11 G4-11
No of pupils: B64 G127
Fees: DAY £4830-£5460

IN LOCO PARENTIS
272 Balham High Road, London SW17
Tel: 0181 767 7109
Head: Ms Emily Dexter MontDip, NNEB
Type: Co-educational Day

JACK IN THE BOX NURSERY SCHOOL
Seacadets Hall, Mellison Road, London SW17
Tel: 0171 622 1106
Head: Miss J Clarke
Type: Co-educational Day

★ LITTLE WANDSWORTH NURSERY
Bertrum House School, London SW17 7AL
Tel: 0181 767 4051
Head: Mrs Marie Cabourn-Smith
Type: Co-educational Day B2-4 G2-4
No of pupils: B43 G37
Fees: DAY £1995

THE MONTESSORI NURSERY-CHILDREN'S HOUSE
St Mary's Church Hall, London SW17
Tel: 0181 947 7359
Head: Samantha Gmaj
Type: Co-educational Day

RED BALLOON NURSERY SCHOOL
St Mary Magdalene Church Hall, London SW17 7SD
Tel: 0181 672 4711/228 4447
Head: Ms T Millington-Drake MontDip
Type: Co-educational Day B2-5 G2-5
Fees: DAY £620-£640

UPPER TOOTING INDEPENDENT HIGH SCHOOL
169 Trinity Road, London SW17 7HL
Tel: 0181 672 5676
Head: Mrs A M Abbott
Type: Co-educational Day B6-16 G6-16
No of pupils: B40 G24
Fees: DAY £2274-£2754

SW18

345 NURSERY SCHOOL
Fitzhugh Community Clubroom, London SW18 4AA
Tel: 0181 870 8441/877 0437
Head: Mrs Annabel Dixon
Type: Co-educational Day

CROSSFIELD KINDERGARTEN
United Reform Church, Earlsfield Road, London SW18 3EJ
Tel: 0181 875 0898
Type: Co-educational Day

HIGHFIELD SCHOOL
256 Trinity Road, London SW18 3RQ
Tel: 0181 874 2778
Head: Mrs V-J F Lowe
Type: Co-educational Day B2-11 G2-11
No of pupils: B82 G44
Fees: DAY £1530-£3660

MELROSE HOUSE NURSERY SCHOOL
39 Melrose Road, London SW18 1LX
Tel: 0181 874 7769
Head: Mrs Ruth Oates NNEB
Type: Co-educational Day B2-5 G2-5
No of pupils: B15 G15

THE PUTNEY KINDERGARTEN
176 Sutherland Grove, London SW18
Tel: 0181 877 3555
Type: Co-educational Day

RIGHT IMPRESSIONS MONTESSORI NURSERY
All Saints Wandsworth Parish, London SW18 1RQ
Tel: 0181 877 9554
Head: Mrs Gul Sherwaram BA(Hons)Econ, MontDip(AMI)
Type: Co-educational Day B0-6 G0-6
Fees: DAY £1800

SQUARE ONE NURSERY SCHOOL
17B Amerland Road, London SW18 1PX
Tel: 0181 871 3377/947 8497
Head: Mrs S J Stewart
Type: Co-educational Day

WANDLE HOUSE NURSERY SCHOOL
25-27 West Hill, London SW18
Tel: 0181 875 0752
Head: Mrs Shirley Stewart MontDip, BEd(Hons)
Type: Co-educational Day

WIMBLEDON PARK MONTESSORI SCHOOL
206 Heythorp Street, London SW18
Tel: 0181 944 8584
Head: Mrs Wilberforce Ritchie
Type: Co-educational Day B2-5 G2-5
Fees: DAY £1620

SW19

THE CASTLE KINDERGARTEN
20 Henfield Road, London SW19
Tel: 0181 544 0089
Head: Mrs Beverley Davis DipEd
Type: Co-educational Day B2-5 G2-5
No of pupils: B34 G34

COSMOPOLITAN DAY NURSERY
65/67 High Street, London SW19
Tel: 0181 544 0758
Type: Co-educational Day

CROWN KINDERGARTENS
Ashcombe Road, London SW19 8JP
Tel: 0181 540 8820
Head: Mrs Acres
Type: Co-educational Day

ELIZABETH RUSSELL SCHOOL OF COOKERY
Flat 5, 18 The Grange, London SW19 4PS
Tel: 0181 947 2144
Heads: Miss A Russell & Mrs E Pilon
Type: Co-educational Day B17-99 G17-99
No of pupils: B8 G8
Fees: DAY £4920

THE GROVE NURSERY
28 Wilton Grove, London SW19
Tel: 0181 540 2388
Head: V Kimber
Type: Co-educational Day
Fees: DAY £1575

HERBERT DAY NURSERY
Park House Hall, London SW19
Tel: 0181 542 7416
Head: Mrs V I Bedford
Type: Co-educational Day

THE HILL KINDERGARTEN
65 Wimbledon Hill Road, London SW19
Tel: 0181 946 7467
Heads: Mrs Dobbs TechCertFroebel &
        Mrs Fox BA(Hons)Soc
Type: Co-educational Day B3-5 G3-5
No of pupils: B51 G44
Fees: DAY £1320-£1560

KING'S COLLEGE SCHOOL
Southside, London SW19 4TT
Tel: 0181 255 5352
Head: A C V Evans
Type: Boys Day B13-18
No of pupils: B720
Fees: DAY £6840

KING'S COLLEGE JUNIOR SCHOOL
Southside, London SW19 4TT
Tel: 0181 255 5335
Head: C Holloway
Type: Boys Day B7-13
No of pupils: B460
Fees: DAY £2110-£2230

MONTESSORI 3-5 NURSERY
58 Queens Road, London SW19 8LR
Tel: 0181 946 8139
Head: Mrs I Hodgson
Type: Co-educational Day B2-6 G2-6
Fees: DAY £1431-£2694

NODDY'S NURSERY SCHOOL
Trinity Church Hall, London SW19 6SP
Tel: 0181 785 9191
Head: Mrs Sarah Edwards NNEB, MontDip
Type: Co-educational Day B2-5 G2-5
No of pupils: B50 G50

THE RAINBOW PLAYGROUP
38 Kingsley Road, London SW19 8HF
Tel: 0181 543 3851
Head: Mrs Sarah Horton
Type: Co-educational Day B2-5 G2-5

THE STUDY PREPARATORY SCHOOL
Wilberforce House, Camp Road, London SW19 4UN
Tel: 0181 947 6969
Head: Mrs L Bond MA(Cantab), FRGS
Type: Girls Day G4-11
No of pupils: G315
Fees: DAY £4098-£4656

TRINITY NURSERY SCHOOL
The Holy Trinity Church Centre, London SW19
Tel: 0181 540 3868
Head: Miss A Turpin
Type: Co-educational Day

WILLINGTON SCHOOL
Worcester Road, London SW19 7QQ
Tel: 0181 944 7020
Head: J A C Hey BA
Type: Boys Day B4-13
No of pupils: B200
Fees: DAY £3900-£4665

WIMBLEDON COMMON PREPARATORY
113 Ridgway, London SW19 4TA
Tel: 0181 946 1001
Head: M G Turner
Type: Co-educational Day & Boarding

WIMBLEDON COLLEGE PREPARATORY SCHOOL
Donhead Lodge, 33 Edge Hill, London SW19 4NP
Tel: 0181 946 7000
Head: D J O'Leary BEd(Hons)
Type: Boys Day B7-13
No of pupils: B260
Fees: DAY £3210

WIMBLEDON HIGH SCHOOL
Mansel Road, London SW19 4AB
Tel: 0181 946 1756
Head: Dr J L Clough BA(London), PhD(Hull)
Type: Girls Day G4-18
No of pupils: G718 VIth143
Fees: DAY £3855-£4920

WIMBLEDON HOUSE SCHOOL
1B & 1C Dorset Road, London SW19 3EY
Tel: 0181 544 1523
Head: Mrs J Tucker
Type: Co-educational Day B3-11 G3-11
No of pupils: B70 G50
Fees: DAY £1425-£3570

THE WIMBLEDON VILLAGE MONTESSORI SCHOOL
26 Lingfield Road, London SW19 4QD
Tel: 0181 944 0772
Head: Paul Nolan
Type: Co-educational Day

SW20

BLOSSOM HOUSE SCHOOL
14 The Drive, London SW20 8TG
Tel: 0181 946 7348
Head: Joann A Burgess
Type: Co-educational Day

HAZELHURST SCHOOL FOR GIRLS
17 The Downs, London SW20 8HF
Tel: 0181 946 1704
Head: Mrs C W M Milner-Williams CertEd, MInstD
Type: Girls Day B4-7 G4-16
No of pupils: B2 G130
Fees: DAY £3240-£4860

THE NORWEGIAN SCHOOL
28 Arterberry Road, London SW20 8AH
Tel: 0181 947 6617
Head: Mrs Valborg Ligard
Type: Co-educational Day B3-16 G3-16
No of pupils: B52 G52

THE ROWANS SCHOOL
19 Drax Avenue, London SW20 0EG
Tel: 0181 946 8220
Head: Mrs J Anderson BSc
Type: Co-educational Day B3-9 G3-9
No of pupils: B75 G45
Fees: DAY £1680-£3240

URSULINE CONVENT PREPARATORY SCHOOL
18 The Downs, London SW20 8HR
Tel: 0181 947 0859
Head: Sr Brendan
Type: Girls Day B3-7 G3-13
No of pupils: B12 G215
Fees: DAY £2400

W1

CAVENDISH COLLEGE
209-212 Tottenham Court Road, London W1P 9AF
Tel: 0171 580 6043
Head: Dr J Sanders BSc, MBA, PhD
Type: Co-educational Day B18-25 G18-25
Fees: DAY £1980-£4200

GREAT BEGINNINGS MONTESSORI SCHOOL
82a Chiltern Street, London W1M 1PS
Tel: 0171 486 2276
Head: Mrs W Innes
Type: Co-educational Day B2-6 G2-6
No of pupils: B25 G25
Fees: DAY £2160-£3150

JUMBO MONTESSORI NURSERY SCHOOL
St James Church Hall, London W1H
Tel: 0171 935 2441
Head: Miss J Barnical
Type: Co-educational Day B2-5 G2-5
No of pupils: B13 G22
Fees: DAY £1785

LONDON MONTESSORI CENTRE LTD
18 Balderton Street, London W1Y 1TG
Tel: 0171 493 0165
Head: Lauren Joffe BA, MontDip, AdDip
Type: Co-educational Day B17-60 G17-60
No of pupils: B10 G290
Fees: DAY £3600

★ **PORTLAND PLACE SCHOOL**
56-58 Portland Place, London W1N 3DG
Tel: 0171 307 8700
Head: R Walker BSc, CChem, MRSC
Type: Co-educational Day B11-18 G11-18
No of pupils: B85 G35
Fees: DAY £5835-£6435

★ **QUEEN'S COLLEGE, LONDON**
43-49 Harley Street, London W1N 2BT
Tel: 0171 636 2446
Head: The Hon Lady Goodhart MA(Oxon)
Type: Girls Day G11-18
No of pupils: G380 VIth100
Fees: DAY £6600

THE RAY COCHRANE BEAUTY SCHOOL
118 Baker Street, London W1M 1LB
Tel: 0171 486 6291
Head: Miss B Suri CIDESCO, CIBTAC
Type: Girls Day G17-50
No of pupils: G23
Fees: DAY £1275-£5295

W2

ABBEY TUTORIAL COLLEGE
28a Hereford Road, London W2 5AJ
Tel: 0171 229 5928
Head: J Burnett BSc
Type: Co-educational Day B18-20 G18-20
No of pupils: B45 G45
Fees: DAY £1700-£8000

CONNAUGHT HOUSE SCHOOL
47 Connaught Square, London W2 2HL
Tel: 0171 262 8830
Heads: Mrs J Hampton & Mr F Hampton MA, RCA
Type: Co-educational Day B4-11 G4-11
No of pupils: B34 G37
Fees: DAY £3750-£4770

CREME DE LA CREME (UK) LTD
32 Edgeware Road, London W2
Tel: 0171 286 6544
Type: Co-educational Day

DAVIES, LAING & DICK
10 Pembridge Square, London W2 4ED
Tel: 0171 727 2797
Head: Ms Elizabeth Rickards BA, MA, PGCE
Type: Co-educational Day B16-19 G16-19
No of pupils: B170 G1358 VIth220
Fees: DAY £1605-£8190

DR ROLFE'S MONTESSORI SCHOOL
10 Pembridge Square, London W2 4ED
Tel: 0171 727 8300
Head: Miss A Arnold NNEB (Dyslexia Therapist)
Type: Co-educational Day B2-5 G2-5
No of pupils: B30 G30
Fees: DAY £2190-£3753

★ **THE HAMPSHIRE SCHOOL**
9 Queensborough Terrace, London W2 3TB
Tel: 0171 229 7065
Head: A G Bray CertEd
Type: Co-educational Day B3-13 G3-13
Fees: DAY £2205-£6930

KINDERLAND MONTESSORI NURSERY SCHOOL
47 Palace Court, London W2 4LF
Tel: 0171 7921964
Head: Ms Elaine Quigley
Type: Co-educational Day

MONTESSORI KINDERLAND NURSERY SCHOOL
47 Palace Court, London W2
Tel: 0171 792 1964
Type: Co-educational Day

PAINT POTS MONTESSORI SCHOOL, BAYSWATER
Bayswater United Reform Church, London W2 5LS
Tel: 0171 792 0433
Head: Miss G Hood MontDip
Type: Co-educational Day B2-5 G2-5
No of pupils: B12 G12
Fees: DAY £2085-£3618

PEMBRIDGE HALL SCHOOL FOR GIRLS
18 Pembridge Square, London W2 4EH
Tel: 0171 229 0121
Head: Mrs L Marani
Type: Girls Day G4-11
No of pupils: G250
Fees: DAY £4425

RAVENSTONE HOUSE
PRE-PREPARATORY SCHOOL & NURSERY
The Long Garden, Albion Street, London W2 2AX
Tel: 0171 262 1190
Head: Mrs A J Saunders
Type: Co-educational Day B1-7 G1-7
No of pupils: B43 G44
Fees: DAY £1600-£6600

ST JOHNS NURSERY SCHOOL
St Johns Church, London W2 2QD
Tel: 0171 402 2529
Head: Ms Nukki Cosh
Type: Co-educational Day B2-5 G2-5
No of pupils: B17 G14
Fees: DAY £2530-£5450

WETHERBY SCHOOL
11 Pembridge Square, London W2 4ED
Tel: 0171 727 9581
Head: Miss F Blair Turner
Type: Boys Day B4-8
No of pupils: B150
Fees: DAY £5370

W3

BARBARA SPEAKE STAGE SCHOOL
East Acton Lane, London W3 7EG
Tel: 0181 743 1306
Heads: Miss B Speake ARAD, MISTD, MIDTA &
   Mr David Speake BA(Hons)
Type: Co-educational Day B4-16 G4-16
No of pupils: B45 G91
Fees: DAY £1725-£1920

EALING MONTESSORI SCHOOL
St Martins Church Hall, London W3
Tel: 0181 992 4513/998 0249
Head: Mrs P Jaffer
Type: Co-educational Day B2-6 G2-6
Fees: DAY £1730-£2595

GREEK CONSULATE SCHOOL
3 Pierrepoint Road, London W3 9JP
Tel: 0181 896 3581
Head: Evangelos Kosmetos
Type: Co-educational Day

★ **INTERNATIONAL SCHOOL OF LONDON**
139 Gunnersbury Avenue, London W3 8LG
Tel: 0181 992 5823
Head: Richard Hermon MA
Type: Co-educational Day B4-18 G4-18
No of pupils: B108 G81 VIth27
Fees: DAY £5550-£8760

THE JAPANESE SCHOOL
87 Creffield Road, London W3 9PU
Tel: 0181 993 7145
Head: Y Tsukamoto
Type: Co-educational Day B6-15 G6-15
No of pupils: B480 G320
Fees: DAY £1170

KING FAHAD ACADEMY
Bromyard Avenue, London W3 7HD
Tel: 0181 743 0131
Head: Dr Ibtissam Al-Bassam
Type: Co-educational Day B3-18 G3-18
No of pupils: B520 G570
Fees: DAY £1672-£2272

THE VILLAGE MONTESSORI NURSERY
All Saints Church, Bollo Bridge Road, London W3
Tel: 0181 993 3540
Head: Miss Kay Bingham
Type: Co-educational Day

W4

★ **THE ARTS EDUCATIONAL SCHOOL**
Cone Ripman House, 14 Bath Road,
Bedford Park, London W4 1LY
Tel: 0181 994 9366
Head: Mrs Anna Sylvester-Johnson BA(Hons), PGCE
Type: Co-educational Day B8-16 G8-16
No of pupils: B27 G88
Fees: DAY £3900-£5750

CATERPILLAR MONTESSORI NURSERY SCHOOL
St Albans Church Hall, South Parade, London W4 3HY
Tel: 0181 747 8531
Head: Mrs M Ward-Niblett
Type: Co-educational Day B2-5 G2-5
Fees: DAY £1560-£1830

CHISWICK & BEDFORD PARK PREPARATORY SCHOOL
Priory House, London W4 1TX
Tel: 0181 994 1804
Head: Mrs M B Morrow
Type: Co-educational Day B4-11 G4-11
No of pupils: B61 G114
Fees: DAY £3195-£3975

ELMWOOD MONTESSORI SCHOOL
St Michaels Church Hall, London W4 3DY
Tel: 0181 9948177
Head: Mrs S Herbert BA
Type: Co-educational Day B2-5 G2-5
No of pupils: B20 G20
Fees: DAY £2025

★ **THE FALCONS PRE-PREPARATORY SCHOOL**
2 Burnaby Gardens, London W4 3DT
Tel: 0181 747 8393
Head: Miss L Wall CertEd
Type: Boys Day B3-8
No of pupils: B163
Fees: DAY £4920

HOMEFIELDS UNDER FIVES CENTRE
Homefields, London W4
Tel: 0181 995 4648
Head: Mrs Sandra Lane
Type: Co-educational Day

THE MEADOWS MONTESSORI SCHOOL
Dukes Meadows Community Centre, London W4 2TD
Tel: 0181 742 1327/995 2621
Head: Mrs S Herbert BA
Type: Co-educational Day B2-5 G2-5
No of pupils: B20 G20
Fees: DAY £2010

ORCHARD HOUSE SCHOOL
16 Newton Grove, London W4 1LB
Tel: 0181 742 8544
Head: Mrs S A B Hobbs BA(Hons), PGCE, AMBDA, MontDip
Type: Co-educational Day B3-8 G3-8
No of pupils: B84 G76
Fees: DAY £2295-£4590

W5

ASTON HOUSE SCHOOL
1 Aston Road, London W5 2RL
Tel: 0181 566 7300
Head: Dr J Cook PhD, MA, MBA
Type: Co-educational Day B2-11 G2-11
No of pupils: B35 G35
Fees: DAY £3150-£4050

★ **BEACON HOUSE SCHOOL**
15 Gunnersbury Avenue, London W5 3XD
Tel: 0181 992 5189
Head: Mrs M Milner BA(Hons)(Lond)
Type: Co-educational Day B3-11 G3-11
No of pupils: B25 G119
Fees: DAY £1440-£3210

BUTTERCUPS NURSERY SCHOOL
Ealing Dance Centre, Pitshanger Lane, London W5
Tel: 0181 998 2774
Head: Mrs C Whitehouse
Type: Co-educational Day

★ **CLIFTON LODGE**
8 Mattock Lane, Ealing, London W5 5BG
Tel: 0181 579 3662
Head: D A P Blumlein BA
Type: Boys Day B4-13
No of pupils: B160
Fees: DAY £4100-£4600

CORFTON HILL EDUCATION ESTABLISHMENT
35 Corfton Road, London W5 2HP
Tel: 0181 248 9051
Head: Mrs G S Levitt CertEd, TEFL(Lond)
Type: Co-educational Day B7-11 G7-11
No of pupils: B6 G1
Fees: DAY £2820

DURSTON HOUSE
12-14-26 Castlebar Road, London W5 2DR
Tel: 0181 997 8795
Head: P D Craze MA, CertEd
Type: Boys Day B4-13
No of pupils: B390
Fees: DAY £4665-£5610

EALING TUTORIAL COLLEGE
28a New Broadway, London W5 2AX
Tel: 0181 579 6668
Head: Mrs G Watt
Type: Co-educational Day B16-19 G16-19
No of pupils: B24 G20
Fees: DAY £1600-£8250

HARVINGTON SCHOOL
20 Castlebar Road, London W5 2DS
Tel: 0181 997 1583
Head: Mrs A Fookes BA
Type: Girls Day G3-16
No of pupils: G205
Fees: DAY £3300-£4155

JUMPERS! NURSERY SCHOOL
25 St Mary's Road, London W5 5RE
Tel: 0181 579 6946
Head: Ann Babb
Type: Co-educational Day

KITE OF EALING MONTESSORI NURSERY
45 Queens Walk, London W5 1TL
Tel: 0181 566 7962
Type: Co-educational Day

LA PETITE FRANCE
Ealing YMCA, 25 St Mary's Road, London W5 5RE
Tel: 0181 579 5076
Head: Miss Beatrice Saison
Type: Co-educational Day

NURSERY LAND
Ninth Ealing Scouts Hall, London W5
Tel: 0181 566 5962
Type: Co-educational Day

PARK VIEW NURSERY SHOOL
Methodist Church Hall, Rooms 1,2 & 3, London W5 1LY
Tel: 0181 575 2199
Head: Mrs Marilyn Blackledge
Type: Co-educational Day B2-5 G2-5

PITSHANGER BUSY BEES NURSERY
181 Pitshanger Lane, London W5 1RQ
Tel: 0181 997 5078
Head: Mrs Marysia Maryniak
Type: Co-educational Day B3-5 G3-5

ST ANGELO PREPARATORY SCHOOL
10 Montpelier Road, London W5 2QP
Tel: 0181 997 3209
Head: D G A Cattini BA, PGCE
Type: Boys Day B4-13
No of pupils: B70
Fees: DAY £3240-£3600

ST AUGUSTINE'S PRIORY
Hillcrest Road, London W5 2JL
Tel: 0181 997 2022
Head: Mrs F J Gumley-Mason MA(Cantab)
Type: Girls Day G4-19
No of pupils: G365 VIth40
Fees: DAY £2505-£3795

ST BENEDICT'S SCHOOL
54 Eaton Rise, London W5 2ES
Tel: 0181 862 2010
Head: Dr A J Dachs MA, PhD(Cantab), FRSA
Type: Boys Day B11-18 G16-18
No of pupils: B407 VIth186
Fees: DAY £5220

ST BENEDICT'S JUNIOR SCHOOL
5 Montpelier Avenue, London W5 2XP
Tel: 0181 862 2050
Head: Fr M Shipperlee OSB, BA, BD
Type: Boys Day B4-11
No of pupils: B230
Fees: DAY £3795-£4110

ST MATTHEWS MONTESSORI SCHOOL
North Common Road, London W5 2QA
Tel: 0181 579 2304
Head: Mrs Y Abdulrahman
Type: Co-educational Day

TORTOISE GREEN NURSERY SCHOOL
43 Castlebar Road, London W5 2DJ
Tel: 0181 998 0638
Head: Mrs Olivia Woodward
Type: Co-educational Day

W6

BAYONNE NURSERY SCHOOL
50 Paynes Walk, London W6
Tel: 0171 385 5366
Head: Ms Madelaine Lee
Type: Co-educational Day B3-5 G3-5

BUTE HOUSE PREPARATORY SCHOOL FOR GIRLS
Bute House, London W6 7EA
Tel: 0171 603 7381
Head: Mrs S Salvidant BEd(Hons)
Type: Girls Day G4-11
No of pupils: G280
Fees: DAY £4350

ECOLE FRANCAISE JACQUES PREVERT
59 Brook Green, London W6 7BE
Tel: 0171 602 6871
Head: M Grolleau
Type: Co-educational Day B4-11 G4-11
No of pupils: B138 G124
Fees: DAY £2257

THE GODOLPHIN AND LATYMER SCHOOL
Iffley Road, London W6 0PG
Tel: 0181 741 1936
Head: Miss M Rudland BSc
Type: Girls Day G11-18
No of pupils: G516 VIth191
Fees: DAY £6285

THE JORDANS NURSERY SCHOOL 2
Holy Innocents Church, London W6
Tel: 0181 746 3144
Head: Mrs S Jordan MontDip, NNEB, RSHDip
Type: Co-educational Day B2-5 G2-5
Fees: DAY £1680-£2016

★ LATYMER UPPER SCHOOL
King Street, Hammersmith, London W6 9LR
Tel: 0181 741 1851
Head: C Diggory BSc, CMath, FIMA, FRSA
Type: Boys Day B7-18 G16-18
No of pupils: B1045 VIth290
Fees: DAY £5424-£6180

RAVENSCOURT PARK PREPARATORY SCHOOL
16 Ravenscourt Avenue, London W6 0SL
Tel: 0181 846 9153
Head: Mrs M Gardener
Type: Co-educational Day B4-13 G4-13
Fees: DAY £4326

RAVENSCOURT THEATRE SCHOOL
Tandy House, 30-40 Dalling Road, London W6 0JB
Tel: 0181 741 0707
Head: Rev Stuart Affleck
Type: Co-educational Day B5-16 G5-16
No of pupils: B45 G48
Fees: DAY £3450

THE RICHFORD STREET DAY NURSERY
50 Richford Gate, London W6 7HZ
Tel: 0181 746 1015
Head: Anna Lee
Type: Co-educational Day B0-5 G0-5
Fees: DAY £1774

THE ROSE MONTESSORI SCHOOL
St Alban's Church Hall, London W6 8HJ
Tel: 0171 381 6002
Head: Ms Marisa Deniya
Type: Co-educational Day B2-5 G2-5
No of pupils: B15 G16
Fees: DAY £1143-£1860

ST PAUL'S GIRLS' SCHOOL
Brook Green, London W6 7BS
Tel: 0171 603 2288
Head: Miss J Gough MA
Type: Girls Day G11-18
No of pupils: G410 VIth200
Fees: DAY £6627

W7

BUTTONS NURSERY SCHOOL
99 Oaklands Road, London W7
Tel: 0181 840 3355
Heads: Jane Loukes SRN, RMN &
Anthony Loukes MA(Oxon)
Type: Co-educational Day B2-5 G2-5
No of pupils: B22 G26
Fees: DAY £300-£3378

MANOR HOUSE SCHOOL
16 Golden Manor, London W7 3EG
Tel: 0181 567 4101
Head: J Carpenter BA(Hons)
Type: Co-educational Day B2-13 G2-13
No of pupils: B104 G50
Fees: DAY £2310-£2965

W8

ALLENDALE SCHOOL
Allen Street, London W8 6BL
Tel: 0171 937 7576
Head: Mrs M E Peake MA
Type: Co-educational Day B5-8 G5-11
No of pupils: B25 G30
Fees: DAY £2700-£3000

★ **ASHBOURNE MIDDLE SCHOOL**
17 Old Court Place, London W8 4PL
Tel: 0171 376 0360
Head: M J Hatchard-Kirby MSc, BApSc
Type: Co-educational Day B10-16 G10-16
No of pupils: 50
Fees: DAY £8625

★ **LADY EDEN'S SCHOOL**
39/41 Victoria Road, London W8 5RJ
Tel: 0171 937 0583
Head: Mrs J A Davies BA, CertEd
Type: Girls Day G3fi-11
No of pupils: G155
Fees: DAY £2595-£5910

LANSDOWNE INDEPENDENT SIXTH FORM COLLEGE
7-9 Palace Gate, London W8 5LS
Tel: 0171 616 4400
Head: P Templeton BSc(Econ)
Type: Co-educational Day B16-19 G16-19
No of pupils: B118 G122
Fees: DAY £5925

LEITH'S SCHOOL OF FOOD & WINE
21 St Alban's Grove, London W8 5BP
Tel: 0171 229 0177
Head: Caroline Waldegrave
Type: Co-educational Day B18-99 G18-99
No of pupils: B15 G81
Fees: DAY £8700

POOH CORNER MONTESSORI NURSERY SCHOOL
Christ Church Vestry, London W8
Tel: 0171 937 1364
Type: Co-educational Day

THOMAS'S PREPARATORY SCHOOL, KENSINGTON
17-19 Cottesmore Gardens, London W8 5PR
Tel: 0171 938 1931
Head: Mr B V R Thomas BA(Hons)
Type: Co-educational Day B4-11 G4-11
No of pupils: B102 G103
Fees: DAY £2120

W9

LITTLE SWEETHEARTS NURSERY SCHOOL LTD
St Saviours Church, London W9
Tel: 0171 266 1616
Head: Mrs Ulker Eaton
Type: Co-educational Day

THE MAIDA VALE DAY NURSERY
235 Lanark Road, London W9 1RA
Tel: 0171 625 1966
Head: Jackie Gardiner
Type: Co-educational Day B2-5 G2-5
Fees: DAY £1664

WINDMILL MONTESSORI NURSERY SCHOOL
Former Caretaker's Cottage, London W9
Tel: 0171 289 3410
Heads: Miss M H Leoni & Miss J Davidson
Type: Co-educational Day
Fees: DAY £2400-£4800

W10

BASSETT HOUSE SCHOOL
60 Bassett Road, London W10 6JP
Tel: 0181 969 0313
Head: Mrs A Landen BEd(Hons)(Warwick), MontDip
Type: Co-educational Day B3-8 G3-8
No of pupils: B70 G50
Fees: DAY £765-£1530

LA PETITE ECOLE FRANCAIS
90 Oxford Gardens, London W10 5UW
Tel: 0181 960 1278
Head: Ms A Stones
Type: Co-educational Day

W11

ACORN NURSERY SCHOOL
2 Lansdowne Crescent, London W11
Tel: 0171 727 2122
Head: Mrs Jane Cameron BEd(Hons)
Type: Co-educational Day B2-5 G2-5
Fees: DAY £2250

DENBIGH UNDER FIVES GROUP
5/7 Denbigh Road, London W11
Tel: 0171 221 5318
Type: Co-educational Day

HOLLAND PARK NURSERY SCHOOL
St Johns Church, London W11
Tel: 0171 221 2194
Head: Mrs Sybil Pagnamenta BA
Type: Co-educational Day B2-5 G2-5
No of pupils: B12 G12
Fees: DAY £2250

KENLEY MONTESSORI SCHOOL
Kenley Walk, London W11 4BA
Tel: 0171 229 2740/0181 876 5021
Head: Isabel Aljovin MontDipAdv
Type: Co-educational Day B2-6 G2-6
No of pupils: B10 G10
Fees: DAY £1560-£1920

LADBROKE SQUARE MONTESSORI SCHOOL
43 Ladbroke Square, London W11 3ND
Tel: 0171 229 0125
Head: Mrs Sophia Russell-Cobb MontDip
Type: Co-educational Day B2-5 G2-5
No of pupils: B60 G40
Fees: DAY £2100-£3750

NORLAND PLACE SCHOOL
162-166 Holland Park Avenue, London W11 4UH
Tel: 0171 603 9103
Head: David Alexander
Type: Co-educational Day B4-8 G4-11
No of pupils: B91 G152
Fees: DAY £3510-£5580

SOUTHBANK INTERNATIONAL SCHOOL
36-38 Kensington Park Road, London W11 3BU
Tel: 0171 229 8230
Head: M E Toubkin BA
Type: Co-educational Day B5-18 G5-18
Fees: DAY £7290-£8910

SQUARE MONTESSORI SCHOOL
18 Holland Park Avenue, London W11 3QU
Tel: 0171 221 6004
Head: Mrs V Lawson-Tancred
Type: Co-educational Day
Fees: DAY £2220

ST PETERS NURSERY SCHOOL
59a Portobello Road, London W11
Tel: 0171 243 2617
Head: Beverley Gibbs
Type: Co-educational Day

W12

BRINGING UP BABY
101 Frithville Gardens, London W12
Tel: 0181 749 1255/6
Type: Co-educational Day

THE JORDANS NURSERY SCHOOL 1
Kelmscott Gardens Community Centre, London W12
Tel: 0181 749 1984
Head: Mrs S Jordan MontDip, NNEB, RSHDip
Type: Co-educational Day B2-5 G2-5
Fees: DAY £1680-£2016

LITTLE PEOPLE OF WILLOW VALE
9 Willow Vale, London W12 0PA
Tel: 0181 749 2877
Head: Miss Jane Gleasure
Type: Co-educational Day

THE SHEPHERD'S BUSH DAY NURSERY
101 Frithville Gardens, London W12 7JQ
Tel: 0181 749 1255/6
Head: Miss Carol Kewley
Type: Co-educational Day B0-5 G0-5
Fees: DAY £1994

W13

★ **AVENUE HOUSE SCHOOL**
70 The Avenue, Ealing, London W13 8LS
Tel: 0181 998 9981
Head: Miss C Barber CertEd
Type: Co-educational Day B2fi-11 G2fi-11
Fees: DAY £1890-£3780

EALING COLLEGE UPPER SCHOOL
83 The Avenue, London W13 8JS
Tel: 0181 997 4346
Head: Mr Barrington Webb MA
Type: Boys Day B11-18 G16-18
No of pupils: B158 G5 VIth60
Fees: DAY £4080

HOLISTIC EARLY LEARNING SCHOOL
2 Amherst Road, London W13
Tel: 0181 998 2723
Head: Teri Farrar
Type: Co-educational Day

JIGSAW NURSERY & MONTESSORI SCHOOL
1 Courtfield Gardens, London W13
Tel: 0181 997 8330
Head: Debbie Clements
Type: Co-educational Day

MIDHURST NURSERY SCHOOL
146 Midhurst Road, London W13 9TP
Tel: 0181 579 4028
Head: Mrs Hawes
Type: Co-educational Day

NOTTING HILL & EALING HIGH SCHOOL
2 Cleveland Road, London W13 8AX
Tel: 0181 997 5744
Head: Mrs S Whitfield MA(Cantab)
Type: Girls Day G5-18
No of pupils: G832 VIth140
Fees: DAY £3864-£4920

W14

BRAMBER NURSERY
Bramber Road, London W14
Tel: 0171 385 5489
Type: Co-educational Day

BRIGHT SPARKS MONTESSORI SCHOOL
25 Minford Gardens, London W14 0AP
Tel: 0171 371 4697
Head: Matilda D'Angelo
Type: Co-educational Day B2-5 G2-5

BUSY BEE NURSERY SCHOOL
Addison Boys Club, London W14
Tel: 0171 602 8905
Type: Co-educational Day

HOLLAND PARK DAY NURSERY
9 Holland Road, London W14 8HJ
Tel: 0171 602 9266
Head: Audrey Bryant
Type: Co-educational Day B0-3 G0-3

HOLLAND PARK DAY NURSERY'S SCHOOL HOUSE
5 Holland Road, London W14
Tel: 0171 602 9066
Head: Sophie Bashall
Type: Co-educational Day

JAMES LEE NURSERY SCHOOL
Gliddon Road, London W14
Tel: 0181 741 8877
Type: Co-educational Day

THE ROYAL BALLET SCHOOL
155 Talgarth Road, London W14 9DE
Tel: 0181 748 6335
Head: J Mitchell
Type: Co-educational Boarding & Day B11-18 G11-18
No of pupils: B70 G181 FB128
Fees: FB £16,323 DAY £9459

SINCLAIR MONTESSORI NURSERY SCHOOL
Garden Flat, London W14 0NL
Tel: 0171 602 3745
Head: Miss Catherine Burnaby-Atkins MontDipEd, SENDip
Type: Co-educational Day B2-5 G2-5
No of pupils: B11 G19
Fees: DAY £1110-£1650

WC1

DAVIES'S COLLEGE
25 Old Gloucester Street, London WC1N 3AF
Tel: 0171 430 1622
Head: Andrew Williams BA, MSc
Type: Co-educational Day B15-50 G15-50
No of pupils: B75 G85
Fees: DAY £4950-£5670

WC2

CHERUBS NURSERY
48 The Market, London WC2E 8RF
Tel: 0171 240 4686
Type: Co-educational Day

KINGSWAY CHILDREN'S CENTRE
70 Great Queen Street, London WC2B
Tel: 0171 831 7460
Type: Co-educational Day

THE URDANG ACADEMY OF BALLET
20-22 Shelton Street, London WC2H 9JJ
Tel: 0171 836 5709
Head: Mrs J Crowther BA(Hons)
Type: Co-educational Day B10-16 G10-16
No of pupils: B3 G20
Fees: DAY £6600

NW1

THE CAMDEN DAY NURSERY
123-127 St Pancras Way, London NW1 0SY
Tel: 0171 284 3600
Head: Sue Timms
Type: Co-educational Day B0-3 G0-3
Fees: DAY £1955

★ **THE CAVENDISH SCHOOL**
179 Arlington Road, London NW1 7EY
Tel: 0171 485 1958
Head: Mrs L J Harris BA
Type: Co-educational Day B3-11 G3-11
No of pupils: B9 G156
Fees: DAY £3870-£4131

★ **FRANCIS HOLLAND SCHOOL**
Clarence Gate, Ivor Place, London NW1 6XR
Tel: 0171 723 0176
Head: Mrs P H Parsonson MA(Oxon)
Type: Girls Day G11-18
No of pupils: G453 VIth87
Fees: DAY £5295

INTERNATIONAL COMMUNITY SCHOOL
4 York Terrace East, London NW1 4PT
Tel: 0171 935 1206
Head: P Hurd
Type: Co-educational Day B3-18 G3-18
Fees: DAY £5100-£6750

NORTH BRIDGE HOUSE PREP SCHOOL
1 Gloucester Avenue, London NW1 7AB
Tel: 0171 485 0661
Head: Miss J Battye
Type: Co-educational Day B8-10 G8-10
No of pupils: B104 G136
Fees: DAY £5616

NORTH BRIDGE HOUSE SENIOR SCHOOL
1 Gloucester Avenue, London NW1 7AB
Tel: 0171 267 6266
Heads: R L Shaw CertEd & J C Lovelock BA(Hons), PGCE
Type: Co-educational Day B10-16 G10-16
No of pupils: B172 G68
Fees: DAY £5616

★ **ST MARKS SQUARE NURSERY SCHOOL**
St Marks Church, London NW1
Tel: 0171 586 8383
Head: Dr Sheema Parsons BEd
Type: Co-educational Day B2-5 G2-5
No of pupils: B14 G14
Fees: £2400

SYLVIA YOUNG THEATRE SCHOOL
Rossmore Road, London NW1 6NJ
Tel: 0171 402 0673
Head: Miss M T Melville
Type: Co-educational Day B9-16 G9-16
No of pupils: B42 G96
Fees: DAY £3000-£4500

NW2

ABBEY NURSERY SCHOOL LTD
The Scout Hut, London NW2
Tel: 0181 208 2202
Type: Co-educational Day

★ **THE LITTLE ARK MONTESSORI**
80 Westbere Road, London NW2 3RU
Tel: 0171 794 6359
Principal: Angela Coyne MontDip
Type: Co-educational Day B2-5 G2-5
No of pupils: B12 G12
Fees: DAY £3360-£6000

MENORAH FOUNDATION SCHOOL
Caddington Road, London NW2 1RP
Tel: 0181 208 0644
Head: Anne Albert
Type: Co-educational Day & Boarding

THE MULBERRY HOUSE SCHOOL
7 Minster Road, London NW2 3SD
Tel: 0181 452 7340
Heads: Ms J Pedder CertEd, BA &
Ms B Lewis-Powell CertEd
Type: Co-educational Day B2-8 G2-8
No of pupils: B70 G65

THE MULBERRY HOUSE SCHOOL
68 Shoot Up Hill, London NW2 3XL
Tel: 0181 452 7340
Heads: Ms J Pedder BA, CertEd &
Mrs B Lewis-Powell CertEd
Type: Co-educational Day B4-8 G4-8
No of pupils: B45 G30

NEASDEN MONTESSORI SCHOOL
St Catherines Church Hall, London NW2 7RX
Tel: 0181 208 1631
Head: Mrs J Sen Gupta BA, MontDip(AMI)
Type: Co-educational Day B2-5 G2-5

**ST MICHAEL'S MONTESSORI
CHILDREN'S HOUSE SCHOOL**
St Michael's Church Hall, London NW2 6XG
Tel: 0181 208 2554
Head: Wendy Cooper-Anderson MontDip(AMI), RGN
Type: Co-educational Day B2-5 G2-5
No of pupils: B3 G9
Fees: DAY £1800-£2400

THE WELSH SCHOOL, LONDON
265 Willesden Lane, London NW2 5JG
Tel: 0181 459 2690
Head: Ms S Edwards BEd(Hons)
Type: Co-educational Day B4-11 G4-11
Fees: DAY £1350

NW3

ANNABEL'S MONTESSORI NURSERY SCHOOL
Recreation Club, Royal Free Hospital, London NW3
Tel: 0171 431 6158
Type: Co-educational Day

CHALCOT MONTESSORI SCHOOL AMI
9 Chalcot Gardens, London NW3 4YB
Tel: 0171 722 1386
Head: J Morfey AMI Dip
Type: Co-educational Day B2-6 G2-6
No of pupils: B12 G12
Fees: DAY £2235

CHERRYFIELDS NURSERY SCHOOL
523 Finchley Road, London NW3
Tel: 0181 905 3350
Type: Co-educational Day

CHURCH ROW NURSERY
Hampstead Parish Church, Church Row, London NW3
Tel: 0171 431 2603
Type: Co-educational Day

★ **DEVONSHIRE HOUSE PREPARATORY SCHOOL**
2 Arkwright Road, London NW3 6AD
Tel: 0171 435 1916
Head: Mrs S Donovan BEd(Hons)
Type: Co-educational Day B2fi-13 G2fi-13
No of pupils: B188 G108
Fees: DAY £3765-£4980

ETON NURSERY MONTESSORI SCHOOL
45 Buckland Crescent, London NW3
Tel: 0171 722 1532
Type: Co-educational Day

FINE ARTS COLLEGE
85 Belsize Park Gardens, London NW3 4NJ
Tel: 0171 586 0312
Heads: Candida Cochrane CFA(Oxon) & Nicholas
        Cochrane CFA(Oxon)
Type: Co-educational Boarding & Day B15-20 G15-20
No of pupils: B40 G60
Fees: DAY £2295-£8985

FRIENDS PRE-SCHOOL
120 Heath Street, London NW3 1DR
Tel: 0171 433 3195
Heads: Mrs Charmain Hunt & Mrs Carmen Tan
Type: Co-educational Day

THE HALL SCHOOL
23 Crossfield Road, London NW3 4NU
Tel: 0171 722 1700
Head: P F Ramage MA(Cantab)
Type: Boys Day B5-13
No of pupils: B406
Fees: DAY £5955

★ **HAMPSTEAD HILL NURSERY & PRE-PREP SCHOOL**
St Stephen's Hall, Pond Street, London NW3 2PP
Tel: 0171 435 6262
Head: Mrs A Taylor
Type: Co-educational Day B2-8 G2-8
No of pupils: 210
Fees: on application

HEATHSIDE PREPARATORY SCHOOL
16 New End, London NW3 1JA
Tel: 0171 794 5857
Heads: Ms Melissa Remus BA & Ms Jill White BSc
Type: Co-educational Day B2-13 G2-13
No of pupils: B46 G39
Fees: DAY £2100-£3960

HEREWARD HOUSE SCHOOL
14 Strathray Gardens, London NW3 4NY
Tel: 0171 794 4820
Head: Mrs L Sampson BA
Type: Boys Day B4-13
No of pupils: B180
Fees: DAY £4920-£5490

THE HILLTOP NURSERY SCHOOL
Christchurch, London NW3 1AB
Tel: 0171 435 7010
Head: Mrs G Tausig BA(Hons), MontDip
Type: Co-educational Day B2-5 G2-5
No of pupils: B12 G12
Fees: DAY £710-£1210

LYNDHURST HOUSE PREPARATORY SCHOOL
24 Lyndhurst Gardens, London NW3 5NW
Tel: 0171 435 4936
Head: M O Spilberg MA(St Edmund Hall,Oxon)
Type: Boys Day B7-13
No of pupils: B135
Fees: DAY £6045

MARIA MONTESSORI CHILDREN'S HOUSE
26 Lyndhurst Gardens, London NW3 5NW
Tel: 0171 435 3646
Head: Mrs L Lawrence
Type: Co-educational Day B2-6 G2-6
Fees: DAY £3300-£3800

MARIA MONTESSORI TRAINING ORGANISATION
26 Lyndhurst Gardens, London NW3 5NW
Tel: 0171 435 3646
Head: Mrs L Lawrence
Type: Co-educational Day B18-0 G18-0
No of pupils: B3 G60
Fees: DAY £3300-£4200

NORTH BRIDGE HOUSE SCHOOL
33 Fitzjohns Avenue, London NW3 5JY
Tel: 0171 435 9641
Head: Ms R Allsopp BEd
Type: Co-educational Day B2-5 G2-5
No of pupils: B115 G103
Fees: DAY £5616

NORTH BRIDGE HOUSE SCHOOL
8 Netherhall Gardens, London NW3 5RR
Tel: 0171 435 2884
Head: Ms Judith Raines
Type: Co-educational Day B5-7 G5-7
No of pupils: B107 G98
Fees: DAY £5616

THE OAK TREE NURSERY
2 Arkwright Road, London NW3 6AD
Tel: 0171 435 1916
Head: Mrs S P T Donovan
Type: Co-educational Day
No of pupils: B15 G15
Fees: DAY £4035

OCTAGON NURSERY SCHOOL
St Saviour's Church Hall, London NW3
Tel: 0171 586 3206
Type: Co-educational Day

OLIVER'S NURSERY SCHOOL
52 Belsize Square, London NW3
Tel: 0171 435 5898
Type: Co-educational Day

PETER PIPER NURSERY SCHOOL
St Lukes Church Hall, London NW3 7SR
Tel: 0171 431 7402/0181 441 8189
Head: Mrs T Vickers
Type: Co-educational Day B2-5 G2-5
No of pupils: B20 G10

THE PHOENIX SCHOOL
36 College Crescent, London NW3 5LF
Tel: 0171 722 4433
Heads: Jonathan Clegg MA(Oxon) & Gillian Clegg
Type: Co-educational Day B3-7 G3-7
No of pupils: B56 G34
Fees: DAY £2400-£4950

READY STEADY GO
12a King Henrys Road, London NW3 3RP
Tel: 0171 586 6289/5862
Head: Jennifer Silverton BA(Hons), PGTC
Type: Co-educational Day B2-5 G2-5
Fees: DAY £3600

★ **THE ROYAL SCHOOL, HAMPSTEAD**
65 Rosslyn Hill, London NW3 5UD
Tel: 0171 794 7707
Head: Mrs C A Sibson BA(Oxon)
Type: Girls Day & Boarding G4-18
No of pupils: G180
Fees: FB £7500-£9300 WB £5760-£7500
DAY £3450-£4050

SARUM HALL
15 Eton Avenue, London NW3 3EL
Tel: 0171 794 2261
Head: Lady Smith-Gordon BEd
Type: Girls Day G3-11
No of pupils: B1 G162
Fees: DAY £990-£1700

SOUTHBANK INTERNATIONAL SCHOOL
16 Netherall Gardens, London NW3 5TH
Tel: 0171 431 1200
Head: Mrs J Treftz
Type: Co-educational Day

★ **SOUTH HAMPSTEAD HIGH SCHOOL GPDST**
3 Maresfield Gardens, London NW3 5SS
Tel: 0171 435 2899
Head: Mrs J G Scott BSc
Type: Girls Day G4-18
No of pupils: G912 VIth155
Fees: DAY £4044-£4920

ST ANTHONY'S SCHOOL
90 Fitzjohns Avenue, London NW3 6NP
Tel: 0171 435 0316
Head: Nigel Pitel BA(Oxon), PGCE
Type: Boys Day B5-13
No of pupils: B290
Fees: DAY £5280-£5430

ST CHRISTOPHER'S SCHOOL
32 Belsize Lane, London NW3 5AE
Tel: 0171 435 1521
Head: Mrs F Cook CertEd
Type: Girls Day G4-11
No of pupils: G223
Fees: DAY £4785-£5085

STEPPING STONE SCHOOL
33 Fitzjohns Avenue, London NW3
Tel: 0171 435 9641
Head: Mrs Robyn Allsopp BEd(Hons)
Type: Co-educational Day B2-6 G2-6
No of pupils: B110 G102
Fees: DAY £535-£1872

★ **ST MARGARET'S SCHOOL**
18 Kidderpore Gardens, London NW3 7SR
Tel: 0171 435 2439
Head: Mrs S Meaden BA(Hons), MBA, PGCE
Type: Girls Day G5-16
No of pupils: G142
Fees: DAY £3690-£4365

★ **ST MARY'S SCHOOL HAMPSTEAD**
47 Fitzjohn's Avenue, London NW3 6PG
Tel: 0171 435 1868
Head: Mrs W Nash BA (CertEd), FCollP
Type: Co-educational Day B3-11 G3-11
No of pupils: B40 G217
Fees: DAY £4425

TREVOR ROBERTS'
55-57 Eton Avenue, London NW3 3ET
Tel: 0171 586 1444/722 3553
Head: C Trevor-Roberts LVO
Type: Co-educational Day B5-13 G5-13
No of pupils: B98 G78
Fees: DAY £3900-£7500

★ **THE VILLAGE SCHOOL**
2 Parkhill Road, Belsize park, London NW3 2YN
Tel: 0171 485 4673
Head: Mrs F M Prior BA Hons(Cantab)
Type: Girls Day G4-11
No of pupils: G130
Fees: DAY £4290-£5310

UNIVERSITY COLLEGE SCHOOL
Frognal, London NW3 6XH
Tel: 0171 435 2215
Head: K J Durham BA
Type: Boys Day B11-18
No of pupils: B500 VIth200
Fees: DAY £6735-£7200

UNIVERSITY COLLEGE SCHOOL (JUNIOR)
11 Holly Hill, London NW3 6QN
Tel: 0171 435 3068
Head: J F Hubbard BSc
Type: Boys Day B7-11
No of pupils: B220
Fees: DAY £6735

WILLOUGHBY HALL SCHOOL
1 Willoughby Road, London NW3 1RP
Tel: 0171 794 3538
Head: Mrs Susan Segal MSc, DipEd
Type: Co-educational Day B3-8 G3-11
No of pupils: B45 G55
Fees: DAY £4125-£4950

NW4

ALBANY COLLEGE
23-24 Queens Road, London NW4 2TL
Tel: 0181 202 9748/5965
Head: R J Arthy MPhil, MRIC
Type: Co-educational Day B13-18 G13-18
No of pupils: B110 G80
Fees: DAY £5000-£7200

HENDON PREPARATORY SCHOOL
20 Tenterdon Grove, London NW4 1TD
Tel: 0181 203 7727
Head: T Lee BEd(Hons)
Type: Co-educational Day B2-13 G2-11
Fees: DAY £4560-£5610

NW5

BLUEBELLS NURSERY
Church Hall, London NW5
Tel: 0171 284 3952
Head: A Pearson
Type: Co-educational Day

CAMDEN COMMUNITY NURSERIES
99 Leighton Road, London NW5
Tel: 0171 485 2105
Type: Co-educational Day

CRESSWOOD NURSERY
215 Queens Crescent, London NW5
Tel: 0171 485 1551
Type: Co-educational Day

LILE AUX ENFANTS
22 Vicars Road, London NW5 4NL
Tel: 0171 267 7119
Head: Ms C Chagny
Type: Co-educational Day

ROOFTOPS NURSERY
Preistly House, Athlone Street, London NW5 4LL
Tel: 0171 267 7949
Head: Mrs Elaine Walton
Type: Co-educational Day

TADPOLE NURSERY
Highgate Road Baptist Chapel, London NW5
Tel: 0171 267 4465
Type: Co-educational Day

YORK RISE NURSERY
St Mary Brookfield Hall, London NW5 1SB
Tel: 0171 485 7962
Head: Miss Becca Coles
Type: Co-educational Day B2-5 G2-5
No of pupils: B10 G10

NW6

AL-SADIQ & AL-ZAHRA SCHOOLS
134 Salusbury Road, London NW6 6PF
Type: Co-educational Day

BEEHIVE MONTESSORI SCHOOL
Christchurch Hall, Christchurch Avenue, London NW6
Tel: 0181 451 5477
Type: Co-educational Day

THE BEEHIVE ON QUEEN'S PARK
147 Chevening Road, London NW6
Tel: 0181 969 2235
Type: Co-educational Day

BROADHURST SCHOOL
19 Greencroft Gardens, London NW6 3LP
Tel: 0171 328 4280
Head: Miss Berkery
Type: Co-educational Day

CCCR NURSERY
160 Mill Lane, London NW6
Tel: 0171 431 1279
Head: Margaret Connolly
Type: Co-educational Day

CHASTON NURSERY SCHOOL
30 Palmerston Road, London NW6
Tel: 0171 372 2120
Type: Co-educational Day

ISLAMIA GIRLS SCHOOL
129 Salisbury Road, London NW6 6RG
Tel: 0171 372 3472
Head: Dr Azam Baig
Type: Co-educational Day

ISLAMIA PRIMARY SCHOOL
129 Salisbury Road, London NW6 6RG
Tel: 0171 372 2532
Head: Dr Azam Baig
Type: Co-educational Day

JEWISH PREPARATORY SCHOOL
2 Andover Place, London NW6 5ED
Tel: 0171 328 2802
Head: Mrs Kathy Peters
Type: Co-educational Day B3-11 G3-11

THE NEW LEARNING CENTRE
211 Sumatra Road, London NW6 1PF
Tel: 0171 794 0321/5328
Head: Noel Janis-Norton
Type: Co-educational Day B5-25 G5-25

RAINBOW MONTESSORI SCHOOL
St James's Hall, Sherriff Road, London NW6 2AP
Tel: 0171 328 8986
Head: Mrs Linda Madden MontDipAdv
Type: Co-educational Day B2-5 G2-5
No of pupils: B15 G15
Fees: DAY £1956-£2559

RAINBOW MONTESSORI JUNIOR SCHOOL
13 Woodchurch Road, London NW6 3PL
Tel: 0171 328 8986
Head: Mrs Linda Madden MontDipAdv
Type: Co-educational Day B2-11 G2-11
No of pupils: B15 G15
Fees: DAY £4512

SOUTH KILBURN RESIDENTS UNDER 5 NURSERY
19 Malvern Road, London NW6
Tel: 0171 625 4014
Head: Miss L Wilson
Type: Co-educational Day

WEST HAMPSTEAD PRE SCHOOL
11 Woodchurch Road, London NW6 3PL
Tel: 0171 328 4787
Head: Tarja Haikdnen
Type: Co-educational Day B2-5 G2-5
Fees: DAY £6480

NW7

BELMONT (MILL HILL JUNIOR SCHOOL)
London NW7 4ED
Tel: 0181 959 1431
Head: J R Hawkins BA, CertEd
Type: Co-educational Day B7-13 G7-13
No of pupils: B303 G12
Fees: DAY £5835

★ GOODWYN SCHOOL
Hammers Lane, Mill Hill, London NW7 4DB
Tel: 0181 959 3756
Head: S W E Robertson
Type: Co-educational Day B3-8 G3-8
No of pupils: B100 G100
Fees: DAY £2070-£4140

LITTLE CHERUBS KINDERGARTEN
2 Accommodation Road, London NW7
Tel: 0181 959 2420
Head: Mrs P Nixon
Type: Co-educational Day

MATHILDA MARKS-KENNEDY SCHOOL
68 Hale Lane, London NW7 3RT
Tel: 0181 959 6089
Head: Mrs J Shindler BEd, DipEd
Type: Co-educational Day B2-11 G2-11
No of pupils: B100 G100
Fees: DAY £2400-£3285

MILL HILL SCHOOL
The Ridgeway, London NW7 1QS
Tel: 0181 959 1176
Head: William R Winfield MA
Type: Boys Boarding & Day B4-18 G4-18
Fees: FB £12,045 DAY £6105-£7815

★ **THE MOUNT SCHOOL**
Milespit Hill, Mill Hill, London NW7 2RX
Tel: 0181 959 3403
Head: Mrs M Pond BSc(Lond), MIBiol
Type: Girls Day G5-18
No of pupils: G340 VIth45
Fees: DAY £3240-£3900

ST MARTIN'S
22 Goodwyn Avenue, London NW7 3RG
Tel: 0181 959 1965
Heads: Mr N Harris & Mrs A Wilson
Type: Co-educational Day B3-7 G3-11
No of pupils: B50 G60
Fees: DAY £1860-£2040

NW8

★ **ABERCORN PLACE SCHOOL**
28 Abercorn Place, London NW8 9XP
Tel: 0171 286 4785
Head: Mrs A Greystoke BA(Hons)
Type: Co-educational Day B2fi-13 G2fi-13
No of pupils: B100 G90
Fees: DAY £3150-£5850

★ **THE AMERICAN SCHOOL IN LONDON**
2-8 Loudoun Road, London NW8 0NP
Tel: 0171 722 0101
Head: Judith R Glickman PhD
Type: Co-educational Day B4-18 G4-18
No of pupils: B643 G598
Fees: DAY £8835-£10,410

ARNOLD HOUSE SCHOOL
3 Loudoun Road, London NW8 0LH
Tel: 0171 286 1100
Head: N M Allen BA, PGCE
Type: Boys Day B5-13
No of pupils: B230
Fees: DAY £5505

ST CHRISTINA'S RC PREPARATORY SCHOOL
25 St Edmunds Terrace, London NW8 7PY
Tel: 0171 722 8784
Head: Sr Mary Corr
Type: Girls Day B3-7 G3-11
No of pupils: B35 G180
Fees: DAY £3300

ST JOHNS WOOD JUNIOR PREPARATORY SCHOOL
St Johns Hall, Lords Roundabout, London NW8 7NE
Tel: 0171 722 7149
Head: Mrs C A Segal BSc, MBA, DipEd
Type: Co-educational Day B3-8 G3-11
No of pupils: B50 G46
Fees: DAY £2025-£3975

TODDLERS INN NURSERY SCHOOL
Cicely Davis Hall, London NW8
Tel: 0171586 0520
Head: Laura McCole
Type: Co-educational Day

NW9

BEIS YAAKOV PRIMARY SCHOOL
373 Edgware Road, London NW9 6NQ
Heads: Caroline Scharfer & Feigy Levenb
Type: Co-educational Day

GOWER HOUSE SCHOOL
Blackbird Hill, London NW9 8RR
Tel: 0181 205 2509
Head: M Keane BSc(Hons), PGCE
Type: Co-educational Day B2-11 G2-11
No of pupils: B125 G100
Fees: DAY £2385-£3450

JOEL NURSERY
214 Colindeep Lane, London NW9 6DF
Tel: 0181 200 0189
Head: Mrs Caroline Lawlor NNEB
Type: Co-educational Day B2-5 G2-5
No of pupils: B24 G18

ST NICHOLAS SCHOOL
22 Salmon Street, London NW9 8PN
Tel: 0181 205 7153
Head: Mrs Y Fisher
Type: Co-educational Day B5-11 G5-11
No of pupils: B35 G35

NW10

BRIDGE PARK KINDER CARE LTD
Bridge Park, Harrow Road, London NW10
Tel: 0181 838 1688
Type: Co-educational Day

THE CHILDREN'S CENTRE
Christ Church, London NW10
Tel: 0181 961 9250
Head: Denise Lepore
Type: Co-educational Day

THE CHILDREN'S CENTRE
40 Nicoll Road, London NW10
Tel: 0181 961 6648
Head: Denise Lepore
Type: Co-educational Day

DOYLE NURSERY SCHOOL
College Road, London NW10
Tel: 0181 969 2179
Type: Co-educational Day

SWAMINARAYAN SCHOOL
260 Brentfield Road, London NW10 8HE
Tel: 0181 965 8381
Head: P F Hancock
Type: Co-educational Day & Boarding

NW11

BETH JACOB GRAMMAR FOR GIRLS
835 Finchley Road, London NW11 8NA
Tel: 0181 455 6497
Head: Ann Devorah Steinberg
Type: Co-educational Day

GOLDERS HILL SCHOOL
666 Finchley Road, London NW11 7NT
Tel: 0181 455 2589
Head: Mrs A Eglash
Type: Co-educational Day B2-8 G2-8
No of pupils: B80 G60
Fees: DAY £1650-£3600

GOLDERS HILL SCHOOL NURSERY
678 Finchley Road, London NW11
Tel: 0181 455 0063
Type: Co-educational Day

★ **THE KING ALFRED SCHOOL**
Manor Wood, North End Road, London NW11 7HY
Tel: 0181 457 5200
Head: F P Moran MA(Cantab), PGCE
Type: Co-educational Day B4-18 G4-18
No of pupils: B213 G235 VIth39
Fees: DAY £3780-£6450

MENORAH GRAMMAR SCHOOL
Beverley Gardens, London NW11 9DG
Tel: 0181 458 8354
Head: Rabbi A M Goldblatt MA(Oxon)
Type: Boys Day B11-18
No of pupils: B115 VIth10
Fees: DAY £3870

MONTESSORI SCHOOL
31 Hoop Lane, London NW11
Tel: 0181 209 0813
Type: Co-educational Day

SPEEDWELL MONTESSORI NURSERY SCHOOL
St Albans Church Hall, London NW11
Tel: 0181 209 0281
Head: Mrs Benedict
Type: Co-educational Day

THE TUITION CENTRE
8 Accommodation Road, London NW11 8ED
Tel: 0181 201 8020
Head: B Canetti BA(Hons), MSc
Type: Co-educational Day B14-20 G14-20
No of pupils: B40 G35
Fees: DAY £1450-£6800

N1

THE CHILDREN'S HOUSE SCHOOL
77 Elmore Street, London N1
Tel: 0171 354 2113
Head: Jane Gibberd DipEd
Type: Co-educational Day B2-5 G2-5
No of pupils: B45 G48
Fees: DAY £2310-£3495

THE COMET NURSERY SCHOOL
20 Halcombe Street, London N1
Tel: 0171 729 0936
Type: Co-educational Day

FLORAL PLACE NURSERY
1 Floral Place, London N1 2PL
Tel: 0171 354 9945
Head: Mrs Susan Haye
Type: Co-educational Day

GOODWILL NURSERY
Hoxton Youth Community Centre, London N1
Tel: 0171 739 3313
Head: Mrs Muriel McClenahan
Type: Co-educational Day

ISLINGTON GREEN NURSERY
327 Upper Street, London N1
Tel: 0171 704 0756
Head: Miss Christina Clayton
Type: Co-educational Day

THE METROPOLITAN THEATRE SCHOOL
Trinity Centre, Bletchley Street, London N1 7QG
Tel: 0171 608 2992
Head: Miss W Beattie MA
Type: Co-educational Day B5-16 G5-16
No of pupils: B7 G36
Fees: DAY £8550-£11,250

SPRIGS & SPROGS DAY NURSERY
Unit 3, Shepperton House, London N1
Tel: 0171 704 6204
Type: Co-educational Day

★ **ST ANDREW'S MONTESSORI**
St Andrew's Church, Thornhill Square, London N1 1BQ
Tel: 0171 700 2961
Head: Charlotte Biss MontDip
Type: Co-educational Day B2fi-5 G2fi-5
No of pupils: B15 G17
Fees: DAY £1950-£3180

STEPS AND STAIRS NURSERY SCHOOL
De Beauvoir Road, London N1
Tel: 0171 249 2554
Head: Pat Holland
Type: Co-educational Day B2-5 G2-5

N2

ANNEMOUNT SCHOOL
18 Holne Chase, London N2 0QN
Tel: 0181 455 2132
Head: Mrs G Tausig BA(Hons), MontDip
Type: Co-educational Day B2-7 G2-7
No of pupils: B35 G35
Fees: DAY £710-£1210

KEREM HOUSE
18 Kingsley Way, London N2 0ER
Tel: 0181 455 7524
Head: Mrs D Rose CertEd
Type: Co-educational Day B3-5 G3-5

THE KEREM SCHOOL
Norrice Lea, London N2 0RE
Tel: 0181 455 0909
Head: Mrs R Goulden MEd, BEd(Hons)
Type: Co-educational Day B4-11 G4-11
No of pupils: B79 G81
Fees: DAY £3609

SUNFLOWER PLAYGROUP
43 Linden Lea, London N2
Tel: 0181 201 8386
Type: Co-educational Day

N3

AKIVA SCHOOL
The Manor House, London N3 2SY
Tel: 0181 3494980
Head: Mrs Linda Bayfield BA(Hons), PGCE
Type: Co-educational Day B4-11 G4-11
No of pupils: B89 G55
Fees: DAY £3645

PARDES GRAMMAR BOYS' SCHOOL
Hendon Lane, London N3 1SA
Tel: 0181 343 3568
Head: Rabbi D Dunner
Type: Boys Day B11-17
No of pupils: B176 VIth20
Fees: DAY £3750

N4

CARIBBEAN COMMUNITY CENTRE NURSERY
416 Seven Sisters Road, London N4
Tel: 0181 802 0550
Type: Co-educational Day

HOLLY PARK MONTESSORI SCHOOL
The Holly Park Methodist Church Hall, London N4 4BY
Tel: 0171 263 6563
Head: Mrs A Lake AMI Montessori Dip
Type: Co-educational Day B2-9 G2-9
Fees: DAY £670-£1090

ST ANGELA DAY NURSERY
34 & 36 Adolphus Road, London N4 2AY
Tel: 0181 800 5228
Type: Co-educational Day

N5

PRIMROSE MONTESSORI SCHOOL
Congregational Church, London N5 2TE
Tel: 0171 359 8985
Head: Mrs L Grandson
Type: Co-educational Day B2-11 G2-11
No of pupils: B12 G14
Fees: DAY £3255

N6

CHANNING SCHOOL
London N6 5HG
Tel: 0181 340 2328
Head: Mrs I R Raphael MA(Cantab)
Type: Girls Day G4-18
No of pupils: G479 VIth71
Fees: DAY £5355-£5880

CHANNING JUNIOR SCHOOL
Fairseat, London N6 5JR
Tel: 0181 340 2328
Head: Mrs E McDonald
Type: Girls Day G5-11
No of pupils: G144
Fees: DAY £4410-£5010

HIGHGATE SCHOOL
Highgate, London N6 4AY
Tel: 0181 340 1524
Head: R P Kennedy MA
Type: Boys Day B13-18
No of pupils: B412 VIth204
Fees: DAY £7515

THE HIGHGATE ACTIVITY NURSERY
1 Church Road, London N6 4QH
Tel: 0181 348 9248
Head: Ms J Crowe NNEB
Type: Co-educational Day B2-5 G2-5
Fees: DAY £6500

HIGHGATE JUNIOR SCHOOL
Cholmeley House, 3 Bishopswood Road,
London N6 4PL
Tel: 0181 340 9193
Head: H S Evers BA, CertEd
Type: Boys Day B7-13
No of pupils: B370
Fees: DAY £6750

HIGHGATE PRE-PREPARATORY SCHOOL
7 Bishopswood Road, London N6 4PH
Tel: 0181 340 9196
Head: Mrs B Rock
Type: Co-educational Day B3-7 G3-7
No of pupils: B99 G33
Fees: DAY £2880-£5925

LIMEWOOD SCHOOL
19 Stanhope Road, London N6 5AW
Tel: 0181 340 6487
Head: J M Sabri-Tabrizi
Type: Co-educational Day

RAINBOW MONTESSORI SCHOOL
Highgate URC, London N6 6BA
Tel: 0171 328 8986
Head: Mrs Linda Madden MontDipAdv
Type: Co-educational Day B2-7 G2-7
No of pupils: B15 G15
Fees: DAY £2109-£3039

N7

CITY COLLEGE OF HIGHER EDUCATION
67-88 Seven Sisters Road, London N7 6BU
Tel: 0171 263 5937
Head: A Andrews MBIM, FFA, FCEA, MABE
Type: Co-educational Day

NORTH CALEDONIAN PRE-SCHOOL CENTRE
577 Caledonian Road, London N7
Tel: 0171 609 7302
Head: Ms Bernadette Doherty
Type: Co-educational Day

THE SAM MORRIS CENTRE
Parkside Crescent, London N7 7JG
Tel: 0171 6091735
Head: Linda Singh
Type: Co-educational Day

N8

THE ARK MONTESSORI NURSERY SCHOOL
42 Turnpike Lane, London N8
Tel: 0181 881 6556
Type: Co-educational Day

LITTLE TREE MONTESSORI NURSERY SCHOOL
143 Ferme Park Road, London N8
Tel: 0181 342 9231
Head: Mrs Kathy Twomey-Brenner
Type: Co-educational Day

NORTH LONDON RUDOLPH STEINER
PO Box 280, London N8 7HT
Tel: 0171 7234400
Type: Co-educational Day & Boarding

N10

★ **THE MONTESSORI HOUSE SCHOOL**
5 Princes Avenue, Muswell Hill, London N10 3LS
Tel: 0181 444 4399
Head: Mrs N Forsyth AMIDip
Type: Co-educational Day B2-7 G2-7
No of pupils: B30 G33
Fees: DAY £1467-£3417

NORFOLK HOUSE SCHOOL
10 Muswell Avenue, London N10 2EG
Tel: 0181 883 4584
Head: R M Howat MA(Ed)
Type: Co-educational Day B4-11 G4-11
No of pupils: B62 G32
Fees: DAY £3609

THE NURSERY MONTESSORI MUSWELL HILL
24 Tetherdown, London N10 1NB
Tel: 0181 883 7958
Head: Mrs E Sweby
Type: Co-educational Day

★ **THE PRINCES AVENUE SCHOOL**
5 Prince's Avenue, London N10 3LS
Tel: 0181 444 4399
Head: Mrs N Forsyth AMIDip
Type: Co-educational Day B2-7 G2-7
No of pupils: B35 G40
Fees: DAY £1600-£4950

N11

★ **WOODSIDE PARK SCHOOL**
Friern Barnet Road, London N11 3DR
Tel: 0181 368 3777
Head: R F Metters BEd
Type: Co-educational Day B11-18 G11-18
No of pupils: B137 G15 VIth3
Fees: DAY £7500

N12

LAUREL WAY PLAYGROUP
Union Church Hall, London N12 7ET
Tel: 0181 445 7514
Head: Mrs Susan Farber
Type: Co-educational Day

TORAH TERMINAH PRIMARY SCHOOL
Wiseman Linden Hall, London N12 8RZ
Tel: 0181 446 3566
Head: Rabbi Ephraim Klyne
Type: Co-educational Day & Boarding

★ **WOODSIDE PARK SCHOOL**
Pre-preparatory & Nursery Dept, London N12 8SY
Tel: 0181 445 9670
Head: R F Metters BEd
Type: Co-educational Day B2-7 G2-7
No of pupils: B105 G59
Fees: DAY £820

★ WOODSIDE PARK SCHOOL
Preparatory Department, London N12 8SY
Tel: 0181 445 2333
Head: R F Metters BEd
Type: Co-educational Day B8-13 G8-13
No of pupils: B130 G44
Fees: DAY £820-£7500

N13

TINY TOTS NURSERY SCHOOL
Lacey Hall, Hazlewoos Lane, London N13
Tel: 0181 447 9516
Head: Mrs Maria Tamalis Mont
Type: Co-educational Day B2-5 G2-5
No of pupils: B16 G8
Fees: DAY £2880

TINY TOTS NURSERY SCHOOL
Montessori Monkey Business, London N13
Tel: 0171 259 5104
Head: Mrs Maria Tamalis Mont
Type: Co-educational Day B2-5 G2-5
Fees: DAY £2880

N14

SALCOMBE PRE-SCHOOL
33 The Green, London N14
Tel: 0181 882 2136
Head: Mrs G Dinner
Type: Co-educational Day

SALCOMBE PREPARATORY SCHOOL
224-226 Chase Side, London N14 4PL
Tel: 0181 441 5282
Head: A J Blackhurst BA(Hons), AdvDipEd
Type: Co-educational Day B2-11 G2-11
No of pupils: B241 G170
Fees: DAY £3450

TINY TOTS NURSERY SCHOOL
Walker Hall, London N14
Tel: 0181 447 9098
Head: Mrs Veronica Gray
Type: Co-educational Day B2-5 G2-5
No of pupils: B24 G24
Fees: DAY £2880

VITA ET PAX SCHOOL
Priory Close, London N14 4AT
Tel: 0181 449 8336
Head: Miss P M Condon
Type: Co-educational Day B4-11 G4-11
No of pupils: B89 G89
Fees: DAY £2595

N15

BETHEL NURSERY
Parish Church Hall, London N15 LR
Tel: 0171 729 4375
Type: Co-educational Day

N16

APPLETREE NURSERY
59A Osbaldeston Road, London N16
Tel: 0181 806 3525
Type: Co-educational Day

BEATTY ROAD NURSERY
162 Albion Road, London N16
Tel: 0171 254 7309
Head: Phylis Seymour
Type: Co-educational Day

BEIS MALKA GIRLS SCHOOL
93 Alkham Road, London N16 6XD
Tel: 0181 806 2070
Head: M Dresdner
Type: Co-educational Day

BEIS ROCHEL D'SATMER GIRLS SCHOOL
51-57 Amhurst Park, London N16 5DL
Tel: 0181 800 9060
Head: Mrs R Goldman
Type: Co-educational Day

COCONUT NURSERY
133 Stoke Newington Church Street, London N16
Tel: 0171 923 0720
Type: Co-educational Day

HACKNEY CARE FOR KIDS
61 Evering Road, London N16
Tel: 0171 923 3471
Head: Mrs Sandra Dowdy
Type: Co-educational Day

LUBAVITCH HOUSE GRAMMAR SCHOOL
107-115 Stamford Hill, London N16 5RP
Tel: 0181 800 0022
Head: Rabbi T M Hertz
Type: Co-educational Day B2-18 G2-16
No of pupils: B350 G150

LUBAVITCH ORTHODOX JEWISH NURSERY
Unit 1, 109-115 Stamford Hill, London N16 5RP
Tel: 0181 800 0022
Head: Mrs F Sudak
Type: Co-educational Day

MECHINAH LIYESHIVAH ZICHRON MOSHE
86 Amhurst Park, London N16 5AR
Tel: 0181 800 5892
Head: Rabbi M Halpern
Type: Co-educational Day & Boarding

THE METHODIST CHURCH MISSION MONTESSORI
Day Nursery, London N16
Tel: 0171 254 6218
Type: Co-educational Day

PHOENIX HOUSE NURSERY SCHOOL
27 Stamford Hill, London N16
Tel: 0181 880 2550
Head: Mrs Barbara MacIntosh
Type: Co-educational Day

RAINBOW NURSERY
Nevill Road, London N16
Tel: 0171 254 7930
Type: Co-educational Day

SMALL STEPS PLAY CENTRE
Scout Hall, London N16
Tel: 0181 809 3518
Type: Co-educational Day

STOKE NEWINGTON DAY NURSERY
104 Stoke Newington High Street, London N16
Tel: 0171 254 8028
Type: Co-educational Day

SUNRISE DAY NURSERY
1 Cazenove Road, London N16
Tel: 0181 806 6279
Head: Miss D D Carmody
Type: Co-educational Day

TALMUD TORAH BOBOV
87 Egerton Road, London N16 6UF
Tel: 0181 800 4389
Heads: Rabbi Abrahams & Rabbi Horovitz
Type: Co-educational Day

TALMUD TORAH JEWISH SCHOOL
112-114 Bethune Road, London N16 5DU
Tel: 0181 802 2512
Head: Mr Leach
Type: Boys Day B3-11
No of pupils: B60

TAYYIBAH GIRLS SCHOOL
88 Filey Avenue, London N16 6JJ
Tel: 0181 880 0085
Head: Mrs N B Qureishi MSc
Type: Girls Day G5-15
No of pupils: G150
Fees: DAY £2370

THUMBELINA NURSERY
171 Green Lanes, London N16 9DB
Head: Ms Carol Jenkinson PPADip, BTEC
Type: Co-educational Day B2-5 G2-5
No of pupils: B17 G11

TTTYY SCHOOL
14 Heathland Road, London N16
Tel: 0181 802 1348
Head: Mr Lubeisky
Type: Co-educational Day & Boarding

YESODEY HATORAH JEWISH SCHOOL
2-4 Amhurst Park, London N16 5AE
Tel: 0181 800 8612
Head: Rabbi Pinter
Type: Co-educational Day B3-16 G3-16
No of pupils: B300 G680

YETEV LEV DAY SCHOOL FOR BOYS
111-115 Cazenove Road, London N16 6AX
Tel: 0181 806 3708
Head: I Greenbaum BA(Hons), ACP
Type: Boys Day B3-13
No of pupils: B240

N17

EXCELSIOR COLLEGE
Selby Centre, Selby Road, London N17 8UL
Tel: 0181 365 1153
Head: Gareth Gilfillian
Type: Co-educational Day

THE JOHN LOUGHBOROUGH SCHOOL
Holcombe Road, London N17 9AD
Tel: 0181 808 7837/0563
Head: Dr Clinton A Valley
Type: Co-educational Day B9-16 G9-16
No of pupils: B109 G95
Fees: DAY £1290-£1950

MONTESSORI PLAYSKOOL
Unit 16, 2 Somerset Road, London N17
Tel: 0181 808 1149
Type: Co-educational Day

PARKSIDE PREPARATORY SCHOOL
Church Lane, Bruce Grove, London N17 7AA
Tel: 0181 808 1451
Head: Mrs Rachel E Horan-Botfield CertEd
Type: Co-educational Day B3-11 G3-11
No of pupils: B32 G24
Fees: DAY £2205

PEMBURY HOUSE NURSERY SCHOOL
Lansdowne Road, London N17
Tel: 0181 801 9914
Head: Mrs Anne Jones
Type: Co-educational Day

SUNRISE PRIMARY SCHOOL
55 Coniston Road, London N17 0EX
Tel: 0181 885 3354
Head: Mrs Meeta Lovage
Type: Co-educational Day B4-12 G4-12
No of pupils: B14 G21
Fees: DAY £0-£3380

N20

PRE-SCHOOL PLAYGROUPS ASSOCIATION
Biboard House, London N20
Tel: 0181 446 4684
Type: Co-educational Day

TINY TOTS NURSERY SCHOOL
United Reformed Church, London N20
Tel: 0181 829 9666
Head: Mrs Tina Antoniades PPA
Type: Co-educational Day B2-5 G2-5
No of pupils: B8 G11
Fees: DAY £2880

N21

GRANGE PARK PREPARATORY SCHOOL
13 The Chine, Grange Park, London N21 2EA
Tel: 0181 360 1469
Head: Mrs R J Jeans
Type: Girls Day G3-11
No of pupils: G105
Fees: DAY £2415

KEBLE SCHOOL
Wades Hill, London N21 1BG
Tel: 0181 360 3359
Head: Gordon Waite BEd
Type: Boys Day B4-13
No of pupils: B180
Fees: DAY £3675-£4995

PALMERS GREEN HIGH SCHOOL
104 Hoppers Road, London N21 3LJ
Tel: 0181 886 1135
Head: Mrs S Grant BMus
Type: Girls Day G3-16
No of pupils: G332
Fees: DAY £1650-£4650

SUPER TOT NURSERY
Highlands Hospital, London N21
Tel: 0181 360 6655
Head: Miss Louise Eden
Type: Co-educational Day

TINY TOTS NURSERY SCHOOL
Methodist Church Hall, London N21
Tel: 0171 259 5104
Head: Mrs Pat Sargent PPA
Type: Co-educational Day B2-5 G2-5
No of pupils: B10 G10
Fees: DAY £2880

N22

KIDS BUSINESS
New River Sports Centre, London N22
Tel: 0181 881 5738
Head: Miss Jurina Ikoloh
Type: Co-educational Day

Geographical Directory of Schools in Greater London

Essex

Corbets Tay

OAKFIELDS MONTESSORI SCHOOL
Harwood Hall, Corbets Tay, Essex RM14 2YG
Tel: 01708 220117
Head: Mrs K Malandreniotis
Type: Co-educational Day & Boarding

Hornchurch

GOODRINGTON SCHOOL
17 Walden Road, Hornchurch, Essex RM11 2JT
Tel: 01708 448349
Head: Mrs J Lauchlan SRN, DipSoc, DipEd
Type: Co-educational Day B3-11 G3-11
No of pupils: B34 G26
Fees: DAY £1200-£1974

RAPHAEL INDEPENDENT SCHOOL
Park Lane, Hornchurch, Essex RM11 1XY
Tel: 01708 744735
Head: N W Malicka BA(Hons)
Type: Co-educational Day B4-16 G4-16
No of pupils: B95 G35
Fees: DAY £2550-£4350

Ilford

BEEHIVE PREPARATORY SCHOOL
233 Beehive Lane, Ilford, Essex IG4 5ED
Tel: 0181 550 3224
Head: Mr C J Beasant BEd
Type: Co-educational Day B4-11 G4-11
No of pupils: B51 G44
Fees: DAY £1680-£2220

CLARKS PREPARATORY SCHOOL
81/85 York Road, Ilford, Essex IG1 3AF
Tel: 0181 478 6510
Head: Margaret Louise Jones
Type: Co-educational Day

★ CRANBROOK COLLEGE
Mansfield Road, Ilford, Essex IG1 3BD
Tel: 0181 554 1757
Head: G T Reading MA, CertEd(Oxon), FRSA
Type: Boys Day B4-16
No of pupils: B221
Fees: DAY £3030-£3885

EASTCOURT INDEPENDENT SCHOOL
1 Eastwood Road, Ilford, Essex IG3 8UW
Tel: 0181 590 5472
Head: Mrs C Redgrave BSc(Hons), DipEd, MEd
Type: Co-educational Day B4-11 G4-11
No of pupils: B149 G180
Fees: DAY £2250

GLENARM COLLEGE
20 Coventry Road, Ilford, Essex IG1 4QR
Tel: 0181 554 1760
Head: Mrs V Mullooly MA
Type: Co-educational Day B4-11 G4-11
No of pupils: B12 G118
Fees: DAY £2625

ILFORD URSULINE HIGH SCHOOL
Morland Road, Ilford, Essex IG1 4QS
Tel: 0181 554 1995
Head: Miss J Reddington CertEd
Type: Girls Day G4-18
No of pupils: G315 VIth54
Fees: DAY £3400-£4575

MANSFIELD LODGE
29 Mansfield Road, Ilford, Essex IG1 3BA
Tel: 0181 553 0212
Head: Anna Meshora
Type: Co-educational Day & Boarding

PARK SCHOOL FOR GIRLS
20 Park Avenue, Ilford, Essex IG1 4RS
Tel: 0181 554 2466
Head: Mrs N O'Brien BA
Type: Girls Day G7-18
No of pupils: G186 VIth19
Fees: DAY £2730-£3630

Romford

GIDEA PARK COLLEGE
2 Balgores Lane, Romford, Essex RM2 5JR
Tel: 01708 740381
Head: Mrs V S Lee BA
Type: Co-educational Day B2-11 G2-11
Fees: DAY £2925

IMMANUEL SCHOOL
Havering Grange Centre, Romford, Essex RM1 4HR
Tel: 01708 764449
Heads: Mrs Hilary Reeves & David Van Rooyen
Type: Co-educational Day B4-16 G4-16
No of pupils: B48 G41
Fees: DAY £2340

KINGS OAK PRIMARY
Salem Baptist Church, Romford, Essex RM7 9AQ
Head: Samuel Selvon
Type: Co-educational Day

ST MARY'S HARE PARK SCHOOL
South Drive, Romford, Essex RM2 6HH
Tel: 01708 761220
Head: Mrs J C Guilford
Type: Girls Day B3-7 G3-11
Fees: DAY £2055

Seven Kings

ILFORD PREPARATORY SCHOOL
Carnegie Buildings, Seven Kings, Essex IG3 8RR
Tel: 0181 599 8822
Head: Mrs B P M Wiggs BSc(Hons), PGCE
Type: Co-educational Day B3-11 G3-11
No of pupils: B85 G85
Fees: DAY £2250-£2850

Woodford Bridge

ST JOHN'S RC SPECIAL SCHOOL
Turpins Lane, Woodford Bridge, Essex IG8 8AX
Tel: 0181 504 1818
Head: Sr Marie Galvin
Type: Co-educational Day

Woodford Green

AVON HOUSE
490 High Road, Woodford Green, Essex IG8 OPN
Tel: 0181 504 1749
Head: Mrs S Ferrari
Type: Co-educational Day B3-11 G3-11
Fees: DAY £2625-£3015

BANCROFT'S SCHOOL
Whitehall Road, Woodford Green, Essex IG8 0RF
Tel: 0181 505 4821
Head: Dr P R Scott MA, DPhil
Type: Co-educational Day B7-18 G7-18
No of pupils: B463 G488 VIth232
Fees: DAY £4308-£5694

ST AUBYN'S SCHOOL
Bunces Lane, Woodford Green, Essex IG8 9DU
Tel: 0181 504 1577
Head: Gordon James MA
Type: Co-educational Day B3-13 G3-7
No of pupils: B290 G50
Fees: DAY £1038-£4119

WOODFORD GREEN PREPARATORY SCHOOL
Glengall Roadane, Woodford Green, Essex IG8 0BZ
Tel: 0181 504 5045
Head: I P Stroud BSc(Hons), DipED, CertEd
Type: Co-educational Day B3-11 G3-11
No of pupils: B176 G200
Fees: DAY £1440-£3060

Hertfordshire

Barnet

★ **LYONSDOWN SCHOOL TRUST LTD**
3 Richmond Road, New Barnet, Hertfordshire EN5 1SA
Tel: 0181 449 0225
Head: Mrs R Miller BA
Type: Co-educational Day B4-11 G4-11
No of pupils: B38 G151
Fees: DAY £2970-£3285

ST MARTHA'S JUNIOR SCHOOL
22 Wood Street, Barnet, Hertfordshire EN5 4BW
Tel: 0181 449 4346
Head: Sr Christina O'Dwyer
Type: Girls Day B4-7 G4-11
No of pupils: G188

★ **ST MARTHA'S SENIOR SCHOOL**
Camlet Way, Hadley, Barnet, Hertfordshire EN5 5PX
Tel: 0181 449 6889
Head: Sr M Cecile Archer BA(Hons), PGCE
Type: Girls Day G11-18
No of pupils: G354 VIth50
Fees: DAY £3150

Kent

Beckenham

EDEN PARK & ELMHURST PREPARATORY SCHOOL
204 Upper Elmers End Road, Beckenham,
Kent BR3 3HE
Tel: 0181 650 0365
Head: Mrs B Hunter
Type: Co-educational Day B3-11 G3-11
No of pupils: B103 G90
Fees: DAY £1680-£2430

ST CHRISTOPHER'S SCHOOL
49 Bromley Road, Beckenham, Kent BR3 2PA
Tel: 0181 650 2200
Head: D Attwood-Bloomfield
Type: Co-educational Day B3-11 G3-11
No of pupils: B110 G105
Fees: DAY £1280-£3516

Bromley

ASHGROVE SCHOOL
116 Widmore Road, Bromley, Kent BR1 3BE
Tel: 0181 460 4143
Head: Dr Patricia Ash CertEd, BSc(Hons), PhD,
    CMath, FIMA
Type: Co-educational Day B3-11 G3-11
No of pupils: B56 G39
Fees: DAY £1180

BASTON SCHOOL
Baston Road, Bromley, Kent BR2 7AB
Tel: 0181 462 1010
Head: Mr C R C Wimble MA(Cantab), PGTC
Type: Girls Day & Boarding G2-18
No of pupils: G193 VIth28 FB24 WB3
Fees: FB £9222 WB £9072 DAY £1005-£4722

BICKLEY PARK SCHOOL
2 Southborough Road, Bromley, Kent BR1 2DY
Tel: 0181 467 2195
Head: D J A Cassell FBIM, DipIAPS, FCollP, JP
Type: Co-educational Day B2-13 G2-13
No of pupils: B364 G13
Fees: DAY £1590-£5490

BICKLEY PARVA SCHOOL
14 Page Heath Lane, Bromley, Kent BR1 2DS
Tel: 0181 460 9800
Head: Mrs M P Dorning
Type: Co-educational Day B2-8 G2-8
No of pupils: B196 G10
Fees: DAY £315-£3180

BISHOP CHALLONER SCHOOL
Bromley Road, Bromley, Kent BR2 0BS
Tel: 0181 460 3546
Head: T Robinson BSc
Type: Co-educational Day B3-18 G3-18
Fees: DAY £2250-£3585

BREASIDE PREPARATORY SCHOOL
41-43 Orchard Road, Bromley, Kent BR1 2PR
Tel: 0181 460 0916
Head: Neil G Murray
Type: Co-educational Day B3-11 G3-11
No of pupils: B162 G53
Fees: DAY £1800-£3366

★ **BROMLEY HIGH SCHOOL GPDST**
Blackbrook Lane, Bromley, Kent BR1 2TW
Tel: 0181 468 7981
Head: Mrs E J Hancock BA
Type: Girls Day G4-18
No of pupils: G729 VIth132
Fees: DAY £3864-£4920

**CONEY HILL SCHOOL & NASH FURTHER
EDUCATION CENTRE**
Croydon Road, Bromley, Kent BR2 7AG
Tel: 0181 462 7419/5493
Head: Mrs Karen Fletcher MEd
Type: Co-educational Boarding & Day B6-25 G6-25
Fees: FB £24,000-£40,000 DAY £16,000-£28,000

HOLY TRINITY COLLEGE
81 Plaistow Lane, Bromley, Kent BR1 3LL
Tel: 0181 313 0399
Heads: Mrs Doreen Bradshaw BA, MA, PGCE &
Miss Anne Murphy CertEd
Type: Girls Day B3-4 G3-18
No of pupils: B30 G546 VIth72
Fees: DAY £1395-£4347

Chislehurst

BABINGTON HOUSE SCHOOL
Grange Drive, Chislehurst, Kent BR7 5ES
Tel: 0181 467 5537
Head: Mrs E V Walter BA(Hons), PGCE, FRSA
Type: Co-educational Day B3-11 G3-16
No of pupils: B55 G175
Fees: DAY £3405-£4350

DARUL-ULOOM LONDON
Foxbury Avenue, Chislehurst, Kent BR7 6SD
Tel: 0181 295 0637
Head: Mukaradam M Musa
Type: Co-educational Day

★ FARRINGTONS & STRATFORD HOUSE
Perry Street, Chislehurst, Kent BR7 6LR
Tel: 0181 467 0256
Head: Mrs B J Stock BA(Hons)
Type: Girls Day & Boarding G11-18
No of pupils: G205 VIth75
Fees: FB £10,278 DAY £5205

★ FARRINGTONS & STRATFORD HOUSE JUNIOR SCHOOL
Perry Street, Chislehurst, Kent BR7 6LR
Tel: 0181 467 0256/0395
Head: Mrs B J Stock BA
Type: Girls Boarding & Day G2fi-11
No of pupils: G208
Fees: FB £8916 DAY £3698

GREENHAYES SCHOOL FOR BOYS
83 Corkscrew Hill, West Wickham, Kent BR4 9BA
Tel: 0181 777 2093
Head: D J Cozens BA, CertEd
Type: Boys Day B4-11
No of pupils: B57
Fees: DAY £2325-£2565

★ ST DAVID'S COLLEGE
Beckenham Road, West Wickham, Kent BR4 0QS
Tel: 0181 777 5852
Principals: Mrs P A Johnson CertEd, FRGS, Mrs F V
Schove & Mrs A Wagstaff BA (Hons)
Type: Co-educational Day B4-11 G4-11
No of pupils: B104 G93
Fees: DAY £2655-£2805

Sidcup

BENEDICT HOUSE PREPARATORY SCHOOL
1-5 Victoria Road, Sidcup, Kent DA15 7HD
Tel: 0181 300 7206
Head: Mrs A Brown
Type: Co-educational Day

HARENC PREPARATORY SCHOOL FOR BOYS
167 Rectory Lane, Sidcup, Kent DA14 5BU
Tel: 0181 309 0619
Head: S H D Cassidy CertEd, ACP, FCollP
Type: Boys Day B3-11
No of pupils: B160
Fees: DAY £1470-£3390

MERTON COURT PREPARATORY SCHOOL
38 Knoll Road, Sidcup, Kent DA14 4QU
Tel: 0181 300 2112
Head: Dominic Price BEd, MBA
Type: Co-educational Day B2-11 G2-11
No of pupils: B155 G135
Fees: DAY £2970-£3300

WEST LODGE SCHOOL LTD
36 Station Road, Sidcup, Kent DA15 7DU
Tel: 0181 300 2489
Head: Mrs J V Barrett
Type: Girls Day B3-7 G3-11
No of pupils: B10 G110
Fees: DAY £1500-£2790

West Wickham

GREENHAYES PREPARATORY SCHOOL
83 Corkscrew Hill, West Wickham, Kent BR4 9BA
Tel: 0181 777 4352
Head: Mrs A Heard NNEB, CNTC
Type: Co-educational Day B3-5 G3-5
No of pupils: B10 G10
Fees: DAY £570-£1140

Middlesex

Ashford

LAURELS PREPARATORY SCHOOL
3 Clarendon Road, Ashford, Middlesex TW15 2QE
Tel: 01784 252681
Head: Miss J Challand
Type: Co-educational Day

ST DAVID'S SCHOOL
Freepost Sea 0837, Ashford, Middlesex TW15 3BR
Tel: 01784 252494
Head: Mrs J G Osborne BA(Hons), DipEd
Type: Girls Day & Boarding G3-18
No of pupils: G360 VIth30 FB25 WB20
Fees: FB £8985 WB £8460 DAY £4950

Brentford

PARK SCHOOL
Syon Park, Brentford, Middlesex TW8 8JF
Tel: 0181 568 4355
Head: Mrs C Whitehouse
Type: Co-educational Day

Edgware

DRIZEN TUTORIAL COLLEGE
Whitchurch Boys Club, Edgware, Middlesex
Head: Stanley Drizen
Type: Co-educational Day

HOLLAND HOUSE
1 Broadhurst Avenue, Edgware, Middlesex HA8 8TP
Tel: 0181 958 6979
Head: Mrs I Tyk BA(Hons)
Type: Co-educational Day B4-11 G4-11
No of pupils: B70 G70
Fees: DAY £2670

NORTH LONDON COLLEGIATE SCHOOL
Canons Drive, Edgware, Middlesex HA8 7RJ
Tel: 0181 952 0912
Head: Mrs J L Clanchy MA
Type: Girls Day G4-18
No of pupils: G1019 VIth227
Fees: DAY £4137-£5124

Enfield

BUSH HILL PARK PRE SCHOOL
2 Queen Anne's Place, Enfield, Middlesex EN1 2PX
Tel: 0181 364 1188
Head: Mrs Elizabeth Broughton
Type: Co-educational Day B2-5 G2-5
Fees: DAY £5340

ST JOHN'S SENIOR SCHOOL
North Lodge, Enfield, Middlesex EN2 8BE
Tel: 0181 363 4439
Head: A Tardios LLB(Hons), BA(Hons), CertEd
Type: Co-educational Day B11-18 G11-18
No of pupils: B51 G58
Fees: DAY £3600-£3900

Feltham

HOUNSLOW COLLEGE
The Old Rectory, Feltham, Middlesex TW13 6PN
Tel: 0181 751 1710
Head: R C Boyd BA, DipPhysEd
Type: Co-educational Day B10-18 G10-18
No of pupils: B17 G18
Fees: DAY £2595

Hampton

ATHELSTAN HOUSE SCHOOL
36 Percy Road, Hampton, Middlesex TW12 2LA
Tel: 0181 979 1045
Head: Elsa Morya Woolf
Type: Co-educational Day

DENMEAD SCHOOL
41-43 Wensleydale Road, Hampton,
Middlesex TW12 2LP
Tel: 0181 979 1844
Head: R P Jeynes BA(Hons) (Dunelm)
Type: Boys Day B2-13 G2-7
No of pupils: B180
Fees: DAY £1650-£4050

GRASSROOTS SCHOOL
The Studio, Hampton, Middlesex TW12 2JA
Tel: 0181 783 1190
Head: Mrs Walters
Type: Co-educational Day B2-5 G2-5
Fees: DAY £2160

★ HAMPTON SCHOOL
Hanworth Road, Hampton, Middlesex TW12 3HD
Tel: 0181 979 5526
Head: B R Martin MA(Cantab), MBA, MIMgt
Type: Boys Day B11-18
No of pupils: B930 VIth280
Fees: DAY £5280

JACK AND JILL SCHOOL
30 Nightingale Road, Hampton, Middlesex TW12 3HX
Tel: 0181 979 3195
Head: Miss K Papirnik BEd(Hons)
Type: Girls Day B3-5 G3-7
No of pupils: B20 G130
Fees: DAY £1860-£3360

THE LADY ELEANOR HOLLES SCHOOL
102 Hanworth Road, Hampton, Middlesex TW12 3HF
Tel: 0181 979 1601
Head: Miss E M Candy BSc, FRSA
Type: Girls Day G7-18
No of pupils: G705 VIth171
Fees: DAY £4620-£5520

★ **TWICKENHAM PREPARATORY SCHOOL**
Beveree, 43 High Street, Hampton,
Middlesex TW12 2SA
Tel: 0181 979 6216
Head: N D Flynn MA(Oxon)
Type: Co-educational Day B4-13 G4-11
No of pupils: B80 G69
Fees: DAY £2670-£4260

Hanwell

LITTLE EDEN SDA PRIMARY SCHOOL
Hanwell SDA Church, Hanwell, Middlesex W7 3QP
Tel: 0181 566 3186
Head: Miss Laura A Osei
Type: Co-educational Day

Harrow

ALPHA PREPARATORY SCHOOL
21 Hindes Road, Harrow, Middlesex HA1 1SH
Tel: 0181 427 1471
Head: P J Wylie BA(Hons), CertEd
Type: Co-educational Day B2-13 G2-13
No of pupils: B143 G24
Fees: DAY £3150-£4275

BUCKINGHAM COLLEGE SENIOR SCHOOL
15 Hindes Road, Harrow, Middlesex HA1 1SH
Tel: 0181 427 1220
Head: D T F Bell MA, PGCE
Type: Boys Day B11-18 G16-18
Fees: DAY £3705-£4335

GREENHILL COLLEGE
Lowlands Road, Harrow,
Middlesex HA1 3AQ
Tel: 0181 422 2388
Type: Co-educational Day

HARROW SCHOOL
1 High Street, Harrow,
Middlesex HA1 3HW
Tel: 0181 869 1200
Head: N R Bomford MA, FRSA
Type: Boys Boarding B13-18
No of pupils: B780 VIth320
Fees: FB £13,830

★ **THE JOHN LYON SCHOOL**
Middle Road, Harrow, Middlesex HA2 0HN
Tel: 0181 422 2046
Head: Rev T J Wright BD, AKC
Type: Boys Day B11-18
No of pupils: B525 VIth136
Fees: DAY £5790

ORLEY FARM SCHOOL
South Hill Avenue, Harrow, Middlesex HA1 3NU
Tel: 0181 422 1525
Head: I S Elliot BA, PGCE
Type: Co-educational Day B4-13 G4-13
No of pupils: B400 G60
Fees: DAY £3840-£5238

THE PURCELL SCHOOL, LONDON
Mount Park Road, Harrow on the Hill,
Middlesex HA1 3JS
Tel: 0181 422 1284
Head: K J Bain MA, FRSA
Type: Co-educational Day & Boarding B8-18 G8-18
No of pupils: B34 G56 VIth59
Fees: FB £12,699-£14,400 DAY £6969-£8514

QUAINTON HALL SCHOOL
91 Hindes Road, Harrow, Middlesex HA1 1RX
Tel: 0181 427 1304
Head: P J Milner MA(Cantab), CertEd
Type: Boys Day B4-13
No of pupils: B215
Fees: DAY £3555-£4770

ROXETH MEAD SCHOOL
Buckholt House, Harrow, Middlesex HA2 0HW
Tel: 0181 422 2092
Head: Mrs A Collins CertEd
Type: Co-educational Day B3-7 G3-7
No of pupils: B28 G32
Fees: DAY £3015

Hayes

GURU NANAK SIKH COLLEGE
Springfield Road, Hayes, Middlesex UB4 0LT
Tel: 0181 573 6085
Head: Rajinder Singh Sandhu
Type: Co-educational Day

Hounslow

HOUNSLOW COLLEGE PREPARATORY SCHOOL
Park Road, Hounslow, Middlesex TW13 6PN
Tel: 0181 751 1710
Head: Mrs J E Greening BEd(Hons)
Type: Co-educational Day B3-10 G3-10
No of pupils: B57 G18
Fees: DAY £2355

Isleworth

ASHTON HOUSE SCHOOL
50-52 Eversley Crescent, Isleworth,
Middlesex TW7 4LW
Tel: 0181 560 3902
Head: Miss Regan BEd(Hons)
Type: Co-educational Day B3-11 G3-11
No of pupils: B35 G35
Fees: DAY £972-£1321

Kenton

BUCKINGHAM COLLEGE LOWER SCHOOL
The Ridgeway, Kenton, Middlesex HA3 OLJ
Tel: 0181 907 1522
Head: N Wilkins BEd(Hons), MA, MCollP
Type: Boys Day B4-11
No of pupils: B110
Fees: DAY £2985-£3975

Northwood

HALL SCHOOL WITHIN THE GRANGE
Rickmansworth Road, Northwood,
Middlesex HA6 2RB
Tel: 01923 822807
Head: Mrs A C Portway
Type: Co-educational Day

MERCHANT TAYLORS' SCHOOL
Sandy Lodge, Northwood, Middlesex HA6 2HT
Tel: 01923 820644
Head: J R Gabitass MA(Oxon)
Type: Boys Day & Boarding B11-18
No of pupils: B492 VIth254
Fees: FB £11,520 DAY £6920

★ NORTHWOOD COLLEGE
Maxwell Road, Northwood, Middlesex HA6 2YE
Tel: 01923 825446
Head: Mrs A Mayou MA
Type: Girls Day G3-18
No of pupils: G725 VIth106
Fees: DAY £3420-£5172

NORTHWOOD HILLS
MONTESSORI NURSERY SCHOOL
St Edmund the King Church Hall, Northwood,
Middlesex HA6 12S
Tel: 0181 868 3782
Head: Mrs S Ranasingha
Type: Co-educational Day B2-5 G2-5
Fees: DAY £370

RNIB SUNSHINE HOUSE SCHOOL
33 Dene Road, Northwood, Middlesex HA6 2DD
Tel: 01923 822538
Head: Mrs Rita Kirkwood
Type: Co-educational Boarding & Day B2-11 G2-11
Fees: FB £28,737 DAY £19,002

★ ST HELEN'S SCHOOL
Eastbury Road, Northwood, Middlesex HA6 3AS
Tel: 01923 828511
Head: Mrs D M Jefkins MA(Cantab), CPhys
Type: Girls Day & Boarding G4-18
No of pupils: G965 VIth168 FB40 WB12
Fees: FB £8103-£9576 DAY £3294-£5082

ST JOHN'S SCHOOL
Potter Street Hill, Northwood, Middlesex HA6 3QY
Tel: 0181 866 0067
Head: Mr C R Kelly BA
Type: Boys Day B4-13
No of pupils: B320
Fees: DAY £3600-£4440

ST MARTIN'S SCHOOL
40 Moor Park Road, Northwood, Middlesex HA6 2DJ
Tel: 01923 825740
Head: M J Hodgson MA, CertEd
Type: Boys Day B3-13
No of pupils: B375
Fees: DAY £4140-£5055

Pinner

★ HEATHFIELD SCHOOL GPDST
Beaulieu Drive, Pinner, Middlesex HA5 1NB
Tel: 0181 868 2346
Head: Miss C M Juett BSc
Type: Girls Day G3-18
No of pupils: G486 VIth68
Fees: DAY £3444-£4920

INNELLAN HOUSE SCHOOL
44 Love Lane, Pinner, Middlesex HA5 3EX
Tel: 0181 866 1855
Head: Mrs R Edwards CertEd
Type: Co-educational Day B3-8 G3-8
No of pupils: B42 G46
Fees: DAY £2415-£2610

REDDIFORD SCHOOL
36-38 Cecil Park, Pinner, Middlesex HA5 5HH
Tel: 0181 866 0660
Head: B J Hembry MA, CertEd
Type: Co-educational Day B3-11 G3-11
No of pupils: B120 G95
Fees: DAY £1425-£3465

Shepperton

★ HALLIFORD SCHOOL
Russell Road, Shepperton, Middlesex TW17 9HX
Tel: 01932 223593
Head: J R Crook CertEd(Lond), BA(Wales)
Type: Boys Day B11-19
No of pupils: B284 VIth53
Fees: DAY £2580-£4680

Southall

THE SYBIL ELGAR SCHOOL
Havelock Court, Southall, Middlesex UB2 4NR
Tel: 0181 813 9168
Head: Chloe Philips
Type: Co-educational Boarding & Day B11-19 G11-19

Staines

★ **STAINES PREPARATORY SCHOOL TRUST**
3 Gresham Road, Staines, Middlesex TW18 2BT
Tel: 01784 450909/452916
Head: P A Monger MA, PGCE
Type: Co-educational Day B3-12 G3-12
No of pupils: B248 G172
Fees: DAY £2730-£3255

Stanmore

PETERBOROUGH & ST MARGARET'S HIGH SCHOOL
Common Road, Stanmore, Middlesex HA7 3JB
Tel: 0181 950 3600
Head: Mrs D M Tomlinson
Type: Girls Day G4-16
No of pupils: G218
Fees: DAY £2928-£4440

Twickenham

THE MALL SCHOOL
185 Hampton Road, Twickenham, Middlesex TW2 5NQ
Tel: 0181 977 2523
Head: T P A MacDonogh MA
Type: Boys Day B4-13
No of pupils: B290
Fees: DAY £3900-£4530

NEWLAND HOUSE SCHOOL
32-34 Waldegrave Park, Twickenham, Middlesex TW1 4TQ
Tel: 0181 892 7479
Head: D J Ott BSc, UED(Rhodes)
Type: Co-educational Day B4-13 G4-13
No of pupils: B271 G146
Fees: DAY £3945-£4600

ST CATHERINE'S CATHOLIC SCHOOL
Cross Deep, Twickenham, Middlesex TW1 4QJ
Tel: 0181 891 2898
Head: Miss D Wynter BA
Type: Girls Day B3-10 G3-16
No of pupils: B5 G303
Fees: DAY £2985-£4050

ST CATHERINE'S PREPARATORY SCHOOL
Pope's Villa, Twickenham, Middlesex TW1 4QJ
Tel: 0181 892 1201
Head: Miss Winter
Type: Girls Day

★ **SUNFLOWER MONTESSORI SCHOOL**
8 Victoria Road, Twickenham, Middlesex TW1 3HW
Tel: 0181 891 2675
Principal: Peter Colbert
Head: Mrs J Yandell
Type: Co-educational Day B2fi-12 G2fi-12
No of pupils: B33 G41
Fees: DAY £1755-£3255

Uxbridge

★ **THE AMERICAN COMMUNITY SCHOOL**
Hillingdon Court, 108 Vine Lane, Hillingdon, Uxbridge,
Middlesex UB10 0BE
Tel: 01895 259771
Head: Paul Berg
Type: Co-educational Day B4-18 G4-18
No of pupils: B290 G288
Fees: On application

PIELD HEATH SCHOOL
Pield Heath Road, Uxbridge, Middlesex UB8 3NW
Tel: 01895 258507
Head: Sr Julie Rose
Type: Co-educational Boarding & Day B7-19 G7-19
No of pupils: B54 G46
Fees: FB £17,397-£20,358 DAY £10,501

ST HELEN'S COLLEGE
Parkway, Uxbridge, Middlesex UB10 9JX
Tel: 01895 234371
Heads: D A Crehan MSc, ARCS &
      Mrs G R Crehan BA, PGCE
Type: Co-educational Day B3-11 G3-11
No of pupils: B131 G135
Fees: DAY £2220-£2475

Wembley

BUXLOW PREPARATORY SCHOOL
5/6 Castleton Gardens, Wembley, Middlesex HA9 7QJ
Tel: 0181 904 3615
Head: Mrs B L Lancaster DipCST
Type: Co-educational Day B4-11 G4-11
No of pupils: B64 G53
Fees: DAY £3060

ST CHRISTOPHER'S SCHOOL
71 Wembley Park Drive, Wembley, Middlesex HA9 8HE
Tel: 0181 902 5069
Head: Mrs S M Morley DipEd
Type: Co-educational Day B4-11 G4-11
No of pupils: B54 G54
Fees: DAY £2775-£3150

Surrey

Cheam

AMBLESIDE SCHOOL
1 West Drive, Cheam, Surrey SM2 7NB
Tel: 0181 642 2862
Head: Mrs L M Vaughan Stevens MontDip
Type: Co-educational Day B3-8 G3-8
No of pupils: B14 G45
Fees: DAY £1638-£3381

GLAISDALE SCHOOL
14 Arundel Road, Cheam,
Surrey SM2 7AD
Tel: 0181 288 1488
Head: Mrs H M Steel BEd(Hons), CertEd
Type: Co-educational Day B3-11 G3-11
No of pupils: B63 G119
Fees: DAY £345-£2670

Croydon

CAMBRIDGE TUTORS COLLEGE
Water Tower Hill, Croydon, Surrey CR0 5SX
Tel: 0181 688 5284/7363
Head: D N Wilson BA, MLitt, MIL, FCollP, FRSA
Type: Co-educational Day &
    Boarding B16-19 G16-19
No of pupils: VIth199
Fees: FB £10,390 DAY £8050

LINK DAY PRIMARY SCHOOL
138 Croydon Road, Croydon, Surrey CR0 4PG
Tel: 0181 688 5239
Head: Geoff Stewart AdvDipSen, CertEd
Type: Co-educational Day B6-12 G6-12
No of pupils: B27 G10
Fees: DAY £10,935

LINK SECONDARY DAY SCHOOL
84 Croydon Road, Croydon, Surrey CR0 4PD
Tel: 0181 688 7691
Head: W E Fuller MSc
Type: Co-educational Day B11-16 G11-16
No of pupils: B33 G2
Fees: DAY £11,601

NEW LIFE CHRISTIAN SCHOOL
Cairo New Road, Croydon, Surrey CR0 1XP
Tel: 0181 680 7671
Head: Mrs Ann C Weiner
Type: Co-educational Day & Boarding

OLD PALACE SCHOOL
Old Palace Road, Croydon, Surrey CR0 1AX
Tel: 0181 688 2027
Head: Miss K L Hilton BA, PGCE
Type: Girls Day G4-18
No of pupils: G820
Fees: DAY £2925-£3978

ROYAL RUSSELL SCHOOL
Coombe Lane, Croydon, Surrey CR9 5BX
Tel: 0181 657 4433
Head: Dr J R Jennings BSc, PhD
Type: Co-educational Boarding & Day B3-18 G3-18
No of pupils: B380 G200 VIth120 FB100 WB50
Fees: FB/WB £10,530 DAY £1305-£5550

★ TRINITY SCHOOL
Shirley Park, Croydon, Surrey CR9 7AT
Tel: 0181 656 9541
Head: B J Lenon MA
Type: Boys Day B10-18
No of pupils: B675 VIth215
Fees: DAY £5622

Kingston upon Thames

BUSHY PARK PRE SCHOOL
Church Grove, Kingston upon Thames,
Surrey KT1 4AL
Tel: 0181 614 8044
Head: Mrs Cook
Type: Co-educational Day B1-5 G1-5
Fees: DAY £5880-£4896

CANBURY SCHOOL
Kingston Hill, Kingston upon Thames,
Surrey KT2 7LN
Tel: 0181 549 8622
Head: J G Wyatt MA
Type: Co-educational Day B10-16 G10-17
No of pupils: B32 G10
Fees: DAY £4425

★ HOLY CROSS PREPARATORY SCHOOL
George Road, Kingston upon Thames,
Surrey KT2 7NU
Tel: 0181 942 0729
Head: Mrs M K Hayes MA
Type: Girls Day G4-11
No of pupils: G245
Fees: DAY £3390

KINGSTON GRAMMAR SCHOOL
70 London Road, Kingston upon Thames,
Surrey KT2 6PY
Tel: 0181 546 5875
Head: C D Baxter MA(Oxon), FRSA
Type: Co-educational Day B10-19 G10-19
No of pupils: B310 G152 VIth138
Fees: DAY £5560-£5830

MARYMOUNT INTERNATIONAL SCHOOL

George Road, Kingston upon Thames, Surrey KT2 7PE
Tel: 0181 949 0571
Head: Sr Rosaleen Sheridan RSHM, MSc
Type: Girls Day & Boarding G11-18
No of pupils: G222 VIth45 FB105 WB9
Fees: FB £13,100-£14,000 WB £12,900-£13,800
DAY £7200-£8100

PARK HILL SCHOOL

8 Queens Road, Kingston upon Thames,
Surrey KT2 7SH
Tel: 0181 546 5496
Head: Mrs M D Christie
Type: Co-educational Day B3-8 G3-11
No of pupils: B45 G75
Fees: DAY £1950-£3525

ROKEBY

George Road, Kingston upon Thames, Surrey KT2 7PB
Tel: 0181 942 2247
Head: R M Moody MA
Type: Boys Day B4-13
No of pupils: B363
Fees: DAY £3495-£5559

SURBITON HIGH SCHOOL

Surbiton Crescent, Kingston upon Thames,
Surrey KT1 2JT
Tel: 0181 546 5245
Head: Miss M G Perry BSc, MEd
Type: Girls Day B4-11 G4-18
No of pupils: B116 G795
Fees: DAY £2901-£4875

New Malden

BRETBY HOUSE SCHOOL

39 Woodlands Avenue, New Malden, Surrey KT3 3UL
Tel: 0181 942 5779
Head: Mrs E R T Myners CertEd(London)
Type: Co-educational Day B3-7 G3-7
No of pupils: B61 G64
Fees: DAY £602-£1312

THE STUDY SCHOOL

57 Thetford Road, New Malden, Surrey KT3 5DP
Tel: 0181 942 0754
Head: J H N Hudson BA
Type: Co-educational Day B3-11 G3-11
No of pupils: B80 G50
Fees: DAY £1455-£3560

WESTBURY HOUSE

80 Westbury Road, New Malden, Surrey KT3 5AS
Tel: 0181 942 5885
Head: Mrs M T Morton CertEd
Type: Co-educational Day B3-11 G3-11
No of pupils: B93 G79
Fees: DAY £1605-£3435

Purley

COMMONWEAL LODGE SCHOOL

Woodcote Lane, Purley, Surrey CR8 3HB
Tel: 0181 660 3179
Head: Mrs S C Law BEd, MA, LRAM, FRSA
Type: Girls Day G3-18
No of pupils: G160 VIth12
Fees: DAY £1515-£4725

DOWNSIDE SCHOOL

Woodcote Lane, Purley, Surrey CR8 3HB
Tel: 0181 660 0558
Head: T M Andrews BA, CertFPS
Type: Boys Day B3-13
No of pupils: B180
Fees: DAY £1755-£4515

LALEHAM LEA PREPARATORY SCHOOL

29 Peaks Hill, Purley, Surrey CR8 3JJ
Tel: 0181 660 3351
Head: A C F Baseley
Type: Co-educational Day B3-11 G3-11
No of pupils: B72 G33
Fees: DAY £800-£2400

OAKWOOD

Godstone Road, Purley, Surrey CR8 2AN
Tel: 0181 668 8080
Head: Mrs P M Shanks
Type: Co-educational Day

REEDHAM PARK

Old Lodge Lane, Purley, Surrey CR8 4DM
Tel: 0181 660 6357
Head: Miss Routledge
Type: Co-educational Day & Boarding

ST DAVID'S SCHOOL

23/25 Woodcote Valley Road, Purley,
Surrey CR8 3AL
Tel: 0181 660 0723
Head: Mrs L Randall BEd
Type: Co-educational Day B3-11 G3-11
No of pupils: B85 G82
Fees: DAY £2130-£2595

WEST DENE SCHOOL

167 Brighton Road, Purley, Surrey CR8 4HE
Tel: 0181 660 2404
Head: Mrs G Charkin CertEd
Type: Co-educational Day B3-8 G3-8
No of pupils: B45 G85
Fees: DAY £1635-£2610

Richmond

BROOMFIELD HOUSE SCHOOL
Broomfield Road, Richmond, Surrey TW9 3HS
Tel: 0181 940 3884
Head: Mrs I O Harrow GTCL, LTCL, AMusTCI
Type: Co-educational Day B3-11 G3-11
No of pupils: B50 G80
Fees: DAY £1875-£3750

THE GERMAN SCHOOL
Douglas House, Richmond, Surrey TW10 7AH
Tel: 0181 948 3410/940 5724
Head: E Backhaus
Type: Co-educational Day B5-19 G5-19
Fees: DAY £1440-£2205

KEW COLLEGE
24-26 Cumberland Road, Richmond,
Surrey TW9 3HQ
Tel: 0181 940 2039
Head: Mrs D Lyness
Type: Co-educational Day B3-11 G3-11
Fees: DAY £1800-£2175

KING'S HOUSE SCHOOL
68 King's Road, Richmond, Surrey TW10 6ES
Tel: 0181 940 1878
Head: R Armitage
Type: Boys Day B4-13
No of pupils: B340
Fees: DAY £3360-£4725

OLD VICARAGE SCHOOL
48 Richmond Hill, Richmond, Surrey TW10 6QX
Tel: 0181 940 0922
Head: Miss J C F Reynolds BEd
Type: Girls Day G4-11
No of pupils: G168
Fees: DAY £3420-£4200

UNICORN SCHOOL
238 Kew Road, Richmond, Surrey TW9 3JX
Tel: 0181 948 3926
Head: Mrs F Timmis CertEd(London)
Type: Co-educational Day B3-11 G3-11
No of pupils: B79 G80
Fees: DAY £2295-£4275

South Croydon

BEECH HOUSE PREPARATORY SCHOOL
15 Church Way, South Croydon, Surrey CR2 OJT
Tel: 0181 651 0446
Head: Mrs M Robinson
Type: Co-educational Day B3-7 G3-7
No of pupils: B20 G20
Fees: DAY £1320-£1815

★ CROHAM HURST SCHOOL
79 Croham Road, South Croydon,
Surrey CR2 7YN
Tel: 0181 680 3064
Head: Miss S C Budgen BA
Type: Girls Day G3-18
No of pupils: G558 VIth63
Fees: DAY £2370-£4890

CROYDON HIGH SCHOOL GPDST
Old Farleigh Road, South Croydon,
Surrey CR2 8YB
Tel: 0181 651 5020
Head: Mrs P E Davies BSc, MEd
Type: Girls Day G4-18
No of pupils: G819 VIth189
Fees: DAY £3036-£4140

★ CUMNOR HOUSE SCHOOL
168 Pampisford Road, South Croydon,
Surrey CR2 6DA
Tel: 0181 660 3445
Head: J T Jenkins MA(Cantab)
Type: Boys Day B4-13
No of pupils: B330
Fees: DAY £3885-£4425

ELMHURST SCHOOL
44-48 South Park Hill Road, South Croydon,
Surrey CR2 7DW
Tel: 0181 688 0661
Heads: B K Dighton CertEd &
   R E Anderson DipEd, ACP
Type: Boys Day B4-11
No of pupils: B230
Fees: DAY £3300-£3900

FOLLY END CHRISTIAN SCHOOL
9 South Park Hill Road, South Croydon,
Surrey CR2 7DY
Tel: 0181 649 9121
Head: S Poole BEd(Hons)
Type: Co-educational Day B4-11 G4-11
No of pupils: B20 G24
Fees: DAY £1512-£1632

RUTHERFORD SCHOOL
1A Melville Avenue, South Croydon, Surrey CR2 7HZ
Tel: 0181 688 7560
Head: Ms R G Hills CertEd
Type: Co-educational Day B2-12 G2-12
No of pupils: B14 G10
Fees: DAY £18270

SANDERSTEAD JUNIOR SCHOOL
29 Purley Oaks Road, South Croydon, Surrey CR2 0NW
Tel: 0181 660 0801
Head: Mrs A Barns
Type: Co-educational Day B4-12 G4-12
Fees: DAY £1755-£3159

WHITGIFT SCHOOL
Haling Park, South Croydon, Surrey CR2 6YT
Tel: 0181 688 9222
Head: Dr C A Barnett MA, DPhil
Type: Boys Day B10-18
No of pupils: B1100
Fees: DAY £5826

Surbiton

LINLEY HOUSE
6 Berrylands Road, Surbiton, Surrey KT5 8RA
Tel: 0181 399 4979
Head: Mrs S M Mallin CertEd(Bristol)
Type: Co-educational Day B3-7 G3-7
No of pupils: B10 G20
Fees: DAY £1860-£2595

SHREWSBURY HOUSE SCHOOL
107 Ditton Road, Surbiton, Surrey KT6 6RL
Tel: 0181 399 3066
Head: Mr C M Ross BA, HDipEd, TCD
Type: Boys Day B7-13
No of pupils: B260
Fees: DAY £5475

SURBITON PREPARATORY SCHOOL
3 Avenue Elmers, Surbiton, Surrey KT6 4SP
Tel: 0181 546 5245
Head: S J Pryce
Type: Co-educational Day B5-11 G5-11
Fees: DAY £2700-£3795

Sutton

HOMEFIELD PREPARATORY SCHOOL
Western Road, Sutton, Surrey SM1 2TE
Tel: 0181 642 0965
Head: P R Mowbray BA
Type: Boys Day B5-13
No of pupils: B280
Fees: DAY £2340-£3870

SEATON HOUSE SCHOOL
67 Banstead Road South, Sutton, Surrey SM2 5LH
Tel: 0181 642 2332
Head: Mrs J R Harrison
Type: Girls Day G3-11
No of pupils: G175
Fees: DAY £1365-£2880

STOWFORD
95 Brighton Road, Sutton, Surrey SM2 5SJ
Tel: 0181 661 9444
Head: R J Shakespeare BA, MA, MA
Type: Co-educational Day B7-17 G7-17
No of pupils: B46 G20
Fees: DAY £2940-£4700

SUTTON HIGH SCHOOL (GPDST)
55 Cheam Road, Sutton, Surrey SM1 2AX
Tel: 0181 642 0594
Head: Mrs Anne Coutts BSc, MEd
Type: Girls Day G4-18
No of pupils: G636 VIth140
Fees: DAY £3864-£4920

Wallington

COLLINGWOOD SCHOOL
3 Springfield Road, Wallington, Surrey SM6 0BD
Tel: 0181 647 4607
Head: D W Sweet BSc(Hons), MEd, FCollP, CertEd
Type: Co-educational Day B3-11 G3-11
No of pupils: B108 G28
Fees: DAY £945-£3030

Geographical Directory of
Schools in the South East

Berkshire

Aldermaston

CEDARS SCHOOL
Church Road, Aldermaston, Berkshire RG7 4LR
Tel: 0174 714251
Head: Mrs A E Ludlow CertEd
Type: Co-educational Day B4-11 G4-11
No of pupils: B18 G18
Fees: DAY £2685

Ascot

★ HEATHFIELD SCHOOL
London Road, Ascot, Berkshire SL5 8BQ
Tel: 01344 882955
Head: Mrs J M Benammar BA, MèsL
Type: Girls Boarding G11-18
No of pupils: G215 VIth57 FB215
Fees: FB £4375

LICENSED VICTUALLERS' SCHOOL
London Road, Ascot, Berkshire SL5 8DR
Tel: 01344 882770
Head: Mr I A Mullins BEd(Hons), MSc, MBIM
Type: Co-educational Boarding & Day B4-18 G4-18
No of pupils: B375 G228 VIth79 FB98 WB66
Fees: FB/WB £8937-£9930 DAY £3699-£5610

MARIST CONVENT JUNIOR SCHOOL
Kings Road, Ascot, Berkshire SL5 7PS
Tel: 01344 26137
Head: Sr Kathleen Kelly
Type: Co-educational Day & Boarding

MARIST SENIOR SCHOOL
Kings Road, Ascot, Berkshire SL5 7PS
Tel: 01344 24291
Head: Mrs K Butwilowska JP, BA, Med
Type: Girls Day G11-18
No of pupils: G331 VIth76
Fees: DAY £4200

PAPPLEWICK
Windsor Road, Ascot, Berkshire SL5 7LH
Tel: 01344 21488
Head: D R LLewellyn BA, DipEd
Type: Boys Boarding & Day B7-14
No of pupils: B190 FB120
Fees: FB £9345 DAY £7176

ST GEORGE'S SCHOOL
Ascot, Berkshire SL5 7DZ
Tel: 01344 20273
Head: Mrs A M Griggs BA, TCert
Type: Girls Boarding & Day G11-18
No of pupils: G214 VIth75
Fees: FB £11,625 DAY £6825

ST MARY'S SCHOOL
St Mary's Road, Ascot, Berkshire SL5 9JF
Tel: 01344 23721/27788
Head: Sr M Frances Orchard IBVM, BA, PGCE
Type: Girls Boarding & Day G11-18
No of pupils: G241 VIth95 FB326
Fees: FB £11,833 DAY £7101

STUBBINGTON HOUSE
Bagshot Road, Ascot, Berkshire SL5 9JU
Tel: 01344 874666
Head: Mrs P E Goodwin CertEd, Froebel, CertInfEd
Type: Co-educational Boarding & Day B2-13 G2-13
No of pupils: B52 G31 FB15
Fees: FB £8100 WB £7200 DAY £2700-£3450

SUNNINGDALE
Ascot, Berkshire SL5 9PY
Tel: 01344 20159
Heads: A J N Dawson & T M E Dawson DipIAPS
Type: Boys Boarding B8-13
No of pupils: B115 FB120
Fees: FB £7350

Bracknell

BRACKNELL MONTESSORI SCHOOL
Berkshire Guide Centre, Bracknell, Berkshire RG42 1GG
Tel: 01344 50922
Head: Mrs E Ashcroft
Type: Co-educational Day B2-6 G2-6
No of pupils: B30 G30
Fees: DAY £1098-£2958

LAMBROOK
Winkfield Row, Bracknell, Berkshire RG42 6LY
Tel: 01344 882717
Head: R Badham-Thornhill BA, PGCE
Type: Co-educational Boarding & Day B4-13 G4-13
No of pupils: B135 G12
Fees: FB £6360-£8925 DAY £3315-£6360

MEADOWBROOK MONTESSORI SCHOOL
Malt Hill Road, Bracknell, Berkshire RG12 6JQ
Tel: 01344 890869
Head: Mrs Helen Watkins
Type: Co-educational Day & Boarding

NEWBOLD SCHOOL
Popeswood Road, Bracknell, Berkshire RG42 4AH
Tel: 01344 421088
Head: M Brooks CertEd
Type: Co-educational Day B3-11 G3-11
No of pupils: B40 G40
Fees: DAY £1410-£1770

SWAAY SCHOOL
Foxhill Centre, Pondmoor Road, Bracknell,
Berkshire RG12 7JZ
Tel: 01344 304013
Head: Mrs P Vigneswaren
Type: Co-educational Day

Brimpton

SEK INTERNATIONAL SCHOOL
Little Park House, Brimpton, Berkshire RG7 4ST
Tel: 01734 713213
Head: J Casavo
Type: Co-educational Day & Boarding

Cookham Dean

HERRIES SCHOOL
Dean Lane, Cookham Dean, Berkshire SL6 9BD
Tel: 01628 483350
Head: D G Hare BEd(Hons)
Type: Co-educational Day B2-13 G2-13
No of pupils: B15 G65
Fees: DAY £470-£1335

Crowthorne

OUR LADY'S PREPARATORY SCHOOL
The Avenue, Crowthorne, Berkshire RG11 6PB
Tel: 01344 773394
Head: Mrs S T Hayden
Type: Co-educational Day & Boarding

WAVERLEY SCHOOL
Ravenswood Avenue, Crowthorne, Berkshire RG45 6AY
Tel: 01344 772379
Head: Stuart G Melton BSc, PGCE
Type: Co-educational Day B3-11 G3-11
No of pupils: B80 G70
Fees: DAY £1620-£3459

WELLINGTON COLLEGE
Crowthorne, Berkshire RG45 7PU
Tel: 01344 771588
Head: C J Driver BA, BEd, MPhil
Type: Boys Boarding & Day B13-18 G16-18
No of pupils: B744 G51 FB690
Fees: FB £12,270 DAY £8955

Hungerford

THE NORLAND COLLEGE
Denford Park, Hungerford, Berkshire RG17 OPQ
Tel: 01488 682252
Head: Mrs L E Davis MPhil, RGN, FRSH
Type: Co-educational Day & Boarding B17-99 G17-99
Fees: FB £11,550 DAY £7410

Maidenhead

CLAIRES COURT SCHOOL
Ray Mill Road East, Maidenhead, Berkshire SL6 8TE
Tel: 01628 411471
Head: D H Course BA
Type: Boys Day B11-18 G16-18
No of pupils: B216 VIth52
Fees: DAY £4605-£5325

HIGHFIELD SCHOOL TRUST LTD
2 West Road, Maidenhead, Berkshire SL6 1PD
Tel: 01628 24918
Head: Mrs C M A Lane
Type: Co-educational Day B2-7 G2-11
No of pupils: B30 G150
Fees: DAY £522-£4110

MAIDENHEAD COLLEGE CLAIRES COURT GIRLS
1 College Avenue, Maidenhead, Berkshire SL6 6AW
Tel: 01628 411480
Head: Mrs A C Pitts CertEd
Type: Girls Day B2-11 G2-18
No of pupils: B54 G214 VIth52
Fees: DAY £3345-£4965

REDROOFS THEATRE SCHOOL
26 Bath Road, Maidenhead, Berkshire SL6 4JT
Tel: 01628 74092
Heads: June Rose FLCM, RADA(Voc) &
        Bridget Jenkins BA(Hons)(Acad)
Type: Co-educational Day B7-16 G7-16
No of pupils: B28 G32
Fees: DAY £3111

RIDGEWAY SCHOOL (CLAIRES COURT JUNIOR)
Maidenhead, Berkshire SL6 3QE
Tel: 01628 822609
Head: K M Boyd
Type: Boys Day B4-11
No of pupils: B229
Fees: DAY £3480-£4425

SILCHESTER HOUSE SCHOOL
Bath Road, Maidenhead, Berkshire SL6 0AP
Tel: 01628 20549
Head: Mrs D J Austen CertEd(London)
Type: Co-educational Day B2-12 G2-12
No of pupils: B61 G72
Fees: DAY £2700-£3960

ST PIRAN'S PREPARATORY SCHOOL
Gringer Hill, Maidenhead, Berkshire SL6 7LZ
Tel: 01628 27316
Head: A P Blumer CertEd
Type: Co-educational Day B3-13 G3-13
No of pupils: B225 G45
Fees: DAY £2760-£5490

WINBURY SCHOOL
Hibbert Road, Maidenhead, Berkshire SL6 1UU
Tel: 01628 27412
Head: Mrs P Prewett CertEd
Type: Co-educational Day B3-8 G3-8
No of pupils: B37 G37
Fees: DAY £1665-£2745

Newbury

BROCKHURST PRE-PREPARATORY SCHOOL
Ridge House, Newbury, Berkshire RG16 9HZ
Tel: 01635 863259
Head: Mrs R A Fleming
Type: Co-educational Day B2-7 G2-7
Fees: DAY £615-£3072

★ CHEAM HAWTREYS
Headley, Newbury, Berkshire RG19 8LD
Tel: 01635 268242
Head: C C Evers BA
Type: Boys Boarding & Day B7-13
No of pupils: B132
Fees: FB £9600 DAY £6780

FALKLAND ST GABRIEL
Sandleford Priory, Newbury, Berkshire RG15 9BB
Tel: 01635 40663
Head: Mrs J H Felton MA
Type: Girls Day B3-7 G3-11
No of pupils: B3 G7
Fees: DAY £1576-£3414

GREENHILL SCHOOL
Horris Hill, Newbury, Berkshire RG20 9DJ
Tel: 01635 40594
Head: Amanda le Quesne
Type: Co-educational Day

HORRIS HILL
Newbury, Berkshire RG20 9DJ
Tel: 01635 40594
Head: N J Chapman BA
Type: Boys Boarding & Day B8-13
No of pupils: B110
Fees: FB £9800 DAY £6600

MARLSTON HOUSE PREPARATORY SCHOOL
Newbury, Berkshire RG16 9UL
Tel: 01635 200293
Head: A J Pudden MA
Type: Girls Day G2-11
No of pupils: G45
Fees: DAY £3300-£6840

PRIOR'S COURT PREPARATORY SCHOOL
Newbury, Berkshire RG18 9NU
Tel: 01635 248209
Head: P B High MA, BSc, DLC, FRGS
Type: Co-educational Boarding & Day B3-13 G3-13
No of pupils: B120 G60 FB70
Fees: FB £9000 DAY £3000-£6000

ST GABRIEL'S SCHOOL
Sandleford Priory, Newbury, Berkshire RG20 9BD
Tel: 01635 40663
Head: D J Cobb BA(Lond)
Type: Girls Day B3-8 G3-18
No of pupils: B14 G350
Fees: DAY £774-£5196

ST MICHAELS SCHOOL
Harts Lane, Newbury, Berkshire RG20 9JW
Tel: 01635 278137/253 209
Head: Fr Paul Morgan
Type: Co-educational Day & Boarding B7-16 G7-16
No of pupils: B37 G38 FB18 WB52
Fees: FB/WB £4500 DAY £1800

THORNGROVE SCHOOL
The Mount, Newbury, Berkshire RG15 9PS
Tel: 01635 253172
Heads: Mr & Mrs N J Broughton
Type: Co-educational Day B2-13 G2-13
No of pupils: B65 G55
Fees: DAY £3555-£4596

Padworth

ALDER BRIDGE SCHOOL
Mill Lane, Padworth, Berkshire RG7 4JU
Type: Co-educational Day

Reading

THE ABBEY SCHOOL
Kendrick Road, Reading, Berkshire RG1 5DZ
Tel: 01734 872256
Head: Miss B C L Sheldon BA, CertEd, ACE
Type: Girls Day B4-7 G4-18
No of pupils: G830 VIth180
Fees: DAY £3525-£4350

THE ARK SCHOOL
School Road, Reading, Berkshire RG7 4JA
Tel: 01734 83 802
Head: J S Hartley MA(Oxon), PGCE
Type: Co-educational Day B2-8 G2-8
No of pupils: B30 G34

BRADFIELD COLLEGE
Reading, Berkshire RG7 6AR
Tel: 01734 744203
Head: Mr P B Smith MA
Type: Boys Boarding B13-18 G16-18
No of pupils: B500 G120
Fees: FB £4275 DAY £3206

CHRISTCHURCH GARDENS KINDERGARTEN
5 Christchurch Gardens, Reading, Berkshire RG2 7AH
Tel: 01734 866301
Type: Co-educational Day

CROSFIELDS SCHOOL
Reading, Berkshire RG2 9BL
Tel: 01734 871810
Head: F G Skipwith
Type: Boys Day B4-13
No of pupils: B345
Fees: DAY £2850-£5190

DOUAI SCHOOL
Reading, Berkshire RG7 5TH
Tel: 01734 715200
Head: Dom E Power OSB, MA, PhD
Type: Co-educational Boarding & Day B10-18 G10-18
No of pupils: B100 G30 VIth70
Fees: FB £10,545 WB £8445 DAY £5535-£6780

ELSTREE SCHOOL
Reading, Berkshire RG7 5TD
Tel: 0118 971 3302
Head: S M Hill MA(Cantab)
Type: Co-educational Day & Boarding B3-13 G3-13
No of pupils: B190 G15 FB100
Fees: FB £9600 DAY £6840

FOXLEY PNEU SCHOOL
Manor Drive, Reading, Berkshire RG10 OPX
Tel: 01734 343578
Head: Miss M J Fallon Montessori Dip
Type: Co-educational Day B3-7 G3-7
No of pupils: B14 G9
Fees: DAY £1922

HEMDEAN HOUSE SCHOOL
Hemdean Road, Reading, Berkshire RG4 8LA
Tel: 01734 472590
Head: Mrs P L Pethybridge BA(Hons)
Type: Co-educational Day B2-16 G2-16
No of pupils: B45 G95
Fees: DAY £2250-£3225

THE HIGHLANDS SCHOOL
Wardle Avenue, Reading, Berkshire RG3 6JR
Tel: 01734 427186
Head: Miss E D Lind-Smith CertEd(Camb)
Type: Co-educational Day B3-8 G3-11
No of pupils: B44 G116
Fees: DAY £2088-£3312

LEIGHTON PARK SCHOOL
Shinfield Road, Reading, Berkshire RG2 7DH
Tel: 01734 872065
Head: J H Dunston MA
Type: Co-educational Boarding & Day B11-18 G11-18
No of pupils: B178 G68 VIth121
Fees: FB £9999-£11,754 DAY £7416-£8820

THE ORATORY PREPARATORY SCHOOL
Great Oaks, Reading, Berkshire RG8 7SF
Tel: 01734 844511
Head: D L Sexon BA, PGCE
Type: Co-educational Day & Boarding B3-13 G3-13
No of pupils: B229 G68
Fees: FB £7965 DAY £1587-£5760

THE ORATORY SCHOOL
Reading, Berkshire RG8 OPJ
Tel: 01491 680207
Head: S W Barrow BA
Type: Boys Boarding & Day B11-18
No of pupils: B276 VIth138
Fees: FB £9255-£11,760 DAY £6675-£8220

PADWORTH COLLEGE
Reading, Berkshire RG7 4NR
Tel: 01734 832644/5
Head: Dr S Villazon MA, PhD, FRSA
Type: Girls Boarding & Day G14-19
No of pupils: G125
Fees: FB £11,262 DAY £5631

PANGBOURNE COLLEGE
Reading, Berkshire RG8 8LA
Tel: 01734 842101/2
Head: A B E Hudson MA(Oxon), DipEd(Lond)
Type: Co-educational Boarding & Day B11-18 G11-18
No of pupils: B191 G8 VIth159
Fees: FB £8625-£11,880 DAY £6030-£8310

PRESENTATION COLLEGE
63 Bath Road, Reading, Berkshire RG30 2BB
Tel: 01734 572861
Head: Rev Terence Hurley BSc, HDE, FPM
Type: Boys Day B4-18 G16-18
No of pupils: B350
Fees: DAY £3240-£3600

QUEEN ANNE'S SCHOOL
6 Henley Road, Reading, Berkshire RG4 6DX
Tel: 0118 947 1582
Head: Mrs D Forbes MA(Oxon)
Type: Girls Boarding & Day G11-18
No of pupils: G320 VIth120
Fees: FB £11,820 DAY £7740

ST ANDREW'S SCHOOL
Buckhold, Reading, Berkshire RG8 8QA
Tel: 0118 974 4276
Head: J M Snow BA, CertEd
Type: Co-educational Day & Boarding B4-13 G4-13
No of pupils: B162 G96
Fees: FB £8400-£8550 WB £7800-£7950
DAY £3450-£6180

ST EDWARD'S SCHOOL
64 Tilehurst Road, Reading, Berkshire RG30 2JH
Tel: 0118 957 4342
Head: R A McComas BA, CertEd
Type: Boys Day B7-13
No of pupils: B116
Fees: DAY £3231-£3360

ST JOSEPH'S CONVENT SCHOOL
64 Upper Redlands Road, Reading, Berkshire RG1 5JT
Tel: 0118 966 1000
Head: Mrs V Brookes BEd
Type: Girls Day G11-18
No of pupils: G287 VIth63
Fees: DAY £4065

ST JOSEPH'S PREPARATORY SCHOOL
66 Upper Redlands Road, Reading, Berkshire RG1 5JT
Tel: 01734 351717
Head: Sr Helen-Marie
Type: Girls Day B3-7 G3-11
No of pupils: B25 G155
Fees: DAY £2160

Slough

ETON END PNEU SCHOOL
35 Eton Road, Slough, Berkshire SL3 9AX
Tel: 01753 541075
Head: Mrs B E Ottley CertEd
Type: Girls Day B3-7 G3-11
No of pupils: B65 G160
Fees: DAY £2955-£3795

LANGLEY MANOR SCHOOL
St Mary's Road, Slough, Berkshire SL3 6BZ
Tel: 01753 825368/77005
Head: Mrs S Eaton BEd
Type: Co-educational Day B3-12 G3-12
No of pupils: B140 G124
Fees: DAY £3237-£3372

LONG CLOSE SCHOOL
Upton Court Road, Slough, Berkshire SL3 7LU
Tel: 01753 520095
Head: M H Kneath BEd
Type: Co-educational Day B3-13 G3-13
No of pupils: B146 G50
Fees: DAY £1775-£5265

ST BERNARD'S PREPARATORY SCHOOL
Hawtrey Close, Slough, Berkshire SL1 1TB
Tel: 01753 521821
Head: Mrs M F Casey
Type: Girls Day B3-12 G3-12
No of pupils: B40 G159
Fees: DAY £3030-£3210

Sonning-on-Thames

READING BLUE COAT SCHOOL
Holme Park, Sonning-on-Thames, Berkshire RG4 6SU
Tel: 0118 944 1005
Head: Rev A C E Sanders MA(Oxon), MEd
Type: Boys Day & Boarding B11-18 G16-18
No of pupils: B545 G45 VIth190 FB25 WB40
Fees: FB £10,050 WB £9735 DAY £5514

Sunningdale

HURST LODGE
Charters Road, Sunningdale, Berkshire SL5 9QG
Tel: 01344 22154
Head: Mrs A Smit
Type: Girls Day & Boarding B2-7 G2-18
No of pupils: B22 G178
Fees: FB £10,485 DAY £1905-£6195

Thatcham

DOWNE HOUSE SCHOOL
Thatcham, Berkshire RG20 9JJ
Tel: 01635 200286
Head: Mrs A Gwatkin MA London
Type: Girls Boarding & Day G11-18
No of pupils: G610 VIth168
Fees: FB £12,915 DAY £9360

Twyford

CEDAR PARK SCHOOL
Bridge Farm Road, Twyford, Berkshire RG10 9PP
Tel: 01734 340118
Head: Mrs C D Christie BSc, PGCE
Type: Co-educational Day B2-7 G2-7
No of pupils: B38 G38
Fees: DAY £690-£4700

Windsor

THE BRIGIDINE SCHOOL
King's Road, Windsor, Berkshire SL4 2AX
Tel: 01753 863779
Head: Mrs M B Cairns BSc
Type: Girls Day B3-7 G3-18
No of pupils: B4 G322 VIth30
Fees: DAY £3210-£4680

ETON COLLEGE
Windsor, Berkshire SL4 6DW
Tel: 01753 671000
Head: John E Lewis MA
Type: Boys Boarding B13-18
No of pupils: B776 VIth502
Fees: FB £13,410

HAILEYBURY JUNIOR SCHOOL
Clewer Manor, Windsor, Berkshire SL4 3RS
Tel: 01753 866330
Head: B J Hare MA, CertEd
Type: Boys Boarding & Day B7-13
No of pupils: B174 FB35 WB11
Fees: FB £7875 DAY £6150

ST GEORGE'S SCHOOL
Windsor Castle, Windsor, Berkshire SL4 1QF
Tel: 01753 865553
Head: Rev Roger Marsh
Type: Boys Boarding & Day B3-13
No of pupils: B70 G8 WB10
Fees: FB £8580 WB £8430 DAY £5790-£6390

ST JOHN'S BEAUMONT
Windsor, Berkshire SL4 2JN
Tel: 01784 432428
Head: D St J Gogarty MA, PGCE
Type: Boys Boarding & Day B4-13
No of pupils: B215 FB17 WB18
Fees: FB/WB £8331-£9954 DAY £3429-£6027

UPTON HOUSE SCHOOL
115 St Leonard's Road, Windsor, Berkshire SL4 3DF
Tel: 01753 862610
Head: Mrs J Woodley BA, CertEd
Type: Girls Day B3-7 G3-11
No of pupils: B63 G143
Fees: DAY £1755-£3990

Wokingham

BEARWOOD COLLEGE
Wokingham, Berkshire RG41 5BG
Tel: 01734 786915
Head: R J Belcher BSc, PhD, CBiol, MIBiol
Type: Co-educational Boarding & Day B11-19 G11-19
No of pupils: B142 G6 VIth69
Fees: FB £9450-£10,500 DAY £5265-£5850

HOLME GRANGE SCHOOL
Heathlands Road, Wokingham, Berkshire RG40 3AL
Tel: 0118 978 1566/0118 977 4524
Head: N J Brodrick BEd
Type: Co-educational Day B3-13 G3-13
No of pupils: B167 G119
Fees: DAY £1800-£4836

LUCKLEY-OAKFIELD SCHOOL
Luckley Road, Wokingham, Berkshire RG40 3EU
Tel: 01734 784175
Head: R C Blake MA(Oxon), MPhil(Soton)
Type: Girls Day & Boarding G11-18
No of pupils: G180 VIth50 FB45 WB45
Fees: FB £8349 WB £8184 DAY £5175

LUDGROVE
Wokingham, Berkshire RG40 3AB
Tel: 01734 789881
Heads: G W P Barber MA & C N J Marston MA
Type: Boys Boarding B8-13
No of pupils: B197 FB190
Fees: FB £9150

WHITE HOUSE PREPARATORY SCHOOL
Finchampstead Road, Wokingham, Berkshire RG11 3HD
Tel: 01734 785151
Head: Mrs M L Blake BA
Type: Co-educational Day B3-7 G3-11
No of pupils: B27 G110
Fees: DAY £1005-£3375

Buckinghamshire

Amersham

THE BEACON SCHOOL
Chesham Bois, Amersham, Buckinghamshire HP6 5PF
Tel: 01494 433654
Head: J V Cross BA(Hons), PGCE
Type: Boys Day B3-13
No of pupils: B310
Fees: DAY £1794-£5745

HEATHERTON HOUSE SCHOOL
Copperkins Lane, Amersham, Buckinghamshire HP6 5QB
Tel: 01494 726433
Head: Mrs P K Thomson BA, CertEd
Type: Girls Day B3-5 G3-12
No of pupils: B20 G135
Fees: DAY £1515-£4185

Aylesbury

ASHFOLD SCHOOL
Aylesbury, Buckinghamshire HP18 9NG
Tel: 01844 238237
Head: D H M Dalrymple
Type: Co-educational Boarding & Day B3-14 G3-14
No of pupils: B120 G50 FB8 WB18
Fees: FB £7965 WB £7965 DAY £1935-£6060

LADYMEDE SCHOOL
Aylesbury, Buckinghamshire HP17 0XP
Tel: 01844 346154
Head: Mrs V Cloutt BEd(Hons), FCollP
Type: Co-educational Day B3-12 G3-12
Fees: DAY £1650-£4440

Beaconsfield

DAVENIES SCHOOL
Station Road, Beaconsfield, Buckinghamshire HP9 1AA
Tel: 01494 674169
Head: J R Jones BEd(Oxon)
Type: Boys Day B4-13
No of pupils: B260
Fees: DAY £4080-£4485

HIGH MARCH SCHOOL
23 Ledborough Lane, Beaconsfield,
Buckinghamshire HP9 2PZ
Tel: 01494 675186
Head: Mrs P A Forsyth MA
Type: Girls Day B3-7 G3-13
No of pupils: B17 G305
Fees: DAY £1440-£4410

Buckingham

AKELEY WOOD SCHOOL
Buckingham, Buckinghamshire MK18 5AE
Tel: 01280 814110
Head: J C Lovelock BA, CertEd
Type: Co-educational Day B10-18 G10-18
No of pupils: B200 G160
Fees: DAY £3795-£4380

STOWE SCHOOL
Buckingham, Buckinghamshire MK18 5EH
Tel: 01280 813164
Head: Jeremy Nichols MA
Type: Boys Boarding & Day B13-18 G16-18
No of pupils: B446 G106 VIth296
Fees: FB £13,500 DAY £9450

Chesham

CHESHAM PREPARATORY SCHOOL
Chesham, Buckinghamshire HP5 3QF
Tel: 01494 782619
Head: R J H Ford DipEd, CertEd
Type: Co-educational Day B5-13 G5-13
No of pupils: B173 G135
Fees: DAY £2985-£3795

Farnham Royal

CALDICOTT
Crown Lane, Farnham Royal, Buckinghamshire SL2 3SL
Tel: 01753 644457
Head: M C B Spens MA
Type: Boys Boarding & Day B7-13
No of pupils: B259
Fees: FB £8910 DAY £6600

DAIR HOUSE SCHOOL TRUST LTD
Bishops Blake, Farnham Royal,
Buckinghamshire SL2 3BY
Tel: 01753 643964
Head: Mrs T A Devonside SRN, SCM Mont Dip Ed
Type: Co-educational Day B3-8 G3-8
No of pupils: B85 G23
Fees: DAY £1536-£3192

Gerrards Cross

GAYHURST SCHOOL
Bull Lane, Gerrards Cross, Buckinghamshire SL9 8RJ
Tel: 01753 882690
Head: Mr A J Simms MA(Cantab)
Type: Boys Day B4-13
No of pupils: B230
Fees: DAY £3420-£4710

HOLY CROSS CONVENT
The Grange, Gerrards Cross, Buckinghamshire SL9 9DW
Tel: 01753 895600
Head: Dr David Walker BA, MEd, Phd
Type: Girls Day & Boarding G4-18
No of pupils: G435 VIth35
Fees: FB £9000 DAY £3030-£3180

KINGSCOTE PRE-PREPARATORY SCHOOL
Oval Way, Gerrards Cross, Buckinghamshire SL9 8PZ
Tel: 01753 885535
Head: Mrs S A Tunstall CertEd
Type: Boys Day B4-7
No of pupils: B108
Fees: DAY £1260

★ MALTMAN'S GREEN SCHOOL
Maltman's Lane, Gerrards Cross,
Buckinghamshire SL9 8RR
Tel: 01753 883022
Head: Mrs M Evans BA(Hons), PGCE
Type: Girls Day G3-13
No of pupils: G370
Fees: DAY £1545-£5028

ST MARY'S SCHOOL
Packhorse Road, Gerrards Cross,
Buckinghamshire SL9 8JQ
Tel: 01753 883370
Head: Mrs F Balcombe BA(Hons), PGCE
Type: Girls Day G3-18
No of pupils: G270 VIth33
Fees: DAY £2765-£5295

THORPE HOUSE SCHOOL
Oval Way, Gerrards Cross, Buckinghamshire SL9 8PZ
Tel: 01753 882474
Head: Dr John Scaife
Type: Boys Day B4-13
No of pupils: B286
Fees: DAY £3780-£4770

Great Missenden

GATEWAY SCHOOL
1 High Street, Great Missenden,
Buckinghamshire HP16 9AA
Tel: 01494 862407
Heads: J L Wade BA, DASE, PGCE &
　　　Mrs J H Wade, BA, PGCE
Type: Co-educational Day B2-13 G2-13
No of pupils: B211 G152
Fees: DAY £1200-£4005

High Wycombe

CROWN HOUSE SCHOOL
19 London Road, High Wycombe,
Buckinghamshire HP11 1BJ
Tel: 01494 529927
Head: L Clark MA(Oxon)
Type: Co-educational Day B4-12 G4-12
No of pupils: B74 G70
Fees: DAY £3240

GODSTOWE PREPARATORY SCHOOL
Shubbery Road, High Wycombe,
Buckinghamshire HP13 6PR
Tel: 01494 529273
Head: Mrs F Henson BA(Hons), PGCE
Type: Girls Boarding & Day B3-8 G3-13
No of pupils: B22 G381 FB120
Fees: FB/WB £9180 DAY £1425-£5100

PIPERS CORNER SCHOOL
High Wycombe, Buckinghamshire HP15 6LP
Tel: 01494 718255
Head: Mrs V M Stattersfield, MA(Oxon), PGCE
Type: Girls Boarding & Day G4-18
No of pupils: G290 VIth60
Fees: FB £8004-£9702 WB £7944-£9582
DAY £2805-£5808

WYCOMBE ABBEY SCHOOL
High Wycombe, Buckinghamshire HP11 1PE
Tel: 01494 520381
Head: Mrs J M Goodland BA(Hons), CertEd
Type: Girls Boarding & Day G11-18
No of pupils: G340 VIth160
Fees: FB £12,780 DAY £9585

Milton Keynes

AKELEYWOOD JUNIOR SCHOOL
Wicken Park, Milton Keynes,
Buckinghamshire MK19 6DA
Tel: 01908 57231
Head: J C Lovelock
Type: Co-educational Day

BURY LAWN SCHOOL
Soskin Drive, Stantonbury Fields, Milton Keynes,
Buckinghamshire MK14 6DP
Tel: 01908 220345/01404 881702
Head: Mrs H W K Kiff BA(Hons), AdvCertEd
Type: Co-educational Day B1-18 G1-18
No of pupils: B177 G156 VIth17
Fees: DAY £3495-£5010

GROVE INDEPENDENT SCHOOL
Redland Drive, Milton Keynes,
Buckinghamshire MK5 8HD
Tel: 01908 664336
Head: Miss Deborah Berkin
Type: Co-educational Day B0-13 G0-13
No of pupils: B122 G118
Fees: DAY £5196

GYOSEI INTERNATIONAL SCHOOL UK
Japonica Lane, V10 Brickhill Street, Milton Keynes,
Buckinghamshire MK15 9JX
Tel: 01908 690100
Head: K Tagawa
Type: Co-educational Boarding & Day B12-18 G12-18
No of pupils: B149 G93 FB33
Fees: FB £11,340 DAY £6340

MILTON KEYNES PREPARATORY SCHOOL
Tattenhoe Lane, Milton Keynes,
Buckinghamshire MK3 7EG
Tel: 01908 642111
Head: Mrs H A Pauley BEd
Type: Co-educational Day B0-13 G0-13
No of pupils: B200 G170
Fees: DAY £4237-£4698

SWANBOURNE HOUSE SCHOOL
Milton Keynes, Buckinghamshire MK17 0HZ
Tel: 01296 720264
Heads: S D Goodhart BEd & Mrs J S Goodhart BEd
Type: Co-educational Boarding & Day B3-13 G3-13
No of pupils: B188 G134 FB15 WB35
Fees: FB/WB £8550 DAY £3090-£6570

THORNTON COLLEGE
Convent of Jesus & Mary, Milton Keynes,
Buckinghamshire MK17 0HJ
Tel: 01280 812610
Head: Mrs E E Speddy BA, DipEd
Type: Girls Day & Boarding B3-7 G3-16
No of pupils: B14 G236
Fees: FB/WB £6680-£8070 DAY £3970-£4980

Princes Risborough

ST TERESA'S SCHOOL
Aylesbury Road, Princes Risborough,
Buckinghamshire HP27 0JW
Tel: 01844 345005
Heads: Mrs C M Sparkes & Mrs A M Broom Smith
Type: Co-educational Day B3-12 G3-12
No of pupils: B75 G85
Fees: DAY £937-£2728

Wexham

TEIKYO SCHOOL UK
Framewood Road, Wexham, Buckinghamshire SL2 4QS
Tel: 01753 663711
Head: A Watanabe BA
Type: Co-educational Day & Boarding B16-18 G16-18
No of pupils: B58 G42

Essex

Billericay

ST JOHN'S SCHOOL
Stock Road, Billericay, Essex CM12 0AR
Tel: 01277 623070
Heads: Mrs S Hillier BA(Hons) & Mrs F Armour BEd(Hons)
Type: Co-educational Day B3-16 G3-16
No of pupils: B170 G150
Fees: DAY £1800-£4320

Brentwood

BRENTWOOD PREPARATORY SCHOOL
Middleton Hall, Brentwood, Essex CM15 8EQ
Tel: 01277 220045
Head: T J G Marchant
Type: Co-educational Day B3-11 G3-11
No of pupils: B302 G36
Fees: DAY £2322-£4647

BRENTWOOD SCHOOL
Ingrave Road, Brentwood, Essex CM15 8AS
Tel: 01277 212271
Head: J A B Kelsall
Type: Co-educational Day & Boarding B7-18 G11-18
No of pupils: FB60
Fees: FB £9615 DAY £5496

HERINGTON HOUSE SCHOOL
Mount Avenue, Brentwood, Essex CM13 2NS
Tel: 01277 211595
Head: R Dudley-Cooke
Type: Co-educational Day B3-11 G3-11
No of pupils: B35 G100
Fees: DAY £1710-£3615

PENIEL ACADEMY
49 Coxtie Green Road, Brentwood, Essex CM14 5PS
Tel: 01277 372996
Head: Rev M S B Reid BD
Type: Co-educational Day

URSULINE PREPARATORY SCHOOL
Old Great Ropers, Great Ropers Lane, Brentwood,
Essex CM133HR
Tel: 01277 202 559
Head: Mrs Pauline Wilson MSc
Type: Co-educational Day B3-11 G3-11
No of pupils: B16 G123
Fees: DAY £1875-£3570

WOODLANDS PREPARATORY SCHOOL
Warley Street, Brentwood, Essex CM13 3LA
Tel: 01277 211699
Head: Linda Tingle
Type: Co-educational Day & Boarding

Buckhurst Hill

THE DAIGLEN SCHOOL
68 Palmerston Road, Buckhurst Hill, Essex IG9 5LG
Tel: 0181 504 7108
Head: David Wood CertEd, CertMus, FCollP
Type: Boys Day B4-11
No of pupils: B150
Fees: DAY £2625

BRAESIDE SCHOOL FOR GIRLS
130 High Road, Buckhurst Hill, Essex IG9 5SD
Tel: 0181 504 1133
Head: Mrs C Naismith BA(Hons), PGCE
Type: Girls Day G4-16
No of pupils: G208
Fees: DAY £3075-£5050

LOYOLA PREPARATORY SCHOOL
103 Palmerston Road, Buckhurst Hill, Essex IG9 5NH
Tel: 0181 504 7372
Head: P G M Nicholson CertEd, BEd(Hons)
Type: Boys Day B3-11
No of pupils: B204
Fees: DAY £1575-£3270

Chelmsford

ELM GREEN PREPARATORY SCHOOL
Parsonage Lane, Chelmsford, Essex CM3 4SU
Tel: 01245 225230
Head: Mrs E L Mimpriss CertEd
Type: Co-educational Day B4-11 G4-11
No of pupils: B115 G105
Fees: DAY £3255

HEATHCOTE SCHOOL
Eves Corner, Chelmsford, Essex CM3 4QB
Tel: 01245 223131
Heads: Mr & Mrs R H Greenland TCE, MIQA
Type: Co-educational Day B2-11 G2-11
No of pupils: B79 G85
Fees: DAY £3030

NEW HALL PREPARATORY SCHOOL
Chelmsford, Essex CM3 3HT
Tel: 01245 467588
Head: Mr Gerard Hudson BSc PGCE
Type: Co-educational Day & Boarding B4-11 G4-11
Fees: FB £10,830 WB £10,620 DAY £3210

NEW HALL SCHOOL
Chelmsford, Essex CM3 3HT
Tel: 01245 467588
Head: Sr Anne Marie CRSS, MA(Cantab)
Type: Girls Boarding & Day G11-18
No of pupils: G420 VIth116
Fees: FB £10,830 WB £10,620 DAY £6930

ST ANNE'S PREPARATORY SCHOOL
New London Road, Chelmsford, Essex CM2 0AW
Tel: 01245 353488
Head: Mrs K Darby CertEd ACP
Type: Co-educational Day B3-11 G3-11
No of pupils: B40 G80
Fees: DAY £2490-£2880

ST CEDD'S SCHOOL EDUCATIONAL TRUST LTD
Maltese Road, Chelmsford, Essex CM1 2PB
Tel: 01245 354380
Head: Dr S A Foster BA, PhD
Type: Co-educational Day B4-11 G4-11
No of pupils: B174 G160
Fees: DAY £2835

ST PHILIP'S PRIORY SCHOOL
178 New London Road, Chelmsford, Essex CM2 0AR
Tel: 01245 284907
Head: Sr Michelle OSM
Type: Co-educational Day B4-11 G4-11
No of pupils: B100 G100
Fees: DAY £2250-£2300

WIDFORD LODGE
Widford Road, Chelmsford, Essex CM2 9AN
Tel: 01245 352581
Head: H C Witham MA(Cantab)
Type: Co-educational Day B2-13 G2-13
No of pupils: B145 G15
Fees: DAY £2820-£3990

Chigwell

CHIGWELL SCHOOL
High Road, Chigwell, Essex IG7 6QF
Tel: 0181 501 5700
Head: D Gibbs
Type: Boys Day & Boarding B7-18 G16-18
No of pupils: B505 VIth195 FB28 WB42
Fees: FB £6711-£9993 WB £6342-£9459
DAY £4275-£6573

GURU GOBIND SINGH KHALSA COLLEGE
Roding Lane, Chigwell, Essex IG7 6BQ
Tel: 0181 559 9160
Head: Mrs Inderjeet Kaur BEng, MTAX, DipCompSc, DipEd
Type: Co-educational Day B3-17 G3-17
No of pupils: B88 G122
Fees: DAY £3900

Clacton-on-Sea

ST CLARE'S DAY NURSERY
18 Holland Road, Clacton-on-Sea, Essex CO15 6EG
Tel: 01255 421236
Head: Sr Carmel
Type: Co-educational Day B3-5 G3-5

Colchester

COLCHESTER BOYS HIGH SCHOOL
Wellesley Road, Colchester, Essex CO3 3HD
Tel: 01206 573389
Head: Mr Andrew T Moore MA(Oxon), PGCE
Type: Co-educational Day B3-16 G3-11
No of pupils: B327 G21
Fees: DAY £2835-£3600

COLCHESTER ROYAL GRAMMAR SCHOOL
Lexden Road, Colchester, Essex CO3 3ND
Tel: 01206 577971/2
Head: Stewart Francis MA
Type: Boys Day & Boarding B11-18
No of pupils: B670 VIth188
Fees: WB £2925

COLNE VALLEY CHRISTIAN SCHOOL
Ramparts, Bakers Lane, Colchester, Essex CO4 5BB
Tel: 01206 845869
Head: Miss Janet Ann Lycett
Type: Co-educational Day

DONYLAND LODGE
Fingringhoe Road, Colchester, Essex CO5 7JL
Tel: 01206 728869
Head: R Meyers
Type: Co-educational Day

DOUCECROFT SCHOOL
163 High Street, Colchester, Essex CO5 9JA
Tel: 01376 570060
Head: Mrs Kathy Cranmer BEd
Type: Co-educational Boarding & Day B3-19 G3-19
No of pupils: B26
Fees: FB £28,920 DAY £18,207

HOLMWOOD HOUSE
Colchester, Essex CO3 5ST
Tel: 01206 574305
Head: H S Thackrah BEd
Type: Co-educational Day & Boarding B4-13 G4-13
No of pupils: B236 G124
Fees: FB £8265-£9270 DAY £4035-£7170

LITTLEGARTH SCHOOL
Horkesley Park, Colchester, Essex CO6 4JR
Tel: 01206 262332
Head: Mrs M-L Harvey CertEd, LCP, FCollP
Type: Co-educational Day B2-12 G2-12
No of pupils: B122 G140
Fees: DAY £1050-£3090

OXFORD HOUSE SCHOOL
2-4 Lexden Road, Colchester, Essex CO3 3NE
Tel: 01206 576686
Head: R P Spendlove CertEd, ACP, FCollP
Type: Co-educational Day B2-11 G2-11
No of pupils: B65 G65
Fees: DAY £1635-£3240

OXLEY PARKER SCHOOL
(Royal Eastern Counties Schools Ltd), Colchester,
Essex CO4 5JF
Tel: 01206 853222
Head: D P King DipEd
Type: Boys Boarding B7-17
No of pupils: B40
Fees: FB £22,200 DAY £14,799

ST MARY'S SCHOOL
Lexden Road, Colchester, Essex CO3 3RB
Tel: 01206 572544
Head: Mrs G Mouser MPhil
Type: Girls Day G4-17
No of pupils: G452
Fees: DAY £2820-£3960

Dunmow

FELSTED PREPARATORY SCHOOL
Felsted, Dunmow, Essex CM6 3JL
Tel: 01371 820252
Head: M P Pomphrey BSc
Type: Co-educational Boarding & Day B4-13 G4-13
No of pupils: B167 G112
Fees: FB £8865 DAY £2655-£6495

FELSTED SCHOOL
Dunmow, Essex CM6 3LL
Tel: 01371 820258
Head: S C Roberts MA
Type: Co-educational Boarding & Day B13-18 G13-18
No of pupils: B180 G86 VIth180
Fees: FB £12,360 DAY £9030

Earls Colne

OGILVY COURT RESIDENTIAL HOME
America Road, Earls Colne, Essex CO6 2LB
Tel: 01787 222355
Head: D Russell-Jones
Type: Co-educational Boarding B18-99 G18-99

Epping

COOPERSALE HALL SCHOOL
Flux's Lane, Epping, Essex CM16 7PE
Tel: 01992 577133
Head: Nicholas Hagger MA(Oxon)
Type: Co-educational Day B3-11 G3-11
No of pupils: B124 G119
Fees: DAY £1987-£3585

Frinton-on-Sea

ST PHILOMENA'S PREPARATORY SCHOOL
Hadleigh Road, Frinton-on-Sea, Essex CO13 9HQ
Tel: 01255 674492
Head: Mrs B Buck
Type: Co-educational Day B3-11 G3-11
Fees: DAY £1494

Great Dunmow

FKS (SCHOOLS) LTD
Greenacre, Great Dunmow, Essex CM6 3AT
Tel: 01371 872854
Head: Mrs Alexandra Orr TCert
Type: Co-educational Day B2-11 G2-11
No of pupils: B105 G116
Fees: DAY £2340-£2805

Halstead

GOSFIELD SCHOOL
Cut Hedge Park, Halstead, Essex CO9 1PF
Tel: 01787 474040
Head: John Shaw MA, MABE
Type: Co-educational Day & Boarding B3-18 G3-18
No of pupils: B79 G43 VIth12
Fees: FB/WB £7605-£9900 DAY £2970-£5310

GREENWOOD
(Royal Eastern Counties Schools Ltd), Halstead,
Essex CO9 2DQ
Tel: 01787 472002
Head: Mrs C A Grandin CertEd, BA, BSc, MSc
Type: Girls Boarding G7-17
No of pupils: G30
Fees: FB £22,200 DAY £14,799

ST MARGARET'S SCHOOL
Gosfield Hall Park, Halstead, Essex CO9 1SE
Tel: 01787 472134
Head: J Dann MA, DipEd
Type: Co-educational Day B2-13 G2-13
No of pupils: B65 G80
Fees: DAY £2514-£3007

Harlow

ST NICHOLAS SCHOOL
Hillingdon House, Harlow, Essex CM17 0NJ
Tel: 01279 429910
Head: G W Brant MA, BEd(Hons), CertEd
Type: Co-educational Day B4-16 G4-16
No of pupils: B134 G148
Fees: DAY £2085-£4215

Ingatestone

LANDRY SCHOOL
Whites Hill, Ingatestone, Essex CM4 9QD
Tel: 01277 840338
Head: Miss E Prior
Type: Co-educational Day B4-8 G4-8
No of pupils: B7 G8
Fees: DAY £1200

Leigh-on-Sea

COLLEGE SAINT-PIERRE
16 Leigh Road, Leigh-on-Sea, Essex SS9 1LD
Tel: 01702 74164
Head: G Bragard
Type: Co-educational Day B3-11 G3-11
No of pupils: B48 G27
Fees: DAY £1230-£2340

ST MICHAEL'S SCHOOL
198 Hadleigh Road, Leigh-on-Sea, Essex SS9 2LP
Tel: 01702 78719
Head: Mrs S V Stokes BA, TCert, MontDip
Type: Co-educational Day B3-11 G3-11
No of pupils: B141 G146
Fees: DAY £2700

Loughton

OAKLANDS SCHOOL
8 Albion Hill, Loughton, Essex IG10 4RA
Tel: 0181 508 3517
Head: N Hagger MA(Oxon)
Type: Co-educational Day B3-11 G3-11
No of pupils: B70 G162
Fees: DAY £2100-£3069

WOODCROFT SCHOOL
Whitakers Way, Loughton, Essex IG10 1SQ
Tel: 0181 508 1369
Head: Mr C D Renehan RMN, BEd
Type: Co-educational Day B2-11 G2-11
Fees: DAY £24,000

Maldon

MALDON COURT PREPARATORY SCHOOL
Silver Street, Maldon, Essex CM9 4QE
Tel: 01621 853529
Head: Mr A G Webb BEd
Type: Co-educational Day B4-11 G4-11
No of pupils: B76 G49
Fees: DAY £2790-£2910

Ongar

SPRINGFIELD PNEU SCHOOL
Stondon Road, Ongar, Essex CM5 9RG
Tel: 01277 362945
Head: Mrs J A Burge CertEd
Type: Co-educational Day B3-11 G3-11
No of pupils: B30 G50
Fees: DAY £2400-£4275

Rochford

CROWSTONE PREPARATORY SCHOOL
(Sutton Annexe), Rochford, Essex SS4 1LL
Tel: 01702 540629
Head: J P Thayer
Type: Co-educational Day B2-11 G2-11
No of pupils: B120 G130
Fees: DAY £1770-£2925

Saffron Walden

DAME JOHANE BRADBURY'S SCHOOL
Ashdon Road, Saffron Walden, Essex CB10 2AL
Tel: 01799 522348
Head: Mrs R M Rainey CertEd, Froebel
Type: Co-educational Day B3-11 G3-11
No of pupils: B113 G159
Fees: DAY £2484-£3291

FRIENDS' SCHOOL
Mount Pleasant Road, Saffron Walden, Essex CB11 3EB
Tel: 01799 525351
Head: Mrs Jane Laing BA
Type: Co-educational Day & Boarding B3-18 G3-18
No of pupils: B155 G151 VIth60 FB87
Fees: FB £6885-£10,614 DAY £2400-£6369

Southend-on-Sea

ALLEYN COURT PREPARATORY SCHOOL
Wakering Road, Southend-on-Sea, Essex SS3 0PW
Tel: 01702 582553
Heads: S Bishop AdvDipEd, CertEd, ACP &
P Green, DipPhysEd, MBIM
Type: Co-educational Day B3-13 G3-13
No of pupils: B187 G92
Fees: DAY £1857-£4788

THORPE HALL SCHOOL
Wakering Road, Southend-on-Sea, Essex SS1 3RD
Tel: 01702 582340
Head: T Fawell CertEd, BEd, FCollP
Type: Co-educational Day B2-16 G2-16
No of pupils: B240 G184
Fees: DAY £2340-£3360

Waltham Forest

LITTLE ACORNS
Higham High Road, Waltham Forest, Essex IG8 9LB
Tel: 0181 504 0045
Head: Mrs Susan Jones
Type: Co-educational Day

Westcliff-on-Sea

CROWSTONE PREPARATORY SCHOOL
121-123 Crowstone Road, Westcliff-on-Sea,
Essex SS0 8LH
Tel: 01702 346758
Head: J P Thayer
Type: Co-educational Day B3-11 G3-11
Fees: DAY £2655

QUEENSLAND PREPARATORY SCHOOL
100 Crowstone Road, Westcliff-on-Sea, Essex SSO 8LQ
Tel: 01702 340664
Head: Miss R G Waltham
Type: Co-educational Day B4-11 G4-11
Fees: DAY £1500-£1590

ST HILDA'S SCHOOL
15 Imperial Avenue, Westcliff-on-Sea, Essex SS0 8NE
Tel: 01702 344542
Head: Mrs V M Tunnicliffe
Type: Girls Day B3-7 G3-16
Fees: DAY £2388-£2940

WESTMINSTER PREPARATORY SCHOOL
9 Westminster Drive, Westcliff-on-Sea, Essex SS0 9SJ
Tel: 01702 74144
Head: Mrs J Perfitt-Harvey
Type: Co-educational Day B4-11 G4-11
Fees: DAY £1350-£1500

Hampshire

Alton

ALTON CONVENT
Anstey Lane, Alton, Hampshire GU34 2NG
Tel: 01420 82070/83878
Heads: F Martin, BA(Hons) & Rev Mother
Madeline de Jesus, BA(Hons), ALCM
Type: Girls Day B4-11 G4-16
No of pupils: B37 G323
Fees: DAY £3090-£3390

MAYFIELD PREPARATORY SCHOOL
103 Anstey Road, Alton, Hampshire GU34 2RN
Tel: 01420 83105
Heads: T T Incles BEd(Hons), CertEd &
Mrs C E Incles CertEd
Type: Co-educational Day B2-11 G2-11
No of pupils: B61 G49
Fees: DAY £2697-£2757

Andover

FARLEIGH SCHOOL
Red Rice, Andover, Hampshire SP11 7PW
Tel: 01264 710766
Head: J E Murphy BSc,PGCE
Type: Co-educational Day & Boarding B3-13 G3-13
No of pupils: B259 G107
Fees: FB £8910 DAY £1452-£6327

ROOKWOOD SCHOOL
Weyhill Road, Andover, Hampshire SP10 3AL
Tel: 01264 352855
Head: Mrs S Hindle BA(Hons), FCollP
Type: Co-educational Day & Boarding B3-16 G3-16
No of pupils: B96 G185
Fees: FB £6840-£9006 WB £6315-£8481
DAY £555-£4731

ST BENEDICT'S CONVENT SCHOOL
Penton Lodge, Andover, Hampshire SP11 0RD
Tel: 01264 772291
Head: Mrs J Taylor
Type: Co-educational Boarding & Day B2-11 G2-16
Fees: FB £5610-£6840 DAY £1500-£2985

Basingstoke

DANESHILL SCHOOL
Basingstoke, Hampshire RG27 0AR
Tel: 01256 882707
Head: S V Spencer CertEd, DipPhysEd
Type: Co-educational Day B3-12 G3-12
No of pupils: B135 G185
Fees: DAY £1350-£3885

KINGS SCHOOL
Sarum Hill, Basingstoke, Hampshire RG21 1ST
Tel: 01256 467092
Head: Richard Britton
Type: Co-educational Day

Bramdean

BROCKWOOD PARK
KRISHNAMURTI EDUCATION CENTRE
Bramdean, Hampshire SO24 0LQ
Tel: 01962 771744
Heads: C Foster & I Peters
Type: Co-educational Boarding B14-19 G14-19
No of pupils: B33 G22
Fees: FB £8000

Catherington

VIKING ASSOCIATES LTD SCHOOL
Catherington House, Catherington, Hampshire PO8 9NJ
Tel: 01705 593251
Head: Mrs J L Easton
Type: Co-educational Day

Chandlers Ford

KINGSMEAD DAY NURSERY
120 Kingsway, Chandlers Ford, Hampshire SO5 1DW
Tel: 01703 253815
Head: Mrs H M Hancock
Type: Co-educational Day B3-8 G3-8
Fees: DAY £930-£1380

WOODHILL SCHOOL
61 Brownhill Road, Chandlers Ford,
Hampshire SO53 2EH
Tel: 01703 268012
Head: Mrs M Dacombe
Type: Co-educational Day B3-11 G3-11
No of pupils: B60 G60
Fees: DAY £1239-£2415

Curdridge

VINE SCHOOL
Church Lane, Curdridge, Hampshire SO32 2DR
Tel: 01489 789123
Head: R W Medway BEd
Type: Co-educational Day B3-11 G3-11
No of pupils: B30 G30
Fees: DAY £2000

Eastleigh

SHERBORNE HOUSE SCHOOL
Lakewood Road, Eastleigh, Hampshire SO53 1EU
Tel: 01703 252440
Heads: G J Clewer BEd(Hon), CertEd &
Mrs L M Clewer CertEd(Hon), MEd
Type: Co-educational Day B2-11 G2-11
No of pupils: B40 G162
Fees: DAY £2670-£3195

Fair Oak

KINGS SCHOOL SENIOR
Lakesmere House, Fair Oak, Hampshire SO50 7DB
Tel: 01703 600956
Head: Paul Trevett
Type: Co-educational Day

Fareham

BOUNDARY OAK SCHOOL
Roche Court, Fareham, Hampshire PO17 5BL
Tel: 01329 280955
Head: R B Bliss CertEd
Type: Co-educational Day & Boarding B3-13 G3-13
No of pupils: B170 G50 FB2 WB35
Fees: FB £6420-£8040 DAY £1560-£5355

HILL HEAD PRE-PREPARATORY SCHOOL
51 Crofton Lane, Fareham, Hampshire PO14 3LW
Tel: 01329 662666
Head: Mrs B M A Barber BEd(Hons)
Type: Co-educational Day B3-8 G3-8
Fees: DAY £1770

MEONCROSS SCHOOL
Burnt House Lane, Fareham, Hampshire PO14 2EF
Tel: 01329 662182
Head: C J Ford BEd(Oxon)
Type: Co-educational Day B2-16 G2-16
No of pupils: B215 G224
Fees: DAY £2961-£4071

SEAFIELD SCHOOL
Westlands Grove, Fareham, Hampshire PO16 9AA
Tel: 01705 377158
Head: Mrs E G Jones CertEd, MIL
Type: Co-educational Day B2-8 G2-8
No of pupils: B30 G25
Fees: DAY £1110-£1440

WEST HILL PARK PREPARATORY SCHOOL
Fareham, Hampshire PO14 4BS
Tel: 01329 842356
Head: E P K Hudson CertEd
Type: Co-educational Boarding & Day B3-13 G3-13
No of pupils: B160 G30 FB70
Fees: FB £7665 DAY £1455-£5670

WYKEHAM HOUSE SCHOOL
East Street, Fareham, Hampshire PO16 0BW
Tel: 01329 280178
Head: Mrs R M Kamaryc BA, MSc, PGCE
Type: Girls Day G2-16
No of pupils: G300
Fees: DAY £1560-£3870

Farnborough

★ FARNBOROUGH HILL
Farnborough Road, Farnborough, Hampshire GU14 8AT
Tel: 01252 545197
Head: Miss R McGeoch MA, MLitt, PGCE
Type: Girls Day G11-18
No of pupils: G526 VIth111
Fees: DAY £4782

RUSHMOOR INDEPENDENT SCHOOL
40 Reading Road, Farnborough, Hampshire GU14 6NB
Tel: 01252 544738
Head: Mrs A V Rendell
Type: Co-educational Day B2-16 G2-16
No of pupils: B49 G17
Fees: DAY £375-£2787

SALESIAN COLLEGE
Reading Road, Farnborough, Hampshire GU14 6PA
Tel: 01252 542919
Head: Rev Br M Delmer SDB, BEd
Type: Boys Day B11-18
No of pupils: B466
Fees: DAY £3234

Fleet

ST NICHOLAS SCHOOL
Redfields House, Redfields Lane, Fleet,
Hampshire GU13 0RE
Tel: 01252 850121
Head: Mrs A V Whatmough BA, CertEd
Type: Girls Day B3-7 G3-16
No of pupils: B20 G339
Fees: DAY £1260-£3900

STOCKTON HOUSE SCHOOL
Stockton Avenue, Fleet, Hampshire GU13 8NS
Tel: 01252 616323
Head: Mrs C Tweedie-Smith
Type: Co-educational Day B2-8 G2-8
Fees: DAY £600-£2085

Fordingbridge

FORRES SANDLE MANOR
Fordingbridge, Hampshire SP6 1NS
Tel: 01425 653181
Head: R P J Moore BA, PGCE
Type: Co-educational Boarding & Day B3-13 G3-13
No of pupils: B140 G105
Fees: FB/WB £7710-£8985 DAY £1920-£6375

Gosport

MARYCOURT SCHOOL
27 Crescent Road, Gosport, Hampshire PO12 2DJ
Tel: 01705 581766
Head: Mrs Margaret Crane BA, CertEd
Type: Co-educational Day B3-11 G3-11
No of pupils: B56 G49
Fees: DAY £1155-£2076

Havant

GLENHURST SCHOOL
16 Beechworth Road, Havant, Hampshire PO9 1AX
Tel: 01705 484054
Head: Mrs E A Newman
Type: Co-educational Day B3-9 G3-9
No of pupils: B61 G33
Fees: DAY £1195-£1485

Hartley Wintney

★ GREY HOUSE SCHOOL
Mount Pleasant, Hartley Wintney, Hampshire RG27 8PW
Tel: 01252 842353
Head: Mrs E M Purse CertEd
Type: Co-educational Day B4-11 G4-11
No of pupils: B75 G72
Fees: DAY £3168-£3900

Hook

LORD WANDSWORTH COLLEGE
Long Sutton, Hook, Hampshire RG29 1TB
Tel: 01256 862482
Head: G de W Waller MA, MSc
Type: Boys Day & Boarding B11-18 G16-18
No of pupils: B322 VIth158
Fees: FB/WB £9456-£9972 DAY £7380-£7752

NORTH FORELAND LODGE
Hook, Hampshire RG27 0HT
Tel: 01256 882431
Head: Miss S R Cameron BA
Type: Girls Boarding & Day G11-18
No of pupils: G141 VIth19 FB108
Fees: FB £11,550 DAY £7050

ST NEOT'S SCHOOL
St Neot's Road, Hook, Hampshire RG27 0PN
Tel: 01734 732118
Head: R J Thorp BA(Dunelm), PGCE(Cantab)
Type: Co-educational Day & Boarding B3-14 G3-14
No of pupils: B120 G60
Fees: WB £8010 DAY £2010-£6120

Lee-on-the-Solent

ST ANNE'S SCHOOL
13 Milvil Road, Lee-on-the-Solent, Hampshire PO13 9LU
Tel: 01705 550820
Head: Mrs J Bottomley BEd
Type: Co-educational Day B3-8 G3-8
No of pupils: B15 G20
Fees: DAY £1710-£2010

Liphook

BROOKHAM SCHOOL
Highfield Lane, Liphook, Hampshire GU30 7LQ
Tel: 01428 722005
Head: Mrs D Jenner CertEd
Type: Co-educational Day B3-8 G3-8
No of pupils: B50 G30
Fees: DAY £4350

HIGHFIELD SCHOOL
Liphook, Hampshire GU30 7LQ
Tel: 01428 722228
Head: N O Ramage MA
Type: Co-educational Boarding & Day B7-13 G7-13
No of pupils: B105 G76 FB140
Fees: FB £8325-£9450 DAY £6300-£7350

LITTLEFIELD SCHOOL
Midhurst Road, Liphook, Hampshire GU30 7HT
Tel: 01428 723187
Head: G Milne BEd(Hons), CertEd, MCollP
Type: Co-educational Day B2-11 G2-11
No of pupils: B60 G82
Fees: DAY £1245-£3300

Lymington

HORDLE HOUSE
Milford-on-Sea, Lymington, Hampshire SO41 0NW
Tel: 01590 642104
Head: Henry Phillips BA(Hons), CertED, LGSM
Type: Co-educational Day & Boarding B2-13 G2-13
No of pupils: B89 G75
Fees: FB £6960-£8190 DAY £3255-£6150

WALHAMPTON SCHOOL
Lymington, Hampshire SO41 5ZG
Tel: 01590 672013
Head: A W S Robinson MA
Type: Co-educational Boarding & Day B3-13 G3-13
No of pupils: B124 G81
Fees: FB £9540 DAY £3435-£7290

New Milton

BALLARD COLLEGE
Fernhill Lane, New Milton, Hampshire BH25 5JL
Tel: 01425 611090
Head: The Rev Andrew Folks BA, DipTh
Type: Co-educational Boarding & Day B11-18 G11-18
No of pupils: VIth20
Fees: FB £8850 WB £8295 DAY £5655

BALLARD LAKE PREPARATORY SCHOOL
Fernhill Lane, New Milton, Hampshire BH25 5JL
Tel: 01425 611153
Head: Miss Gill Morris
Type: Co-educational Boarding & Day B2-13 G2-13
No of pupils: FB20
Fees: FB £8205 WB £7395 DAY £3105-£5550

DURLSTON COURT
Becton Lane, New Milton, Hampshire BH25 7AQ
Tel: 01425 610010
Head: E G Liston BSc, CertEd
Type: Co-educational Day & Boarding B3-14 G3-14
No of pupils: B80 G60
Fees: FB £8310 DAY £1740-£5880

Petersfield

BEDALES SCHOOL
Church Road, Petersfield, Hampshire GU32 2DG
Tel: 01730 300100
Head: Mrs Alison Willcocks MA, BMus
Type: Co-educational Boarding & Day B8-18 G8-18
No of pupils: B200 G200 FB346
Fees: FB £12,996 DAY £9567

CHURCHERS COLLEGE
Portsmouth Road, Petersfield, Hampshire GU31 4AS
Tel: 01730 263033
Head: G W Buttle BA, PGCE, MA, FRSA
Type: Co-educational Day B4-18 G4-18
No of pupils: B341 G221 VIth141
Fees: DAY £2790-£5250

DITCHAM PARK SCHOOL
Ditcham Park, Petersfield, Hampshire GU31 5RN
Tel: 01730 825659
Head: Mrs P M Holmes DipEd
Type: Co-educational Day B4-16 G4-16
No of pupils: B162 G139
Fees: DAY £3180-£5340

DUNHURST (BEDALES JUNIOR SCHOOL)
Alton Road, Petersfield, Hampshire GU31 2DP
Tel: 01730 300200
Heads: M L Heslop MA, PGCE &
      Mrs H A Heslop BA, PGCE
Type: Co-educational Boarding & Day B8-13 G8-13
No of pupils: B80 G80
Fees: FB £9297-£9696 DAY £6360-£6780

Portsmouth

THE PORTSMOUTH GRAMMAR SCHOOL
High Street, Portsmouth, Hampshire PO1 2LN
Tel: 01705 819125
Head: A C V Evans MA, MPhil, FIL
Type: Co-educational Day B4-18 G4-18
No of pupils: B677 G274 VIth198
Fees: DAY £3048-£4755

Ringwood

AVONLEA SCHOOL
8 Broadshard Lane, Ringwood, Hampshire BH24 1RR
Tel: 01425 473994
Head: P Lewis BA
Type: Co-educational Day B2-11 G2-11
No of pupils: B30 G50
Fees: DAY £1350-£1950

MOYLES COURT SCHOOL
Moyles Court, Ringwood, Hampshire BH24 3NF
Tel: 01425 472856/473197
Head: Mr Dean
Type: Co-educational Day & Boarding B3-16 G3-16
No of pupils: B83 G63 FB61
Fees: FB £6690-£7740 DAY £3285-£4650

RINGWOOD WALDORF SCHOOL
Folly Farm Lane, Ringwood, Hampshire BH24 2NN
Tel: 01425 472664
Type: Co-educational Day B3-14 G3-14
No of pupils: B60 G60
Fees: DAY £750-£3600

Romsey

EMBLEY PARK SCHOOL
Embley Park, Romsey, Hampshire SO51 6ZE
Tel: 01794 512206
Head: D F Chapman BA(Dunelm), FCollP
Type: Co-educational Boarding & Day B3-18 G3-18
No of pupils: B243 G129 VIth57
Fees: FB £4785-£10,395 DAY £1470-£5835

STANBRIDGE EARLS SCHOOL
Stanbridge Lane, Romsey, Hampshire SO51 0ZS
Tel: 01794 516777
Head: H Moxon MA, DipEd
Type: Co-educational Boarding & Day B11-18 G11-18
No of pupils: B151 G40 VIth48
Fees: FB £11,070-£12,120 DAY £8310-£9090

THE STROUD SCHOOL
Highwood House, Romsey, Hampshire SO51 9ZH
Tel: 01794 513231
Head: Alastair J L Dodds MA(Cantab)
Type: Co-educational Day B3-13 G3-13
No of pupils: B194 G72
Fees: DAY £1695-£6009

Southampton

THE ATHERLEY SCHOOL
Hill Lane, Southampton, Hampshire SO16 5RG
Tel: 01703 772898
Head: Miss A Burrows
Type: Girls Day B3-11 G3-19
No of pupils: B69 G365
•*Fees:* DAY £3198-£4482

FAIRLANDS MONTESSORI SCHOOL
Church Road, Southampton, Hampshire SO3 2HW
Tel: 01489 784842
Head: Mrs J Howard
Type: Co-educational Day

THE GREGG SCHOOL
Townhill Park House, Southampton,
Hampshire SO18 2GF
Tel: 01703 472133
Head: R D Hart BEd
Type: Co-educational Day B11-16 G11-16
No of pupils: B135 G93
Fees: DAY £4425

GROVE PLACE, THE ATHERLEY JUNIOR SCHOOL
Upton Lane, Southampton, Hampshire SO16 0AB
Tel: 01703 732406
Head: Mrs D A Hitchcock
Type: Co-educational Day B3-11 G3-11
No of pupils: B51 G126
Fees: DAY £1016-£1424

KING EDWARD VI SCHOOL
Kellett Road, Southampton, Hampshire SO15 7UQ
Tel: 01703 704561
Head: P B Hamilton
Type: Co-educational Day B11-18 G11-18
No of pupils: B753 G200
Fees: DAY £5016

KINGS PRIMARY SCHOOL
26 Quob Lane, Southampton, Hampshire SO3 3HN
Tel: 01703 472266
Head: S Williams
Type: Co-educational Day

SOUTHAMPTON SMALL SCHOOL
2 Brookvale Road, Southampton, Hampshire SO17 1QL
Tel: 01703 322538
Head: Mrs J R Brennan BEd, MAEd
Type: Co-educational Day B2-11 G2-11
No of pupils: B22 G20
Fees: DAY £1500-£2500

ST CHRISTOPHER'S SCHOOL
Tamarisk Gardens, Southampton, Hampshire SO18 4RA
Tel: 01703 672010
Head: Mrs Julia A Naulin BEd
Type: Co-educational Day B3-8 G3-8
Fees: DAY £1920

ST MARY'S COLLEGE
57 Midanbury Lane, Southampton, Hampshire SO9 4TG
Tel: 01703 671267
Head: The Rev Br Peter
Type: Boys Day B3-18
No of pupils: B450
Fees: DAY £1095-£3285

ST WINIFRED'S SCHOOL
17-19 Winn Road, Southampton, Hampshire SO17 1EJ
Tel: 01703 557352
Head: Mrs J K Collins BA(Hons)
Type: Co-educational Day B2-11 G2-11
No of pupils: B80 G51
Fees: DAY £2835

WARSASH PRE SCHOOL
The Old School, 128 Church Road, Southampton,
Hampshire SO3 9GF
Tel: 01489 582844
Head: Patricia Lewin
Type: Co-educational Day B1-5 G1-5
Fees: DAY £4560

WESSEX TUTORS
44 Shirley Road, Southampton, Hampshire SO1 3EU
Tel: 01703 334719
Head: Mrs J E White BA(London)
Type: Co-educational Day B14-21 G14-21
No of pupils: B20 G20
Fees: DAY £8225

WESTWOOD PARK PRE SCHOOL
27 Winn Road, Southampton, Hampshire SO2 1EJ
Tel: 01703 672551
Head: Avril Howard
Type: Co-educational Day B2-5 G2-5
Fees: DAY £4704

WOODHILL PREPARATORY SCHOOL
Brook Lane, Southampton, Hampshire SO30 2ER
Tel: 01489 781112
Heads: Mrs M Dacombe & Mr M Raisborough
Type: Co-educational Day B3-11 G3-11
No of pupils: B70 G70
Fees: DAY £1239-£2415

Southsea

MAYVILLE HIGH SCHOOL
35 St Simons Road, Southsea, Hampshire PO5 2PE
Tel: 01705 734847
Head: Mrs L Owens BEd
Type: Girls Day B2-8 G2-16
No of pupils: B22 G177
Fees: DAY £2550-£3750

PORTSMOUTH HIGH SCHOOL GPDST
Kent Road, Southsea, Hampshire PO5 3EQ
Tel: 01705 826714
Head: Mrs J M Dawtrey BA
Type: Girls Day G4-18
No of pupils: G625 VIth90
Fees: DAY £3036-£4140

ST JOHN'S COLLEGE
Grove Road South, Southsea, Hampshire PO5 3QW
Tel: 01705 815118
Head: Mr G Morgan
Type: Co-educational Day & Boarding B4-18 G4-18
No of pupils: B555 G55 VIth90 FB85
Fees: FB £7140-£8100 DAY £2820-£4050

YAGO SCHOOL
West End House, St Johns College Campus, Southsea,
Hampshire PO5 3QW
Tel: 01705 865112
Head: R Resa
Type: Co-educational Day

Tadley

INHURST HOUSE SCHOOL
Baughurst, Tadley, Hampshire RG26 5JJ
Tel: 0118 981 3388
Head: Mrs M Smallwood BEd(Hons)
Type: Co-educational Day B3-8 G3-11
No of pupils: B40 G90
Fees: DAY £3635-£3935

Waterlooville

WOODSIDE HOUSE SCHOOL
Woodside House, Waterlooville, Hampshire PO7 5RT
Tel: 01705 230024
Heads: Mrs L J Ractliffe BEd &
       Mrs M J Vernon-Harcourt BEd, DAES
Type: Co-educational Day B3-11 G3-11
No of pupils: B45 G30
Fees: DAY £2190-£2310

Wickham

ROOKESBURY PARK SCHOOL
Wickham, Hampshire PO17 6HT
Tel: 01329 833108
Head: Miss L A Appleyard MAEd, CertEd
Type: Girls Day & Boarding G3-13
No of pupils: G135 FB45 WB5
Fees: FB £6870-£8295 DAY £1605-£5760

Winchester

KINGSMEAD DAY NURSERY
Kingsgate Road, Winchester, Hampshire SO23 9PG
Tel: 01962 862266
Head: Mrs H M Hancock
Type: Co-educational Day

NETHERCLIFFE SCHOOL
Hatherley Road, Winchester, Hampshire SO22 6RS
Tel: 01962 854570
Head: R F G Whitfield TCert
Type: Co-educational Day B3-11 G3-11
No of pupils: B81 G46
Fees: DAY £1605-£3636

Hertfordshire

THE PILGRIMS' SCHOOL
3 The Close, Winchester, Hampshire SO23 9LT
Tel: 01962 854189
Head: M E K Kefford MA, DipEd
Type: Boys Boarding & Day B8-13
No of pupils: B180 FB80
Fees: FB £8490 DAY £6195

PRINCE'S MEAD SCHOOL
43 Edgar Road, Winchester, Hampshire SO23 9TN
Tel: 01962 853416
Head: Mrs D Moore
Type: Co-educational Day B3-11 G3-11
No of pupils: B118 G137
Fees: DAY £2874-£4122

★ **ST SWITHUN'S JUNIOR SCHOOL**
Alresford Road, Winchester, Hampshire SO21 1HA
Tel: 01962 852634
Head: Mrs V A M Lewis MA, MSc, DipEd
Type: Co-educational Day B3-8 G3-11
No of pupils: B42 G166
Fees: DAY £1875-£4725

★ **ST SWITHUN'S SCHOOL**
Alresford Road, Winchester, Hampshire SO21 1HA
Tel: 01962 861316
Head: Dr H L Harvey BSc, Phd(London)
Type: Girls Boarding & Day G11-18
No of pupils: G450 VIth115
Fees: FB £11,130 DAY £6720

TWYFORD SCHOOL
Winchester, Hampshire SO21 1NW
Tel: 01962 712269
Head: P R D Gould CertEd(London)
Type: Co-educational Day & Boarding B3-13 G3-13
No of pupils: B192 G70 FB70
Fees: FB £9285 DAY £1890-£6810

WESSEX TUTORS
14/18 Parchment Street, Winchester,
Hampshire SO23 8AZ
Tel: 01962 853964
Head: Mrs E Backhouse MA(Cantab)
Type: Co-educational Day B15-99 G15-99
No of pupils: B45 G45
Fees: DAY £960-£1920

WINCHESTER COLLEGE
College Street, Winchester, Hampshire SO23 9NA
Tel: 01962 854328
Head: J P Sabben-Clare MA
Type: Boys Boarding & Day B13-18
No of pupils: B406 VIth284
Fees: FB £13,290 DAY £9966

Aldenham Village

EDGE GROVE SCHOOL
Aldenham Village, Hertfordshire WD2 8BL
Tel: 01923 855724
Head: K J Waterfield CertEd
Type: Boys Boarding & Day B7-13
No of pupils: B140
Fees: FB/WB £8250-£8550 DAY £4800-£6150

ST CHRISTOPHER'S EDGE GROVE
Aldenham Village, Hertfordshire WD2 8BL
Tel: 01923 855745
Head: Mrs E S Cornelissen LESM, LRAM
Type: Co-educational Day B2-7 G2-7
No of pupils: B79 G43
Fees: DAY £1800-£3300

Barnet

NORFOLK LODGE PREPARATORY SCHOOL
Dancers Hill Road, Barnet, Hertfordshire EN5 4RP
Tel: 0181 447 1565
Head: Mrs Lauren Beirne MD, AdvMontDip
Type: Co-educational Day B2-11 G2-11
No of pupils: B40 G45
Fees: DAY £535-£1170

Berkhamsted

BERKHAMSTED JUNIOR SCHOOL
Castle Street, Berkhamsted, Hertfordshire HP4 2BB
Tel: 01442 863236
Head: E T Sneddon MA, PGCE
Type: Boys Day & Boarding B5-13
No of pupils: B265
Fees: FB £9850 DAY £3690-£5900

BERKHAMSTED SCHOOL
Castle Street, Berkhamsted, Hertfordshire HP4 2BB
Tel: 01442 863236
Type: Boys Day & Boarding B7-18 G16-18
No of pupils: B730 G14
Fees: FB £11,034 DAY £6774

BERKHAMSTED SCHOOL FOR GIRLS
Kings Road, Berkhamsted, Hertfordshire HP4 3BG
Tel: 01442 862168
Head: Dr P Chadwick MA(Cantab), MA(London),
      PhD(London)
Type: Girls Day & Boarding B3-7 G3-18
No of pupils: B19 G410 VIth88 FB24 WB21
Fees: FB/WB £9327 DAY £3474-£5487

EGERTON-ROTHESAY SCHOOL
Durrants Lane, Berkhamsted, Hertfordshire HP4 3UJ
Tel: 01442 865275
Head: J R Adkins BSc(Hons), PGCE
Type: Co-educational Day B2-18 G2-18
No of pupils: B283 G171 VIth21
Fees: DAY £534-£5490

HARESFOOT SCHOOL
Chesham Road, Berkhamsted, Hertfordshire HP4 2SZ
Tel: 01442 872742
Head: Mrs G R Waterhouse DipPe
Type: Co-educational Day B2-12 G2-12
No of pupils: B95 G122
Fees: DAY £468-£3570

HARESFOOT SENIOR SCHOOL
The Common, Berkhamsted, Hertfordshire HP4 2QF
Tel: 01442 877215
Head: D L Davies MA
Type: Co-educational Day B11-18 G11-18
No of pupils: B44 G14 VIth3
Fees: DAY £4800-£5850

MARLIN MONTESSORI SCHOOL
1 Park View Road, Berkhamsted, Hertfordshire HP4 3EY
Tel: 01442 866290
Head: Mrs S O'Neill
Type: Co-educational Day B1-7 G1-7
Fees: DAY £555-£5000

Bishop's Stortford

BISHOP'S STORTFORD COLLEGE
Maze Green Road, Bishop's Stortford,
Hertfordshire CM23 2QZ
Tel: 01279 838575
Head: S G G Benson
Type: Boys Boarding & Day B13-18 G16-18
No of pupils: B318 G30 FB160
Fees: FB £10,020 DAY £7230

BISHOP'S STORTFORD COLLEGE JUNIOR SCHOOL
Maze Green Road, Bishop's Stortford,
Hertfordshire CM23 2PH
Tel: 01279 653616
Head: D J Defoe BSc, CChem, MRSC
Type: Co-educational Day & Boarding B4-13 G4-13
No of pupils: B252 G38 FB40 WB12
Fees: FB/WB £7200-£7860 DAY £3600-£5970

CHRISTIAN SCHOOL (TAKELEY)
Dunmow Road, Brewers End, Bishop's Stortford,
Hertfordshire CM22 6QH
Tel: 01279 871182
Head: M E Humphries
Type: Co-educational Day B5-16 G5-16
No of pupils: B20 G14

HOWE GREEN HOUSE SCHOOL
Great Hallingbury, Bishop's Stortford,
Hertfordshire CM22 7UF
Tel: 01279 657706
Head: Mrs N R J Garrod CertEd
Type: Co-educational Day B3-11 G3-11
No of pupils: B61 G78
Fees: DAY £2865-£4620

**MONTESSORI NURSERY &
PRE-PREPARATORY SCHOOL**
High House Farm, Mill End, Bishop's Stortford,
Hertfordshire CM22 6PL
Tel: 01279 870898
Head: Mrs Geraldine Gibson
Type: Co-educational Day & Boarding

Borehamwood

HABERDASHERS' ASKE'S SCHOOL
Butterfly Lane, Borehamwood, Hertfordshire WD6 3AF
Tel: 0181 207 4323
Head: Mr J W R Golding MA
Type: Boys Day B7-18
No of pupils: B1300
Fees: DAY £5136-£5601

HABERDASHERS' ASKE'S SCHOOL FOR GIRLS
Aldenham Road, Borehamwood, Hertfordshire WD6 3BT
Tel: 0181 953 4261
Head: Mrs P A Penney BA, FRSA, FIMgt, MINstD
Type: Girls Day G4-18
No of pupils: G1145 VIth240
Fees: DAY £4410

Bushey

C K H R IMMANUEL COLLEGE
87/91 Elstree Road, Bushey, Hertfordshire WD2 3RH
Tel: 0181 950 0604
Head: Myrna Jacobs BA(Hons)
Type: Co-educational Day B11-18 G11-18
No of pupils: B166 G128 VIth29
Fees: DAY £5650

LITTLE ACORNS MONTESSORI SCHOOL
International University Grounds, Bushey,
Hertfordshire WD2 2LN
Tel: 01923 230705
Heads: Jean Nugent & Ruby Lau
Type: Co-educational Day B2-12 G2-12
Fees: DAY £2010

LONGWOOD SCHOOL
Aldenham Road, Bushey, Hertfordshire WD2 2ER
Tel: 01923 253715
Head: Mrs Satoula Livesey CertEd
Type: Co-educational Day B3-8 G3-8
No of pupils: B35 G42
Fees: DAY £2655

ST ANDREW'S MONTESSORI PREP SCHOOL
Aldenham Road, Bushey, Hertfordshire WD2 3TS
Tel: 01442 866290
Head: Mrs S O'Neill
Type: Co-educational Day B2-12 G2-12
No of pupils: B35 G32
Fees: DAY £1590-£4050

ST HILDA'S SCHOOL
High Street, Bushey, Hertfordshire WD2 3DA
Tel: 0181 950 1751
Head: Mrs L Cavanagh BA(Hons), DipCE
Type: Girls Day G3-11
No of pupils: B8 G150
Fees: DAY £2925-£4140

ST MARGARET'S SCHOOL
Merryhill Road, Bushey, Hertfordshire WD2 1DT
Tel: 0181 9501548
Head: Miss M de Villiers BA
Type: Girls Boarding & Day G4-18
No of pupils: G438 VIth66
Fees: FB £7935-£9210 DAY £3240-£5625

Bushey Heath

WESTWOOD SCHOOL
6 Hartsbourne Road, Bushey Heath,
Hertfordshire WD2 1JH
Tel: 0181 950 1138
Head: Mrs J Hill
Type: Co-educational Day B4-7 G4-7
No of pupils: B35 G37
Fees: DAY £3261

Elstree

ALDENHAM SCHOOL
Elstree, Hertfordshire WD6 3AJ
Tel: 01923 858122
Head: S R Borthwick BSc, CPhys, MInstP
Type: Boys Boarding & Day B11-18 G16-18
No of pupils: B375 VIth120 FB100
Fees: FB £8316-£11,910 DAY £5196-£8175

Harpenden

ALDWICKBURY SCHOOL
Wheathampstead Road, Harpenden,
Hertfordshire AL5 1AE
Tel: 01582 713022
Head: P H Jeffery BA
Type: Boys Day & Boarding B4-13 G4-7
No of pupils: B278 G20 WB46
Fees: WB £6045-£6375 DAY £4470-£4800

HARPENDEN PREPARATORY SCHOOL
53 Luton Road, Harpenden, Hertfordshire AL5 2UE
Tel: 01582 712361
Head: Mrs Elizabeth R Broughton CertEd
Type: Co-educational Day B2-11 G2-11
No of pupils: B47 G43
Fees: DAY £2676-£3237

KINGS SCHOOL
Elmfield, Harpenden, Hertfordshire AL5 4DA
Tel: 01582 767566
Head: Michael John Vincent
Type: Co-educational Day B5-16 G5-16
No of pupils: B80 G76
Fees: DAY £6300

ST HILDA'S SCHOOL
28 Douglas Road, Harpenden, Hertfordshire AL5 2ES
Tel: 01582 712307
Head: Mrs M Piachaud BA, CertEd
Type: Girls Day G2-11
No of pupils: G168
Fees: DAY £3045-£3135

Hatfield

QUEENSWOOD SCHOOL
Shepherd's Way, Hatfield, Hertfordshire AL9 6NS
Tel: 01707 652262
Head: Clarissa Farr MA
Type: Girls Boarding & Day G11-18
No of pupils: G288 VIth102
Fees: FB £10,974-£11,958 DAY £6768-£7374

Hemel Hempstead

★ **ABBOTS HILL SCHOOL**
Bunkers Lane, Hemel Hempstead,
Hertfordshire HP3 8RP
Tel: 01442 240333
Head: Mrs K Lewis MA(Cantab), BSc, PGCE, FRSA, MIMgt
Type: Girls Boarding & Day G11-16
No of pupils: 165
Fees: FB £10,710 WB £10,635 DAY £6330

LOCKERS PARK
Lockers Park Lane, Hemel Hempstead,
Hertfordshire HP1 1TL
Tel: 01442 251712
Head: D R Lees-Jones
Type: Boys Boarding & Day B7-13
No of pupils: B115 FB87
Fees: FB £8235 DAY £5085-£5985

ST NICHOLAS HOUSE
Bunkers Lane, Hemel Hempstead,
Hertfordshire HP3 8RP
Tel: 01442 211156
Head: Mrs D A Harrison BA, PGCE
Type: Girls Day B3-7 G3-11
No of pupils: B20 G105
Fees: DAY £3075-£3795

WESTBROOK HAY SCHOOL
London Road, Hemel Hempstead, Hertfordshire HP1 2RF
Tel: 01442 256143
Head: Keith Young BEd(Hons)Exeter
Type: Co-educational Day & Boarding B2-13 G2-13
No of pupils: B140 G46 FB30
Fees: FB £8625 DAY £3495-£6195

Hertford

DUNCOMBE SCHOOL
4 Warren Park Road, Hertford, Hertfordshire SG14 3JA
Tel: 01992 582653
Head: Miss R M Martin
Type: Co-educational Day B4-11 G4-11
No of pupils: B109 G116
Fees: DAY £1524-£4287

HAILEYBURY
Hertford, Hertfordshire SG13 7NU
Tel: 01992 463353
Head: S A Westley MA
Type: Boys Boarding & Day B11-18 G16-18
No of pupils: B298 VIth283 FB420
Fees: FB £13,338 DAY £6405-£9672

HEATH MOUNT SCHOOL
Woodhall Park, Hertford, Hertfordshire SG14 3NG
Tel: 01920 830230
Head: Rev H J Matthews MA, BSc, PGCE
Type: Co-educational Boarding & Day B3-13 G3-13
No of pupils: B178 G86 FB50
Fees: FB £6810-£7620 DAY £1650-£6060

ST JOSEPH'S IN THE PARK
St Mary's Lane, Hertford, Hertfordshire SG14 2LX
Tel: 01992 581378
Head: Mrs J King
Type: Co-educational Day B3-11 G3-11
No of pupils: B52 G53
Fees: DAY £1185

Hitchin

KINGSHOTT
Hitchin, Hertfordshire SG4 7JX
Tel: 01462 432009
Head: Rev D Highton BA
Type: Co-educational Day B4-13 G4-13
No of pupils: B221 G110
Fees: DAY £3180-£4260

★ **THE PRINCESS HELENA COLLEGE**
Temple Dinsley, Preston, Hitchin, Hertfordshire SG14 7RT
Tel: 01462 432100
Head: John F Jarvis OBE, BA, MSc, FIPD, FIMgt, FRGS
Type: Girls Boarding & Day G10-18
No of pupils: G140 VIth43
Fees: FB £8328-£10,410 DAY £5796-£7245

Kings Langley

RUDOLF STEINER SCHOOL
Langley Hill, Kings Langley, Hertfordshire WD4 9HG
Tel: 01923 262505
Type: Co-educational Day B3-19 G3-19
Fees: DAY £2145-£3450

Letchworth

★ **ST CHRISTOPHER SCHOOL**
Barrington Road, Letchworth, Hertfordshire SG6 3JZ
Tel: 01462 679301
Head: Colin Reid MA
Type: Co-educational Day & Boarding B2fi-18 G2fi-18
No of pupils: B310 G206 VIth95
Fees: FB £9171-£11,454 DAY £1620-£6489

ST FRANCIS' COLLEGE
The Broadway, Letchworth, Hertfordshire SG6 3PJ
Tel: 01462 670511
Head: Miss M Hegarty BA, HDipEd, DHS
Type: Girls Day & Boarding B3-7 G3-18
No of pupils: B13 G282 VIth52 FB60
Fees: FB £8325-£10,410 WB £6825-£10,200
DAY £2685-£5355

Much Hadham

BARN SCHOOL
Tower Hill, Much Hadham, Hertfordshire SG10 6DL
Tel: 01279 842502
Head: Mrs M Renny
Type: Co-educational Day B3-11 G3-11
No of pupils: B22 G35
Fees: DAY £2025-£3450

Potters Bar

LOCHINVER HOUSE SCHOOL
Heath Road, Potters Bar, Hertfordshire EN6 1LW
Tel: 01707 653064
Head: P C E Atkinson BSc, CBiol, PGCE
Type: Boys Day B4-13
No of pupils: B315
Fees: DAY £3570-£4755

ST JOHN'S PREPARATORY SCHOOL
The Ridgeway, Potters Bar, Hertfordshire EN6 5QT
Tel: 01707 657294
Head: C Tardios BA(Hons)
Type: Co-educational Day B4-11 G4-11
No of pupils: B81 G75
Fees: DAY £3120-£3600

STORMONT
The Causeway, Potters Bar, Hertfordshire EN6 5HA
Tel: 01707 654037
Head: Mrs M E Johnston BA(Hons), PGCE
Type: Girls Day G4-11
No of pupils: G170
Fees: DAY £3690-£4230

Radlett

MANOR LODGE SCHOOL
Rectory Lane, Radlett, Hertfordshire WD7 9BG
Tel: 01707 642424
Head: Mrs Judith Smart CertEd, BA(Open)
Type: Co-educational Day B4-11 G4-11
No of pupils: B193 G131
Fees: DAY £3420-£4200

RADLETT NURSERY AND INFANTS SCHOOL
Cobden Hill, Radlett, Hertfordshire WD7 2JL
Tel: 01923 856374
Head: Mrs Jenny Briggs
Type: Co-educational Day & Boarding

RADLETT PREPARATORY SCHOOL
Kendal Hall, Radlett, Hertfordshire WD7 7LY
Tel: 01923 856812
Head: W N Warren BEd(Hons)
Type: Co-educational Day B5-11 G5-11
No of pupils: B260 G230
Fees: DAY £3300

Redbourn

RAVENSTONE HOUSE PRE-PREP AND NURSERY
South Common, Redbourn, Hertfordshire AL3 7NB
Tel: 01582 792060
Head: Mrs Mary Hall CertEd
Type: Co-educational Day B0-5 G0-5
No of pupils: B33 G24
Fees: DAY £2530-£4533

Rickmansworth

NORTHWOOD PREPARATORY SCHOOL
Moor Farm, Rikmansworth, Hertfordshire WD3 1LW
Tel: 01923 825648
Head: N D Flynn MA(Oxon), PGCE(Exeter)
Type: Boys Day B4-13
No of pupils: B270
Fees: DAY £3780-£4560

THE RICKMANSWORTH MASONIC SCHOOL
Rickmansworth Park, Rickmansworth,
Hertfordshire WD3 4HF
Tel: 01923 773168
Head: Mrs I M Andrews MA(Oxon)
Type: Girls Day & Boarding G4-18
No of pupils: G680
Fees: FB £5229-£8811 WB £5154-£8736
DAY £2760-£5361

RICKMANSWORTH PNEU SCHOOL
88 The Drive, Rickmansworth, Hertfordshire WD3 4DU
Tel: 01923 772101
Head: Mrs S K Marshall-Taylor BSc
Type: Girls Day G3-11
No of pupils: G136
Fees: DAY £1155-£3315

YORK HOUSE SCHOOL
Redheath, Rickmansworth, Hertfordshire WD3 4LW
Tel: 01923 772395
Head: P B Moore BA, MCollP
Type: Co-educational Day B2-13 G2-13
No of pupils: B229 G8
Fees: DAY £2889-£4554

St Albans

BEECHWOOD PARK
St Albans, Hertfordshire AL3 8AW
Tel: 01582 840333
Head: D S Macpherson MA
Type: Boys Day & Boarding B4-13 G4-7
No of pupils: B258 G49 FB51 WB4
Fees: FB £7725 WB £7305 DAY £3915-£5355

HOMEWOOD INDEPENDENT SCHOOL
Hazel Road, St Albans, Hertfordshire AL2 2AH
Tel: 01727 873542
Head: Mrs Carol Erwin CertEd
Type: Co-educational Day B2-8 G2-8
No of pupils: B40 G30
Fees: DAY £1740-£2925

SACRED HEART JUNIOR SCHOOL
8 King Harry Lane, St Albans, Hertfordshire AL3 4AW
Tel: 01727 862616
Head: Br Roger L Bosse
Type: Co-educational Day & Boarding

ST ALBANS HIGH SCHOOL
Townsend Avenue, St Albans, Hertfordshire AL1 3SJ
Tel: 01727 853800
Head: Mrs C Y Daly BSc, FRSA
Type: Girls Day G7-18
No of pupils: G730 VIth132
Fees: DAY £4170-£5040

ST ALBANS SCHOOL
Abbey Gateway, St Albans, Hertfordshire AL3 4HB
Tel: 01727 855521
Head: Mr A R Grant MA(Cantab)
Type: Boys Day B11-18 G16-18
No of pupils: B430 VIth220
Fees: DAY £5865

ST ALBANS TUTORS
30 Beaconsfield Road, St Albans, Hertfordshire AL1 3RB
Tel: 01727 842348
Head: Mrs Hilary Beskeen BA(Hons)
Type: Co-educational Day

ST COLUMBA'S COLLEGE
King Harry Lane, St Albans, Hertfordshire AL3 4AW
Tel: 01727 855185
Head: J Stuart MA(Oxon)
Type: Boys Day B11-18
No of pupils: B500
Fees: DAY £4140

Tring

★ **THE ARTS EDUCATIONAL SCHOOL**
Tring Park, Tring, Hertfordshire HP23 5LX
Tel: 01442 824255
Principal: Mrs J D Billing GGSM(London), CertEd, FRSA
Type: Co-educational Boarding & Day B8-18 G8-18
No of pupils: 220 FB160
Fees: FB £9108-£11,901 DAY £5253-£7353

ST FRANCIS DE SALES INDEPENDENT RC SCHOOL
Aylesbury Road, Tring, Hertfordshire HP23 4DL
Tel: 01442 822315
Head: Sr Miriam Elizbeth BA, DipEd, DipRel
Type: Girls Day B2-11 G2-17
No of pupils: B39 G101
Fees: DAY £2400-£3750

Ware

★ **ST EDMUND'S COLLEGE**
Old Hall Green, Ware, Hertfordshire SG11 1DS
Tel: 01920 821504
Head: D J J McEwen MA(Oxon), FRSA
Type: Co-educational Day & Boarding B3-18 G3-18
No of pupils: B315 G205 VIth130 FB106 WB12
Fees: FB £8340-£10,320 DAY £4050-£6480

Watford

BHAKTIVEDANTA MANOR SCHOOL
Letchmore Heath, Watford, Hertfordshire WD2 8EP
Tel: 01923 857244
Type: Co-educational Day

NORTHFIELD SCHOOL
Church Road, Watford, Hertfordshire WD1 3QB
Tel: 01923 229758
Head: Mrs P Hargreaves BSc, MEd
Type: Girls Day B2-7 G2-18
No of pupils: B20 G100
Fees: DAY £3180-£4023

STANBOROUGH SCHOOL
Stanborough Park, Watford, Hertfordshire WD2 6JT
Tel: 01923 673268
Head: Dr A Luxton PhD
Type: Co-educational Day & Boarding B3-18 G3-18
Fees: FB £5890-£6690 DAY £2790-£2790

Welwyn

SHERRARDSWOOD SCHOOL
Lockleys, Welwyn, Hertfordshire AL6 0BJ
Tel: 01438 714282
Head: Martin Lloyd MA
Type: Co-educational Day & Boarding B4-18 G4-18
No of pupils: B159 G138 VIth20
Fees: FB £6804-£8385 DAY £2706-£4437

Kent

Ashford

ASHFORD JUNIOR SCHOOL
East Hill, Ashford, Kent TN24 8PB
Tel: 01233 625171
Head: P H Power BSc, CertEd
Type: Girls Boarding & Day G3-11
No of pupils: G158
Fees: FB £9747 DAY £626-£4941

ASHFORD SCHOOL
East Hill, Ashford, Kent TN24 8PB
Tel: 01233 625171/2
Head: Mrs P Metham BA(Hons) Bristol
Type: Girls Day & Boarding G11-18
No of pupils: G366 VIth111
Fees: FB £9747-£11,319 DAY £626-£6513

FRIARS SCHOOL
Ashford, Kent TN23 3DJ
Tel: 01233 620493
Head: P M Ashley BA, CertEd
Type: Co-educational Boarding & Day B2-13 G2-13
No of pupils: B118 G36 FB4 WB8
Fees: WB £7800 DAY £1260-£5595

HOLLINGTON SCHOOL
Hollington Place, Ashford, Kent TN24 8UN
Tel: 01233 621000
Head: Mrs M J Cox BA(Hons)
Type: Co-educational Day B2-11 G2-11
No of pupils: B22 G25
Fees: DAY £2715-£2865

SPRING GROVE SCHOOL
Harville Road, Ashford, Kent TN25 5EX
Tel: 01233 812337
Head: N Washington-Jones BA
Type: Co-educational Day B2-11 G2-11
No of pupils: B80 G84
Fees: DAY £1500-£4200

WYE HIGH SCHOOL
Oxenturn House, Ashford, Kent TN25 5AW
Tel: 01233 812244
Head: Mrs E P M Fenner
Type: Co-educational Day

Broadstairs

DAVENPORT ACTIVITY CENTRE
Davenport House School, Margate Road, Broadstairs,
Kent CT10 2QD
Head: N Barnsby
Type: Co-educational Day

HADDON DENE SCHOOL
57 Gladstone Road, Broadstairs, Kent CT10 2HY
Tel: 01843 861176
Heads: Dr & Mrs P J Smith
Type: Co-educational Day B3-11 G3-11
No of pupils: B105 G95
Fees: DAY £1830-£2190

WELLESLEY HOUSE
114 Ramsgate Road, Broadstairs, Kent CT10 2DG
Tel: 01843 862 991
Head: R R Steel BSc
Type: Co-educational Boarding & Day B7-13 G7-13
No of pupils: B102 G53 FB95 WB36
Fees: FB £9225 WB £8925 DAY £6825

Canterbury

KENT COLLEGE
Whitstable Road, Canterbury, Kent CT2 9DT
Tel: 01227 763231
Head: E B Halse BSc
Type: Co-educational Day & Boarding B3-18 G3-18
No of pupils: B307 G218 VIth160
Fees: FB £8481-£10,770 DAY £6048

KING'S JUNIOR SCHOOL
Milner Court, Canterbury, Kent CT2 0AY
Tel: 01227 714000
Head: R G Barton MA
Type: Co-educational Boarding & Day B4-13 G4-13
No of pupils: B175 G104 FB40 WB18
Fees: FB/WB £8460 DAY £3300-£5910

THE KING'S SCHOOL, CANTERBURY
Canterbury, Kent CT1 2ES
Tel: 01227 595501
Head: Rev Keith Wilkinson BA, MA, FRSA
Type: Co-educational Boarding & Day B13-18 G13-18
No of pupils: B438 G302
Fees: FB £13,440 DAY £9285

PERRY COURT RUDOLF STEINER SCHOOL
Garlinge Green, Canterbury, Kent CT4 5RU
Tel: 01227 738285
Type: Co-educational Day B4-17 G4-17
No of pupils: B110 G90
Fees: DAY £2832-£3342

ST CHRISTOPHER'S SCHOOL
48 New Dover Road, Canterbury, Kent CT1 3DT
Tel: 01227 462960
Head: J D Archer BEd(Hons)
Type: Co-educational Day B2-11 G2-11
No of pupils: B62 G78
Fees: DAY £960-£2307

ST EDMUND'S JUNIOR SCHOOL
St Thomas Hill, Canterbury, Kent CT2 8HU
Tel: 01227 454575
Head: D C Gahan MA
Type: Co-educational Day & Boarding B4-13 G4-13
No of pupils: FB58
Fees: FB £8100 DAY £2985-£5655

ST EDMUND'S SCHOOL
Canterbury, Kent CT2 8HU
Tel: 01227 454575
Head: A N Ridley MA(Oxon)
Type: Co-educational Day & Boarding B3-18 G3-18
No of pupils: B320 G170 VIth120
Fees: FB £12,030 DAY £3090-£8310

ST FAITHS AT ASH SCHOOL
5 The Street, Canterbury, Kent CT3 2HH
Tel: 01304 813409
Head: Mrs J A Dredge BEd
Type: Co-educational Day B3-11 G3-11
No of pupils: B90 G100
Fees: DAY £945-£2895

VERNON HOLME
(Kent College Infant & Junior School), Canterbury,
Kent CT2 9AQ
Tel: 01227 762436
Head: T J Smith BA
Type: Co-educational Day & Boarding B3-11 G3-11
No of pupils: B109 G96 FB9 WB1
Fees: FB £8481 DAY £2928-£5862

Cranbrook

BEDGEBURY SCHOOL
Bedgebury Park, Cranbrook, Kent TN17 2SH
Tel: 01580 211221/211954
Head: Mrs L J Griffin BA, BPhil
Type: Girls Boarding & Day B3-7 G3-18
No of pupils: B13 G257 VIth97
Fees: FB £7425-£11,301 DAY £1747-£6996

BENENDEN SCHOOL
Cranbrook, Kent TN17 4AA
Tel: 01580 240592
Head: Mrs G duCharme MA
Type: Girls Boarding G11-18
No of pupils: G440 VIth140
Fees: FB £13,260

BETHANY SCHOOL
Cranbrook, Kent TN17 1LB
Tel: 01580 211273
Head: W M Harvey MA(Oxon) DipEd
Type: Co-educational Boarding & Day B11-18 G11-18
No of pupils: B245 G50 VIth84
Fees: FB/ WB £9819-£10,353 DAY £6282-£6813

★ **DULWICH PREPARATORY SCHOOL**
Coursehorn, Cranbrook, Kent TN17 3NP
Tel: 01580 712179
Head: M C Wagstaffe BA(Hons), PGCE
Type: Co-educational Day & Boarding B3-13 G3-13
No of pupils: B276 G257
Fees: FB £8775-£8985 DAY £2025-£5850

Deal

DON BUSS LEARNING CENTRE
The Old School, Ringwould Road, Deal, Kent CT14 8DW
Head: Mrs V Norman
Type: Co-educational Day

NORTHBOURNE PARK SCHOOL
Betteshanger, Deal, Kent CT14 0NW
Tel: 01304 611215/218
Head: F Roche BEd(Hons), MA
Type: Co-educational Day & Boarding B3-13 G3-13
Fees: FB/WB £8535-£9225 DAY £3375-£6045

Dover

DOVER COLLEGE
Effingham Crescent, Dover, Kent CT17 9RH
Tel: 01304 205969
Head: M P G Wright BA, JP
Type: Co-educational Boarding & Day B11-18 G11-18
No of pupils: B130 G120 VIth100
Fees: FB/WB £9450-£11,820 DAY £3900-£6450

DUKE OF YORK'S ROYAL MILITARY SCHOOL
Dover, Kent CT15 5EQ
Tel: 01304 245024
Head: Col G H Wilson BA, DipEd, MEd, FRSA
Type: Co-educational Boarding B11-18 G11-18
No of pupils: VIth120
Fees: FB £795

Edenbridge

ST ANDREW'S PREPARATORY SCHOOL
Eden Hall, Edenbridge, Kent TN8 5NN
Tel: 01342 850388
Head: Mrs A Jones BA, PGCE
Type: Co-educational Day B3-11 G3-11
No of pupils: B59 G48
Fees: DAY £1440-£2700

Faversham

LORENDON PREPARATORY SCHOOL
Painter's Forstal, Faversham, Kent ME13 0EN
Tel: 01795 590030
Head: Mrs Anne Hannaford BA(Hons),DipEd
Type: Co-educational Day B3-11 G3-11
No of pupils: B60 G60
Fees: DAY £2730-£3675

Folkestone

SIBTON PARK GIRLS' PREPARATORY SCHOOL
Sibton Park, Folkestone, Kent CT18 8HB
Tel: 01303 862284
Heads: Mrs P F E Blackwell MA(Hons) &
          Mr C Blackwell BA(Hons)
Type: Girls Boarding & Day B1-8 G1-13
No of pupils: B20 G95
Fees: FB £7170-£9390 DAY £360-£6150

ST MARY'S COLLEGE
Ravenlea Road, Folkestone, Kent CT20 2JU
Tel: 01303 851363
Head: Sr B Milligan
Type: Co-educational Day B4-16 G4-16
No of pupils: B51 G69
Fees: DAY £2010-£5367

WESTBROOK HOUSE PREPARATORY SCHOOL
Westbrook House, Folkestone, Kent CT20 2NQ
Tel: 01303 851222
Head: Christopher FitzGerald BA, CertEd, ACP
Type: Co-educational Day & Boarding B3-13 G3-13
No of pupils: B71 G53
Fees: FB £6300-£8160 DAY £2000-£5385

Gillingham

BRYONY SCHOOL
Marshall Road, Gillingham, Kent ME8 0AJ
Tel: 01634 231511
Heads: D E & Mrs M P Edmunds
Type: Co-educational Day B2-11 G2-11
No of pupils: B99 G120
Fees: DAY £2060-£2349

Gravesend

BRONTE SCHOOL
5-7 Parrock Road, Gravesend,
Kent DA12 1PY
Tel: 01474 533805
Head: Mrs R M Roberts CertEd
Type: Co-educational Day B2-11 G2-11
No of pupils: B46 G40
Fees: DAY £2750

COBHAM HALL SCHOOL
Gravesend, Kent DA12 3BL
Tel: 01474 823371/824 319
Head: Mrs R McCarthy BA
Type: Girls Boarding & Day G11-18
No of pupils: G200 VIth70 FB160 WB10
Fees: FB £12,855 DAY £6600-£8250

CONVENT PREPARATORY SCHOOL
46 Old Road East, Gravesend, Kent DA12 1NR
Tel: 01474 533012
Head: Sr Anne
Type: Co-educational Day B3-11 G3-11
No of pupils: B127 G119
Fees: DAY £2100

Hawkhurst

MARLBOROUGH HOUSE SCHOOL
High Street, Hawkhurst, Kent TN18 4PY
Tel: 01580 753555
Head: David Hopkins MA(Oxon), PGCE
Type: Co-educational Day & Boarding B3-13 G3-13
No of pupils: B115 G69
Fees: FB £8805 WB £8745 DAY £1785-£6705

ST RONAN'S
Hawkhurst, Kent TN18 5DJ
Tel: 01580 752271
Head: Sir J R Vassar-Smith Bt
Type: Co-educational Boarding & Day B3-13 G3-13
No of pupils: B86 G14
Fees: FB/WB £8640 DAY £1044-£6360

Longfield

STEEPHILL SCHOOL
Off Castle Hill, Longfield, Kent DA3 7BG
Tel: 01474 702107
Head: Mrs Linda Bramley BA(Hons), PGCE
Type: Co-educational Day B3-11 G3-11
No of pupils: B41 G34
Fees: DAY £2250

Maidstone

SHERNOLD SCHOOL
Hill Place, Maidstone, Kent ME16 0ER
Tel: 01622 752868
Head: Mrs C Birtwell BSc, MBA
Type: Co-educational Day B3-5 G3-11
Fees: DAY £1563-£3015

SUNRISE INDEPENDENT SCHOOL
Sutton Road, Maidstone, Kent ME17 3ND
Tel: 01622 861325
Head: Mrs J Bowyer
Type: Co-educational Day B0-5 G0-5
Fees: DAY £4160

SUTTON VALENCE SCHOOL WITH UNDERHILL
Maidstone, Kent ME17 3HN
Tel: 01622 842281
Head: N A Sampson MA
Type: Co-educational Day & Boarding B3-19 G3-19
No of pupils: B373 G277 VIth125 FB115 WB4
Fees: FB £8850-£11,700 DAY £3150-£7485

Margate

HONITON HOUSE PREPARATORY SCHOOL
Sweyn Road, Margate, Kent CT9 2DG
Tel: 01843 221819
Head: Mrs Mary Bate
Type: Co-educational Day B3-11 G3-11
No of pupils: B43 G40

Otham

EYLESDEN COURT PREPARATORY SCHOOL
Gore Court, Otham, Kent
Tel: 01622 737845
Head: R G Dean-Hughes LLM
Type: Co-educational Day B3-13 G3-13
Fees: DAY £2520-£3885

Ramsgate

ST LAWRENCE COLLEGE IN THANET
Ramsgate, Kent CT11 7AE
Tel: 01843 587666
Head: Mark Slater, MA
Type: Co-educational Boarding & Day B4-18 G4-18
No of pupils: B321 G204 VIth132 FB230
Fees: FB £8880-£11,835 DAY £5820-£7905

THE JUNIOR SCHOOL, ST LAWRENCE COLLEGE
College Road, Ramsgate, Kent CT11 7AF
Tel: 01843 591788
Head: Rev D D R Blackwall BSc
Type: Co-educational Day & Boarding B4-13 G4-13
No of pupils: B85 G64 FB58
Fees: FB £8880 DAY £2070-£5820

Rochester

CEDARS SCHOOL
219 Maidstone Road, Rochester, Kent ME1 3BU
Tel: 01634 847163
Head: Mrs B M V Gross
Type: Co-educational Day

GAD'S HILL SCHOOL
Rochester, Kent ME3 7PA
Tel: 01474 822366
Head: Mrs A Everitt BA(Hons), AKC, PGCE
Type: Co-educational Day B3-11 G3-18
No of pupils: B40 G110 VIth1
Fees: DAY £1338-£2925

KING'S PREPARATORY SCHOOL
King Edward Road, Rochester, Kent ME1 1UB
Tel: 01634 843657
Head: Mr C J Nickless BA
Type: Co-educational Day & Boarding B8-13 G8-13
No of pupils: B194 G51 FB16
Fees: FB/WB £9735-£10,560 DAY £5475-£6300

★ **KING'S SCHOOL, ROCHESTER**
Satis House, Rochester, Kent ME1 1TE
Tel: 01634 843913
Head: Dr I R Walker BA, PhD, LTh, ABIA, FCollP, FRSA
Type: Co-educational Day & Boarding B4-18 G4-18
No of pupils: B511 G180 VIth117
Fees: FB £9735-£12,375 DAY £3510-£7110

ROCHESTER TUTORS INDEPENDENT COLLEGE
New Road House, Rochester, Kent ME1 1BD
Tel: 01634 828115
Heads: B Pain BSc(Hons) & Simon De Belder BA(Hons)
Type: Co-educational Day & Boarding B14-50 G14-50
No of pupils: B75 G75
Fees: FB £3150 DAY £6900

ST ANDREW'S SCHOOL
24-28 Watts Avenue, Rochester, Kent ME1 1SA
Tel: 01634 843479
Head: L Smith
Type: Co-educational Day B4-11 G4-11
No of pupils: B140 G160
Fees: DAY £2070-£2310

Sevenoaks

APPLE TREE COTTAGE SCHOOL
Seal Chart, Sevenoaks, Kent TN15 OES
Tel: 01732 61097
Head: Mrs M May
Type: Co-educational Day

★ **COMBE BANK SCHOOL**
Sevenoaks, Kent TN14 6AE
Tel: 01959 563720
Heads: Miss N Spurr BSc, FRSA & Mrs E Marsden BA
Type: Girls Day B3-5 G3-18
No of pupils: B17 G389 VIth47
Fees: DAY £1950-£6030

THE GRANVILLE SCHOOL
2 Bradbourne Park Road, Sevenoaks, Kent TN13 3LJ
Tel: 01732 453039
Head: Mrs J D Evans CertEd(Cantab)
Type: Girls Day B3-4 G3-11
No of pupils: B12 G178
Fees: DAY £1575-£3960

MARGARET MAY SCHOOLS LIMITED
Apple Tree Cottage School, Sevenoaks, Kent TN15 0ES
Tel: 01732 761097
Head: Mrs M May
Type: Co-educational Day B3-8 G3-8
No of pupils: B17 G18
Fees: DAY £1050

THE NEW BEACON SCHOOL
Brittains Lane, Sevenoaks, Kent TN13 2PB
Tel: 01732 452131
Head: R Constantine MA(Cantab)
Type: Boys Day & Boarding B5-13
No of pupils: B390
Fees: WB £7260 DAY £2625-£4650

RUSSELL HOUSE SCHOOL
Station Road, Sevenoaks, Kent TN14 5QU
Tel: 01959 522352
Heads: Mrs E Lindsay BA, CertEd &
     Mr A Duffy BEd(Hons)
Type: Co-educational Day B3-11 G3-11
No of pupils: B95 G95
Fees: DAY £2025-£4155

SEVENOAKS PREPARATORY SCHOOL
Fawke Cottage, Sevenoaks, Kent TN15 0JU
Tel: 01732 762336
Head: E H Oatley
Type: Co-educational Day B2-13 G2-13
No of pupils: B220 G60
Fees: DAY £2910-£4410

SEVENOAKS SCHOOL
Sevenoaks, Kent TN13 1HU
Tel: 01732 455133
Head: R P Barker MA
Type: Co-educational Day & Boarding B11-18 G11-18
No of pupils: B525 G415 FB331
Fees: FB £11,178-£11,961 DAY £6804-£7587

SOLEFIELD SCHOOL
Solefield Road, Sevenoaks, Kent TN13 1PH
Tel: 01732 452142
Head: J R Baugh BEd
Type: Boys Day B4-13
No of pupils: B200
Fees: DAY £870-£1480

ST MICHAEL'S SCHOOL
Offord Court, Sevenoaks, Kent TN14 5SA
Tel: 01959 522137
Head: Dr P A Roots PhD
Type: Co-educational Day B2-13 G2-13
No of pupils: B220 G130 WB8
Fees: DAY £3000-£4500

WALTHAMSTOW HALL
Sevenoaks, Kent TN13 3UL
Tel: 01732 451334
Head: Mrs J S Lang MA(Oxford)
Type: Girls Day & Boarding G3-18
No of pupils: G370 VIth110
Fees: FB/WB £10,035-£12,360 DAY £285-£6660

WEST HEATH SCHOOL
Sevenoaks, Kent TN13 1SR
Tel: 01732 452541
Head: Mrs A Williamson BSc, FRSA
Type: Girls Boarding & Day G11-18
No of pupils: G75 VIth30
Fees: FB £11,040 DAY £7755

Sheerness

ELLIOTT PARK SCHOOL CHARITABLE TRUST
18-20 Marina Drive, Sheerness, Kent ME12 2DP
Tel: 01795 873372
Head: Richard E Fielder CertEd, DipEdACP
Type: Co-educational Day B4-11 G4-11
Fees: DAY £1950-£2040

Sittingbourne

INTEGRATED SUPPORT PROGRAMME
Church Street, Sittingbourne, Kent ME10 3EG
Tel: 01795 428097
Head: Miss B M Gorman
Type: Co-educational Day

Tonbridge

FOSSE BANK NEW SCHOOL
Coldharbour Lane, Tonbridge, Kent TN11 9LE
Tel: 01732 834212
Head: Mrs M Wells MA, DipEd
Type: Co-educational Day B2-11 G2-11
No of pupils: B46 G47
Fees: DAY £1974-£3348

HILDEN GRANGE SCHOOL
62 Dry Hill Park Road, Tonbridge, Kent TN10 3BX
Tel: 01732 352706
Heads: J A Stewart & J Withers
Type: Co-educational Day B3-13 G3-13
No of pupils: B208 G79
Fees: DAY £3105-£4968

HILDEN OAKS SCHOOL
38 Dry Hill Park Road, Tonbridge, Kent TN10 3BU
Tel: 01732 353941
Head: Mrs H J Bacon
Type: Co-educational Day B3-7 G3-11
No of pupils: B21 G119
Fees: DAY £1530-£3390

THE OLD VICARAGE
Marden, Tonbridge, Kent TN12 9AG
Tel: 01622 832200
Head: Mrs P G Stevens LRAM(S&D)
Type: Girls Day & Boarding G16-50
No of pupils: G10
Fees: FB £6900 DAY £3975

SACKVILLE SCHOOL
Tonbridge Road, Tonbridge, Kent TN11 9HN
Tel: 01732 838888
Head: Mrs M Sinclair MA
Type: Co-educational Day B11-18 G11-18
No of pupils: B100 G16 VIth3
Fees: DAY £4806-£6024

★ **SOMERHILL PRE-PREP, DERWENT LODGE, YARDLEY COURT**
Somerhill, Tonbridge, Kent TN11 0NJ
Tel: 01732 352124
Head: J S M Morris
Type: Co-educational Day B3-13 G3-13
No of pupils: B236 G164
Fees: DAY £1950-£6225

TONBRIDGE SCHOOL
Tonbridge, Kent TN9 1JP
Tel: 01732 365555
Head: J M Hammond MA
Type: Boys Boarding & Day B13-18
No of pupils: B696 VIth275 FB430
Fees: FB £13,620 DAY £9612

Tunbridge Wells

BEECHWOOD SACRED HEART
12 Pembury Road, Tunbridge Wells, Kent TN2 3QD
Tel: 01892 532747
Head: T S Hodkinson
Type: Girls Day & Boarding B2-11 G2-18
No of pupils: B8 G151 VIth54
Fees: FB £8280-£11,211 DAY £2535-£6675

BRETLANDS BEAUTY TRAINING CENTRE
Baden-Powell Place, Tunbridge Wells, Kent TN4 8XD
Tel: 01892 533161
Head: Mrs J Thornycroft CIDESCO, BABTAC, C&G
Type: Girls Day G17-55
Fees: DAY £1410-£5288

HOLMEWOOD HOUSE
Tunbridge Wells, Kent TN3 0EB
Tel: 01892 862088
Head: D G Ives MA(Oxon)
Type: Co-educational Day & Boarding B3-13 G3-13
No of pupils: B302 G162 FB62
Fees: FB/WB £10,980 DAY £1995-£7380

KENT COLLEGE JUNIOR SCHOOL
Aultmore House, Old Church Road, Tunbridge Wells,
Kent TN2 4AX
Tel: 01892 820204
Head: Mrs Diana Dunham
Type: Girls Day & Boarding B4-11 G4-11
No of pupils: B92 G81
Fees: FB £9627 DAY £5400

KENT COLLEGE, PEMBURY
Tunbridge Wells, Kent TN2 4AX
Tel: 01892 822006
Head: Miss B J Crompton BSc, CPhys, MInstP
Type: Girls Boarding & Day G3-18
No of pupils: G327 VIth63 FB68 WB32
Fees: FB £8760-£11,700 WB £7710-£10,905
DAY £3345-£6960

THE MEAD SCHOOL
16 Frant Road, Tunbridge Wells, Kent TN2 5SN
Tel: 01892 525837
Head: Mrs A Culley CertEd(Oxon)
Type: Co-educational Day B3-11 G3-11
No of pupils: B27 G28
Fees: DAY £1440-£3480

ROSE HILL SCHOOL
Tunbridge Wells, Kent TN4 9SY
Tel: 01892 525591
Head: J G L Parker BA, JP
Type: Co-educational Day B2-13 G2-13
No of pupils: B191 G77
Fees: DAY £1800-£5850

Westerham

CROFT HALL SCHOOL
London Road, Westerham, Kent TN16 2DU
Tel: 01959 563381
Head: Miss P Wilkinson CertEd
Type: Co-educational Day B3-7 G3-7
No of pupils: B16 G24
Fees: DAY £1575-£2790

THE HILL SCHOOL
Pilgrims' Way, Westerham, Kent TN16 2DU
Tel: 01959 563381
Head: N J R Sanceau BEd, FCollP, CertEd
Type: Co-educational Day B3-13 G3-13
No of pupils: B60 G30
Fees: DAY £1665-£4320

Westgate-on-Sea

CHARTFIELD SCHOOL
45 Minster Road, Westgate-on-Sea, Kent CT8 8DA
Tel: 01843 831716
Head: Mrs J L Prebble CertEd
Type: Co-educational Day B4-11 G4-11
No of pupils: B38 G36
Fees: DAY £1650-£1680

URSULINE COLLEGE
225 Canterbury Road, Westgate-on-Sea, Kent CT8 8LX
Tel: 01843 834431
Head: Sr Alice Montgomery OSU, MEd
Type: Co-educational Boarding & Day B5-18 G5-18
No of pupils: B130 G190 VIth120
Fees: FB £9969-£11,124 DAY £3750-£5640

Surrey

Ashtead

CITY OF LONDON FREEMEN'S SCHOOL
Ashtead Park, Ashtead, Surrey KT21 1ET
Tel: 01372 277933
Head: D C Haywood MA
Type: Co-educational Day & Boarding B7-18 G7-18
No of pupils: B295 G326 VIth120 FB26 WB21
Fees: FB £8286-£9888 WB £7893-£9585
DAY £4689-£6291

PARSONS MEAD SCHOOL
Ottways Lane, Ashtead, Surrey KT21 2PE
Tel: 01372 276401
Head: Miss E B Plant BA(Hons), PGCE
Type: Girls Day & Boarding G3-18
No of pupils: G355 VIth40 WB12
Fees: WB £7940 DAY £3090-£5280

Bagshot

HALL GROVE SCHOOL
Bagshot, Surrey GU19 5HZ
Tel: 01276 473059
Head: A R Graham BSc, PGCE
Type: Boys Day B4-13
No of pupils: B230
Fees: DAY £3615-£4530

Banstead

GREENACRE SCHOOL
Sutton Lane, Banstead, Surrey SM7 3RA
Tel: 01737 352114
Head: Mrs P M Wood BA
Type: Girls Day G3-18
No of pupils: G351 VIth46
Fees: DAY £1350-£5250

OAKLAND NURSERY SCHOOL
Palmersfield Road, Banstead, Surrey SM7 2LD
Tel: 01737 351157
Head: Mrs M Dollimore CertEd
Type: Co-educational Day B3-5 G3-5
No of pupils: B32 G32
Fees: DAY £750-£1245

PRIORY SCHOOL
Bolters Lane, Banstead, Surrey SM7 2AJ
Tel: 01737 354479
Head: I R Chapman MA, BEd
Type: Boys Day B3-13
No of pupils: B195
Fees: DAY £2775-£4095

Camberley

CLEWBOROUGH HOUSE PREPARATORY SCHOOL
Clewborough Drive, Camberley, Surrey GU15 1NX
Tel: 01276 64799
Head: Lt Col Donald A R Clark
Type: Co-educational Day B7-13 G7-13
No of pupils: B60 G36
Fees: DAY £3930-£4245

CLEWBOROUGH HOUSE SCHOOL AT CHESWYCKS
Guildford Road, Camberley, Surrey GU16 6PB
Tel: 01252 835669
Head: Lt Col D A R Clark
Type: Co-educational Day B2-7 G2-7
No of pupils: B84 G53
Fees: DAY £1725-£3615

EAGLE HOUSE
Sandhurst, Camberley, Surrey
Tel: 01344 772134
Head: S J Carder MA
Type: Co-educational Day B4-13 G4-13
No of pupils: B163 G17 FB23 WB24
Fees: FB £9060 DAY £3705-£6375

ELMHURST BALLET SCHOOL
Heathcote Road, Camberley, Surrey GU15 2EV
Tel: 01276 65301
Head: John McNamara BA, MPhil
Type: Co-educational Boarding & Day B9-19 G9-19
No of pupils: B15 G134 VIth72 FB193
Fees: FB £9570 DAY £7020

HAWLEY PLACE SCHOOL
Fernhill Road, Camberley, Surrey GU17 9HU
Tel: 01276 32028
Heads: T G Pipe MA & Mrs M L Pipe LèsL
Type: Co-educational Day B2-11 G2-16
No of pupils: B30 G116
Fees: DAY £3090-£3990

LYNDHURST SCHOOL
Sumner Lodge, Camberley, Surrey GU15 3NE
Tel: 01276 22895
Head: R L Cunliffe CertEd
Type: Co-educational Day B3-12 G3-12
No of pupils: B97 G86
Fees: DAY £1575-£3795

ST CATHERINE'S SCHOOL
Park Road, Camberley, Surrey GU15 2LL
Tel: 01276 23511
Heads: R W Burt BSc, AdvDipEd &
Mrs H M Burt BA, DipEd
Type: Girls Day B2-5 G2-11
No of pupils: B14 G108
Fees: DAY £1575-£4050

YATELEY MANOR SCHOOL
51 Reading Road, Camberley, Surrey GU17 7UQ
Tel: 01252 873298
Head: F G F Howard MA(Cantab), DipEd(Oxon)
Type: Co-educational Day B3-13 G3-13
No of pupils: B322 G175
Fees: DAY £1476-£4932

Caterham

★ CATERHAM PREPARATORY SCHOOL
Harestone Valley Road, Caterham, Surrey CR3 6YB
Tel: 01883 342097
Head: A D Moy BSc, MIBiol
Type: Co-educational Day B3-11 G3-11
No of pupils: 170
Fees: DAY £1755-£5100

★ CATERHAM SCHOOL
Harestone Valley, Caterham, Surrey CR3 6YA
Tel: 01883 343028
Head: R A Davey MA(Dublin)
Type: Co-educational Day & Boarding B3-18 G3-18
No of pupils: 710 VIth220
Fees: FB £11,130-£11,730 DAY £1740-£6090

ESSENDENE LODGE SCHOOL
Essendene Road, Caterham, Surrey CR3 5PB
Tel: 01883 348349
Heads: Mrs S A Haydock & J G Davies
Type: Co-educational Day B2-11 G2-11
Fees: DAY £700-£2100

OAKHYRST GRANGE SCHOOL
160 Stanstead Road, Caterham, Surrey CR3 6AF
Tel: 01883 343344
Head: Mrs D F Cooper CertEd
Type: Boys Day B3-11
No of pupils: B115 G10
Fees: DAY £410-£1025

Chertsey

SIR WILLIAM PERKINS'S SCHOOL
Guildford Road, Chertsey, Surrey KT16 9BN
Tel: 01932 562161
Head: Miss S A Ross BSc
Type: Girls Day G11-18
No of pupils: G460 VIth130
Fees: DAY £4170

Chobham

FLEXLANDS SCHOOL
Station Road, Chobham, Surrey GU24 8AG
Tel: 01276 858841/857341
Head: Mrs Sarah Shaw BA(Hons), PGCE
Type: Girls Day G3-11
No of pupils: G165
Fees: DAY £1860-£4395

Cobham

★ AMERICAN COMMUNITY SCHOOLS
Heywood, Portsmouth Road, Cobham, Surrey KT11 1BL
Tel: 01932 867251
Head: T Lehman
Type: Co-educational Boarding & Day B3-18 G3-18
No of pupils: B666 G584
Fees: On application

THE COBHAM MONTESSORI NURSERY SCHOL
23 Spencer Road, Cobham, Surrey KT11 2AF
Tel: 01306 876465
Head: Mrs S Hall IntMontDip
Type: Co-educational Day B2-5 G2-5
No of pupils: B20 G20
Fees: DAY £630-£3000

FELTONFLEET SCHOOL
Cobham, Surrey KT11 1DR
Tel: 01932 862264
Head: D T Cherry
Type: Co-educational Day & Boarding B3-13 G3-13
No of pupils: B194 G16 FB10 WB28
Fees: FB/WB £7650 DAY £3600-£5685

NOTRE DAME PREPARATORY SCHOOL
Burwood House, Cobham, Surrey KT11 1HA
Tel: 01932 862152
Head: Sr J Lanaghan TCert
Type: Girls Day B3-6 G3-11
No of pupils: B9 G291
Fees: DAY £1575-£4500

NOTRE DAME SENIOR SCHOOL
Burwood House, Cobham, Surrey KT11 1HA
Tel: 01932 863560
Head: Sr Faith Ede MA
Type: Girls Day G11-18
No of pupils: G300 VIth57
Fees: DAY £4500-£4734

PARKSIDE SCHOOL
The Manor, Cobham, Surrey KT11 3PX
Tel: 01932 862749
Head: R L Shipp FCP, BA, CertEd
Type: Boys Day & Boarding B2-14 G3-5
No of pupils: B290 G20 FB8 WB24
Fees: FB £8700 DAY £3690-£5670

REED'S SCHOOL
Sandy Lane, Cobham, Surrey KT11 2ES
Tel: 01932 863076
Head: D E Prince MA(Cantab)
Type: Boys Boarding & Day B11-18 G16-18
No of pupils: B340 VIth75
Fees: FB £8277-£9894 DAY £6207-£7479

YEHUDI MENUHIN SCHOOL
Stoke Road, Cobham, Surrey KT11 3QQ
Tel: 01932 864739
Head: N Chisholm MA
Type: Co-educational Boarding B8-18 G8-18
No of pupils: B20 G30 VIth15 FB57
Fees: FB £20,205

Cranleigh

★ CRANLEIGH PREPARATORY SCHOOL
Horseshoe Lane, Cranleigh, Surrey GU6 8QH
Tel: 01483 274199
Head: M R Keppie MA, PGCE
Type: Boys Boarding & Day B7-13
No of pupils: B185
Fees: FB £8700 DAY £6465

★ CRANLEIGH SCHOOL
Horseshoe Lane, Cranleigh, Surrey GU6 8QQ
Tel: 01483 273997
Head: G de W Waller MA, MSc, FRSA
Type: Boys Boarding & Day B13-18 G16-18
No of pupils: B415 G71 VIth247
Fees: FB £12,990 DAY £9615

DUKE OF KENT SCHOOL
Peaslake Road, Cranleigh, Surrey GU6 7NS
Tel: 01483 277313
Head: R K Wilson MA
Type: Co-educational Boarding & Day B4-13 G4-13
No of pupils: B108 G50
Fees: FB/WB £7725-£8640 DAY £2355-£6045

Dorking

ABINGER HAMMER VILLAGE SCHOOL
Hackhurst Lane, Dorking, Surrey RH5 6SE
Tel: 01306 730343
Head: Mrs Barbara Turner BEd(Hons), DipEd
Type: Co-educational Day B2-8 G2-8
No of pupils: B7 G3

BELMONT PREPARATORY SCHOOL
Feldemore, Dorking, Surrey RH5 6LQ
Tel: 01306 730852
Head: D St Clair Gainer BEd(Hons)(Lond)
Type: Co-educational Boarding & Day B4-13 G4-13
No of pupils: B191 G69
Fees: FB £8720 DAY £2835-£5230

BOX HILL SCHOOL
Dorking, Surrey RH5 6EA
Tel: 01372 373382
Head: Dr R A S Atwood BA, PhD
Type: Co-educational Boarding & Day B11-18 G11-18
No of pupils: B176 G93 FB140 WB23
Fees: FB £10,530 WB £10,080 DAY £5100-£6300

HURTWOOD HOUSE
Dorking, Surrey RH5 6NU
Tel: 01483 277416
Head: K R B Jackson MA, FRSA
Type: Co-educational Day

NOWER LODGE SCHOOL
Coldharbour Lane, Dorking, Surrey RH4 3BT
Tel: 01306 882448
Head: Mrs S Watt CertEd
Type: Co-educational Day B3-13 G3-13
No of pupils: B81 G43
Fees: DAY £1485-£3975

ST TERESA'S SCHOOL
Effingham Hill, Dorking, Surrey RH5 6ST
Tel: 01372 452037
Head: L Allan BA, MEd
Type: Girls Boarding & Day G3-18
No of pupils: G580
Fees: FB £8250-£9330 DAY £2250-£4590

STANWAY SCHOOL
Chichester Road, Dorking, Surrey RH4 1LR
Tel: 01306 882151
Head: Mrs C A Belk BA, DipEd
Type: Girls Day G3-13
No of pupils: B40 G140
Fees: DAY £678-£4290

Effingham

ST TERESA'S PREPARATORY SCHOOL
Grove House, Effingham, Surrey KT24 5QA
Tel: 01372 453456
Head: Mrs M Head CertEd, RTC
Type: Girls Boarding & Day B2-11 G2-11
No of pupils: FB6
Fees: FB/WB £9285 DAY £1500-£3735

Egham

★ **AMERICAN COMMUNITY SCHOOLS, ENGLAND**
Woodlee, London Road, Egham, Surrey TW20 0HS
Tel: 01784 430611
Principal: Mrs K Alderdice
Type: Co-educational Day B3-14 G3-14
No of pupils: B155 G105
Fees: On application

**SCAITCLIFFE & VIRGINIA WATER
PREPARATORY SCHOOL**
Bishopsgate Road, Egham, Surrey TW20 0YJ
Tel: 01784 432109
Heads: W A Constable BA(Hons), PGCE &
        Mrs S Winson BA, TC, DipRD(Open)
Type: Co-educational Day B3-13 G3-11
No of pupils: B125 G45
Fees: WB £2520 DAY £1095-£1863

Epsom

CORNERSTONE SCHOOL
22 West Hill, Epsom, Surrey KT19 8JD
Tel: 01372 742940
Head: G R Davies
Type: Co-educational Day B5-16 G5-16
No of pupils: B28 G16

EPSOM COLLEGE
Epsom, Surrey KT17 4JQ
Tel: 01372 723621
Head: A H Beadles MA
Type: Co-educational Boarding & Day B13-18 G13-18
No of pupils: B335 VIth316
Fees: FB £11,595 WB £11,436 DAY £8616

EWELL CASTLE SCHOOL
Church Street, Epsom, Surrey KT17 2AW
Tel: 0181 393 1413
Head: R A Fewtrell MA, JP
Type: Co-educational Day B3-18 G3-11
No of pupils: B350 G20 VIth60
Fees: DAY £2352-£4425

KINGSWOOD HOUSE SCHOOL
56 West Hill, Epsom, Surrey KT19 8LG
Tel: 01372 723590
Head: P R Brooks MA, BEd(Hons)
Type: Boys Day B3-13
No of pupils: B200
Fees: DAY £3150-£4515

LYNTON PREPARATORY SCHOOL
Epsom Road, Epsom, Surrey KT17 1LJ
Tel: 0181 393 4169
Head: Mrs V M A Thorns
Type: Co-educational Day B4-12 G4-12
No of pupils: B44 G106
Fees: DAY £1920-£2190

ST CHRISTOPHER'S SCHOOL
6 Downs Road, Epsom, Surrey KT18 5HE
Tel: 01372 721807
Head: Miss J A Luckman (NFF)
Type: Co-educational Day B3-7 G3-7
No of pupils: B74 G67
Fees: DAY £1476-£2856

STUDY ASSOCIATES INTERNATIONAL
Gold Peak House, Epsom, Surrey KT18 7EH
Tel: 01372 275005
Head: Mrs B A Legge
Type: Co-educational Day

Esher

CLAREMONT FAN COURT SCHOOL
Claremont Drive, Esher, Surrey KT10 9LY
Tel: 01372 467841
Head: Mrs P B Farrar TCert
Type: Co-educational Day & Boarding B3-18 G3-18
No of pupils: B285 G297 VIth63
Fees: FB £9090-£9435 DAY £3495-£5970

EMBERHURST SCHOOL
94 Ember Lane, Esher, Surrey KT10 8EN
Tel: 0181 2240843
Head: Mrs P Chadwick BEd
Type: Co-educational Day B3-8 G3-8
Fees: DAY £1300-£2400

GRANTCHESTER HOUSE SCHOOL
5 Hinchley Way, Esher, Surrey KT10 0BD
Tel: 0181 398 1157
Head: Mrs A E M Fry CertEd, BEd(Hons)
Type: Co-educational Day B3-7 G3-7
No of pupils: B35 G55
Fees: DAY £1890-£3450

MILBOURNE LODGE JUNIOR SCHOOL
22 Milbourne Lane, Esher, Surrey KT10 9EA
Tel: 01372 462781
Head: Mrs J Hinchliffe
Type: Co-educational Day B3-8 G3-8
No of pupils: B148 G12
Fees: DAY £1815-£4140

MILBOURNE LODGE SCHOOL
43 Arbrook Lane, Esher, Surrey KT10 9EG
Tel: 01372 462737
Head: N R Hale MA
Type: Boys Day B8-13
No of pupils: B181 G21
Fees: DAY £4500-£5000

ROWAN PREPARATORY SCHOOL
Fitzalan Road, Esher, Surrey KT10 0LX
Tel: 01372 462627
Head: Mrs E J Brown BA, CertEd
Type: Girls Day G3-11
No of pupils: G310
Fees: DAY £1750-£4845

Farnham

BARFIELD SCHOOL
Runfold, Farnham, Surrey GU10 1PB
Tel: 01252 782271
Head: B J Hoar BA, CertEd, IAPS
Type: Co-educational Day B3-13 G3-13
No of pupils: B160 G100
Fees: DAY £1825-£5595

EDGEBOROUGH
Farnham, Surrey GU10 3AH
Tel: 01252 792495
Head: R A Jackson MA, PGCE
Type: Co-educational Boarding & Day B3-13 G3-13
No of pupils: B200 G65 FB30
Fees: FB £8265-£9210 DAY £3855-£7020

FRENSHAM HEIGHTS SCHOOL
Farnham, Surrey GU10 4EA
Tel: 01252 792134
Head: P de Voil MA, FRSA
Type: Co-educational Boarding & Day B3-18 G3-18
No of pupils: B123 G130 VIth86
Fees: FB £11,985 DAY £7770

ST GEORGE'S SCHOOL
Brackenhill, Long Road, Farnham, Surrey GU10 4DS
Tel: 01252 792006
Head: Mr Andrew Melbourne
Type: Co-educational Day B2-11 G2-11
No of pupils: B25 G20
Fees: DAY £2334-£2937

Godalming

ALDRO SCHOOL
Shackleford, Godalming, Surrey GU8 6AS
Tel: 01483 810266
Head: I M Argyle BEd
Type: Boys Boarding & Day B7-13
No of pupils: B216
Fees: FB £8505 DAY £6570

BARROW HILLS SCHOOL
Roke Lane, Godalming, Surrey GU8 5NY
Tel: 01428 683639
Head: M Connolly BSc, BA, MEd
Type: Co-educational Day B4-13 G4-13
No of pupils: B113 G23
Fees: DAY £4080-£6240

CHARTERHOUSE
Godalming, Surrey GU7 2DX
Tel: 01483 291601
Head: Rev John Witheridge MA
Type: Boys Boarding & Day B13-18 G16-18
No of pupils: B627 G78 FB679
Fees: FB £13,341 DAY £11,022

★ KING EDWARD'S SCHOOL WITLEY
Petworth Road, Godalming, Witley, Wormley,
Surrey GU8 5SG
Tel: 01428 682572
Head: R J Fox MA, CMath, FIMA
Type: Co-educational Boarding & Day B11-18 G11-18
No of pupils: B159 G153 VIth146
Fees: FB £8970 DAY £6240

★ **PRIOR'S FIELD SCHOOL**
Priorsfield Road, Godalming, Surrey GU7 2RH
Tel: 01483 810551
Head: Mrs J M McCallum BA
Type: Girls Boarding & Day G11-18
No of pupils: G228 VIth45
Fees: FB £3429 DAY £2289

ST HILARY'S SCHOOL
Holloway Hill, Godalming, Surrey GU7 1RZ
Tel: 01483 416551
Head: Mrs M I Thomas
Type: Co-educational Day B3-8 G3-12
No of pupils: B75 G260
Fees: DAY £2505-£3795

Guildford

APPLE ORCHARD EDUCATION UNIT
Apple Orchard, Birtley Green, Guildford, Surrey GU5 0LE
Tel: 01483 904075
Head: Mr A J Money
Type: Co-educational Day

DRAYTON HOUSE SCHOOL
35 Austin Road, Guildford, Surrey GU1 3NP
Tel: 01483 504707
Head: Mrs J Tyson-Jones
(Froebel CertEd London University)
Type: Co-educational Day B2-7 G2-7
Fees: DAY £2160-£3605

GUILDFORD HIGH SCHOOL
London Road, Guildford, Surrey GU1 1SJ
Tel: 01483 561440
Head: Mrs S H Singer BA
Type: Girls Day G4-18
No of pupils: G679 VIth132
Fees: DAY £3024-£5100

GUILDFORD PRE-SCHOOL & NURSERY
56 Epsom Road, Guildford, Surrey GU1 3LG
Tel: 01483 440299
Head: Miss Hilary Lowe
Type: Co-educational Day

LANESBOROUGH
Maori Road, Guildford, Surrey GU1 2EL
Tel: 01483 502060
Head: S Deller CertEd
Type: Boys Day B4-13
No of pupils: B325
Fees: DAY £1830-£4800

LONGACRE SCHOOL
Shamley Green, Guildford, Surrey GU5 0NQ
Tel: 01483 893225
Head: Mrs L Prince
Type: Co-educational Day B3-8 G3-11
No of pupils: B65 G100
Fees: DAY £690-£3660

PEASLAKE SCHOOL
c/o Ridgmount, Lawbrook Lane, Guildford,
Surrey GU5 9QW
Head: Mrs C Doubleday
Type: Co-educational Day & Boarding

ROYAL GRAMMAR SCHOOL
High Street, Guildford, Surrey GU1 3BB
Tel: 01483 502424
Head: T M S Young MA
Type: Boys Day B11-18
No of pupils: B600 VIth250
Fees: DAY £5715-£5985

RYDES HILL PREPARATORY SCHOOL
Rydes Hill House, Guildford, Surrey GU2 6BP
Tel: 01483 563160
Head: Mrs Joan Lenahan BEd(Hons), MA
Type: Girls Day B3-7 G3-11
No of pupils: B14 G140
Fees: DAY £410-£1280

ST CATHERINE'S SCHOOL
Bramley, Guildford, Surrey GU5 0DF
Tel: 01483 893363
Head: Mrs C M Oulton MA(Oxon)
Type: Girls Day & Boarding G4-18
No of pupils: G664 VIth103
Fees: FB £8685-£10,350 DAY £2985-£6300

TORMEAD SCHOOL
27 Cranley Road, Guildford, Surrey GU1 2JD
Tel: 01483 575101
Head: Mrs H E M Alleyne
Type: Girls Day G5-18
No of pupils: G615
Fees: DAY £2625-£4860

Haslemere

HASLEMERE PREPARATORY SCHOOL
The Heights, Haslemere, Surrey GU27 2JP
Tel: 01428 642350
Head: A C Morrison BEd, CertEd
Type: Boys Day B5-13
No of pupils: B200
Fees: DAY £3900-£4980

THE ROYAL SCHOOL
Farnham Lane, Haslemere, Surrey GU27 1HQ
Tel: 01428 605805
Head: C Brooks BA(Hons), AdDipEd, CertEd,
    FRGS, FRMetS
Type: Girls Day & Boarding G4-18
No of pupils: G395 VIth65 FB100 WB63
Fees: FB £7290-£10,017 DAY £3636-£6363

ST IVES
Three Gates Lane, Haslemere, Surrey GU27 2ES
Tel: 01428 643734
Head: Mrs M S Greenway LLB
Type: Girls Day G3-11
No of pupils: G140
Fees: DAY £3675-£4755

TIMBERS PRE-SCHOOL & NURSERY
College Hill, Haslemere, Surrey GU27 2JH
Tel: 01428 645001
Head: Debbie Greatrex
Type: Co-educational Day

★ **WISPERS SCHOOL**
High Lane, Haslemere, Surrey GU27 1AD
Tel: 01428 643646
Head: L H Beltran BA(Hons), PGCE
Type: Girls Boarding & Day G11-18
No of pupils: G120
Fees: On application

Hindhead

AMESBURY SCHOOL
Hazel Grove, Hindhead, Surrey GU26 6BL
Tel: 01428 604322
Head: N Taylor MA
Type: Co-educational Day & Boarding B3-13 G3-13
No of pupils: B170 G30 WB20
Fees: FB/ WB £6465-£7305 DAY £2400-£5925

ST EDMUND'S SCHOOL
Portsmouth Road, Hindhead, Surrey GU26 6BH
Tel: 01428 604808
Head: A Fowler-Watt MA
Type: Boys Boarding & Day B5-13
No of pupils: B110
Fees: FB £7050 DAY £3600

Horley

REDEHALL PREPARATORY SCHOOL
Redehall Road, Horley, Surrey RH6 9QL
Tel: 01342 842987
Head: Mrs E Blow
Type: Co-educational Day B4-11 G4-11
No of pupils: B45 G45

Leatherhead

CRANMORE SCHOOL
West Horsley, Leatherhead, Surrey KT24 6AT
Tel: 01483 284137
Head: K A Cheney BA(Hons), PGCE
Type: Boys Day B3-13
No of pupils: B455
Fees: DAY £2595-£4485

DOWNSEND SCHOOL
Leatherhead Road, Leatherhead, Surrey KT22 8TJ
Tel: 01372 372197
Head: C J Linford MA(Oxon), DipEd(Oxon)
Type: Co-educational Day B2-13 G2-13
No of pupils: B500 G300
Fees: DAY £930-£4530

GLENESK SCHOOL
Ockham Road North, Leatherhead, Surrey KT24 6NS
Tel: 01483 282329
Head: Mrs S P Johnson
Type: Co-educational Day B2-8 G2-8
No of pupils: B71 G92
Fees: DAY £300-£4000

MANOR HOUSE SCHOOL
Manor House Lane, Leatherhead, Surrey KT23 4EN
Tel: 01372 458538
Head: Mrs L A Mendes BA
Type: Girls Day & Boarding G2-16
No of pupils: G255
Fees: WB £6840-£8190 DAY £1620-£5640

ST JOHN'S SCHOOL
Epsom Road, Leatherhead, Surrey KT22 8SP
Tel: 01372 372021
Head: C H Tongue MA
Type: Boys Boarding & Day B13-18 G16-18
No of pupils: B350 G50 VIth186 FB25 WB100
Fees: FB/WB £10,500 DAY £7200

Lingfield

NOTRE DAME JUNIOR SCHOOL
Racecourse Road, Lingfield, Surrey RH7 6PH
Tel: 01342 833372
Head: Mrs N Shepley
Type: Co-educational Day

NOTRE DAME SCHOOL
Lingfield, Surrey RH7 6PH
Tel: 01342 833176
Head: Mrs N E Shepley BA
Type: Co-educational Day B2-18 G2-18
Fees: DAY £2190-£4440

Oxshott

DANES HILL SCHOOL
Leatherhead Road, Oxshott, Surrey KT22 0JG
Tel: 01372 842509
Head: R Parfitt MA, MSc
Type: Co-educational Day B2-13 G2-13
No of pupils: B400 G277
Fees: DAY £256-£1787

Oxted

HAZELWOOD SCHOOL
Wolf's Hill, Oxted, Surrey RH8 0QU
Tel: 01883 712194
Head: A M Synge MA(Oxon), PGCE
Type: Co-educational Day & Boarding B3-13 G3-13
No of pupils: B234 G105
Fees: WB £7545 DAY £1680-£5700

LAVEROCK SCHOOL
19 Bluehouse Lane, Oxted, Surrey RH8 0AA
Tel: 01883 714171
Head: Mrs A C Paterson DipEd
Type: Girls Day G3-11
No of pupils: G158
Fees: DAY £1635-£3750

Redhill

DOODS BROW SCHOOL
54 High Street, Redhill, Surrey RH1 4HQ
Tel: 01737 823372
Head: Mrs G Hitchens
Type: Co-educational Day B2-11 G2-11
No of pupils: B56 G51
Fees: DAY £615-£2250

THE HAWTHORNS SCHOOL
Pendell Court, Redhill, Surrey RH1 4QJ
Tel: 01883 743048
Head: T R Johns BA, PGCE, FRGS
Type: Co-educational Day B2-13 G2-13
No of pupils: B244 G95
Fees: DAY £1080-£4755

Reigate

BURYS COURT SCHOOL
Reigate, Surrey RH2 8RE
Tel: 01306 611372
Head: D V W White BA
Type: Co-educational Day B3-13 G3-13
No of pupils: B100 G50
Fees: DAY £1800

CONISTON SCHOOL
22 Alma Road, Reigate, Surrey RH2 0DL
Tel: 01737 243370
Head: Mrs M H Harvey BA(Hons)
Type: Co-educational Day B2-7 G2-7
No of pupils: B43 G48
Fees: DAY £1026-£2604

DUNOTTAR SCHOOL
High Trees Road, Reigate, Surrey RH2 7EL
Tel: 01737 761945
Head: Miss M Skinner JP, BSc(Hons
Type: Girls Day G4-18
No of pupils: G413 VIth63
Fees: DAY £2970-£4875

MICKLEFIELD SCHOOL
10/12 Somers Road, Reigate, Surrey RH2 9DU
Tel: 01737 242615
Head: Mrs C Belton BA, CertEd
Type: Co-educational Day B2-11 G2-11
No of pupils: B37 G196
Fees: DAY £747-£3756

REIGATE GRAMMAR SCHOOL
Reigate Road, Reigate, Surrey RH2 0QS
Tel: 01737 222231
Head: P V Dixon MA
Type: Co-educational Day B10-18 G10-18
No of pupils: B488 G98 VIth219
Fees: DAY £5160

REIGATE ST MARY'S PREPARATORY & CHOIR SCHOOL
Chart Lane, Reigate, Surrey RH2 7RN
Tel: 01737 244880
Head: A Hart BA(Hons)(Dunelm)
Type: Boys Day B3-13
No of pupils: B248
Fees: DAY £867-£4320

Ripley

RIPLEY COURT SCHOOL
Rose Lane, Ripley, Surrey GU23 6NE
Tel: 01483 225217
Head: J W N Dudgeon MA(TCD), BA(Open)
Type: Boys Boarding B4-13 G4-13
No of pupils: B226 G20 FB12 WB22
Fees: FB/WB £6324 DAY £2559-£4116

Tadworth

ABERDOUR SCHOOL
Brighton Road, Tadworth, Surrey KT20 6AJ
Tel: 01737 354119
Head: A Barraclough CertEd
Type: Co-educational Day B3-13 G3-13
No of pupils: B210 G30
Fees: DAY £595-£1550

BRAMLEY SCHOOL
Chequers Lane, Tadworth, Surrey KT20 7ST
Tel: 01737 812004
Head: Mrs B Johns CertEd
Type: Girls Day G3-11
No of pupils: G118
Fees: DAY £550-£1210

CHINTHURST SCHOOL
Tadworth Street, Tadworth, Surrey KT20 5QZ
Tel: 01737 812011
Head: T J Egan MEd
Type: Boys Day B3-13
No of pupils: B364
Fees: DAY £1260-£3675

ST JOHN'S NURSERY SCHOOL
59 The Avenue, Tadworth, Surrey KT20 5PB
Tel: 01737 813032
Head: Mrs V Hollander
Type: Co-educational Day B3-5 G3-5
No of pupils: B15 G15
Fees: DAY £855

Thames Ditton

WESTON GREEN SCHOOL
Weston Green Road, Thames Ditton, Surrey KT7 0JN
Tel: 0181 398 2778
Head: Mrs J Winser MA, BEd(Hons)
Type: Co-educational Day B3-8 G3-8
Fees: DAY £660-£1120

Thorpe

★ **TASIS ENGLAND AMERICAN SCHOOL**
Coldharbour Lane, Thorpe, Surrey TW20 8TE
Tel: 01932 565252
Type: Co-educational Boarding & Day B4-18 G4-18

Walton-on-Thames

DANESFIELD PREPARATORY SCHOOL
Rydens Avenue, Walton-on-Thames, Surrey KT12 3JB
Tel: 01932 220930
Head: Mrs T Yates
Type: Co-educational Day B4-11 G4-11
No of pupils: B52 G90
Fees: DAY £1530-£3015

WESTWARD PREPARATORY SCHOOL
47 Hersham Road, Walton-on-Thames, Surrey KT12 1LE
Tel: 01932 220911
Head: Mrs P Townley
Type: Co-educational Day B3-11 G3-11
No of pupils: B75 G75
Fees: DAY £1305-£2790

Warlingham

WARLINGHAM PARK SCHOOL
Chelsham Common, Warlingham,
Surrey CR6 9PB
Tel: 01883 626844
Head: M R Donald BSc
Type: Co-educational Day B2-11 G2-11
No of pupils: B63 G55
Fees: DAY £1560-£2925

Weybridge

ST GEORGE'S COLLEGE
Weybridge Road, Weybridge, Surrey KT15 2QS
Tel: 01932 854811
Head: Joseph A Peake MA(Oxon), PGCE
Type: Boys Day B11-18 G16-18
No of pupils: B350 VIth190
Fees: DAY £5985-£6795

ST GEORGE'S COLLEGE JUNIOR SCHOOL
Weybridge Road, Weybridge, Surrey KT15 2QS
Tel: 01932 845784
Head: Fr Martin Ashcroft CJ
Type: Co-educational Day B2-11 G2-11
No of pupils: B225 G25
Fees: DAY £576-£4830

ST MAUR'S SCHOOL
Thames Street, Weybridge, Surrey KT13 8NL
Tel: 01932 851411
Head: Mrs M E Dodds BA(Hons), MA
Type: Girls Day G2-18
No of pupils: G509 VIth50
Fees: DAY £1395-£4725

WALLOP SCHOOL
28 Hangar Hill, Weybridge, Surrey KT13 9YD
Tel: 01932 852885
Head: P D Westcombe BA, PGCE
Type: Co-educational Day B2-13 G2-11
Fees: DAY £2946-£4986

Windlesham

WOODCOTE HOUSE SCHOOL
Snows Ride, Windlesham, Surrey GU20 6PF
Tel: 01276 472115
Head: N H K Paterson BA(Hons), PGCE
Type: Boys Boarding & Day B7-14
No of pupils: B95 FB100
Fees: FB £7600 DAY £5400

Woking

CABLE HOUSE SCHOOL
Horsell Rise, Woking, Surrey GU21 4AY
Tel: 01483 760759
Head: R D G Elvidge BSc
Type: Co-educational Day B3-11 G3-11
No of pupils: B48 G50
Fees: DAY £1590-£3255

COWORTH PARK SCHOOL
Valley End, Woking, Surrey GU24 8TE
Tel: 01276 855707
Head: Mrs P S Middleton CertEd
Type: Co-educational Day B3-7 G3-11
No of pupils: B30 G130
Fees: DAY £1935-£4260

GREENFIELD SCHOOL
Brooklyn Road, Woking, Surrey GU22 7TP
Tel: 01483 772525
Head: Mrs J Becker BA(Hons), BEd(Hons), CertEd
Type: Co-educational Day B3-11 G3-11
No of pupils: B84 G92
Fees: DAY £1665-£2880

HALSTEAD PREPARATORY SCHOOL
Woodham Rise, Woking, Surrey GU21 4EE
Tel: 01483 772682
Head: Mrs A Hancock BA, ACP, FRSA
Type: Girls Day G3-11
No of pupils: G210
Fees: DAY £2000-£4100

HOE BRIDGE SCHOOL & TREES SCHOOLS
Hoe Place, Old Woking Road, Woking,
Surrey GU22 8JE
Tel: 01483 760018/772194
Heads: R W K Barr BEd(Oxon) & Mrs L M Renfrew MA
Type: Co-educational Boarding & Day B2-14 G2-14
No of pupils: B323 G82
Fees: FB £7890-£8715 DAY £750-£6075

OAKFIELD SCHOOL
Coldharbour Road, Woking, Surrey GU22 8SJ
Tel: 01932 342465
Head: Mrs R C Brothers
Type: Co-educational Day B2-11 G2-16
No of pupils: B30 G120
Fees: DAY £3372-£5241

PRINS WILLEM-ALEXANDER SCHOOL
Old Woking Road, Woking, Surrey GU22 8HY
Tel: 01483 750409
Head: Peter Wassink
Type: Co-educational Day & Boarding

★ **ST ANDREW'S SCHOOL**
Church Hill House, Horsell, Woking, Surrey GU21 4QW
Tel: 01483 760943
Head: B Pretorius BEd
Type: Co-educational Day B3-13 G3-13
No of pupils: B165 G15
Fees: DAY £2340-£6285

THE TREES PRE-PREPARATORY SCHOOL
Hoe Place, Woking, Surrey GU22 8JE
Tel: 01483 772194
Head: Mrs L M Renfrew MA
Type: Co-educational Day B3-7 G3-7
No of pupils: B118 G56
Fees: DAY £1687-£3720

Woldingham

WOLDINGHAM SCHOOL
Marden Park, Woldingham, Surrey CR3 7YA
Tel: 01883 349431
Head: Dr P Dineen BA, PhD
Type: Girls Boarding & Day G11-18
No of pupils: G410 VIth140
Fees: FB £12,009 DAY £7281

East Sussex

Battle

BATTLE ABBEY SCHOOL
Battle, East Sussex TN33 0AD
Tel: 01424 772385
Head: D J A Teall BSc(Newcastle)
Type: Co-educational Day & Boarding B2-18 G2-18
No of pupils: B95 G95 VIth20 FB60 WB12
Fees: FB £7590-£9465 DAY £3225-£5865

WILTON HOUSE SCHOOL
Catsfield Place, Battle, East Sussex TN33 9BS
Tel: 01424 830234
Head: J Shrine MA
Type: Co-educational Boarding & Day B13-18 G13-18
Fees: FB £6327-£7950 DAY £2880-£4638

Bexhill-on-Sea

AMBERLEY SCHOOL
9 Buckhurst Road, Bexhill-on-Sea,
East Sussex TN40 1QF
Tel: 01424 212472
Head: Mr Albon
Type: Co-educational Day B3-7 G3-7
Fees: DAY £800-£1100

YOUNG SUSSEX SCHOOL
Belle Hall, Bexhill-on-Sea, East Sussex TN40 2AA
Tel: 01424 730575
Head: Betty Joan Smith
Type: Co-educational Day & Boarding

Brighton

BARTHOLOMEWS TUTORIAL COLLEGE
22-23 Prince Albert Street, Brighton,
East Sussex BN1 1HF
Tel: 01273 205965/205141
Head: W A Duncombe BSc
Type: Co-educational Boarding & Day B16-19 G16-19
No of pupils: VIth40 FB4 WB3
Fees: FB £12,500 DAY £10,000

BRIGHTON & HOVE HIGH SCHOOL
Montpellier Road, Brighton, East Sussex BN1 3AT
Tel: 01273 734112
Head: Miss R A Woodbridge MA
Type: Girls Day G4-18
No of pupils: G641 VIth102
Fees: DAY £3036-£4140

BRIGHTON COLLEGE
Eastern Road, Brighton, East Sussex BN2 2AL
Tel: 01273 704202
Head: J D Leach MA
Type: Co-educational Day & Boarding B13-18 G13-18
No of pupils: B334 G141
Fees: FB £12,450 WB £11,130 DAY £8190

BRIGHTON COLLEGE JUNIOR SCHOOL
Walpole Lodge, Brighton, East Sussex BN2 2EU
Tel: 01273 606845
Head: G Brown DipMus, CertEd, LTCL
Type: Co-educational Day & Boarding B8-13 G8-13
No of pupils: B246 G107
Fees: WB £8850 DAY £1455-£6165

BRIGHTON COLLEGE JUNIOR SCHOOL PRE-PREP
Brighton College, Brighton, East Sussex BN2 2EQ
Tel: 01273 603495
Head: Mrs S P Wicks
Type: Co-educational Day B3-8 G3-8
No of pupils: B98 G48
Fees: DAY £1455-£6165

BRIGHTON STEINER SCHOOL LTD
363 Ditchling Road, Brighton, East Sussex BN1 6JU
Tel: 01273 386300
Type: Co-educational Day

DHARMA SCHOOL
20 Queens Park Rise, Brighton,
East Sussex BN2 2ZF
Tel: 01273 502055
Head: Linda Maria Medhina BA, CertEd
Type: Co-educational Day B3-11 G3-11
No of pupils: B10 G11
Fees: DAY £2250

MONTESSORI HOUSE FOR CHILDREN IN BRIGHTON
67 Stanford Avenue, Brighton, East Sussex BN1 6FB
Tel: 01273 702485
Head: Miss D Cockburn AmiMonteDipl
Type: Co-educational Day B2-9 G2-9
No of pupils: B18 G24
Fees: DAY £1500-£3300

MONTESSORI HOUSE FOR CHILDREN IN KEMP
1 Chesham Place, Brighton, East Sussex BN2 1FB
Tel: 01273 558155
Head: Miss D Cockburn AmiMonteDipl
Type: Co-educational Day B2-6 G2-6
No of pupils: B10 G10
Fees: DAY £1500-£3300

MONTESSORI SCHOOL, BRIGHTON & HOVE
67 Stanford Avenue, Brighton, East Sussex BN1 6FB
Tel: 01273 702485
Head: Daisy Cockburn AMI MontDip
Type: Co-educational Day B2-11 G2-11
Fees: DAY £1500-£3000

ROEDEAN SCHOOL
Brighton, East Sussex BN2 5RQ
Tel: 01273 603181
Head: Mrs A R Longley MA
Type: Girls Boarding & Day G10-18
No of pupils: G450
Fees: FB £13,635 DAY £7740

ST AUBYNS
76 High Street, Brighton, East Sussex BN2 7JN
Tel: 01273 302170
Head: J A L James DipEd
Type: Co-educational Boarding & Day B4-13 G4-13
No of pupils: B120 G8
Fees: FB £9180 DAY £6750

ST MARY'S HALL
Eastern Road, Brighton, East Sussex BN2 5JF
Tel: 01273 606061
Head: Mrs P J James BA
Type: Girls Day & Boarding B3-8 G3-18
No of pupils: B5 G352 VIth51
Fees: FB £9315 WB £6975-£8940 DAY £1230-£6180

WINDLESHAM SCHOOL TRUST LTD
190 Dyke Road, Brighton, East Sussex BN1 5AA
Tel: 01273 553645
Head: Mrs Angele Julie Marie Garner
Type: Co-educational Day & Boarding

Crowborough

JAMEAH ISLAMEYAH
Catts Hill, Crowborough, East Sussex TN6 3NJ
Tel: 01892 853009
Head: Kassim Sowdani
Type: Co-educational Day

Eastbourne

EASTBOURNE COLLEGE
Old Wish Road, Eastbourne, East Sussex BN21 4JX
Tel: 01323 452300
Head: C M P Bush MA
Type: Co-educational Boarding & Day B13-18 G13-18
No of pupils: B224 G38 VIth234
Fees: FB £12 DAY £8936

HARROW HOUSE
1 Silverdale Road, Eastbourne, East Sussex BN20 7AA
Tel: 01323 730851
Head: Mrs J E Jenion BEd, MIHEC
Type: Girls Boarding & Day G16-99
No of pupils: G90
Fees: FB £3200 DAY £2400

MOIRA HOUSE JUNIOR SCHOOL
Upper Carlisle Road, Eastbourne,
East Sussex BN20 7TE
Tel: 01323 644144
Head: Mrs A Harris BEd(Hons), ARCM
Type: Girls Day & Boarding G2-11
No of pupils: G75 FB10
Fees: FB £8700 DAY £3810-£5700

MOIRA HOUSE SCHOOL
Upper Carlisle Road, Eastbourne,
East Sussex BN20 7TD
Tel: 01323 644144
Head: A R Underwood BA(Hons), MA
Type: Girls Boarding & Day G11-18
No of pupils: G230 VIth70 FB130
Fees: FB £11,340 WB £10,320 DAY £3810-£7320

ST ANDREW'S SCHOOL
Meads, Eastbourne, East Sussex BN20 7RP
Tel: 01323 733203
Head: H Davies Jones MA
Type: Co-educational Day & Boarding B3-13 G3-13
No of pupils: B265 G160 FB75
Fees: FB/WB £8625 DAY £1800-£6090

ST BEDE'S CO-ED PREPARATORY SCHOOL
Duke's Drive, Eastbourne, East Sussex BN20 7XL
Tel: 01323 734222
Head: P Pyemont DipEd
Type: Co-educational Day & Boarding B2-13 G2-13
No of pupils: B260 G170
Fees: FB £9510 DAY £1800-£6015

Forest Row

ASHDOWN HOUSE SCHOOL
Forest Row, East Sussex RH18 5JY
Tel: 01342 822574
Head: M V C Williams MA(Cantab)
Type: Co-educational Boarding & Day B8-13 G8-13
No of pupils: B148 G54
Fees: FB £8010 DAY £7200

GREENFIELDS SCHOOL EDUCATIONAL TRUST LTD
Priory Road, Forest Row, East Sussex RH18 5JD
Tel: 01342 822845
Head: Mr A M McQuade MA(Oxon)
Type: Co-educational Day & Boarding B3-18 G3-18
No of pupils: B88 G77
Fees: FB/WB £8979-£9801 DAY £969-£5247

MICHAEL HALL SCHOOL
Kidbrooke Park, Forest Row, East Sussex RH18 5JB
Tel: 01342 822275
Head: E Van-Manen
Type: Co-educational Day & Boarding B3-18 G3-18
No of pupils: B232 G264 VIth55
Fees: FB £6075-£8100 DAY £2310-£3750

Hailsham

ST BEDE'S SCHOOL
Upper Dicker, Hailsham, East Sussex BN27 3QH
Tel: 01323 843252
Head: R A Perrin MA
Type: Co-educational Boarding & Day B12-18 G12-18
No of pupils: B295 G155 VIth180
Fees: FB £11,925 DAY £7200

Hastings

BROOMHAM SCHOOL
Guestling, Hastings, East Sussex TN35 4LT
Tel: 01424 814456
Head: J Auer BA(Hons), ASC(Ed)
Type: Co-educational Boarding & Day B2-18 G2-18
No of pupils: B78 G60
Fees: FB £6150-£8580 DAY £2229-£3600

MERCELLES
St Peters, Hastings, East Sussex TN35 4BP
Tel: 01424 813330/812002
Head: Miss S A Mercel
Type: Co-educational Day

Hove

DEEPDENE SCHOOL
195 New Church Road, Hove, East Sussex BN3 4ED
Tel: 01273 418984
Head: Miss N Webber
Type: Girls Day B3-8 G3-11
Fees: DAY £1296-£3000

THE FOLD SCHOOL
201 New Church Road, Hove, East Sussex BN3 4ED
Tel: 01273 410901
Head: Mrs B Drake BEd, MSR
Type: Co-educational Day B3-9 G3-9
No of pupils: B35 G35
Fees: DAY £1850-£2100

MOWDEN SCHOOL
The Droveway, Hove, East Sussex BN3 6LU
Tel: 01273 503452
Head: C E M Snell
Type: Boys Day & Boarding B7-13
No of pupils: B101 WB20
Fees: WB £6360 DAY £5325

SHANDY STAGE SCHOOL
56A Livingstone Road, Hove, East Sussex BN3 3WL
Tel: 01273 822244
Head: Mr Lindsdale
Type: Co-educational Day & Boarding

ST CHRISTOPHER'S SCHOOL
33 New Church Road, Hove, East Sussex BN3 4AD
Tel: 01273 735404
Head: R J M Saunders
Type: Boys Day B4-14
No of pupils: B230
Fees: DAY £2760

STONELANDS SCHOOL OF BALLET
3 Hove Business Centre, Hove, East Sussex BN3 6HL
Tel: 01273 770445
Head: Mrs D Carteur
Type: Co-educational Day

TORAH ACADEMY
31 New Church Road, Hove, East Sussex BN3 4AD
Tel: 01273 328675
Head: P Efune
Type: Co-educational Day & Boarding

Lewes

THE OLD GRAMMAR SCHOOL
High Street, Lewes, East Sussex BN7 1XS
Tel: 01273 472634
Head: Dr A N L Hodd MA(Cantab), PhD(Dundee)
Type: Co-educational Day B4-18 G4-18
No of pupils: B277 G129 VIth69
Fees: DAY £2460-£4437

Mayfield

HILLHOUSE PREPARATORY SCHOOL
Mayfield College, Mayfield, East Sussex TN20 6PL
Tel: 01435 872041
Head: Mr Brian Smith BA(Hons), PGCE
Type: Co-educational Day B3-11 G3-11
No of pupils: B59 G58
Fees: DAY £2250

SKIPPERS HILL MANOR PREP SCHOOL
Five Ashes, Mayfield, East Sussex TN20 6HR
Tel: 01825 830234
Head: T W Lewis BA(Exon), PGCE(London)
Type: Co-educational Day B2-13 G2-13
No of pupils: B88 G62
Fees: DAY £1785-£5430

ST LEONARDS-MAYFIELD SCHOOL
The Old Palace, Mayfield, East Sussex TN20 6PH
Tel: 01435 873055
Head: Sr J Sinclair BSc, PGCE
Type: Girls Boarding & Day G11-18
No of pupils: G525
Fees: FB £9735 DAY £6490

Robertsbridge

BODIAM MANOR SCHOOL
Robertsbridge, East Sussex TN32 5UJ
Tel: 01580 830225
Heads: P L & Mrs Northen BEd
Type: Co-educational Day B2-13 G2-13
Fees: DAY £2607-£4764

VINEHALL SCHOOL
Robertsbridge, East Sussex TN32 5JL
Tel: 01580 880413
Head: D C Chaplin BA, CertEd
Type: Co-educational Boarding & Day B4-13 G4-13
No of pupils: B159 G99 FB90
Fees: FB £8550 DAY £3660-£6360

Seaford

NEWLANDS PRE-PREPARATORY & NURSERY SCHOOL
Eastbourne Road, Seaford, East Sussex BN25 4NP
Tel: 01323 896461
Head: Mrs A Morgan BEd(Hons), ACP, FCollP
Type: Co-educational Day B2-8 G2-8
No of pupils: B64 G67
Fees: DAY £201-£2985

NEWLANDS SCHOOL
Eastbourne Road, Seaford, East Sussex BN25 4NP
Tel: 01323 892334
Head: B F Underwood MA, DipEd(Oxon)
Type: Co-educational Boarding & Day B2-18 G2-18
No of pupils: B424 G228 VIth70
Fees: FB £8430-£9300 DAY £4380-£5895

OWLETS MONTESSORI SCHOOL
The Old School, Seaford, East Sussex BN25 1HH
Tel: 01323 492123
Head: Mrs A Golledge MontDip
Type: Co-educational Day B2-11 G2-11
No of pupils: B62 G63
Fees: DAY £546-£2340

St Leonards-on-Sea

CLAREMONT SCHOOL
Ebdens Hill, St Leonards-on-Sea,
East Sussex TN37 7PW
Tel: 01424 751555
Head: M Beaumont BSc
Type: Co-educational Day B2-14 G2-14
No of pupils: B120 G120
Fees: DAY £1500-£4500

SHELAGAR TUTORIAL CENTRE
1 Avon Court, St Leonards-on-Sea,
East Sussex TN38 0SY
Tel: 0142501
Head: P Shelton-Agar DipAM
Type: Co-educational Day

ST LEONARDS COLLEGE
Hollington Park Road, St Leonards-on Sea,
East Sussex TN38 0SE
Tel: 01424 440761
Head: Mrs P K Wheeler CertEd
Type: Co-educational Day B11-18 G11-18
No of pupils: B28 G38
Fees: DAY £4950

WINTON HOUSE SCHOOL
4 Dane Road, St Leonards-on-Sea,
East Sussex TN38 0QU
Tel: 01424 424850
Head: Mrs G K Connor
Type: Co-educational Day B4-11 G4-11
No of pupils: B25 G25
Fees: DAY £1980

Uckfield

BUCKSWOOD GRANGE
Uckfield, East Sussex TN22 3PU
Tel: 01825 761666
Head: M B Reiser
Type: Co-educational Day & Boarding B4-16 G4-16
No of pupils: FB70
Fees: FB £6825 WB £6525 DAY £2445-£3210

TEMPLE GROVE SCHOOL
Heron's Ghyll, Uckfield, East Sussex TN22 4DA
Tel: 01825 712112
Head: Mrs J E Lee BA, CertEd
Type: Co-educational Day & Boarding B3-13 G3-13
No of pupils: B85 G85
Fees: FB £6885-£8190 DAY £3795-£6690

Wadhurst

★ BELLERBYS COLLEGE MAYFIELD AND WADHURST
Mayfield Lane, Wadhurst, East Sussex TN5 6JA
Tel: 01892 782000
Heads: Jörg Muller MA & Eric Reynolds BA(Hons),
    PGCE
Type: Co-educational Boarding & Day B11-18 G11-18
No of pupils: B133 G184 VIth71
Fees: FB £12,600 DAY £3000-£6420

BRICKLEHURST MANOR PREPARATORY
Bardown Road, Wadhurst, East Sussex TN5 7EL
Tel: 01580 200448
Heads: Mrs R A Lewis & Dr P W Lewis
Type: Co-educational Day B4-8 G4-11
No of pupils: B24 G83
Fees: DAY £3645-£3825

SACRED HEART RC PRIMARY SCHOOL
Mayfield Lane, Wadhurst, East Sussex TN5 6DQ
Tel: 01892 783414
Head: Mrs H Castle
Type: Co-educational Day B3-11 G3-11
No of pupils: B50 G50
Fees: DAY £900-£2430

West Sussex

Arundel

SLINDON COLLEGE
Slindon House, Arundel, West Sussex BN18 0RH
Tel: 01243 814320
Head: P D Morris BEd, MA(Oxon)
Type: Boys Boarding & Day B11-18
No of pupils: B70 VIth15
Fees: FB £9495 DAY £5985

Burgess Hill

BURGESS HILL SCHOOL FOR GIRLS (JUNIOR)
Keymer Road, Burgess Hill, West Sussex RH15 0AQ
Tel: 01444 241050
Head: Mrs R F Lewis BSc
Type: Girls Day & Boarding G3-10
No of pupils: G208
Fees: FB £9675 DAY £2664-£5730

BURGESS HILL SCHOOL FOR GIRLS (SENIOR)
Keymer Road, Burgess Hill, West Sussex RH15 0EG
Tel: 01444 241050
Head: Mrs R F Lewis BSc
Type: Girls Day & Boarding G11-18
No of pupils: G280 VIth60 FB56
Fees: FB £9675 DAY £2664-£5730

ST PETER'S SCHOOL
Upper St John's Road, Burgess Hill,
West Sussex RH15 8HB
Tel: 01444 235880
Head: Mrs R H Stevens MA(Oxon)
Type: Co-educational Day B2-8 G2-8
No of pupils: B83 G76
Fees: DAY £426-£2748

Chichester

★ **GREAT BALLARD SCHOOL**
Eartham, Chichester, West Sussex PO18 0LR
Tel: 01243 814236
Head: R E T Jennings CertEd
Type: Co-educational Boarding & Day B2-13 G2-13
No of pupils: 155
Fees: FB £7176-£7677 DAY £3025-£5418

LAVANT HOUSE ROSEMEAD
Chichester, West Sussex PO18 9AB
Tel: 01243 527211
Head: Mrs S E Watkins BA
Type: Girls Day & Boarding B3-8 G3-18
No of pupils: B5 G146 FB30
Fees: FB/WB £8325-£10,425 DAY £1425-£5850

LITTLEMEAD GRAMMAR SCHOOL
Woodfield House, Chichester, West Sussex PO20 6EU
Tel: 01243 787551
Head: I F A Bowler
Type: Co-educational Day & Boarding B3-16 G3-16
No of pupils: FB15 WB10
Fees: FB £5985-£6951 WB £5505-£6471
DAY £1248-£4251

NORTHGATE HOUSE SCHOOL
38 North Street, Chichester, West Sussex PO19 1LX
Tel: 01243 784828
Head: Mrs W E Shoesmith
Type: Co-educational Day B4-8 G4-8
Fees: DAY £190-£290

OAKWOOD SCHOOL
Oakwood, Chichester, West Sussex PO18 9AN
Tel: 01243 575209
Head: Simon J E Whittle BA(Hons), PGCE
Type: Co-educational Boarding & Day B2-11 G2-11
No of pupils: B80 G70
Fees: FB £7725 WB £7140 DAY £690-£5385

THE PREBENDAL SCHOOL
53 West Street, Chichester, West Sussex PO19 1RT
Tel: 01243 782026
Head: Rev G C Hall MA(Oxon)
Type: Co-educational Day & Boarding B3-13 G3-13
Fees: FB £7128 WB £6804 DAY £1170-£5232

WESTBOURNE HOUSE SCHOOL
Shopwyke, Chichester, West Sussex PO20 6BH
Tel: 01243 782739
Head: S L Rigby BA, PGCE
Type: Co-educational Boarding & Day B3-13 G3-13
No of pupils: B182 G59 FB97
Fees: FB £7725 DAY £3120-£6240

Crawley

COPTHORNE SCHOOL TRUST
Effingham Lane, Crawley, West Sussex RH10 3HR
Tel: 01342 712311
Head: D Newton BA(Hons)
Type: Co-educational Day & Boarding B4-13 G4-13
No of pupils: B147 G70
Fees: WB £7560 DAY £3420-£6210

WORTH SCHOOL
Crawley, West Sussex RH10 4SD
Tel: 01342 710200
Head: Rev P C Jamison MA(Oxon)
Type: Boys Boarding & Day B10-18
No of pupils: B256 VIth129
Fees: FB £8490-£11,952 DAY £5892-£8109

East Grinstead

BRAMBLETYE
Brambletye, East Grinstead,
West Sussex RH19 3PD
Tel: 01342 321004
Head: D G Fowler-Watt MA, JP
Type: Boys Boarding & Day B7-14
No of pupils: B216 FB160
Fees: FB £9225 DAY £6750

FONTHILL
Coombe Hill Road, East Grinstead,
West Sussex RH9 4LY
Tel: 01342 321635
Head: Mrs J Griffiths MA, CertEd
Type: Co-educational Day B2-8 G2-11
No of pupils: B55 G121
Fees: DAY £525-£1650

STOKE BRUNSWICK SCHOOL
Ashurstwood, East Grinstead,
West Sussex RH19 3PF
Tel: 01342 822233
Head: W M Ellerton CertEd
Type: Co-educational Boarding & Day B3-13 G3-13
No of pupils: B100 G55 FB20 WB10
Fees: FB £8145 DAY £1545-£5925

Findon

VALE HOUSE EDUCATION CENTRE
The Vale House, Findon, West Sussex BN14 0RA
Tel: 01903 877448
Head: Mrs J Packham
Type: Co-educational Day

Hassocks

HURSTPIERPOINT COLLEGE
Hassocks, West Sussex BN6 9JS
Tel: 01273 833636
Head: S D A Meek MA
Type: Co-educational Boarding & Day B6-18 G6-18
No of pupils: B415 G86 VIth161
Fees: FB £8025-£11,940 DAY £5955-£9330

HURSTPIERPOINT JUNIOR SCHOOL
Hurstpierpoint, Hassocks, West Sussex BN6 9JS
Tel: 01273 834975
Head: A G Gobat BSc
Type: Co-educational Day & Boarding B7-13 G7-13
No of pupils: B117 G37
Fees: FB £8025 DAY £4800-£5955

Haywards Heath

ARDINGLY COLLEGE
Haywards Heath, West Sussex RH17 6SQ
Tel: 01444 892577/892429
Head: J W Flecker MA
Type: Co-educational Boarding & Day B13-18 G13-18
No of pupils: B256 G191 FB292
Fees: FB £11,085 DAY £8805

ARDINGLY COLLEGE JUNIOR SCHOOL
Haywards Heath, West Sussex RH17 6SQ
Tel: 01444 892279
Head: Peter Thwaites
Type: Co-educational Day & Boarding B2-13 G2-13
No of pupils: B70 G75 FB51
Fees: FB £8250 DAY £1200-£5400

CUMNOR HOUSE SCHOOL
Danehill, Haywards Heath, West Sussex RH17 7HT
Tel: 01825 790347
Head: N J Milner-Gulland MA(Cantab), CertEd
Type: Co-educational Boarding & Day B4-13 G4-13
No of pupils: B100 G99
Fees: FB £2960-£3115 DAY £1065-£2390

GREAT WALSTEAD SCHOOL
Lindfield, Haywards Heath, West Sussex RH16 2QL
Tel: 01444 483528
Head: H J Lowries BA(Bristol)
Type: Co-educational Boarding & Day B2-13 G2-13
No of pupils: B215 G122 FB56
Fees: FB £7350 WB £7200 DAY £495-£6000

★ HANDCROSS PARK SCHOOL
Handcross, Haywards Heath, West Sussex RH17 6HF
Tel: 01444 400526
Head: W J Hilton BA, CertEd
Type: Co-educational Day & Boarding B2fi-13 G2fi-13
No of pupils: B132 G106
Fees: FB £7380 DAY £5250-£6105

TAVISTOCK & SUMMERHILL SCHOOL
Summerhill Lane, Haywards Heath,
West Sussex RH16 1RP
Tel: 01444 450256
Head: M Barber
Type: Co-educational Day B3-13 G3-13
No of pupils: B94 G49
Fees: DAY £2400-£4500

Horsham

CHRIST'S HOSPITAL
Horsham, West Sussex RH13 7LS
Tel: 01403 252547/211293
Head: Peter C D Southern MA, PhD
Type: Co-educational Boarding B11-18 G11-18
No of pupils: B351 G237 VIth244 FB804
Fees: FB £11,124

FARLINGTON SCHOOL
Strood Park, Horsham, West Sussex RH12 3PN
Tel: 01403 254967
Head: Mrs P M Mawer BA
Type: Girls Day & Boarding G4-18
No of pupils: G351 VIth46
Fees: FB £8730-£9870 DAY £2655-£6090

PENNTHORPE SCHOOL
Horsham, West Sussex RH12 3HJ
Tel: 01403 822391
Head: Simon Moll BEd(Hons)
Type: Co-educational Day B2-13 G2-13
No of pupils: B177 G89
Fees: DAY £2250-£5910

RIKKYO SCHOOL IN ENGLAND
Guildford Road, Horsham, West Sussex RH12 3BE
Tel: 01403 822107
Head: Yasuhiko Soeda
Type: Co-educational Day & Boarding

Lancing

ARDMORE SCHOOL
Wembley Gardens, Lancing, West Sussex BN15 9LA
Tel: 01903 755583
Heads: Mrs Williams & Mrs Cragg
Type: Co-educational Day

LANCING COLLEGE
Lancing, West Sussex BN15 0RW
Tel: 01273 452213
Head: C J Saunders MA
Type: Boys Boarding & Day B13-18 G16-18
No of pupils: B450 G70
Fees: FB £12,030 DAY £9045

SOMPTING ABBOTTS PREPARATORY SCHOOL
Church Lane, Lancing, West Sussex BN15 0AZ
Tel: 01903 235960
Head: R M Johnson CertEd
Type: Boys Day & Boarding B3-13
No of pupils: B150
Fees: WB £6000 DAY £2160-£4050

Littlehampton

THE NEW WEST PRESTON MANOR
39 Park Drive, Littlehampton, West Sussex BN16 3DY
Tel: 01903 784282
Head: Mrs J M Drury
Type: Co-educational Day B2-5 G2-5

Midhurst

CONIFERS SCHOOL
Midhurst, West Sussex GU29 9BG
Tel: 01730 813243
Head: Mrs J Peel
Type: Co-educational Day B3-11 G3-11
No of pupils: B60 G70
Fees: DAY £1425-£2760

ST MARGARET'S JUNIOR CONVENT OF MERCY
Petersfield Road, Midhurst, West Sussex GU29 9JN
Tel: 01730 813956
Head: Sr M Joan
Type: Co-educational Day B3-11 G3-11
No of pupils: B163 G245
Fees: DAY £1125-£2025

ST MARGARET'S SENIOR
SCHOOL CONVENT OF MERCY
Petersfield Road, Midhurst, West Sussex GU29 9JN
Tel: 01730 813899
Head: Sr Aguinas BA, PGCE
Type: Girls Day G11-16
No of pupils: G300
Fees: DAY £2475

Pease Pottage

★ COTTESMORE SCHOOL
Buchan Hill, Pease Pottage, West Sussex RH11 9AU
Tel: 01293 520648
Head: M A Rogerson MA(Cantab)
Type: Co-educational Boarding B7-13 G7-13
No of pupils: B100 G45 FB140
Fees: FB £9150

Petworth

SEAFORD COLLEGE
Lavington Park, Petworth, West Sussex GU28 0NB
Tel: 01798 867392
Head: R C Hannaford BSc, MIBiol, CertEd
Type: Boys Boarding B11-18 G16-18
No of pupils: B324
Fees: FB £7935-£9255 DAY £4950-£5550

Pulborough

ARUNDALE PREPARATORY SCHOOL
Lower Street, Pulborough, West Sussex RH20 2BX
Tel: 01798 872520
Head: Miss K M Lovejoy BEd(Hons), ADBEd
Type: Co-educational Day B3-11 G3-11
No of pupils: B20 G86
Fees: DAY £1425-£4425

DORSET HOUSE SCHOOL
The Manor, Church Lane, Pulborough,
West Sussex RH20 1PB
Tel: 01798 831456
Head: A L James BA(Oxon)
Type: Boys Boarding & Day B4-13
No of pupils: B130
Fees: FB £7500-£8445 DAY £3495-£7050

★ WINDLESHAM HOUSE
Washington, Pulborough, West Sussex RH20 4AY
Tel: 01903 873207
Head: Philip J Lough MA(Oxon), PGCE(Dunelm)
Type: Co-educational Boarding B7-13 G7-13
No of pupils: B155 G106 FB251
Fees: FB £9435

Selsey

ACORNS SCHOOL
33 James Street, Selsey, West Sussex PO20 0JG
Head: Mrs E Hobson
Type: Co-educational Day

Shoreham-by-Sea

SHOREHAM COLLEGE
St Julians Lane, Shoreham-by-Sea,
West Sussex BN43 6YW
Tel: 01273 592681
Head: D R Jarman BA(UCNW), MEd(Reading), CertEd,
   DipPE(Leeds), FCP
Type: Co-educational Day B3-16 G3-16
No of pupils: B148 G61
Fees: DAY £2610-£5805

Steyning

SOUTHDOWN SCHOOL & NURSERY
Jarvis Lane, Steyning, West Sussex BN44 3GL
Tel: 01903 814581
Head: Mrs R A Hoare DipEd
Type: Co-educational Day B3-8 G3-8
No of pupils: B18 G20
Fees: DAY £520-£1650

THE TOWERS
Convent of the Blessed Sacrement, Steyning,
West Sussex BN44 3TF
Tel: 01903 812185
Head: Sr M Andrew RSS BA
Type: Co-educational Day & Boarding B3-8 G3-16
No of pupils: B3 G187 FB68
Fees: FB/WB £5646-£5958 DAY £1800-£3324

Storrington

ST JOSEPH'S DOMINICAN SCHOOL
The Abbey, Storrington, West Sussex RH20 4HE
Tel: 01903 743279
Head: Sr Loretta OP, BEd(Hons)
Type: Co-educational Day B4-11 G4-11
No of pupils: B40 G80
Fees: DAY £2592

Worthing

BROADWATER MANOR SCHOOL
Broadwater Road, Worthing, West Sussex BN14 8HU
Tel: 01903 20488
Head: D Telfer
Type: Co-educational Day B2-13 G2-13
No of pupils: B269 G191
Fees: DAY £285-£3300

OUR LADY OF SION SCHOOL
Gratwicke Road, Worthing, West Sussex BN11 4BL
Tel: 01903 204063
Head: B Sexton MA, BEd
Type: Co-educational Day B2-18 G2-18
No of pupils: B216 G262
Fees: DAY £2985-£4455

SANDHURST SCHOOL
101 Brighton Road, Worthing, West Sussex BN11 2EL
Tel: 01903 201933
Head: Mrs A B Flover CertEd
Type: Co-educational Day B2-13 G2-13
No of pupils: B80 G100
Fees: DAY £1515-£1755

Geographical Directory of
International Schools

London

THE AMERICAN SCHOOL IN LONDON
2-8 Loudoun Road, London NW8 0NP
Tel: 0171 722 0101
Head: Judith R Glickman PhD
Type: Co-educational Day B4-18 G4-18
No of pupils: B643 G598
Fees: DAY £8835-£10,410

INTERNATIONAL SCHOOL OF LONDON
139 Gunnersbury Avenue, London W3 8LG
Tel: 0181 992 5823
Head: Richard Hermon MA
Type: Co-educational Day B4-18 G4-18
No of pupils: B108 G81 VIth27
Fees: DAY £5550-£8760

SOUTHBANK INTERNATIONAL SCHOOL
36-38 Kensington Park Road, London W11 3BU
Tel: 0171 229 8230
Head: M E Toubkin BA
Type: Co-educational Day B5-18 G5-18
Fees: DAY £7290-£8910

WOODSIDE PARK SCHOOL
Friern Barnet Road, London N11 3DR
Tel: 0181 368 3777
Head: R F Metters BEd
Type: Co-educational Day B11-18 G11-18
No of pupils: B364 G123 VIth3
Fees: DAY £6000-£9000

Sussex

BUCKSWOOD GRANGE
Uckfield, East Sussex TN22 3PU
Tel: 01825 761666
Head: M B Reiser BSc(Econ)
Type: Co-educational Day & Boarding B4-16 G4-16
No of pupils: FB70
Fees: FB £6825 WB £6525 DAY £2445-£3210

Kent

SEVENOAKS SCHOOL
Sevenoaks, Kent TN13 1HU
Tel: 01732 455133
Head: R P Barker MA
Type: Co-educational Day & Boarding B11-18 G11-18
No of pupils: B525 G415 FB331
Fees: FB £11,178-£11,961 DAY £6804-£7587

Middlesex

AMERICAN COMMUNITY SCHOOL
Hillingdon Court, Uxbridge, Middlesex UB10 0BE
Tel: 01895 259771
Head: Paul Berg
Type: Co-educational Day B4-18 G4-18
No of pupils: B290 G288

Surrey

AMERICAN COMMUNITY SCHOOLS
Heywood, Cobham, Surrey KT11 1BL
Tel: 01932 867251
Head: T Lehman
Type: Co-educational Boarding & Day B3-18 G3-18
No of pupils: B666 G584

AMERICAN COMMUNITY SCHOOLS, ENGLAND
Woodlee, Egham, Surrey TW20 0HS
Tel: 01784 430611
Head: Mrs K Alderdice
Type: Co-educational Day B3-14 G3-14
No of pupils: B155 G105

MARYMOUNT INTERNATIONAL SCHOOL
George Road, Kingston-upon-Thames, Surrey KT2 7PE
Tel: 0181 949 0571
Head: Sr Rosaleen Sheridan RSHM, MSc
Type: Girls Day & Boarding G11-18
No of pupils: G222 VIth45 FB105 WB9
Fees: FB £13,100-£14,000 WB £12,900-£13,800
DAY £7200-£8100

TASIS ENGLAND AMERICAN SCHOOL
Coldharbour Lane, Egham, Surrey TW20 8TE
Tel: 01932 565252
Head: L D Rigg BA, MA, EdM
Type: Co-educational Boarding & Day B4-18 G4-18
No of pupils: B324 G309
Fees: FB £11,850-£12,160 DAY £6730-£7685

Geographical Directory
of Tutorial Colleges and
Colleges of Further Education

Central London

E1

THE ACADEMY DRAMA SCHOOL
189 Whitechapel Road, London E1 1DN
Tel: 0171 377 8735
Head: T Reynolds RADA

E14

WESTERN INTERNATIONAL UNIVERSITY
18 Ensign House, London E14 9RN
Tel: 0171 537 3388

EC1

CITY BUSINESS COLLEGE
178 Goswell Road, London EC1V 7DT
Tel: 0171 251 6473
Head: M Nowaz BA, MABE, AIFA, ACII

ITALIA CONTI ACADEMY OF THEATRE ART
23 Goswell Road, London EC1M 7AJ
Tel: 0171 608 0047
Head: C K Vote BA, DipEd

LONDON COLLEGE OF ENGLISH & ADVANCED STUDIES
178 Goswell Road, London EC1V 7DT
Tel: 0171 250 0610
Head: M Nowaz BA, MABE, AIFA, ACII

SANDRA TUTORIAL COLLEGE OF SECRETARIAL & COMPUTER STUDIES
Sandra House, London EC1R 5ET
Tel: 0171 833 3101
Head: Mr David

EC2

GUILDHALL SCHOOL OF MUSIC & DRAMA
Barbican, London EC2Y 8DT
Tel: 0171 628 2571

SE1

FOULKS LYNCH
6 Avonmouth Street, London SE1 6NX
Tel: 0181 831 9990
Head: D Rosebery

LONDON CITY COLLEGE
Royal Waterloo House, London SE1 8TX
Tel: 0171 928 0029/0938/0901
Head: N Kyritsis MA, DMS, MCIM

MORLEY COLLEGE
61 Westminster Bridge Road, London SE1 7HT
Tel: 0171 928 8501

SCHILLER INTERNATIONAL UNIVERSITY
Royal Waterloo House, London SE1 8TX
Tel: 0171 928 1372
Head: Dr Richard Taylor PhD

SE3

BLACKHEATH TUTORIAL CENTRE
Suter Lodge, London SE3 0TG
Tel: 0181 297 9599
Head: I R Laslett

SE10

GREENWICH COLLEGE
Meridian House, London SE10 8RT
Tel: 0181 853 4484
Head: W G Hunt BEd, MA

SE11

CITY & GUILDS OF LONDON ART SCHOOL
124 Kennington Park Road, London SE11 4DJ
Tel: 0171 735 2306/5210
Head: Michael Kenny RA

SE13

SOUTH LONDON COLLEGE OF HAIRDRESSING
26 Lewis Grove, London SE13
Tel: 0181 852 7693
Head: Mr A Ross

SE14

LABAN CENTRE FOR MOVEMENT AND DANCE
Laurie Grove, London SE14 6NH
Tel: 0181 692 4070
Head: Dr Marion North MA, PhD, Hon D'Arts

SE21

IVOR SPENCER INTERNATIONAL SCHOOL
12 Little Bornes, London SE21 8SE
Tel: 0181 670 5585/8424
Head: I Spencer

SW1

ABBEY SCHOOL FOR SPEAKERS
16 Gayfere Street, London SW1P 3HP
Tel: 0171 222 6037
Head: Thelma Seear MA

THE BRITISH SCHOOL OF OSTEOPATHY
1/4 Suffolk Street, London SW1Y 4HG
Tel: 0171 930 9254
Head: Clive Standen MA, DO, MRO

★ **INCHBALD SCHOOL OF DESIGN**
7 Eaton Gate, London SW1 9BA
Tel: 0171 730 5508
Head: Mrs Jacqueline Duncan IIDA, FIDDA

WEBSTER UNIVERSITY
5 Grosvenor Gardens, London SW1W 0BD
Tel: 0171 487 7433
Head: Dr James Evans

SW3

JOAN PRICE'S FACE PLACE BEAUTY SCHOOL
33 Cadogan Street, London SW3 3PP
Tel: 0171 589 4226
Head: Mrs T Quayyum BABTAC, ITEC, CIDESCO

SW4

LONDON ACADEMY OF ADMINISTRATIVE STUDIES
Maritime House, London SW4 OJP
Tel: 0171 627 1299
Head: Mr Filani

SW5

COLLINGHAM
23 Collingham Gardens, London SW5 0HL
Tel: 0171 244 7414
Heads: G Hattee MA(Oxon),DipEd & Mrs G Green MSc

LONDON ACADEMY OF MUSIC & DRAMATIC ART
Tower House, London SW5 0SR
Tel: 0171 373 9883
Head: Peter James

LONDON ELECTRONICS COLLEGE
20 Penywern Road, London SW5 9SU
Tel: 0171 373 8721
Head: M D Spalding BSc(Hons), MSc, CEng, MIEE,
    PGCE, MCybSoc, FRSA

PHOTOGRAPHIC TRAINING CENTRE
52/54 Kenway Road, London SW5
Tel: 0171 373 4227
Head: A S Fox

ST JAMES'S SECRETARIAL COLLEGE
4 Wetherby Gardens, London SW5 0JN
Tel: 0171 373 3852
Head: N C E Knight

SW6

BLOOMSBURY COLLEGE
52a Walham Grove, London SW6 1QR
Tel: 0171 381 0213
Head: S Howse BSc, MSc

KENSINGTON COLLEGE OF BUSINESS
52a Walham Grove, London SW6 1QR
Tel: 0171 381 6360
Head: I R Pirie BA

LONDON ACADEMY OF PERFORMING ARTS
2 Effie Road, London SW6 1TB
Tel: 0171 736 0121
Head: Miss C Hocking RADA

★ **LONDON STUDY CENTRE**
Munster House, 676 Fulham Road, London SW6 5SA
Tel: 0171 731 3549/736 4990
Principal: Colin D Gordon MA (Oxon)

SW7

BILINGUAL SECRETARIAL COLLEGE OF THE FRENCH INSTITUTE
14 Cromwell Place, London SW7 2JR
Tel: 0171 589 6211
Head: Michel Richard

CHRISTIE'S EDUCATION
63 Old Brompton Road, London SW7 3JS
Tel: 0171 581 3933
Head: R Cumming

DAVID GAME TUTORIAL COLLEGE
86 Old Brompton Road, London SW7 3LQ
Tel: 0171 584 9097/7580
Head: D T P Game MA, MPhil

DUFF MILLER
59 Queen's Gate, London SW7 5JP
Tel: 0171 225 0577
Head: C Denning BSc, PGCE

HURON UNIVERSITY USA IN LONDON
58 Prince's Gate, London SW7 2PG
Tel: 0171 584 9696
Head: Ms Fay Poosti

INSTITUT FRANCAIS
14 Cromwell Place, London SW7 2JR
Tel: 0171 581 2701 or 0171 58962
Head: Mrs L Towers

LUCIE CLAYTON SECRETARIAL COLLEGE
4 Cornwall Gardens, London SW7 4AJ
Tel: 0171 581 0024
Head: Mrs Denise Perry

MANDER PORTMAN WOODWARD
108 Cromwell Road, London SW7 4ES
Tel: 0171 835 1355
Heads: Dr Nigel Stout MA, DPhil &
 Miss Fiona Dowding MA

MANDER PORTMAN WOODWARD
24 Elvaston Place, London SW7 5NL
Tel: 0171 584 8555
Heads: Miss Fiona Dowding & Dr Nigel Stout

QUEEN'S BUSINESS & SECRETARIAL COLLEGE
24 Queensberry Place, London SW7 2DS
Tel: 0171 589 8583/581 8331
Head: Mrs C Bickford

VACANI SCHOOL OF DANCING
38-42 Harrington Road, London SW7 3ND
Tel: 0171 589 6110
Heads: Miss E Eden & Miss M Stassinopoulos

WEBBER DOUGLAS ACADEMY DRAMATIC ART
30-36 Clareville Street, London SW7 5AP
Tel: 0171 370 4154
Head: R B Jago

WESTMINSTER INDEPENDENT SIXTH FORM COLLEGE
82 Old Brompton Road, London SW7 3LQ
Tel: 0171 584 1288
Head: Mrs Jane Darwin MA, BLit

SW10

THE HEATHERLEY SCHOOL OF FINE ART
Upcerne Road, London SW10 OSH
Tel: 0171 351 4190
Head: J Walton RP, DFA(Lond)

SW11

COLLEGE OF ROYAL ACADEMY OF DANCING
36 Battersea Square, London SW11 3RA
Tel: 0171 223 0091
Head: Miss S Danby LRAD, ARAD

SW17

LONDON EXECUTIVE COLLEGE
Bank Chambers, London SW17 7BA
Tel: 0181 682 1011

SW18

ACADEMY OF LIVE & RECORDED ARTS
Royal Victoria Building, London SW18 3SX
Tel: 0181 870 6475
Head: Sorrel Carson

SW19

ELIZABETH RUSSELL SCHOOL OF COOKERY
Flat 5, 18 The Grange, London SW19 4PS
Tel: 0181 947 2144
Heads: Miss A Russell & Mrs E Pilon

W1

ALAN D SCHOOL OF HAIRDRESSING
61-62 East Castle Street, London W1P 3RE
Tel: 0171 580 3323
Head: Tina Jerrom

AMERICAN COLLEGE IN LONDON
110 Marylebone High Street, London W1M 5FP
Tel: 0171 486 1772
Head: M A Barnette

BLAKE COLLEGE
162 New Cavendish Street, London WIM 7FJ
Tel: 0171 636 0658
Head: D A J Cluckie BA, BSc

BUILDING CRAFTS COLLEGE
153 Great Titchfield Street, London W1P 7FR
Tel: 0171 636 0480
Head: P Quick

CAVENDISH COLLEGE
209-212 Tottenham Court Road, London W1P 9AF
Tel: 0171 580 6043
Head: Dr J Sanders BSc, MBA, PhD

COLLEGE OF CENTRAL LONDON
213-215 Tottenham Court Road, London W1 4US
Tel: 0171 636 2212
Head: N Kailides

COLLEGE OF DATA PROCESSING
213-215 Tottenham Court Road, London W1 4US
Tel: 0171 636 2212
Head: J Kay

HOTEL & TRAVEL TRAINING COLLEGE
287 Oxford Street, London W1R 1LB
Tel: 0171 629 1762
Head: Dr D A Samarakoon

LE CORDON BLEU CULINARY ACADEMY
114 Marylebone Lane, London W1M 6HH
Tel: 0171 935 3503
Head: Miss L Grey

MODERN TUTORIAL COLLEGE
Kilburn Lane, London W1D 4AA
Tel: 0181 960 5899/969 1269
Head: W B Moore BSc

THE RAY COCHRANE BEAUTY SCHOOL
118 Baker Street, London W1M 1LB
Tel: 0171 486 6291
Head: Miss B Suri CIDESCO, CIBTAC

ROBERT FIELDING SCHOOL OF HAIRDRESSING
61-62 East Castle Street, London WIP 3RE
Tel: 0171 580 3323
Head: Tina Jerrom

ROYAL ACADEMY SCHOOLS
Burlington House, London W1V 0DS
Tel: 0171 439 7438
Head: Norman Adams

THE SCHOOL OF COMPUTER TECHNOLOGY
213-215 Tottenham Court Road, London W1 4US
Tel: 0171 636 6441/2
Head: N Kay

SOTHEBY'S EDUCATIONAL STUDIES
30 Oxford Street, London W1R 1RE
Tel: 0171 323 5775
Head: Mrs Anne Ceresole

STEINER SCHOOL OF BEAUTY THERAPY
193 Wardour Street, London W1U 3FA
Tel: 0171 434 4534/4564
Head: Mrs J Wackett

**VIDAL SASSOON ACADEMY
SCHOOL OF HAIRDRESSING**
15 Davies Mews, London W1Y 1AS
Tel: 0171 318 5202
Head: S Ellis

WEST LONDON COLLEGE
Avon House, London W1N 9HA
Tel: 0171 491 1841
Head: P Rainey MA, MSc, MBCS

WORLD-WIDE EDUCATION SERVICE(PNEU)
St Georges House, London W1P 3FP
Tel: 0171 6372644
Head: Miss C Stephenson CertEd

W2

★ **ABBEY TUTORIAL COLLEGE**
28a Hereford Road, London W2 5AJ
Tel: 0171 229 5928
Head: J Burnett BSc

DAVIES, LAING & DICK
10 Pembridge Square, London W2 4ED
Tel: 0171 727 2797
Head: Ms Elizabeth Rickards BA, MA, PGCE

LONDON ACADEMY OF DRESSMAKING
3rd Floor, London W2 4UA
Tel: 0171 727 0221/2850
Head: Mrs P A Parkinson MA

W3

BROADWAY SECRETARIAL TRAINING CENTRE
30-31 The Broadway, London W3 2NP
Tel: 0181 840 2762
Head: Ms J Mattson

W5

DRAMA STUDIO LONDON
Grange Court, London W5 5QN
Tel: 0181 579 3897
Head: P Layton

EALING TUTORIAL COLLEGE
28a New Broadway, London W5 2AX
Tel: 0181 579 6668
Head: Mrs G Watt

W6

RAVENSCOURT TUTORIAL COLLEGE
28 Studland Street, London W6 0JS
Tel: 0181 846 8542
Head: Miss P M Saw

W8

★ **ASHBOURNE INDEPENDENT SIXTH FORM COLLEGE**
17 Old Court Place, London W8 4PL
Tel: 0171 937 3858
Head: Mr M J Hatchard-Kirby MSc, BApSc

CAMPBELL HARRIS TUTORS
185 Kensington High Street, London W8 6SH
Tel: 0171 937 0032
Heads: Mark Harris & Ms Claire Campbell

KENSINGTON COLLEGE
41 Kensington High Street, London W8 5ED
Tel: 0171 937 8886
Head: E B Robinson BSc, DipEd

LANSDOWNE INDEPENDENT SIXTH FORM COLLEGE
7-9 Palace Gate, London W8 5LS
Tel: 0171 616 4400
Head: P Templeton BSc(Econ)

LANSDOWNE SECRETARIAL COLLEGE
7-9 Palace Gate, London W8 5LS
Tel: 0171 581 4866
Head: P Templeton BSc(Econ)

LEITH'S SCHOOL OF FOOD & WINE
21 St Alban's Grove, London W8 5BP
Tel: 0171 229 0177
Head: Caroline Waldegrave

**UNIVERSAL LANGUAGES/
BUSINESS LANGUAGE SERVICES**
45 High Street, London W8 5EB
Tel: 0171 938 1225
Head: A Deniaud

W11

BABEL TECHNICAL COLLEGE
69 Notting Hill Gate, London W11 3JS
Tel: 0171 221 1483
Head: M H Kubba BSc, MSc, MACM, MBCS

WEST LONDON SCHOOL OF THERAPEUTIC MASSAGE
41a St Luke's Road, London W11 1DD
Tel: 0171 229 4672
Head: C Chabrier LTPhys, MIPTI

W12

BRIERLEY PRICE PRIOR LTD
BBP House, Aldine Place, London W12 8AA
Tel: 0181 740 2222

W14

HOLBORN COLLEGE
200 Greyhound Road, London W14 9RY
Tel: 0171 385 3377
Head: John Grenier

KLC DESIGN TRAINING
KLC House, London W14 0AE
Tel: 0171 602 8592
Head: Mrs Jennifer Gibbs MCSD, FRSA

WC1

**ARCHITECTURAL ASSOCIATION
SCHOOL OF ARCHITECTURE**
34-36 Bedford Square, London WC1B 3ES
Tel: 0171 636 0974
Head: Mohsen Mostafavi AADipl, RIBA

DAVIES'S COLLEGE
25 Old Gloucester Street, London WC1N 3AF
Tel: 0171 430 1622
Head: Andrew Williams BA, MSc

INNS OF COURT SCHOOL OF LAW
39 Eagle Street, London WC1R 4AJ
Tel: 0171 404 5787
Head: Mrs M A Phillips

LONDON CONTEMPORARY DANCE SCHOOL
The Place, London WC1H 9AT
Tel: 0171 387 0152
Head: Dr R Ralph

MODERN ART STUDIES
39 Bedford Square, London WC1B 3EG
Tel: 0171 436 3630
Head: Jean Hodgins

PITMAN CENTRAL COLLEGE
154 Southampton Row, London WC1B 5AX
Tel: 0171 837 4481
Head: Mrs J Almond

ROYAL ACADEMY OF DRAMATIC ART
62-64 Gower Street, London WC1E 6ED
Tel: 0171 636 7076
Head: N Barter

WC2

LONDON INTERNATIONAL FILM SCHOOL
24 Shelton Street, London WC2H 9HP
Tel: 0171 836 9642
Head: Martin M Amstell

OFFICE SKILLS CENTRE UK LTD
Dragon Court, London WC2B 5LX
Tel: 0171 242 0566
Head: Jamie Dickson

NW3

CENTRAL SCHOOL OF SPEECH AND DRAMA
Embassy Theatre, London NW3 3HY
Tel: 0171 722 8183
Head: Mr B Fowler

FINE ARTS COLLEGE
85 Belsize Park Gardens, London NW3 4NJ
Tel: 0171 586 0312
Heads: Candida Cochrane CFA(Oxon) &
Nicholas Cochrane CFA(Oxon)

LAKEFIELD CATERING & EDUCATIONAL CENTRE
41a Maresfield Gardens, London NW3 5RY
Tel: 0171 433 3454
Head: Miss J E Gardner

MARIA MONTESSORI TRAINING ORGANISATION
26 Lyndhurst Gardens, London NW3 5NW
Tel: 0171 435 3646
Head: Mrs L Lawrence

STELLA MANN SCHOOL OF DANCING
343a Finchley Road, London NW3
Tel: 0171 435 9317
Head: Miss M Breen ARAD, AISTD

NW4

ALBANY COLLEGE
23-24 Queens Road, London NW4 2TL
Tel: 0181 202 9748/5965
Head: R J Arthy MPhil, MRIC

NW5

DRAMA CENTRE
176 Prince of Wales Road, London NW5 3PT
Tel: 0171 267 1177
Head: C Fettes

NW11

THE TUITION CENTRE
8 Accommodation Road, London NW11 8ED
Tel: 0181 201 8020
Head: B Canetti BA(Hons), MSc

N1

THE LONDON SCHOOL OF INSURANCE
53-55 East Road, London N1 6AH
Tel: 0171 251 5858
Head: R Sampat BSc, MBIM

LONDON STUDIO CENTRE
42-50 York Way, London N1 9AB
Tel: 0171 837 7741
Head: N Espinosa

UKCOSA
9-17 St Albans Place, London N1 0NX
Tel: 0171 226 3762

N6

MARIE LECKO SCHOOL OF FASHION & DESIGN
12 North Grove, London N6 4SL
Tel: 0181 348 1440
Head: Mme Marie King Lecko

N7

CITY COLLEGE OF HIGHER EDUCATION
67-88 Seven Sisters Road, London N7 6BU
Tel: 0171 263 5937
Head: A Andrews MBIM, FFA, FCEA, MABE

THE DESIGN SCHOOL
United House, London N7 9DP
Tel: 0171 607 5566
Head: Iris Dunbar BA, FCSD

EMILE WOOLF COLLEGE
457-463 Caledonian Road, London N7 9BA
Tel: 0171 700 6438

LONDON INTERNATIONAL COLLEGE
67/83 Seven Sisters Road, London N7 6BU
Tel: 0171 263 9729/6464
Head: G Cleo

N8

MOUNTVIEW THEATRE SCHOOL
104 Crouch Hill, London N8 9EA
Tel: 0181 340 5885/0097
Head: Peter Coxhead

REGENT'S COLLEGE
Inner Circle, London NW1 4NS
Tel: 0171 487 7505
Head: J Payne

N15

SUPREME SCHOOL OF HAIR & BEAUTY CONSULTANCY
12 West Green Road, London N15 5NN
Tel: 0181 800 7459/802 4599
Head: Mrs J Sam

N16

LONDON ACADEMY OF HEALTH & BEAUTY
53 Alkham Road, London N16 7AA
Tel: 0181 806 2788
Head: Mrs Penina Katsch

N19

BYAM SHAW SCHOOL OF ART
2 Elthorne Road, London N19 4AG
Tel: 0171 281 4111
Head: A Warman

Greater London

Essex

ROGENE SCHOOL OF BEAUTY THERAPY
Rogene House, Ilford, Essex IG1 1BX
Tel: 0181 478 2728
Head: Mrs C Gibson

Kent

**CONEY HILL SCHOOL &
NASH FURTHER EDUCATION CENTRE**
Croydon Road, Bromley, Kent BR2 7AG
Tel: 0181 462 7419/5493
Head: Mrs Karen Fletcher MEd

BECKENHAM SECRETARIAL COLLEGE
31 Beckenham Road, Beckenham, Kent BR3 4PR
Tel: 0181 650 3321
Head: Mrs E Wakeling

SCHILLER INTERNATIONAL ACADEMY
Wickham Court, West Wickham, Kent BR4 9HW
Tel: 0181 777 8069
Head: Louise Cody BA(Hons), DipSocAd, PGCE(TEFL)

DOREEN BIRD COLLEGE OF PERFORMING ARTS
Birkbeck Centre, Sidcup, Kent DA14 4DE
Tel: 0181 300 6004 or 3031
Head: Miss D Bird

ROSE BRUFORD COLLEGE OF SPEECH & DRAMA
Lamorbey Park, Sidcup, Kent DA15 9DF
Tel: 0181 300 3024
Head: Robert Ely

Middlesex

DRIZEN TUTORIAL COLLEGE
Whitchurch Boys Club, Edgware, Middlesex
Head: Stanley Drizen

**RAMBERT SCHOOL OF BALLET
& CONTEMPORARY DANCE**
West London Institute of Higher Education, Gordon House,
Twickenham, Middlesex
Tel: 0181 891 8200
Head: R McKim

HARROW SECRETARIAL COLLEGE
72 Station Road, Harrow, Middlesex HA1 2SQ
Tel: 0181 427 2939
Head: Mrs R Bluston

GREENHILL COLLEGE
Lowlands Road, Harrow, Middlesex HA1 3AQ
Tel: 0181 422 2388

Surrey

CAMBRIDGE TUTORS COLLEGE
Water Tower Hill, Croydon, Surrey CR0 5SX
Tel: 0181 688 5284/7363
Head: D N Wilson BA, MLitt, MIL, FCollP, FRSA

RENBARDOU SCHOOL OF BEAUTY THERAPY
Acorn House, Croydon, Surrey CR0 6BA
Tel: 0181 686 4781
Head: Renee Tanner

PURLEY SCHOOL OF COMMERCE
13 High Street, Purley, Surrey CR2 2AF
Tel: 0181 660 5060/2568
Head: Miss P W Kent

PURLEY SECRETARIAL & LANGUAGE COLLEGE
14 Brighton Road, Purley, Surrey CR8 3AB
Tel: 0181 660 5060/2568
Head: Miss P W Kent

THE ROYAL BALLET SCHOOL
White Lodge, Richmond, Surrey TW10 5HR
Tel: 0181 876 5547
Head: Mr Mitchell

**RICHMOND COLLEGE
AMERICAN INTERNATIONAL UNIVERSITY**
Queen's Road, Richmond, Surrey TW10 6JP
Tel: 0181 940 9762
Head: Dr W J Petrek BA, STL, PhD

RICHMOND LANGUAGE CENTRE
27/28 George Street, Richmond upon Thames,
Surrey TW9 1HY
Tel: 0181 948 3333/1306
Head: J Mitchell BEd

SCHOOL OF HORTICULTURE
Royal Botanic Gardens, Richmond, Surrey TW9 3AB
Tel: 0181 332 5545
Head: Ian Leese BSc, MHort(RHS), DipHort(Kew),
CertEd, FIHort

South East

Berkshire

THE NORLAND COLLEGE
Denford Park, Hungerford, Berkshire RG17 OPQ
Tel: 01488 682252
Head: Mrs L E Davis Mphil, RGN, FRSH

CHILTERN NURSERY TRAINING COLLEGE
16 Peppard Road, Reading, Berkshire RG4 8JZ
Tel: 01734 471847
Head: Mrs E Sadek

PADWORTH COLLEGE
Reading, Berkshire RG7 4NR
Tel: 01734 832644/5
Head: Dr S Villazon MA, PhD, FRSA

Essex

OGILVY COURT RESIDENTIAL HOME
America Road, Earls Colne, Essex CO6 2LB
Tel: 01787 222355
Head: D Russell-Jones

EAST 15 ACTING SCHOOL
Hatfields, Loughton, Essex IG10 3RU
Tel: 0181 508 5983
Head: Mrs M Walker

CROWN SECRETARIAL COLLEGE
121-129 North Road, Westcliff-on-Sea, Essex SS0 7AH
Tel: 01702 340121
Head: Ms T Corsiwi

Hampshire

WESSEX TUTORS
44 Shirley Road, Southampton, Hampshire SO1 3EU
Tel: 01703 334719
Head: Mrs J E White BA(London)

WESSEX TUTORS
14/18 Parchment Street, Winchester,
Hampshire SO23 8AZ
Tel: 01962 853964
Head: Mrs E Backhouse MA(Cantab)

Hertfordshire

ST ALBANS TUTORS
30 Beaconsfield Road, St Albans,
Hertfordshire AL1 3RB
Tel: 01727 842348
Head: Mrs Hilary Beskeen BA(Hons)

JUSTIN CRAIG EDUCATION
Craig House, 13 High Street, St Albans,
Hertfordshire AL4 0NS
Tel: 01727 827000
Head: Mrs M Craig

**CHAMPNEYS INTERNATIONAL
COLLEGE OF HEALTH & BEAUTY**
Chesham Road, Tring, Hertfordshire HP23 6HY
Tel: 01442 873326
Head: Mrs S Page ITEC, CGTC

Kent

ROCHESTER TUTORS INDEPENDENT COLLEGE
New Road House, Rochester, Kent ME1 1BD
Tel: 01634 828115
Heads: B Pain BSc(Hons) & Simon De Belder BA(Hons)

THE OLD VICARAGE
Marden, Tonbridge, Kent TN12 9AG
Tel: 01622 832200
Head: Mrs P G Stevens LRAM(S&D)

THE ZOBEL SECRETARIAL COLLEGE
18 Pembroke Road, Sevenoaks, Kent TN13 1XR
Tel: 01732 451595
Head: Miss D H C Zobel

BRETLANDS BEAUTY TRAINING CENTRE
Baden-Powell Place, Tunbridge Wells, Kent TN4 8XD
Tel: 01892 533161
Head: Mrs J Thornycroft CIDESCO, BABTAC, C&G

Surrey

GUILDFORD SECRETARIAL COLLEGE
19 Chapel Street, Guildford, Surrey GU1 3UL
Tel: 01483 564885
Head: Mrs D E White

SURREY COLLEGE
53 Woodbridge Road, Guildford, Surrey GU1 4RF
Tel: 01483 565887
Head: R Carstairs BA, MSc

GUILDFORD SCHOOL OF ACTING
Millmead Terrace, Guildford, Surrey GU2 5AT
Tel: 01483 560701
Head: G McDougall MA, FRSA

TANTE MARIE SCHOOL OF COOKERY
Woodham House, Woking, Surrey GU21 4HF
Tel: 01483 726957
Head: Mrs B A Childs FIHEC

CAMPANA INTERNATIONAL COLLEGE
Moor Park House, Farnham, Surrey GU9 8EN
Tel: 01252 727111
Head: Mrs M A P Frost, Licenci, eΠs Lettres

COLLINS SECRETARIAL TRAINING
Victoria House, Epsom, Surrey KT17 1HH
Tel: 01372 728823
Head: Mrs. Brooks

STUDY ASSOCIATES INTERNATIONAL
Gold Peak House, Epsom, Surrey KT18 7EH
Tel: 01372 275005
Head: Mrs B A Legge

ROYAL SCHOOL OF NEEDLEWORK
Appartment 12A, Hampton Court Palace,
Surrey KT8 9AU
Tel: 0181 943 1432
Head: Mrs E Elvin

**RAWORTH COLLEGE FOR SPORTS THERAPY
AND NATURAL MEDICINE**
Dorking, Surrey RH4 2HG
Tel: 01306 742150
Head: Mrs N A Williams

HURTWOOD HOUSE
Dorking, Surrey RH5 6NU
Tel: 01483 277416
Head: K R B Jackson MA, FRSA

East Sussex

BARTHOLOMEWS TUTORIAL COLLEGE
22-23 Prince Albert Street, Brighton,
East Sussex BN1 1HF
Tel: 01273 205965/205141
Head: W A Duncombe BSc

DOMINO GROUP HAIR ACADEMY
1 St James's Street, Brighton, East Sussex BN2 1RE
Tel: 01273 681929
Head: Mrs J A Faulkner

HARROW HOUSE
1 Silverdale Road, Eastbourne,
East Sussex BN20 7AA
Tel: 01323 730851
Head: Mrs J E Jenion BEd, MIHEC

HOVE BUSINESS COLLEGE
1-2 Ventnor Villas, Hove, East Sussex BN3 3DD
Tel: 01273 731352/727102
Head: Mrs P Humphrey

SHANDY STAGE SCHOOL
56A Livingstone Road, Hove, East Sussex BN3 3WL
Tel: 01273 822244
Head: Mr Lindsdale

THE BRITISH ENGINEERIUM
off Nevill Road, Hove, East Sussex BN3 7QA
Tel: 01273 559583
Head: J E Minns

THE COUNTRY HOUSE COURSE
Holmstall, Mayfield, East Sussex TN20 6NJ
Tel: 01435 872275
Head: Mrs M Biron DipIntDes, CertEd, FIDDA

MERCELLES
St Peters, Hastings, East Sussex TN35 4BP
Tel: 01424 813330/812002
Head: Miss S A Mercel

SHELAGAR TUTORIAL CENTRE
1 Avon Court, St Leonards-on-Sea,
East Sussex TN38 0SY
Tel: 01424 435501
Head: P Shelton-Agar DipAM

West Sussex

WEST DEAN COLLEGE
West Dean, Chichester, West Sussex PO18 0QZ
Tel: 01243 811301
Head: David Leigh

The Assisted Places Scheme

At the time of going to press, there is uncertainty about the future of the Scheme. Until now, up to 9800 places have been made available each year at certain independent schools in England and Wales for academically able children whose parents cannot afford the full tuition fees. There is an assisted places scheme in Scotland also, but with certain significant differences. Information about it can be obtained from the Scottish Office Industry and Education Department, Assisted Places Scheme, Area 2A, Victoria Quay, Edinburgh EH6 6QQ, or telephone (0131) 244 0942.

Is my child eligible for an assisted place?

The scheme is open to boys and girls. The normal age of entry will usually be at 11 or 13, but will vary from school to school.

Some assisted places are also available for pupils going straight into the sixth form and, for the first time from September 1996, at ages 5, 7 and 8.

Pupils may get assisted places at other ages but only if they are to be admitted into a class with other assisted pupils who entered in a previous school year.

Pupils may get assisted places whatever type of school they have attended beforehand, although schools are required to offer a majority of assisted places to pupils from state schools.

To be eligible for an assisted place a pupil must have been ordinarily resident in the United Kingdom, the Channel Islands or the Isle of Man for two years before taking up the assisted place. (A child who has been abroad for all or part of that period, *eg* with parents working temporarily overseas, may still count as 'ordinarily resident' in the country. Provision is also made for children of workers from the UK and other countries in the European Economic Area moving within the Area and to refugees.)

What assistance is available?

Assistance with tuition fees is available on a sliding scale linked to family income. Some families may also be eligible for help with other expenses - school meals and uniform and travel to and from school. More information about the help available is given below.

Under the scheme, no assistance is available with boarding fees, but if you would like your child to board, some schools which offer assisted places may themselves be willing to offer you help with boarding fees.

What shall I have to pay towards tuition fees?

The following notes are intended to give you an idea of whether you would qualify for assistance, and some indication of how much you might have to pay.

The parental contribution to fees will depend upon the family's 'relevant income'.

Relevant income will normally be the total of the income (before tax) from all sources of both parents and any unearned income of their dependent children (whether they hold an assisted place or not) less an allowance (of £1200 in 1996-97) for each dependent child other than the assisted place holder and for each other dependent relative of the parents in the same household. Relevant income does not include income from child benefit, mobility allowance, some other social security benefits or the amount of any dependent child's or parent's scholarship or student award.

Relevant income is normally assessed for the income tax year before the school year in question (*eg* relevant income for the school year 1996-97 will be based on income in the tax year 1995-96. Parents will be required to provide documentary evidence, *eg* P60 or a Schedule D or E tax assessment, as appropriate, as a condition of being granted an assisted place. Special rules apply where the parents are divorced or separated (see below); where certain disability benefits are payable; and where income is derived from a business with a special accounting year.

For the school year 1996-97 parents do not have to pay anything if relevant income for the tax year 1995-96 is £9,873 or less. If income exceeds that amount they will have to pay an increasing share up to the full fee. As a guide, the table below gives some examples of what parents will have to pay in the school year 1996-97 if there are one or two assisted place holders in the family. The tables can be extended beyond the £25,000 maximum shown. If you have three or more assisted pupils, a different scale will apply. The schools in the scheme have the complete scales of contributions and will calculate the amount which you will have to pay. You will normally be asked to pay your share of the fees in equal instalments at the start of each term.

The amount of assistance will be reviewed annually and parents will be required to provide details of their income each year to enable their contribution to the fees to be re-assessed.

Parents contribution to fees:
1996-97 school year

Relevant income 1995-96 tax year (after allowances for dependents)	One assisted place holder	For each of two assisted place holders
£	£	£
9874	15	9
10000	24	18
11000	129	96
12000	267	98
13000	417	312
14000	618	462
15000	828	621
17000	1284	963
19000	1764	1323
21000	2409	1806
23000	3069	2301
25000	3729	2796

Relevant income can be higher depending on the fee levels at schools.

What help is available with other expenses?

Pupils whose parents are receiving income support are eligible for free school meals. Grants of £43 - £169 towards the cost of school uniform are available where relevant income is not more than £11,056. For pupils living more than three miles from the school assistance with the cost of public transport will be available on a sliding scale linked to relevant income.

What happens if my income falls suddenly?

In cases of hardship - for example, if income falls because a parent dies or is out of work - the parents' share of the fees may be calculated on current income, rather than income a year earlier. This can be arranged in the first year your child holds an assisted place, or in later years if circumstances change.

What about divorced or separated parents?

In such cases the parental contribution will be assessed on the basis of the relevant income of the parent with whom the child normally resides; plus - if he or she has remarried - that of his or her spouse. This applies where parents are separated by a decree of judicial separation or a legal deed (or there is a court order for custody or access or maintenance, or prohibiting one parent from entering the matrimonial home); and it applies where they are divorced. Maintenance is included in parental income.

How do I apply for an assisted place?

The selection of pupils will (subject to the eligibility rules outlined above) be undertaken by the schools themselves. There is only a limited number of assisted places at each school and most schools will require applicants to take an entrance examination or test and probably to attend for interview. Since schools' selection arrangements and closing dates for applications vary, you should get in touch as soon as possible with the school or schools of your choice. The schools will provide all the necessary application forms and information about their selection arrangements. If you have any further questions about the scheme, please contact the DFEE, Assisted Places Team, Mowden Hall, Darlington, County Durham DL3 9BG; telephone 01325 392163.

Below is a list - the most up-to-date at the time of publication - of schools, by region, participating in the scheme. For each school the normal ages of entry at which assisted places are available are given: 11, 12 or 13. Sixth form entry is indicated by 'VI'. Boys' schools are shown by the letter 'B', girls' schools by 'G' and mixed schools by 'M'. Some single-sex schools have mixed entry sixth forms; these are marked '(M)'. With the Scottish schools the letter 'P' denotes a preparatory school. In a few cases entry at age 11 will be to a junior department or an associated preparatory school with transfer to the main school at 13. Schools which have been authorised to offer boarding places to assisted pupils are indicated by the letter 'b'. Enquiries about boarding and about possible assistance with the boarding element of schools' fees should be addressed to the school concerned. Enquiries about assisted places at a particular school or schools should be addressed to the headmaster or headmistress.

SOUTH AND SOUTH EAST

Berkshire, Buckinghamshire and Hampshire
Wellington College, Crowthorne, Berks B(M)b 5, 11, 13 & VI
The Abbey School, Reading G 5, 11 & VI
Bradfield College, Reading B(M)b VI
Douai School, Reading Mb 11
St Joseph's RC Convent School, Reading G 11 & VI
Leighton Park School, Reading Mb 11 & 13
Pangbourne College, Reading Bb 11, 12 & 13
Reading Blue Coat School, Sonning-on-Thames B 11 & VI
Downe House School, Newbury Gb 11 & 12
Stowe School, Nr Buckingham B(M)b VI
Marist Convent Senior School, Ascot G 5, 11 & VI
Salesian RC College, Farnborough B 11, 13 & VI
Farnborough Hill, Farnborough G 11, 12, 13 & VI
Lord Wandsworth College, Long Sutton, Basingstoke B(M)b 11,
    12, 13 & VI
Winchester College, Bb 13 & VI
St Swithun's School, Winchester Gb VI
King Edward VI School, Southampton M 11, 13 & VI
The Atherley School, Southampton G 5, 11 & VI
Bedales School, Petersfield Mb VI
Churcher's College, Petersfield Mb 5, 11, 12, 13 & VI
St John's RC College, Southsea B(M)b 11, 12, 13 & VI
Portsmouth High School, Southsea G 5, 11 & VI
The Portsmouth Grammar School M 5, 11 & VI
Ryde School, Isle of Wight M 5, 11

Middlesex, Hertfordshire, Essex
Hampton School, Middlesex B 11, 13 & VI
Heathfield School GPDST, Pinner, Middx G 5, 11 & VI
St David's School, Ashford, Middx G 5, 11 & VI
The Lady Eleanor Holles School, Hampton, Middx G 11 & VI
North London Collegiate School, Edgware G 11 & VI
Haileybury College Bb(M) 11 & VI
The John Lyon School, Harrow B 11, 13 & VI
Northwood College G 5, 11 & VI
Merchant Taylors' School, Northwood Bb 11, 13 & VI
St Helen's School for Girls, Northwood Gb 5, 11, 12 & VI
Aldenham School, Elstree B(M)b 13 & VI
Haberdashers' Aske's School for Girls, Elstree G 11 & VI
Haberdashers' Aske's School, Borehamwood B 11 & VI
Queenswood School, Hatfield G 11 & VI
St Columba's College, St Albans B 11

St Albans School B(M) 11 & VI
St Albans High School G 5, 11 & VI
St Margaret's School, Bushey Gb 5, 11 & 13
Berkhamsted School Bb 11, 13 & VI
Berkhamsted School for Girls G 11 & VI
St Edmund's College, Ware Mb 11 & VI
Bancroft's School, Woodford Green M 5, 11 & VI
Chigwell School B(M)b 5, 11, 13 & VI
Ilford Ursuline High School, Ilford G 11 & VI
Brentwood School Mb 5, 11 & VI
Felsted School, Dunmow Mb 5, 11, 13 & VI
Bishop's Stortford College B(M)b 5, 11 & VI
Friends' School, Saffron Walden Mb 11, 12, 13 & VI
New Hall School, Chelmsford G 5, 11 & VI

Surrey, Kent and Sussex

City of London Freemen's School, Ashstead Mb 5, 13 & VI
Parsons Mead School, Ashtead G 5, 11 & VI
Claremont Fan Court School, Esher M 11 & VI
Frensham Heights School, Rowledge, Farnham M 11
King Edward's School, Witley, Nr Godalming Mb 11, 12, 13 & VI
Charterhouse, Godalming B(M)b VI
Cranleigh School B(M)b 11, 13 & VI
St Catherine's School, Bramley Gb 5, 11, 12 & VI
Royal Grammar School, Guildford B 5, 11 & VI
Guildford High School for Girls G 5, 11 & VI
Tormead School G 11 & VI
Reed's School, Cobham B(M)b 11 & 13
Sir William Perkins's School, Chertsey G 11 & VI
St Maur's Convent School, Weybridge Gb 5, 11, 12 & VI
St George's RC College, Addlestone B(M)b 5, 11 & VI
Epsom College B(M)b 11, 13 & VI
St John's School, Leatherhead B(M)b 13 & VI
Notre Dame School, Lingfield M 5, 11 & VI
Notre Dame Senior School, Cobham G 11 & VI
Kingston Grammar School M 11, 13 & VI
Sutton High School, Cheam Rd, Sutton G 5, 11 & VI
Surbiton High School G 11
Croham Hurst School, Croydon G 5, 11
Croydon High School, South Croydon G 5, 11 & VI
Old Palace School of John Whitgift, Croydon G 5, 11 & VI
Trinity School of John Whitgift, Croydon B 5, 11 & VI
Whitgift School, South Croydon B 5, 11 & VI
Reigate Grammar School B 5, 11 & VI
Caterham School B(M)b 5, 11, 12, 13 & VI
Bromley High School, Bromley, Kent G 11 & VI
Holy Trinity College, Bromley G 11 & VI
Dover College Mb 11
St Lawrence College in Thanet, Ramsgate Mb 11
Cobham Hall School, Gravesend G 11 & VI
Sevenoaks School Mb 11

Walthamstow Hall, Sevenoaks Gb 5, 11 & VI
King's School, Rochester Mb 5, 11, 13 & VI
Tonbridge School Bb VI
Sutton Valence School, Nr Maidstone Mb 5, 11, 13 & VI
Ashford School, East Hill, Ashford, Kent Gb 5, 11 & VI
St Edmund's School, Canterbury M 5, 11 & VI
Kent College, Canterbury Mb 11, 12, 13 & VI
Ursuline Convent School, Kent G 11
Eastbourne College M VI
Brighton College Mb 5, 11 & VI
Brighton and Hove High School, Brighton G 5, 11, 12 & VI
Roedean School, Brighton G 11 & VISt Mary's Hall, Brighton Gb 11,
    12, 13 & VI
Lancing College B 11 & VI
Ardingly College, Haywards Heath Mb 5, 11 & VI
Burgess Hill School Gb 5, 11 & VI
Christ's Hospital, Horsham Mb 5, 11 & VI
Farlington School, Horsham G 5, 11 & VI
Hurstpierpoint College, Hassocks Mb 5, 11, 13 & VI
Worth School, Turners Hill, Crawley B 11 & VI

London
City of London School, Victoria Embankment EC4 B 11 & VI
City of London School for Girls, Barbican EC2 G 11 & VI
Forest School, Snaresbrook, E17 Bb 5, 11 & VI
Channing School, N6 G 11 & VI
Highgate School, N6 Bb 11 & VI
Francis Holland School, NW1 G 11 & VI
South Hampstead High School, NW3 G 11 & VI
University College School, Hampstead NW3 B 5, 11 & VI
Mill Hill School, NW7 B(M)b 5, 11, 13 & VI
King Alfred School, NW11 M 5, 11 & VI
Blackheath High School, SE3 G 11 & VI
St Dunstan's College, Catford SE6 B 5, 11 & VI
Eltham College, SE9 B(M)b 5, 11, 12, 13 & VI
Colfe's School, Lee SE12 B(M) 5, 11, 13 & VI
Dulwich College, SE21 Bb 5, 11, 13 & VI
James Allen's Girls' School, Dulwich SE22 G 11, 13 & VI
Alleyn's School, Dulwich SE22 M 5, 11, 13 & VI
Sydenham High School, Westwood Hill, SE26 G 5, 11 & VI
Westminster School, SW1 B(M)b 11
Hellenic College, SW1X M 5, 11 & VI
More House School, SW1X G 11 & VI
Streatham Hill and Clapham High School, SW2 G 5, 11 & VI
Emanuel School, Battersea Rise, SW11 B 11, 12, 13 & VI
St Paul's School, Barnes, SE13 Bb 5, 11, 13 & VI
Putney High School, Putney Hill, SW15 G 5, 11 & VI
King's College School, Wimbledon, SE19 B 11, 13 & VI
Wimbledon High School, Mansel Road, SW19 G 11 & VI
Queen's College, Harley Street, W1 G 11 & VI
St Benedict's School, Ealing, W5 B(M) 5, 11 & VI

St Augustine's Priory School, W5 5, 11 & VI
The Godolphin and Latymer School, Hammersmith, W6 G 11 & VI
Latymer Upper School, Hammersmith, W6 B 11 & VI
St Paul's Girls' School, Hammersmith, W6 G 11 & VI
Notting Hill and Ealing High School, W13 G 5, 11 & VI

Bursaries

CO-EDUCATIONAL SCHOOLS

Alleyn's School, London
American Community School, Uxbridge
American Community Schools, Cobham
American Community Schools, Egham
Ardingly College Junior School,
    Haywards Heath
The Arts Educational London Schools, London
Ashbourne Middle School, London

Babington House School, Chislehurst
Barrow Hills School, Godalming
Battle Abbey School, Battle
Bearwood College, Wokingham
Bedales School, Petersfield
Bellerbys, Mayfield and Wadhurst
Bellerbys College Mayfield and Wadhurst,
    Wadhurst
Bertrum House School, London
Bickley Park School, Bromley
Bishop's Stortford College Junior School,
    Bishop's Stortford
Bodiam Manor School, Robertsbridge
Brighton College, Brighton
Brighton College Junior School, Brighton
Broomham School, Hastings
Broomwood Hall School, London
Bury Lawn School, Milton Keynes

C K H R Immanuel College, Bushey
Cambridge Tutors College, Croydon
Caterham School, Caterham
Churchers College, Petersfield
City of London Freemen's School, Ashtead
Claremont Fan Court School, Esher
Claremont School, St Leonards-on-Sea
Clewborough House Prep School, Camberley
Cottesmore School, Pease Pottage

Danes Hill School, Oxshott
Davies's College, London
Devonshire House Preparatory School,
    London
Dolphin School, London
Douai School, Reading

Dover College, Dover
Duke of Kent School, Cranleigh
Durlston Court, New Milton

Eastbourne College, Eastbourne
Edgeborough, Farnham
Elmhurst Ballet School, Camberley
Emanuel School, London
Embley Park School, Romsey
Epsom College, Epsom
Ewell Castle School, Epsom

Fonthill, East Grinstead
Forres Sandle Manor, Fordingbridge
Frensham Heights School, Farnham

Gad's Hill School, Rochester
Gatehouse School G E T Ltd, London
Great Ballard School, Chichester
Great Walstead School, Haywards Heath
The Gregg School, Southampton

The Hampshire School, London
The Hampshire School,
    Knightsbridge, London
Haresfoot School, Berkhamsted
Haresfoot Senior School, Berkhamsted
Hawley Place School, Camberley
Heath House Preparatory School, London
Heath Mount School, Hertford
Hellenic College of London, London
Hemdean House School, Reading
Highfield School, Maidenhead
Hilden Grange School, Tonbridge
Hollington School, Ashford
Holme Grange School, Wokingham
Hordle House, Lymington
Hurstpierpoint College, Hassocks

International School of London

The Junior School,
    St Lawrence College, Ramsgate

Kent College, Canterbury
King Edward's School Witley, Godalming

King Edward VI School, Southampton
King's Preparatory School, Rochester
King's School, Rochester
Kingshott, Hitchin

Ladymede School, Aylesbury
Lambrook, Bracknell
Leighton Park School, Reading
Licensed Victuallers' School, Ascot
Littlefield School, Liphook
Long Close School, Slough
Lyndhurst School, Camberley

Mathilda Marks-Kennedy School, London
Mayfield Preparatory School, Alton
Meoncross School, Fareham
Michael Hall School, Forest Row

Newland House School, Twickenham
Newlands School, Seaford
Normanhurst School, London
Notre Dame School, Lingfield

Oakwood, Purley
The Octagon School, London
Our Lady of Sion School, Worthing

Pangbourne College, Reading
Pennthorpe School, Horsham
The Prebendal School, Chichester
Prior's Court Preparatory School, Newbury
The Purcell School, London,
    Harrow on the Hill

Ringwood Waldorf School, Ringwood
Riverston School, London
The Roche School, London
Rochester Tutors Independent College,
    Rochester
Rookwood School, Andover
Rose Hill School, Tunbridge Wells

Sackville School, Tonbridge
Scaitcliffe & Virginia Water Prep School,
    Egham
Shernold School, Maidstone
Sherrardswood School, Welwyn
Silchester House School, Maidenhead
St Andrew's School, Reading
St Andrew's School, Woking
St Aubyns, Brighton

St Bede's School, Hailsham
St Christopher's School, Beckenham
St Dunstan's College, London
St James Independent Schools, London
St John's College, Southsea
St Lawrence College in Thanet, Ramsgate
St Leonards College, St Leonards-on-Sea
St Michaels School, Newbury
Stanbridge Earls School, Romsey
Stubbington House, Ascot
Sutton Valence School with Underhill,
    Maidstone
Swanbourne House School, Milton Keynes

Thomas's Preparatory School,
    Battersea, London
Thomas's Preparatory School,
    Kensington, London
Thomas's Preparatory School
    Clapham, London
Thorngrove School, Newbury
The Towers, Steyning
Twyford School, Winchester

Ursuline College, Westgate-on-Sea

Wallop School, Weybridge
Warlingham Park School, Warlingham
Wellesley House, Broadstairs
Westbrook Hay School, Hemel Hempstead
Westbrook House Preparatory School,
    Folkestone
Willoughby Hall School, London
Woodside Park School, London

Yehudi Menuhin School, Cobham
York House School, Rickmansworth

BOY'S SCHOOLS

Aldenham School, Elstree

Caldicott, Farnham Royal
City of London School
Colfe's School, London

Davenies School, Beaconsfield
Dorset House School, Pulborough
Downside School, Purley
Dulwich College, London

Dulwich College Preparatory School, London
Durston House, London

Ealing College Upper School, London
Eaton House The Manor, London
Edge Grove School, Aldenham Village
Eltham College, London
Eton College, Windsor

Haileybury, Hertford
Halliford School, Shepperton
Hampton School, Hampton
Harrow School, Harrow
Highgate School, London
Horris Hill, Newbury

Keble School, London
King's College Junior School, London
Kingswood House School, Epsom

Lancing College, Lancing
Latymer Upper School, London
Lord Wandsworth College, Hook

The Mall School, Twickenham
Mayfield College, Mayfield and Wadhurst
Menorah Grammar School, London
Merchant Taylors' School, Northwood
Mill Hill School, London

Northcote Lodge, London

The Oratory School, Reading

Reading Blue Coat School,
    Sonning-on-Thames

Salesian College, Farnborough
Slindon College, Arundel
Solefield School, Sevenoaks
St Albans School, St Albans
St Columba's College, St Albans
St Edmund's School, Hindhead
St George's College, Weybridge
St George's School, Windsor
St John's School, Leatherhead
St Paul's Cathedral Choir School, London
St Philip's School, London
Stowe School, Buckingham

Trinity School, Croydon

University College School, London

Wellington College, Crowthorne
Westminster School, London
Worth School, Crawley

GIRL'S SCHOOLS

The Abbey School, Reading
Abbots Hill School, Hemel Hempstead
The Atherley School, Southampton

Baston School, Bromley
Bedgebury School, Cranbrook
Beechwood Sacred Heart, Tunbridge Wells
Berkhamsted School for Girls, Berkhamsted
Blackheath High School GPDST, London
Brighton & Hove High School, Brighton
The Brigidine School, Windsor
Bromley High School GPDST, Bromley

Channing School, London
City of London School for Girls, London
Cobham Hall School, Gravesend
Commonweal Lodge School, Purley
Croydon High School GPDST, South Croydon

Derwent Lodge School for Girls, Tonbridge

Farlington School, Horsham
Farringtons & Stratford House, Chislehurst

Garden House School, London
The Godolphin and Latymer School, London
The Granville School, Sevenoaks
Greenacre School, Banstead
Guildford High School, Guildford

Haberdashers' Aske's School for Girls,
    Borehamwood
Heathfield School GPDST, Pinner
Hurst Lodge, Sunningdale

Kent College, Pembury, Tunbridge Wells

The Lady Eleanor Holles School, Hampton
Lavant House Rosemead, Chichester

Manor House School, Leatherhead
Marist Senior School, Ascot
Marlston House Preparatory School, Newbury
Moira House Junior School, Eastbourne
Moira House School, Eastbourne
More House School, London

North Foreland Lodge, Hook
North London Collegiate School, Edgware
Northfield School, Watford
Notre Dame Senior School, Cobham
Notting Hill & Ealing High School, London

Padworth College, Reading
Palmers Green High School, London
Pipers Corner School, High Wycombe
Portsmouth High School GPDST, Southsea
The Princess Helena College, Hitchin
Prior's Field School, Godalming
Putney High School, London

Queen Anne's School, Reading
Queen's College, London
Queenswood School, Hatfield

The Rickmansworth Masonic School,
    Rickmansworth
Rickmansworth PNEU School,
    Rickmansworth
Roedean School, Brighton
Rookesbury Park School, Wickham
The Royal School, Hampstead, London
The Royal School, Haslemere

Sarum Hall, London

Sibton Park Girls' Preparatory School,
    Folkestone
Sir William Perkins's School, Chertsey
South Hampstead High School GPDST,
    London
St Albans High School, St Albans
St Catherine's Catholic School, Twickenham
St David's School, Ashford
St Francis' College, Letchworth
St George's School, Ascot
St Helen's School for Girls, Northwood
St Joseph's Convent School, Reading
St Margaret's School, Watford
St Mary's Hall, Brighton
St Mary's School, Ascot
St Mary's School, Gerrards Cross
St Maur's School, Weybridge
St Nicholas School, Fleet
St Paul's Girls' School, London
Stormont, Potters Bar
Streatham Hill & Clapham High Sch, London
Surbiton High School, Kingston upon Thames
Sutton High School (GPDST), Sutton
Sydenham High School GPDST, London

Thornton College, Milton Keynes

Virgo Fidelis Convent, London

Walthamstow Hall, Sevenoaks
West Heath School, Sevenoaks
Wimbledon High School, London
Woldingham School, Woldingham
Wykeham House School, Fareham

Reserved Entrance Awards

This list is extensive, but not comprehensive, and is based upon information provided by the schools concerned. Awards which specify an academic subject (*eg* Classics), a particular locality or such like or which are reserved for the children of Old Boys or Old Girls are not listed.

For a list of schools offering Assisted Places, see page 295.

A-Art
AA-Academic ability
C-Choral
D-Drama
E-Christian Missionary or full-time worker
F-Her Majesty's Forces*
FO-Foreign Office
G-Games

H-Financial or domestic hardship
I-Instrumental music
M-Medical profession
O-All round ability
S-Science
T-Teaching
+-Clergy
6-VIth Form entry

* F1-The Royal Navy F2-The Royal Marines F3-The Army F4-The Royal Air Force.

BOYS

The Abbey School, Westgate-on-Sea AA F FO G H I O M T
Aberdour School, Tadworth + AA
Aldenham School, Elstree 6 A AA F G H I O
Aldro School, Godalming H
Aldwickbury School, Harpenden AA
Alpha Preparatory School, Harrow T
Arnold House School, London H
Atholl School, Pinner H

Barfield School, Farnham O
Barrow Hills School, Godalming AA O
Bearwood College, Wokingham 6 A AA D F G H I O
Beechwood Park, St Albans + AA F H I
Belmont (Mill Hill Junior School), London I
Berkhamsted Junior School, Berkhamsted AA H
Berkhamsted School, Berkhamsted 6 A AA F3 H I M T
Bishop Challoner School, Bromley 6 AA
Bishop's Stortford College, Bishop's Stortford 6 A AA H I O T
Boundary Oak School, Fareham AA I
Bradfield College, Reading 6 A AA I O
Brockhurst School, Newbury AA F

Buckingham College Senior School, Harrow 6 AA H

Cannock School, Orpington F
Caterham School Preparatory, Caterham + AA E F FO H I O T
Charterhouse, Godalming 6 A AA H I
Chigwell School, Chigwell 6 A AA F FO I
City of London School, London 6 AA H I O
Claires Court School, Maidenhead AA O
Colchester Boys High School A AA G H I O T
Colfe's School, London 6 A AA H I
Cranbrook College, Ilford T
Cranleigh Preparatory School, Cranleigh AA
Cranleigh School, Cranleigh 6 A AA F FO I
Cumnor House School, South Croydon AA G I

Denmead School, Hampton + E
Dorset House School, Pulborough F H I T
Dulwich College, London 6 A AA I
Dulwich College Preparatory School, London H
Durston House, London AA H

Eagle House, Camberley AA I
Ealing College Upper School, London AA H
Eastbourne College, Eastbourne 6 A AA I
Eaton House The Manor, London H
Edge Grove School, Aldenham H
Edinburgh House School, New Milton A AA G H I O
Elstree School, Reading + T
Eltham College, London 6 AA E H I
Emanuel School, London 6 AA H I T
Epsom College, Epsom 6 A AA H I M O
Eton College, Windsor 6 AA H I
Ewell Castle School, Epsom 6 AA G H O

Forest Junior School, London + AA F I
Forest School, London + 6 AA F I
Friern Barnet Grammar School, London AA

Gayhurst School, Gerrards Cross + E H T

Haberdashers' Aske's School, Elstree AA H I
Haileybury College, Hertford + 6 A AA F3 H I O T
Hampden Manor School, Great Missenden AA O T

Hampton School, Hampton A AA H I
Harrow School, Harrow + A AA E H I T
Haslemere Preparatory School T
Hereward House School, London +
Highgate Junior School, London + T
Highgate School, London + 6 AA H I T
Homefield Preparatory School, Sutton AA
Horris Hill, Newbury H

The Junior School, Bishop's Stortford College,
    Bishop's Stortford + A AA E I O

King's College Junior School, London AA I
King's College School, London 6 AA H I
Kingswood House School, Epsom + AA H T

Lambrook, Bracknell + A AA F G H I O T
Lancing College, Lancing + 6 A AA F1 F2 H I O
Lanesborough, Guildford I
Latymer Upper School, London 6 AA I O
Lockers Park, Hemel Hempstead A AA F G I O
Lord Wandsworth College, Basingstoke 6 A AA H I O

The Mall School, Twickenham + H
Mayfield College, Mayfield 6 AA F G H I O
Merchant Taylors' School, Northwood 6 AA H I T
Milbourne Lodge School, Esher + AA I
Mill Hill School, London + AA F I O
Mowden School, Hove + H T

The Oratory School, Reading A AA I
Orley Farm School, Harrow +

Pangbourne College, Reading 6 A AA G H I O
Papplewick, Ascot AA I
Parkside School, Cobham AA F FO H
The Pilgrims School, Winchester I +
Presentation College, Reading H
Priory School, Banstead H

Quinton Hall School, Harrow + H T

Reading Blue Coat School, Reading 6 AA H I
Reed's School, Cobham 6 A AA H I

Reigate St Mary's Preparatory and Choir School H I
Rokeby School, Kingston upon Thames A AA G I T
Royal Grammar School, Guildford 6 AA H I

St Albans School AA I
St Andrew's School, Woking AA G H I
St Aubyn's, Brighton + AA G T
St Augustine's College, Westgate-on-Sea
    AA F H I O
St Benedict's School, London H
St Columba's college, St Albans 6 AA H
St George's College, Weybridge 6 AA G I
St George's School, Windsor I
St John's School, Leatherhead + 6 A AA I
St Paul's Cathedral Choir School, London I
St Paul's Preparatory School, London H I
St Paul's School, London 6 AA H I
St Philip's School, London H O
Salesian College, Farnborough A H
Scaitcliffe School, Egham H
Seaford College, Petworth 6 A AA F G H I O
Shrewsbury House School, Surbiton T
Slindon College, Arundel 6 AA F H O
Solefield School, Sevenoaks T
Stowe School, Buckingham 6 A AA H I O
Streete Court School, Godstone F

Tonbridge School, Tonbridge A AA H I
Trinity School, Croydon + AA H I

University College School, London AA H I

Wellington College, Crowthorne 6 A AA H I S
Westminster Abbey Choir School, London I
Westminster Cathedral Choir School, London H I
Westminster School, London AA H I T
Westminster Under School, London AA I
Whitgift School, South Croydon + 6 AA H I
Willington School, London E H
Winchester College, Winchester 6 AA I
Worth School, Crawley 6 AA I O S

Yardley Court, Tonbridge + AA H I
York House School, Rickmansworth AA H T

CO-EDUCATIONAL

Abercorn Place School, London O

Aberdour School, Tadworth + AA

Alleyn Court and Eton House School,
    Southend-on-Sea + A AA G H I T

Alleyn's School, London 6 A AA H I

The American Community Schools, Uxbridge + E H

The American School in London, London T

Amesbury School, Hindhead AA G I

Ardingly College, Haywards Heath + 6 A AA D F G H I O S

Ardingly College Junior School, Haywards Heath + AA F G H I T

The Arts Educational School, Tring D I

The Arts Educational Schools, London D

Ashbourne Middle School, London AA H

Ashdown House School, Forest Row + T

Ashfold School, Aylesbury A AA F G I

Babington House School, Chislehurst AA O

Bancrofts School, Woodford Green 6 AA H I

Battle Abbey School, Battle AA F

Bedales School, Petersfield H I S

Belmont School, Dorking AA

Bethany School, Cranbrook + 6 A AA E F G I

Bishop Challoner School, Bromley 6 AA

Bodiam Manor School, Robertsbridge AA G I

Box Hill School, Dorking 6 A AA G H I O

Breaside Preparatory School, Bromley AA

Brentwood School, Brentwood A AA F H I

Bricklehurst Manor Preparatory, Wadhurst H

Brighton College, Brighton + 6 A AA F3 G H I O T

Brighton College Junior School, Brighton + F3

Buckswood Grange, Uckfield AA F I O

Bury Lawn School, Milton Keynes H I

Burys Court School, Reigate I

Canbury School, Kingston-upon-Thames AA H O

Caterham School, Caterham + 6 AA E F FO H I T

Caterham School Preparatory, Caterham + AA E F FO H I O T

The Cavendish School, London H

Cheswycks School, Camberley +

Christ's College, London + 6 AA E F H I O S

Christs Hospital, Horsham + F1 F2 F4 H

Churchers College, Petersfield 6 AA H I

City of London Freemen's School, Ashtead 6 AA H I O
Claremont Fan Court School, Esher 6 AA H I O
Claremont School, St Leonards-on-Sea A AA D G H I O
Clewborough House Preparatory School, Camberley F H
Collingham, London 6 H
Copthorne School, Crawley AA H
Cottesmore School, Pease Pottage H
Coworth Park School, Woking +
Croft Hall (Hill School Junior Department),
    Westerham + F G H O T

Dallington School, London H
Dame Johane Bradbury's School, Saffron Walden H
Daneshill House, Basingstoke AA H I T
Ditcham Park School, Petersfield AA T
Dolphin School, Reading A AA D H I
Douai School, Reading 6 A AA H I S
Dover College, Dover 6 A AA F G H I M O T
Dover College Preparatory School, Folkestone + AA F G I
Drayton House School, Guildford H
Duke of Kent School, Cranleigh F O
Duke of York's Royal Military School, Dover F
Dunhurst (Bedales Junior School), Petersfield H I
Durlston Court, New Milton A AA F G H I

Edgeborough, Farnham O
Egerton-Rothesay School, Berkhamsted A AA H I G
Elmhurst Ballet School, Camberley F1 F3 F4 H
Engley Park School, Romsey + 6 A AA E F G H I O T
Essendene Lodge School, Caterham H O

Felsted Preparatory School, Dunmow AA
Felsted School, Dunmow 6 A AA I
Feltonfleet School, Cobham AA I O
Finton House School, London H
The Fold School, Hove AA H
Fonthill, East Grinstead H
Forres Sandle Manor, Fordingbridge AA F I O
Frensham Heights School, Farnham 6 A AA D H I O S
Friars School, Ashford AA F FO
Friends' School, Saffron Walden 6 O

Gatehouse School, London AA
Gateway School, Great Missenden O

Great Ballard School, Chichester A AA D F G I O
Great Walstead, Haywards Heath + AA E F G H I T
Greenfields School, Forest Row A AA D G I O
The Gregg School, Southampton AA H I

The Hampshire School, London O
The Hampshire School (Kensington Gardens), London AA I O
The Hampshire School (Knightsbridge), London AA I O
Hampstead Hill Nursery and Pre-Preparatory School, London H
Handcross Park School, Haywards Heath AA F G I
Haresfoot School, Berkhamsted A AA D O
Haresfoot Senior School, Berkhamsted AA O
The Hawthorns School, Redhill +
Heath Mount School, Hertford AA F I O T
Heathside Preparatory School, London A AA H I O T
Hellenic College of London, London 6 H
Hemdean House School, Reading AA H I O
Herries School, Maidenhead AA
Highfield PNEU School, Maidenhead AA H
Highfield School, Liphook + E
Highfield School, East Grinstead H
Hilden Grange School, Tonbridge A AA H I T
The Hill Preparatory School, Westerham F H T
Holmewood House, Tunbridge Wells A AA F G I O
Holmwood House, Colchester A AA D G H I O
Hordle House, Lymington AA H I
Hurstpierpoint College, Hassocks + 6 A AA E F G H I T

Ibstock Place, The Froebel School, London I
International School of London, London 6 H O
Italia Conti Academy of Theatre Arts, London D

Junior King's School, Canterbury +
The Junior School, St. Lawrence College, Ramsgate + AA F

Kent College, Canterbury + 6 AA F H I O
The King Alfred School, London O
King Edward VI School, Southampton
King Edward's School Witley, Godalming + 6 A AA F H I
King Fahad Academy, London H
King's Preparatory School, Rochester + AA I T
King's School, Rochester + A AA I T
The King's School, Canterbury 6 A AA I

Kingshott, Hitchin AA
Kingston Grammar School, Kingston upon Thames 6 A AA G H I

Leighton Park School, Reading + 6 A AA H I
Licensed Victuallers' School, Ascot 6 AA H O S
The Little Folks Lab, Stevenage H
Littlefield School, Liphook AA H O
Long Close School, Slough AA H O
Lycee Francais Charles de Gaulle, London 6
Lyndhurst School, Camberley AA H

Mander Portman Woodward, London H T
Marlborough House School, Hawkhurst + A AA F G I O T
Mayfield Preparatory School, Alton AA F3 F4 H O T
Meoncross School, Fareham AA H I O T
Merton Court Preparatory School, Sidcup AA D G H I T
Milton Keynes Preparatory School AA H
Moyles Court School, Ringwood AA F H O

Newland House School, Twickenham AA H I O
Newlands Manor School, Seaford 6 A AA F FO G H I O S T
Newlands Preparatory School, Seaford A AA F G H I O S
Newton Preparatory School, London AA S
Normanhurst School, London AA
Northbourne Park School, Deal A AA F G H I O
The Norwegian School, London F FO

Oakfield, Woking A AA H O
Oakwood School, Chichester AA D F1 F3 F4 G H I
The Old Grammar School, Lewes 6
The Oratory Preparatory School, Reading AA G H I
Our Lady of Sion School, Worthing 6 A AA D G H I O S

Pennthorpe School, Horsham AA F
Perry Court Rudolph Steiner School, Canterbury H
The Portsmouth Grammar School, Portsmouth A AA H I
The Prebendal School, Chichester I
Prince's Mead School, Winchester AA I
Priors Court Preparatory School, Newbury + AA E F H
The Purcell School, Harrow H I

Raphael School, Romford H
Reigate Grammar School, Reigate AA I

Riverston School, London + AA G I O
The Roche School, London AA H
Rose Hill School, Tunbridge Wells A AA G H I O
Royal Ballet School, London H
Royal Caledonian Schools, Watford 6 F
Royal Russell School, Croydon 6 AA

Sackville School, Tonbridge A AA D G H I O S
St Andrew's School, Eastbourne AA F O
St Andrew's School, Reading + I
St Bede's, Eastbourne A AA D G I O
St Bede's School, Hailsham 6 A AA D F G H I O T
St Cedd's School, Chelmsford I
St Christopher's School, Canterbury O
St Dunstan's College, London 6 AA F H I S
St Edmund's College, Ware 6 F I
St Edmund's Junior School, Canterbury
    + A AA F FO G I O
St Edmund's School, Canterbury + A AA F FO I
St Hilary's School, Godalming AA I
St John's School, Billericay AA H
St Lawrence College in Thanet, Ramsgate + 6 AA E F I
St Mary's College, Folkstone I
St Michael's School, Leigh-on-Sea +
St Michael's School, Sevenoaks A AA E F FO G H I T
St Nicholas School, Harlow AA H T
St Peter's School, Burgess Hill H
St Piran's Preparatory School, Maidenhead AA E H
Sevenoaks School, Sevenoaks 6 A AA G H I O S
Shaftesbury Independent School, Purley + 6 AA E H
Sherrardswood School, Welwyn Garden City 6 AA F
Shoreham College, Shoreham-by-Sea + 6 AA F I
Sinclair House School, London H O
Skippers Hill Manor Preparatory School, Mayfield AA H O
Southbank International School, London H O
Stanborough School, Watford 6
Stanbridge Earls School, Romsey A H
Stoke Brunswick, East Grinstead AA F H I O
The Stroud School, Romsey + AA
Stubbington House, Ascot AA G H O
Sutton Valence School, Maidstone 6 A AA F G H I T
Swanbourne House School, Milton Keynes
    + A AA F G I O
Sylvia Young Theatre School, London D H I

Temple Grove with St Nicholas School,
    Uckfield A AA G H I O
Thorngrove School, Newbury AA I
Trevor Roberts', London H I

Underhill Preparatory School, Maidstone AA

Vernon Holme (Kent College Infant & Junior School),
    Canterbury + E F H
Vinehall School, Robertsbridge + AA E F I O

Walhampton School, Lymington + E H
Wellesley House School, Broadstairs + H T
West Hill Park Preparatory School, Fareham H
Westbourne House School, Chichester I
Westbrook Hay, Hemel Hempstead AA F O
Westerleigh, St Leonards-on-sea AA H I O T
Willoughby Hall School, London H
Wilton House School, Battle F FO
Windlesham House, Pulborough AA G I
Winton School, Croydon 6 AA
Woodside Park School, London AA G H I O

Yateley Manor Preparatory School, Camberley AA I
Yehudi Menuhin School, Cobham H I

GIRLS

The Abbey School, Reading 6 AA H
Abbot's Hill, Hemel Hempstead + A AA F H I S
Ashford School, Ashford 6 AA I
The Atherley School for Girls, Southampton + 6

Baston School, Bromley I O
Bedgebury School, Cranbrook + 6 A AA F G H I
Beechwood School Sacred Heart, Tunbridge Wells 6 AA G H I O
Bell House School, Brentwood AA
Benenden School, Cranbrook 6 A AA I
Berkhamsted School for Girls, Berkhamsted AA H I
Blackheath High School GPDST, London 6 A H I O S
Brighton and Hove High School GPDST 6 AA H
The Brigidine School, Windsor H
Bromley High School GPDST, Bromley 6 AA H I
Burgess Hill School, Burgess Hill 6 AA H I

Channing School, London + 6 AA H
Charters-Ancaster School GPDST, Bexhill-on-Sea 6 AA H I
City of London School for Girls, London 6 AA H I
Cobham Hall School, Gravesend 6 AA H O
Combe Bank School, Sevenoaks 6 O
Commonweal Lodge School, Purley 6 AA H O
Croham Hurst School, South Croydon 6 AA
Croydon High School GPDST, South Croydon 6 AA H

Derwent Lodge School for Girls, Tonbridge + AA H
Downe House School, Newbury 6 AA H I
Dunottar School, Reigate 6 AA H I

Falkner House, London I
Farlington School, Horsham 6 AA I
Farnborough Hill, Farnborough 6 AA H
Farringtons & Stratford House, Chislehurst + 6 AA F H I
Fernhill Manor School, New Milton 6 AA I
Forest Girls' School, London + 6 AA I
Francis Holland School, London + 6 AA H
Francis Holland School, London + 6 I

Garden House School, London AA H I O
The Godolphin and Latymer School, London H I
Greenacre School for Girls, Banstead 6 AA F H
The Grove School, Hindhead 6 H I O
Guildford High School (Church Schools Co Ltd) + 6 AA H I

Haberdashers' Aske's School for Girls, Elstree + AA H I
Halstead Preparatory School, Woking H
Hawley Place School, Camberley A AA D G I O S
Hazelhurst School for Girls, London AA
Hetherton House School, Amersham H T
Heathfield School, Ascot 6 A AA D G H I O S
Heathfield School, Pinner 6 AA H I
High March School, Beaconsfield AA
Holy Trinity College, Bromley 6 AA H I
Hurst Lodge, Sunningdale 6 A AA D F FO I O

Ilford Ursuline High School, Ilford AA H I O

James Allen's Girls' School, London 6 A AA H I O

Kent College, Pembury + 6 AA D E F H I O

The Lady Eleanor Holles School, Hampton 6 AA H I O
Ladymede, Aylesbury + F
La Sagesse Convent, Romsey H O
Lavant House School, Chichester 6 AA F H
Luckley-Oakfield School, Wokingham 6 AA

Maidenhead College Claires Court Girls AA I
Manor House School, Leatherhead AA G O
Maltmans Green School, Gerrards Cross AA
Marist Convent Senior School, Ascot 6
Marymount International School, Kingston upon Thames AA H
Mayville High School, Southsea AA
Micklefield Wadhurst incorporating the Legat School of Classical
    Ballet, Wadhurst + 6 A AA D E F G H I S
Moira House Junior School, Eastbourne + F H O T
Moira House Senior School, Eastbourne + AA E F H I T
More House, London AA H I
The Mount School, London 6 AA H O

New Hall School, Chelmsford 6 A AA D F FO H I O S
North Foreland Lodge, Basingstoke S
North London Collegiate School, Edgware AA H I
Northfield School, Watford 6
Northwood College, Northwood 6 AA
Notre Dame School, Lingfield 6 AA O
Notre Dame Senior School, Cobham 6 AA H O
Notting Hill and Ealing High School GPDST, London 6 AA H I O

Padworth College, Reading 6 AA F H
Palmers Green High School, London AA H I
Park School for Girls, Ilford AA
Parsons Mead, Ashtead + 6 AA F
Pipers Corner School, High Wycombe 6 F I
Portsmouth High School GPDST, Southsea 6 AA
The Princess Helena College, Hitchin + 6 AA F I
Prior's Field School, Godalming 6 A AA D F H I
Putney High School, London 6 AA H I
Putney Park School, London A AA H I

Queen Anne's School, Reading + A AA I O T
Queen's College, London 6 A AA H I S
Queen's Gate School, London 6 O

Queenswood, Hatfield 6 AA G I

The Rickmansworth Masonic School, Rickmansworth 6 A AA I
Roedean School, Brighton 6 A AA H I
Rookesbury Park School, Wickham AA F H I
Rookwood School, Andover AA
Rosemead School, Littlehampton A AA D F G I
The Royal Naval School for Girls, Haslemere 6 AA D F1 F2 H I O S
Royal School, Hampstead, London F FO

St Albans High School, Newbury + 6 H I O
St Benedict's Convent School, Andover H
St Catherine's School, Guildford 6 AA G H I
St Catherine's School, Twickenham H
St Christina's RC Preparatory School, London H
St David's School, Ashford 6 A AA F H I
St Francis' College, Letchworth 6 AA H I
St Gabriel's School, Newbury O
St George's School, Ascot AA I
St Helen's School for Girls, Northwood 6 AA H I
St James Independent School for Girls, London H
St Joseph's Convent School, Reading 6 AA H
St Leonards-Mayfield School, Mayfield A AA H I
St Margaret's School, Watford + 6 A AA F H I O S
St Margaret's Senior School Convent of Mercy, Midhurst +
St Mary's Hall, Brighton + 6 AA F H I
St Mary's School, Ascot 6 H I S
St Mary's School, Gerrards Cross + 6 AA
St Mary's School Colchester O
St Maur's Convent School, Weybridge 6 AA H I O
St Michael's School, Oxted + AA F
St Nicholas School, Fleet + 6 AA I
St Paul's Girls' School, London A AA H I
St Swithun's School, Winchester 6 AA H I
St Teresa's Preparatory School, Effingham AA H
St Teresa's School, Dorking 6 A AA H I O T
Sarum Hall, London H
Sibton Park, Folkestone + AA F H I O
Sir William Perkins's School, Chertsey 6 AA H
South Hampstead High School, London 6 AA H
Stormont, Potters Bar AA
Streatham Hill and Clapham High School, London 6 AA H I
Surbiton High School, Kingston upon Thames + 6 AA G H I

Sutton High School (GPDST), Sutton 6 AA H O
Sydenham High School, London 6 AA H I

Thornton College Convent of Jesus and Mary, Milton Keynes AA
Tormead School, Guildford 6 AA H

Upton House School, Windsor H
Ursuline Convent School, Westgate-on-Sea F

The Village School, London + AA H

Walthamstow Hall, Sevenoaks + 6 AA E H I
West Heath School, Sevenoaks 6 AA H
Wimbledon High School, London 6 AA H
Wispers School, Haslemere 6 AA I
Wycombe Abbey School, High Wycombe 6 AA I
Wykeham House School, Fareham AA

Schools & Colleges offering A level entry at 16

Berkshire
The Abbey School, Reading
Bearwood College, Wokingham
Bradfield College, Reading
The Brigidine School, Windsor
Claires Court School, Maidenhead
Douai School, Reading
Downe House School, Thatcham
Eton College, Windsor
Heathfield School, Ascot
Hurst Lodge, Sunningdale
Leighton Park School, Reading
Licensed Victuallers' School, Ascot
Luckley-Oakfield School, Wokingham
Maidenhead College Claires Court Girls,
    Maidenhead
Marist Senior School, Ascot
The Oratory School, Reading
Padworth College, Reading
Pangbourne College, Reading
Presentation College, Reading
Prior's Court Preparatory School, Newbury
Queen Anne's School, Reading
Reading Blue Coat School, Sonning-on-Thames
St George's School, Ascot
St Joseph's Convent School, Reading
St Mary's School, Ascot
Wellington College, Crowthorne

Buckinghamshire
Akeley Wood School, Buckingham
Bury Lawn School, Milton Keynes
Gyosei International School UK, Milton Keynes
Pipers Corner School, High Wycombe
St Mary's School, Gerrards Cross
Stowe School, Buckingham
Wycombe Abbey School, High Wycombe

Essex
Bancroft's School, Woodford Green
Chigwell School, Chigwell
Felsted School, Great Dunmow
Friends' School, Saffron Walden
Gosfield School, Halstead
New Hall School, Chelmsford
Park School for Girls, Ilford

Hampshire
The Atherley School, Southampton

Bedales School, Petersfield
Brockwood Park Krishnamurti Educational
    Centre, Bramdean
Churchers College, Petersfield
Embley Park School, Romsey
Farnborough Hill, Farnborough
King Edward VI School, Southampton
Lord Wandsworth College, Hook
North Foreland Lodge, Hook
Portsmouth High School GPDST, Southsea
The Portsmouth Grammar School, Portsmouth
Salesian College, Farnborough
St John's College, Southsea
St Swithun's School, Winchester
Stanbridge Earls School, Romsey
Wessex Tutors, Winchester
Wessex Tutors, Southampton
Winchester College, Winchester

Hertfordshire
The Arts Educational School, Tring
Aldenham School, Elstree
Berkhamsted School for Girls, Berkhamsted
C K H R Immanuel College, Bushey
Egerton-Rothesay School, Berkhamsted
Haberdashers' Aske's School for Girls,
    Borehamwood
Haileybury, Hertford
Haresfoot Senior School, Berkhamsted
Northfield School, Watford
The Princess Helena College, Hitchin
Queenswood School, Hatfield
The Rickmansworth Masonic School,
    Rickmansworth
Sherrardswood School, Welwyn
St Albans High School, St Albans
St Albans School, St Albans
St Christopher School, Letchworth
St Columba's College, St Albans
St Francis' College, Letchworth
St Margaret's School, Watford
St Martha's Senior School, Barnet
Stanborough School, Watford

Kent
Ashford School, Ashford
Baston School, Bromley
Bedgebury School, Cranbrook
Beechwood Sacred Heart, Tunbridge Wells
Bromley High School GPDST, Bromley

Cobham Hall School, Gravesend
Combe Bank School, Sevenoaks
Dover College, Dover
Duke of York's Royal Military School, Dover
Farringtons & Stratford House, Chislehurst
Gad's Hill School, Rochester
Holy Trinity College, Bromley
Kent College, Canterbury
Kent College, Pembury, Tunbridge Wells
The King's School, Canterbury
King's School, Rochester
The Old Vicarage, Tonbridge
Rochester Tutors Independent College, Rochester
Sackville School, Tonbridge
St Lawrence College in Thanet, Ramsgate
Sutton Valence School with Underhill, Maidstone
Ursuline College, Westgate-on-Sea
Walthamstow Hall, Sevenoaks
West Heath School, Sevenoaks

London
Albany College, London
Alleyn's School, London
The Arts Educational London Schools, London
Ashbourne Middle School, London
Blackheath High School GPDST, London
Bloomsbury College, London
Channing School, London
City of London School, London
City of London School for Girls, London
Colfe's School, London
Davies's College, London
Davies, Laing & Dick, London
Dulwich College, London
Ealing College Upper School, London
Eltham College, London
Emanuel School, London
Fine Arts College, London
Francis Holland School, London NW1
Francis Holland School, London SW1
The Godolphin and Latymer School, London
Hellenic College of London
Highgate School, London
Italia Conti Academy of Theatre Art, London
James Allen's Girls' School, London
King Alfred School, London
King Fahad Academy, London
King's College School, London
Latymer Upper School, London
Lycee Francais Charles de Gaulle, London
Menorah Grammar School, London
Mill Hill School, London
More House School, London
The Mount School, London
Notting Hill & Ealing High School, London
Pardes Grammar Boys' School, London

Portland Place School, London
Putney High School, London
Queen's College, London
Queen's Gate School, London
The Royal School, Hampstead, London
South Hampstead High School GPDST, London
St Augustine's Priory, London
St Benedict's School, London
St Dunstan's College, London
St James Independent Schools, London
St Paul's Girls' School, London
St Paul's School, London
Streatham Hill & Clapham High School, London
Sydenham High School GPDST, London
University College School, London
Westminster School, London
Wimbledon High School, London

Middlesex
Halliford School, Shepperton
Hampton School, Hampton
Harrow School, Harrow
Heathfield School GPDST, Pinner
Hounslow College, Feltham
The John Lyon School, Harrow
The Lady Eleanor Holles School, Hampton
Merchant Taylors' School, Northwood
North London Collegiate School, Edgware
Northwood College, Northwood
The Purcell School, London, Harrow on the Hill
St David's School, Ashford
St Helen's School for Girls, Northwood
St John's Senior School, Enfield

Surrey
Cambridge Tutors College, Croydon
Caterham School, Caterham
City of London Freemen's School, Ashtead
Claremont Fan Court School, Esher
Commonweal Lodge School, Purley
Croham Hurst School, South Croydon
Croydon High School GPDST, South Croydon
Dunottar School, Reigate
Elmhurst Ballet School, Camberley
Epsom College, Epsom
Ewell Castle School, Epsom
Frensham Heights School, Farnham
Greenacre School, Banstead
Guildford High School, Guildford
King Edward's School Witley, Godalming
Kingston Grammar School, Kingston upon Thames
Notre Dame School, Lingfield
Notre Dame Senior School, Cobham
Oakwood, Purley
Parsons Mead School, Ashtead
Prior's Field School, Godalming

Reigate Grammar School, Reigate
The Royal School, Haslemere
Royal Grammar School, Guildford
Royal Russell School, Croydon
Sir William Perkins's School, Chertsey
St Catherine's School, Guildford
St George's College, Weybridge
St John's School, Leatherhead
St Maur's School, Weybridge
Surbiton High School, Kingston upon Thames
Sutton High School (GPDST), Sutton
Trinity School, Croydon
Woldingham School, Woldingham
Yehudi Menuhin School, Cobham

East Sussex

Battle Abbey School, Battle
Bellerbys, Brighton
Bellerbys College Mayfield and Wadhurst,
  Wadhurst
Brighton & Hove High School, Brighton
Brighton College, Brighton

Broomham School, Hastings
Eastbourne College, Eastbourne
Greenfields School Educ Trust Ltd, Forest Row
Mayfield College, Mayfield
Michael Hall School, Forest Row
Moira House School, Eastbourne
Newlands School, Seaford
Roedean School, Brighton
St Bede's School, Hailsham
St Mary's Hall, Brighton
The Old Grammar School, Lewes

West Sussex

Burgess Hill School for Girls (Senior), Burgess Hill
Christ's Hospital, Horsham
Farlington School, Horsham
Hurstpierpoint College, Hassocks
Lancing College, Lancing
Lavant House Rosemead, Chichester
Our Lady of Sion School, Worthing
Slindon College, Arundel
Worth School, Crawley

Schools offering entry at 16 to Vocational Courses

Berkshire
Hurst Lodge, Sunningdale
Licensed Victuallers' School, Ascot
Luckley-Oakfield School, Wokingham
The Norland College, Hungerford
Padworth College, Reading
Redroofs Theatre School, Maidenhead

Buckinghamshire
Pipers Corner School, High Wycombe
St Mary's School, Gerrards Cross
Teikyo School UK, Wexham

Essex
Thorpe Hall School, Southend-on-Sea

Hampshire
The Atherley School, Southampton
St John's College, Southsea
Stanbridge Earls School, Romsey

Hertfordshire
The Arts Educational School, Tring
The Rickmansworth Masonic School,
    Rickmansworth

Kent
Bedgebury School, Cranbrook

Bretlands Beauty Training Centre,
    Tunbridge Wells
Combe Bank School, Sevenoaks
Duke of York's Royal Military School, Dover
Farringtons & Stratford House, Chislehurst
Gad's Hill School, Rochester
West Heath School, Sevenoaks

London
The Arts Educational London Schools, London
Barbara Speake Stage School, London
Italia Conti Academy of Theatre Art, London
The Metropolitan Theatre School, London
Ravenscourt Theatre School, London

Surrey
Dunottar School, Reigate
Elmhurst Ballet School, Camberley
The Royal School, Haslemere
St Maur's School, Weybridge

East Sussex
Broomham School, Hastings
Michael Hall School, Forest Row
St Bede's School, Hailsham

West Sussex
Slindon College, Arundel

Schools offering Learning Support

Berkshire
Bracknell Montessori School, Bracknell
The Brigidine School, Windsor
Elstree School, Reading
Eton End PNEU School, Slough
The Highlands School, Reading
Holme Grange School, Wokingham
Horris Hill, Newbury
Hurst Lodge, Sunningdale
Lambrook, Bracknell
Leighton Park School, Reading
Licensed Victuallers' School, Ascot
Long Close School, Slough
Newbold School, Bracknell
Pangbourne College, Reading
Presentation College, Reading
Prior's Court Preparatory School, Newbury
St Edward's School, Reading
St Gabriel's School, Newbury
St Joseph's Convent School, Reading
St Piran's Preparatory School, Maidenhead
Stubbington House, Ascot
Waverley School, Crowthorne

Buckinghamshire
Bury Lawn School, Milton Keynes
Crown House School, High Wycombe
Heatherton House School, Amersham
Ladymede School, Aylesbury
St Mary's School, Gerrards Cross
Stowe School, Buckingham
Thornton College, Milton Keynes

Essex
Alleyn Court Preparatory School, Southend-on-Sea
Avon House, Woodford Green
Brentwood Preparatory School, Brentwood
College Saint-Pierre, Leigh-on-Sea
Dame Johane Bradbury's School, Saffron Walden
Felsted Preparatory School, Dunmow
Friends' School, Saffron Walden
Gosfield School, Halstead
Heathcote School, Chelmsford
Herington House School, Brentwood
Holmwood House, Colchester
Maldon Court Preparatory School, Maldon

Hampshire
Boundary Oak School, Fareham
Churchers College, Petersfield
Durlston Court, New Milton
Embley Park School, Romsey

Farleigh School, Andover
The Gregg School, Southampton
Grove Place, The Atherley Junior School, Southampton
Hordle House, Lymington
Inhurst House School, Tadley
Lord Wandsworth College, Hook
Meoncross School, Fareham
Nethercliffe School, Winchester
North Foreland Lodge, Hook
Rookesbury Park School, Wickham
Rookwood School, Andover
Rushmoor Independent School, Farnborough
St Anne's School, Lee-on-the-Solent
St Nicholas School, Fleet
St Swithun's Junior School, Winchester
Stanbridge Earls School, Romsey
Wessex Tutors, Winchester
Woodside House School, Waterlooville
Wykeham House School, Fareham

Hertfordshire
The Arts Educational School, Tring
Berkhamsted Junior School, Berkhamsted
Haresfoot School, Berkhamsted
Haresfoot Senior School, Berkhamsted
Heath Mount School, Hertford
Kings School, Harpenden
Norfolk Lodge Preparatory School, Barnet
Northfield School, Watford
St Christopher School, Letchworth
St Joseph's in The Park, Hertford
Stanborough School, Watford

Kent
Ashgrove School, Bromley
Baston School, Bromley
Bedgebury School, Cranbrook
Bethany School, Cranbrook
Bickley Park School, Bromley
Bretlands Beauty Training Centre, Tunbridge Wells
Cobham Hall School, Gravesend
Combe Bank School, Sevenoaks
Convent Preparatory School, Gravesend
Dover College, Dover
Dulwich Preparatory School, Cranbrook
Friars School, Ashford
Gad's Hill School, Rochester
King's Junior School, Canterbury
King's Preparatory School, Rochester
King's School, Rochester

Lorendon Preparatory School, Faversham
The New Beacon School, Sevenoaks
Rochester Tutors Independent College, Rochester
Rose Hill School, Tunbridge Wells
Sackville School, Tonbridge
Sibton Park Girls' Preparatory School, Folkestone
Solefield School, Sevenoaks
St Andrew's Preparatory School, Edenbridge
St Faiths at Ash School, Canterbury
St Michael's School, Sevenoaks
Sutton Valence School with Underhill, Maidstone
Ursuline College, Westgate-on-Sea
Vernon Holme, Canterbury
Westbrook House Preparatory School,
   Folkestone
Yardley Court, Tonbridge

London

Ashbourne Middle School, London
Calder House School, London
Cameron House, London
Elizabeth Russell School of Cookery, London
Francis Holland School, London
The Hampshire Schools, London
Harvington School, London
Heath House Preparatory School, London
Hellenic College of London, London
The Hilltop Nursery School, London
Hornsby House School, London
International School of London
Kenley Montessori School, London
Ladbroke Square Montessori School, London
Maria Montessori Training Organisation, London
Mathilda Marks-Kennedy School, London
Menorah Grammar School, London
The Metropolitan Theatre School, London
The Mount School, London
The New Learning Centre, London
Newton Preparatory School, London
Normanhurst School, London
Northcote Lodge, London
The Octagon School, London
Parkgate House School, London
Portland Place School, London
Primrose Montessori School, London
Ravenscourt Theatre School, London
Red Balloon Nursery School, London
Riverston School, London
South London Montessori School, London
St Augustine's Priory, London
St Dunstan's College, London
St Margaret's School, London
St Mary's School Hampstead, London
Westminster Cathedral Choir School, London
Willoughby Hall School, London
The Willow School, London

Wimbledon High School, London
Woodentops Pre-Prep School, London
Woodside Park School, London

Greater London

Buckingham College Lower School, Kenton
Hounslow College, Feltham
Hounslow College Preparatory School, Hounslow
Peterborough & St Margaret's High School,
   Stanmore
St David's School, Ashford
Staines Preparatory School Trust, Staines

Surrey

American Community Schools England, Egham
Barfield School, Farnham
Barrow Hills School, Godalming
The Cobham Montessori Nursery School, Cobham
Commonweal Lodge School, Purley
Coworth Park School, Woking
Downside School, Purley
Duke of Kent School, Cranleigh
Elmhurst Ballet School, Camberley
Frensham Heights School, Farnham
Glenesk School, Leatherhead
Halstead Preparatory School, Woking
Notre Dame School, Lingfield
Prior's Field School, Godalming
Royal Russell School, Croydon
The Royal School, Haslemere
St Edmund's School, Hindhead
St George's College, Weybridge
Sutton High School (GPDST), Sutton
Warlingham Park School, Warlingham
West Dene School, Purley
Woldingham School, Woldingham
Woodcote House School, Windlesham

East Sussex

Battle Abbey School, Battle
Bellerbys College Mayfield and Wadhurst,
   Wadhurst
Bricklehurst Manor Preparatory, Wadhurst
Brighton College, Brighton
Claremont School, St Leonards-on-Sea
Mayfield College, Mayfield
Moira House Junior School, Eastbourne
Moira House School, Eastbourne
Montessori School, Brighton & Hove,
   Brighton
Newlands Pre-Preparatory & Nursery School,
   Seaford
Skippers Hill Manor Prep School, Mayfield
St Aubyns, Brighton
St Bede's School, Hailsham
Arundale Preparatory School, Pulborough

West Sussex

Brambletye, East Grinstead
Burgess Hill School for Girls (Senior), Burgess Hill
Conifers School, Midhurst
Cumnor House School, Haywards Heath
Dorset House School, Pulborough
Great Ballard School, Chichester
Great Walstead School, Haywards Heath
Handcross Park School, Haywards Heath

Hurstpierpoint College, Hassocks
Oakwood School, Chichester
Sandhurst School, Worthing
Shoreham College, Shoreham-by-Sea
Slindon College, Arundel
Southdown School & Nursery, Steyning
St Margaret's Junior Convent of Mercy, Midhurst
Windlesham House School, Pulborough
Worth School, Crawley

Educational Associations

Educational Associations

The Allied Schools
Provision of financial and administrative support services and advice to member schools (Stowe School, Wrekin College, Canford School, Harrogate Ladies' College, Westonbirt School, Riddlesworth Hall School) and of secretariat for the Governing Bodies of those schools.
General Manager, David Harris,
42 South Bar Street, Banbury,
Oxon OX16 9XL
(01295 256441)

The Association of British Riding Schools
An independent body of proprietors and principals of riding establishments, aiming to look after their interests and those of the riding public, to raise standards of management, instruction and animal welfare.
General Secretary, Association of British Riding Schools,
Queens Chambers, 38-40 Queen Street, Penzance,
Cornwall TR18 4BH
(Tel 01736 69440 Fax 01736 51390)

The Association of Heads of Independent Schools
Membership is open to all Heads of Girls' and Co-Educational Junior Independent Schools which are accredited by the ISJC (Independent Schools Joint Council).
Honorary Secretary: Mrs A Holyoak,
Queen's Gate School,
133 Queen's Gate,
London SW7 5LE

The Association of Nursery Training Colleges
For information on Careers in Child Care, Careers as Nannies, Careers as Nursery Workers and on NVQ in Child Care and Education offered in the three independent Nursery Training Colleges, please contact:
The Princess Christian College,
26 Wilbraham Road, Fallowfield,
Manchester M14 6JX
(0161 224 4560)

The Association of Tutors Incorporated
This Association is the professional body to further the interests of tutors. Members include tutors teaching every academic and vocational subject at all levels of education, including tutorial college principals and independent tutors.
Enquiries to: Dr D J Cornelius, PhD, BSc,
Sunnycroft, 63 King Edward Road,
Northampton NN1 5LY
(01604 24171)

The Boarding Schools Association
The BSA is concerned that boarding education remains a healthy and relevant resource readily available to all who want or need it, within the range of educational provision in this country.
General Secretary: Michael Kirk,
Ysgol Naut, Valley Road,
Llanfairfechan,
Gwynedd LL33 0ES

British Association for Commercial and Industrial Education
A member organisation concerned with all aspects of vocational education and training. Further information from:
The Librarian,
British Association for Commercial and Industrial Education,
35 Harbour Exchange Square,
London E14 9GE
(0171 987 8989)

The British Association for Early Childhood Education
A Charitable Association prepared to give advice on matters concerned with the care and education of young children from birth to nine years. Publishes booklets and organises conferences for those interested in Early Years Education.
The Secretary, BAECE Headquarters,
111 City View House,
463 Bethnal Green Road,
London E2 9QY
(0171 739 7594)

The Choir Schools' Association
Schools which educate Cathedral and Collegiate choristers.
The Administrator
The Minster School
Deangate, York YO1 2JA
Tel (01904 625217)
Fax (01904 632418)

Common Entrance Examinations

Details of the Common Entrance examinations, which provide common entrance papers for boys and girls transferring from junior to senior schools at 11+, 12+ and 13+ are available from The Administrator at the address below. Copies of syllabuses and past papers are obtainable from CE Publications Ltd at the same address.

Independent Schools Examinations Board,
Jordan House, Christchurch Road,
New Milton, Hants BH25 6QJ
(01425 621111 Fax: 01425 620044)

CIFE
(Conference for Independent Further Education)

CIFE is the professional association for independent sixth form and tutorial colleges accredited by the British Accreditation Council for Independent Further and Higher Education (BAC) or the Independent Schools Joint Council. Colleges seeking to be accredited by either body within three years can be admitted to candidate membership. Member colleges specialise in preparing students (mainly over statutory school-leaving age) for GCSE and A and A/S Level examinations and for university entrance. The aim of the association is to provide a forum for the exchange of information and ideas, and for the promotion of best practice, and to safeguard adherence to strict standards of professional conduct and ethical propriety. Information published by member colleges as to their exam results is subject to regulation and to validation by BAC as academic auditor to CIFE.
Further information from:

Myles Glover MA,
Buckhall Farm,
Bull Lane, Bethersden,
near Ashford,
Kent TN26 3HB
(01233 820 797)

The Dyslexia Institute Ltd

A registered, educational charity which has established teaching, assessment and teacher-training centres throughout England. The aim of these Institutes is to help dyslexics of all ages to overcome their difficulties in learning to read, write and spell and to achieve their potential. (Leaflets supplied with SAE).

Information Officer:
The Dyslexia Institute Head Office,
133 Gresham Road,
Staines TW18 2AJ
(01784 463851)

Girls' Schools Association

130 Regent Road, Leicester LE1 7PG
(Tel: 0116 254 1619 Fax: 0116 255 3792)
(E-mail: gsa@dial.pipex.com)
President: Mrs Jacqueline Lang
General Secretary: Ms Sheila Cooper

The Girls' Schools Association exists to represent the 230 schools whose Heads are in membership. Its direct aim is to promote excellence in the education of girls. This is achieved through a clear understanding of the individual potential of girls and young women. 110,000 pupils are educated in schools which cover day and boarding, large and small, city and country, academically elite and broad based education.
Scholarships, bursaries or Assisted Places are available in most schools.

The Girls Public Day School Trust

26 Queen Anne's Gate,
London SW1H 9AN
Tel: 0171 222 9595

The Trust was founded in 1872 and was a pioneer of education for girls. Today the pupils in its 28 independent schools (listed below) number about 19,000.

BATH HIGH SCHOOL AND THE ROYAL SCHOOL,
   Bath BA1 5ES
BIRKENHEAD HIGH SCHOOL, 86 Devonshire Place, Birkenhead,
   Merseyside L43 1TY
BLACKHEATH HIGH SCHOOL, Vanbrugh Park, London SE3 7AG
BRIGHTON AND HOVE HIGH SCHOOL, The Temple,
   Montpelier Road, Brighton, Sussex BN1 3AT
BROMLEY HIGH SCHOOL, Blackbrook Lane, Bickley, Bromley,
   Kent BR1 2TW
CROYDON HIGH SCHOOL, Old Farleigh Road, Selsdon,
   South Croydon CR2 8YB
HEATHFIELD SCHOOL, Beaulieu Drive, Pinner,
   Middlesex HA5 1NB
HOWELLS SCHOOL, Llandaff, Cardiff CF5 2YD
IPSWICH HIGH SCHOOL, Woolverstone Hall, Ipswich,
   Suffolk IP4 2UH
KENSINGTON PREPARATORY SCHOOL FOR GIRLS,
   FulhamRoad, London SW6
LIVERPOOL: THE BELVEDERE SCHOOL, 17 Belvidere Road,
   Princes Park, Liverpool L8 3TF
NEWCASTLE: CENTRAL NEWCASTLE HIGH SCHOOL,
   Fulham Road, Newcastle upon Tyne NE2 4DS

NORWICH HIGH SCHOOL, 95 Newmarket Road, Norwich,
Norfolk NR2 2HU
NOTTINGHAM HIGH SCHOOL FOR GIRLS, 9 Arboretum Street,
Nottingham NG1 4JB
NOTTING HILL & EALING HIGH SCHOOL, 2 Cleveland Road,
Ealing, London W13 8AX
**OXFORD HIGH SCHOOL WITH GREYCOTES & THE SQUIRREL
PREP SCHOOLS,** Oxford OX2 6XA
PORTSMOUTH HIGH SCHOOL, Kent Road, Southsea,
Hampshire PO5 3EQ
PUTNEY HIGH SCHOOL, 35 Putney Hill, London SW15 6BH
SHEFFIELD HIGH SCHOOL, 10 Rutland Park, Sheffield S10 2PE
SHREWSBURY HIGH SCHOOL, 32 Town Walls, Shrewsbury,
Shropshire SY1 1TN
SOUTH HAMPSTEAD HIGH SCHOOL, 3 Maresfield Gardens,
London NW3 5SS
STREATHAM HILL & CLAPHAM HIGH SCHOOL,
Abbotswood Road, London SW16 1AW
SUTTON HIGH SCHOOL, 55 Cheam Road, Sutton,
Surrey SM2 2AX
SYDENHAM HIGH SCHOOL, 19 Westwood Hill, London SE26 6BL
WIMBLEDON HIGH SCHOOL, Mansel Road, London SW19 4AB

The schools are not denominational. Entry is by interview and test
appropriate to the pupil's age.

All schools have a Junior Department. Kensington is a preparatory
school only. The Royal School, Bath has boarding facilities.

The schools participate in the Government's Assisted Places Scheme,
offering places at 11+ and at Sixth Form level.

For further details please contact the schools direct, or there is a
general prospectus available from the GPDST office giving the
addresses of all the schools, together with the current fees, and other
general information.

The Girls Public Day School Trust is a charity Reg. No. 1026057 which
exists to provide high quality education for girls.

**The Governing Bodies Association & The Governing Bodies
of Girls Schools Association**
The objects of the Association are to advance education in
Independent Schools, to discuss matters concerning the policy
and administration of Independent Schools, and to encourage co-
operation between their governing bodies.
Enquiries to: D G Banwell, BA,
The Coach House, Pickforde Lane, Ticehurst,
East Sussex TN5 7BJ
Telephone & Fax (01580 200855)

The Headmasters' and Headmistresses' Conference (HMC)
Membership (240) consists of Heads of major boys' and co-educational independent schools. The objects of the annual meeting are to discuss matters of common interest to members.
Membership Secretary: R N P Griffiths,
1 Russell House,
Bepton Road, Midhurst,
West Sussex, GU29 9NB
Secretary: V S Anthony
130 Regent Road,
Leicester LE1 7PG

The Incorporated Association of Preparatory Schools
IAPS is the professional association of headmasters and headmistresses of preparatory schools in the UK and overseas. Membership is open to suitably qualified heads and deputy heads of schools accredited by the Independent Schools Joint Council. Further information from:
The General Secretary:
John Morris,
11 Waterloo Place,
Leamington Spa,
Warwickshire CV32 5LA
(01926 887833)

Independent Beauty Schools Association
The functions of the Association are to help maintain high standards of training in the member schools; to liaise with examining boards; to be represented on the Health and Beauty Therapy Training Board. Please write for a list of member schools and a copy of
A Guide to Training In Beauty Therapy.
PO Box 781,
London SW3 2PN

Independent Business Training Association
IBTA has been established as an association of the leading private business and secretarial colleges with the objective of promoting the highest possible standards of commercial training in the UK.
The Association also offers a free advisory service to prospective students to help them select a suitable course and College of study.
Marilyn Coles,
IBTA,
15 King Edward Street,
Oxford, OX1 4HT
(01865 791908)

The Independent Schools Association

Membership is limited to the Heads of Schools which are not under the direct control of the Department for Education & Employment. The Association aims to co-operate with other bodies which stand for professional freedom in education and to maintain for Independent Schools due recognition by government and the general public of their place in the educational life of the nation.

Secretary: Timothy Ham, MA, DipEd,
Boys' British School,
East Street,
Saffron Walden,
Essex CB10 1LS
(01799 523619)

The Independent Schools Bursars' Association

Membership: 600 independent secondary schools. Objectives include promotion of administrative efficiency and exchange of information between member schools.

Secretary: D J Bird,
Woodlands, Closewood Road,
Denmead,
Waterlooville,
Hants PO7 6JD
(01705 264506)

The Independent Schools Careers Organisation

The organisation's objects are: to assist careers staff in schools, to assist employers in making career opportunities and qualifications known, to advise children and their parents on careers, higher education and opportunities available, and to arrange courses for staff and pupils.

Administrative Director,
The Independent Schools Careers Organisation,
12a Princess Way,
Camberley,
Surrey GU15 3SP
(01276 21188 Fax: 01276 691833)

The Independent Schools Information Service

Established by the leading Associations of Independent Schools to provide information about schools to parents and the media.

Director: D J Woodhead,
ISIS National Headquarters,
56 Buckingham Gate,
London SW1E 6AG
(0171 630 8793/4)

The Independent Schools Joint Council

The ISJC considers matters of policy and administration common to its members and when required speaks collectively on their behalf. It represents its constituent members in joint discussions with the Department for Education and with other organisations.

ISJC is a federation of the following associations:

Governing Bodies Association   (GBA)
Governing Bodies of Girls' Schools Associations   (GBGSA)
Headmasters' and Headmistresses' Conference   (HMC)
Girls' Schools Association   (GSA)
Society of Headmasters and Headmistresses of
Independent Schools   (SHMIS)
Incorporated Association of Preparatory Schools   (IAPS)
Independent Schools' Association Incorporated   (ISAI)
Independent Schools Bursars' Association   (ISBA)

Their combined membership comprises about 1,350 schools.

General Secretary: Dr Arthur Hearnden OBE,
Grosvenor Gardens House,
35-37 Grosvenor Gardens,
London SW1W 7BS
(0171 630 0144 Fax: 0171 931 0036)

The Montessori Training Organisation

Affiliated to the Association Montessori Internationale. Further information from:
The Secretary,
The Maria Montessori Training Organisation,
26 Lyndhurst Gardens,
Hampstead,
London NW3 5NW
(0171 435 3646)

The Round Square Schools

An international group of schools following the principles of Kurt Hahn, the founder of Salem School in Germany, and Gordonstoun in Scotland was formed in 1967. The Round Square, named after Gordonstoun's 17th century circular building in the centre of the school, now has 25 member schools in nine countries: Australia, Canada, England, Germany, India, Kenya, Scotland, Switzerland and the United States.

Member schools arrange regular exchange visits for pupils and undertake aid projects in India, Kenya, Venezuela and Eastern Europe. All schools in the group uphold the five principles of outdoor adventure, community service, education for democracy, international understanding and environmental conservation.

The member schools in the United Kingdom are:

GIRLS	CO-EDUCATIONAL
Cobham Hall, Kent	Abbotsholme, Derbyshire
St Anne's, Cumbria	Box Hill, Surrey
Westfield, Newcastle upon Tyne	Gordonstoun, Scotland
	Rannoch,Scotland
	Wellington, Berks

For more information about Round Square Schools, please contact:
Kay Holland, Secretary,
The Round Square, Box Hill School,
Dorking, Surrey RH5 6EA
(01372 377812)

Round Square Office
(01737 246108 Fax: 01737 240416)

The Secondary Heads Association
An association representing the majority of Principals, Heads and
Deputy Heads in all types of secondary schools and colleges.
General Secretary: J Sutton, MA, FRSA, FIMgt
130 Regent Road,
Leicester LE1 7PG
(0116 247 1797 Fax: 0116 247 1152)

**The Society of Headmasters and Headmistresses of
Independent Schools**
A society of some 70 schools, most of which have a strong boarding
element.
Secretary: I D Cleland, BA, MPhil, DipEd, FRSA
The Coach House, 34A Heath Road,
Upton, Chester CH2 1HX
(01244 379649 Fax: 01244 379649)

Steiner Fellowship
Representing Rudolf Steiner Waldorf Education in the UK and Eire.
The 26 schools affiliated to the Fellowship are to be distinguished from
the curative homes and schools, also based on the work of Steiner,
which are for emotionally disturbed and handicapped children.
The Secretary,
Steiner Schools Fellowship,
Kidbrooke Park, Forest Row,
Sussex RH18 5JB
(01342 822115 Fax: 01342 826004)

UCAS
PO Box 67, Cheltenham GL50 3SF
(01242 222444 Fax: 01242 221622)

WES - World-Wide Education Service, Home School
The WES Home School Service enables parents to teach their
own children at home, either overseas or in the UK. Full courses of
study or single subjects to support local schooling are available for
children aged 3-12 years. All courses are consistent with the National
Curriculum. For further information contact:
The World-Wide Education Service,
St George's House,
14-17 Wells Street,
London W1P 3FP
(0171 637 2644 Fax: 0171 637 3411)

WES - World-Wide Education Service Ltd
The objectives of the service, which was established over a century
ago, are (1) to provide full professional support to overseas British and
International Schools which includes inspection, in-service teacher
training, curriculum and management advice, feasibility studies and
setting up new schools; (2) to undertake OFSTED UK inspections at
both primary and Secondary level and to offer advice and support to
UK Schools, particularly to 'clustered' groups;
(3) recruitment of teaching staff to overseas schools.
WES World-wide Education Service,
Canada House,
272 Field End Road,
Eastcote,
Middlesex HA4 9NA
(0181 866 4400 Fax: 0181 429 4838)

The Woodard Schools
In 1848 Nathaniel Woodard founded Lancing College and by 1891,
when he died, had established seven schools. The Woodard
Corporation now has 35 schools throughout the country, including
14 associated or affiliated schools. All have an Anglican foundation and
together form the largest group of Church Schools in England and
Wales. Further information from:
The Registrar,
The Woodard Schools,
1 The Sanctuary, Westminster,
London SW1P 3JT
(0171 222 5381)

London Postal Areas, Greater London & Home Counties

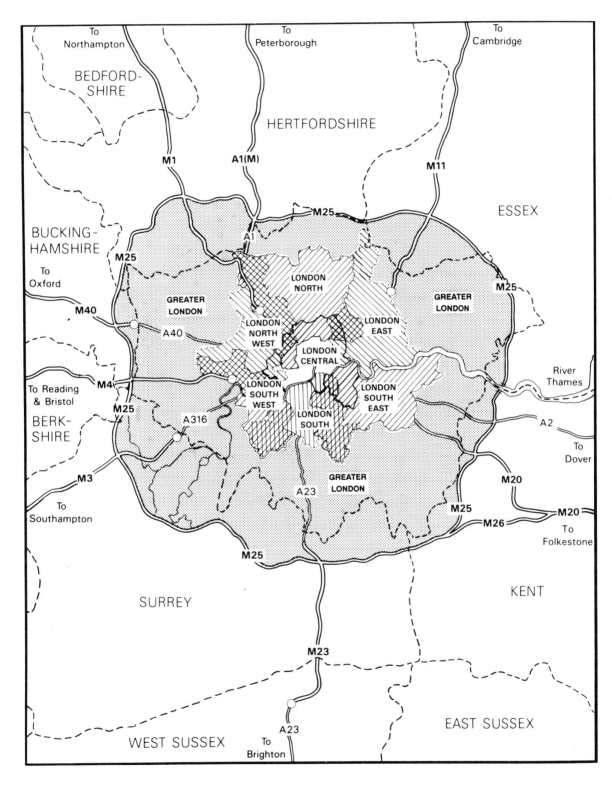

London and the South-East

Index

Please use this form if you would welcome the support of our advisory service and telephone us if you have any questions on how best to proceed.

THIS FORM MAY BE PHOTOCOPIED TO BE FAXED OR MAILED

Please complete in CAPITALS

To: **John Catt Educational Ltd**
Great Glemham
Saxmundham
Suffolk IP17 2DH

From:

Fax No: **01728 663 415**
Tel No: **01728 663 666**

Fax No:
Tel No:

In response to the information provided below please suggest the names of three schools which could fulfil my requirements and request them to send me their prospectuses and any other specific information relevant to my needs.

I understand that this form, when completed, may be faxed to the schools concerned.

Details of pupil

1. Family Name: ....
2. First Name(s): ....
3. Male/Female: ....
4. Date of Birth: ....
5. Nationality: ....
6. Religion: ....
7. First Language: ....
8. Competence in English (if not first language): ....
9. Current School & Dates: ....

   Previous Schools & Dates ....
10. Examinations & Certificates: ....
11. Special Achievements: ....
12. Special Needs: ....
13. Reason for seeking new school: ....

School required

14. Type (Full/Weekly Boarding, Day, Co-ed, Single Sex): ....
15. Proposed Starting Date: ....
16. Area of UK preferred (relatives, friends and travel considerations): ....
17. Examinations sought: GCSE/'A' Level, I.B., Vocational: ....
18. Is Guardianship required: ....

Signature: .... Relationship to pupil: ....

Date: ....